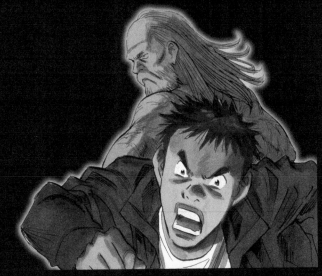

NAOKI URASAWA'S
20th CENTURY BOYS

VOL 07
THE TRUTH

Story & Art by

NAOKI URASAWA

With the cooperation of

Takashi NAGASAKI

PROFILES

NAOKI URASAWA'S 20th CENTURY BOYS

Neo Tokyo in the year 2014, when the Friends are in complete control! To rip off the mask of peace and prosperity...and save his "final hope"...a man who survived what happened on Bloody New Year's Eve is about to pull off the jailbreak of the century and escape from the maximum-security island fortress in Tokyo Bay!!

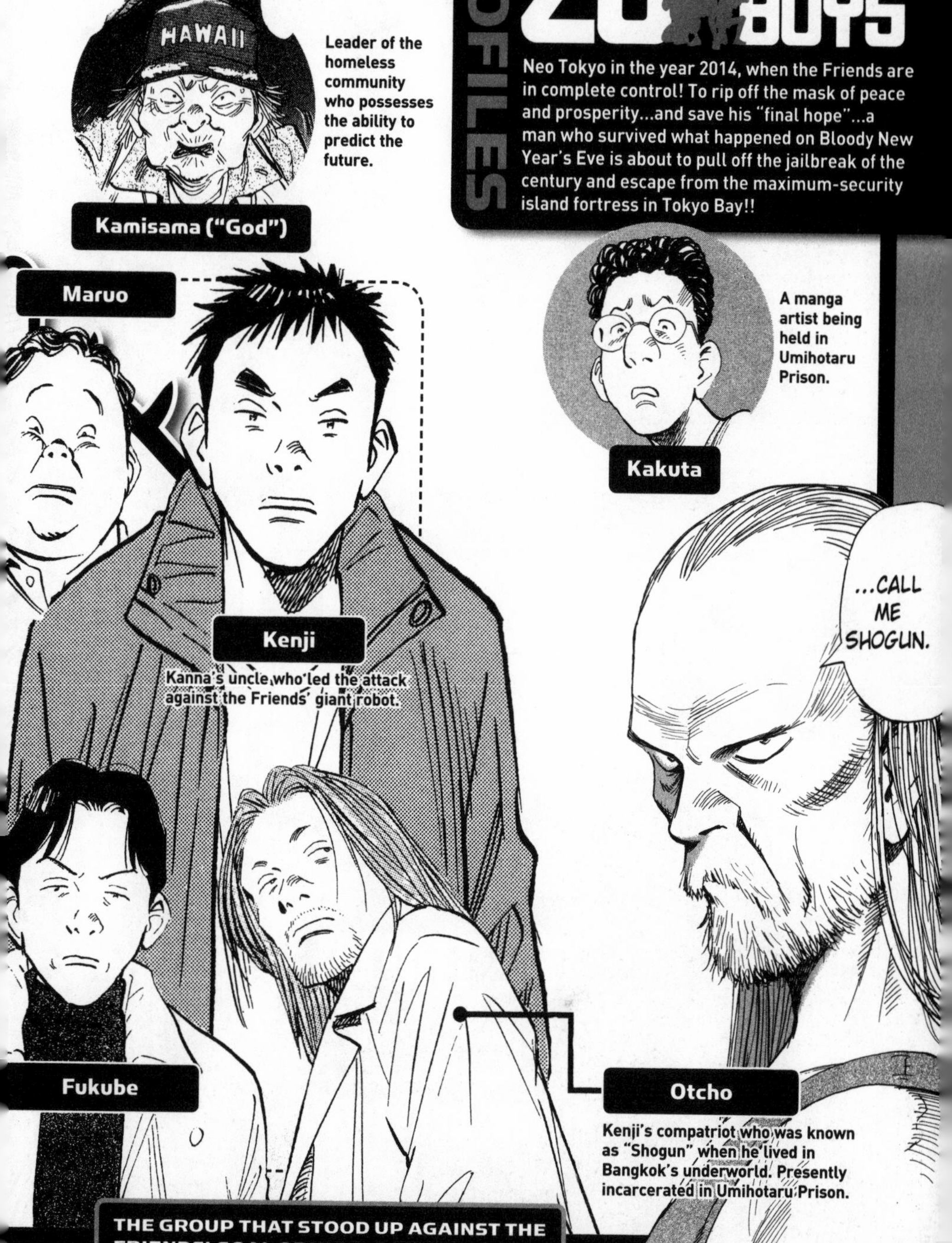
HAWAII
Leader of the homeless community who possesses the ability to predict the future.
Kamisama ("God")
A manga artist being held in Umihotaru Prison.
Kakuta
Maruo
Kenji
Kanna's uncle who led the attack against the Friends' giant robot.
...CALL ME SHOGUN.
Fukube
Otcho
Kenji's compatriot who was known as "Shogun" when he lived in Bangkok's underworld. Presently incarcerated in Umihotaru Prison.
THE GROUP THAT STOOD UP AGAINST THE FRIENDS' GOAL OF WORLD DESTRUCTION.

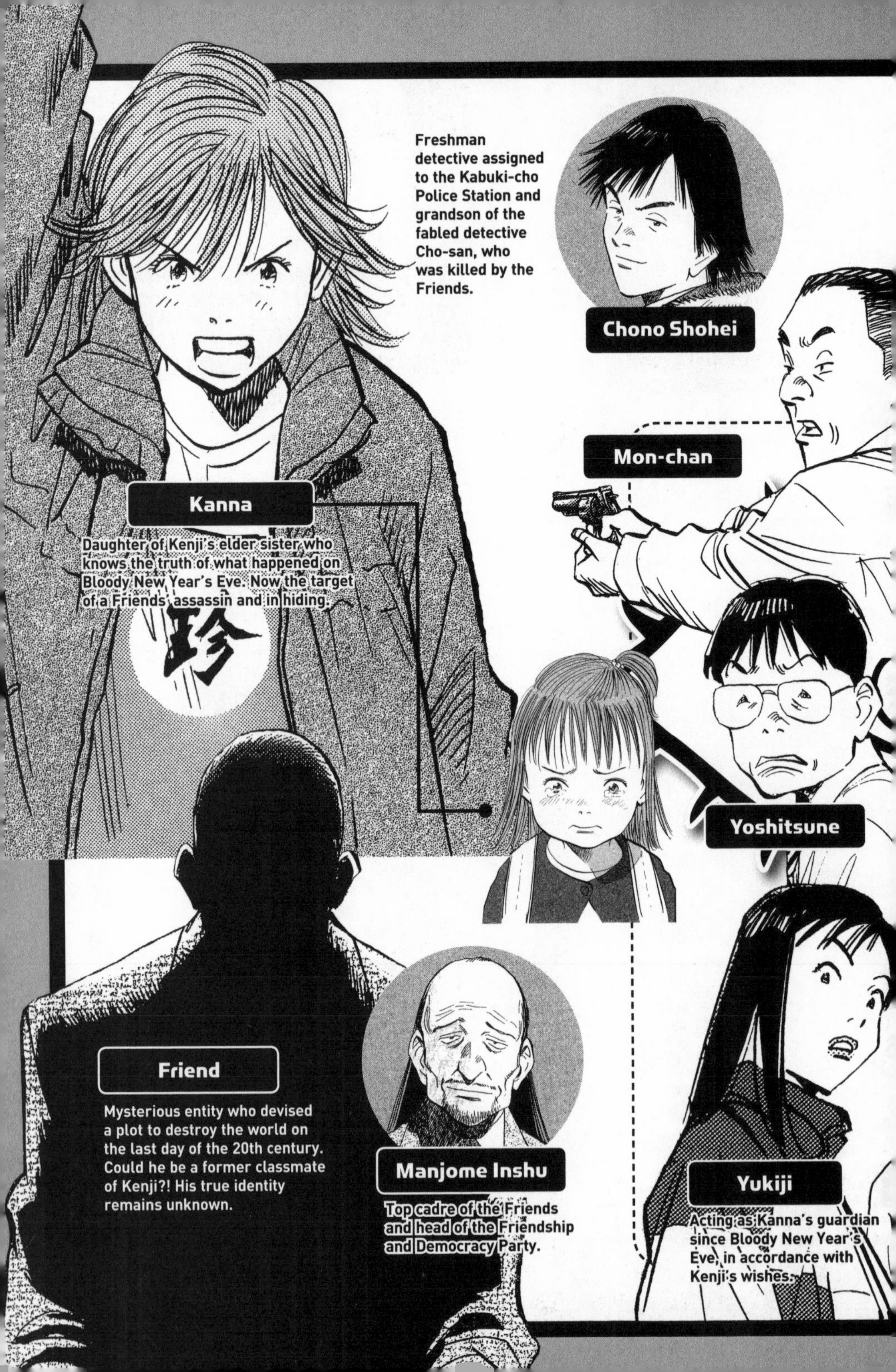
Freshman detective assigned to the Kabuki-cho Police Station and grandson of the fabled detective Cho-san, who was killed by the Friends.
Chono Shohei
Mon-chan
Kanna
Daughter of Kenji's elder sister who knows the truth of what happened on Bloody New Year's Eve. Now the target of a Friends' assassin and in hiding.
Yoshitsune
Yukiji
Acting as Kanna's guardian since Bloody New Year's Eve, in accordance with Kenji's wishes.
Manjome Inshu
Top cadre of the Friends and head of the Friendship and Democracy Party.
Friend
Mysterious entity who devised a plot to destroy the world on the last day of the 20th century. Could he be a former classmate of Kenji?! His true identity remains unknown.

CONTENTS
VOL 07
THE TRUTH

NAOKI URASAWA'S

20th CENTURY BOYS

Chapter 1 Escape

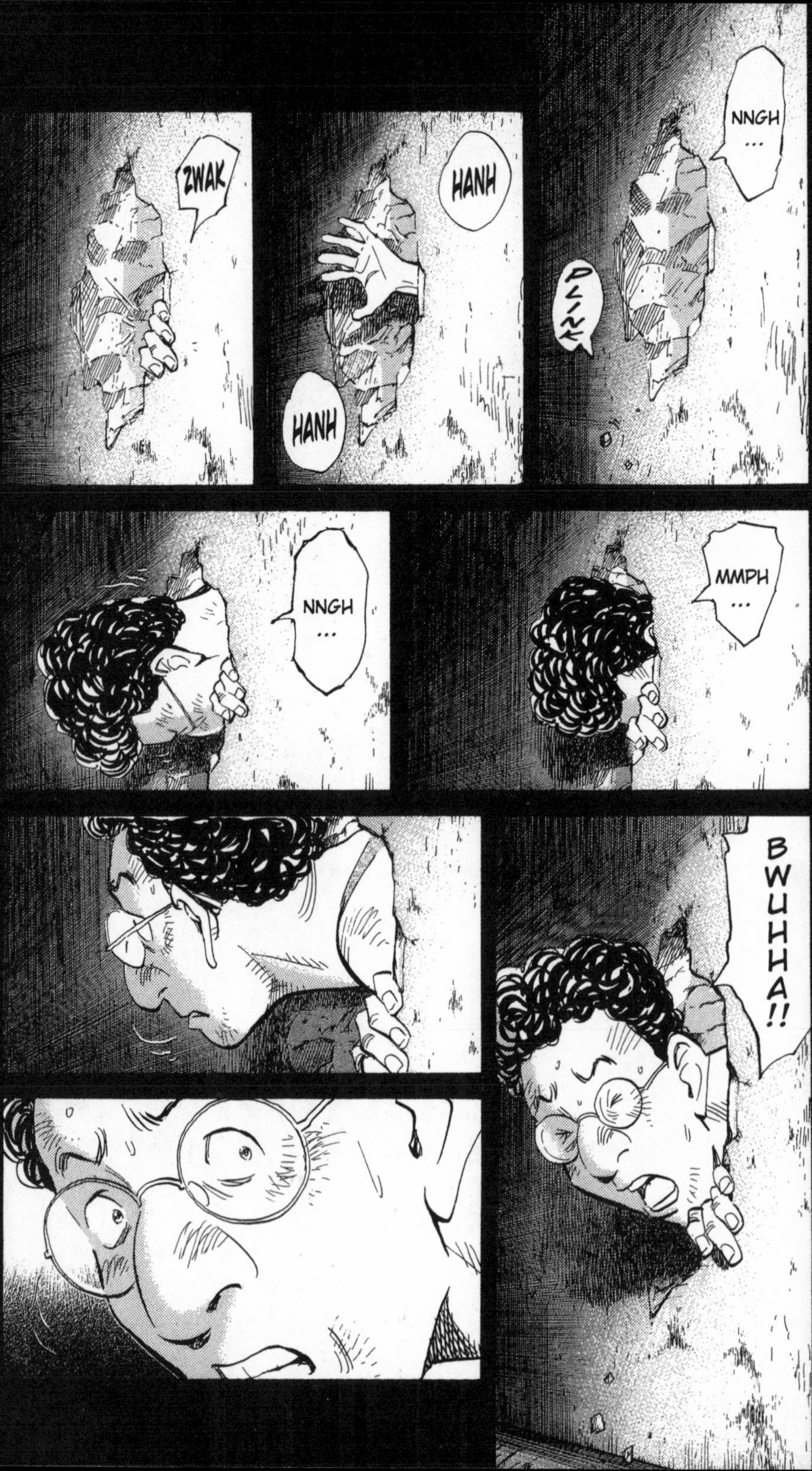
NNGH ...
PLINK
HANH
HANH
ZWAK
MMPH ...
NNGH ...
BWUHHA!!

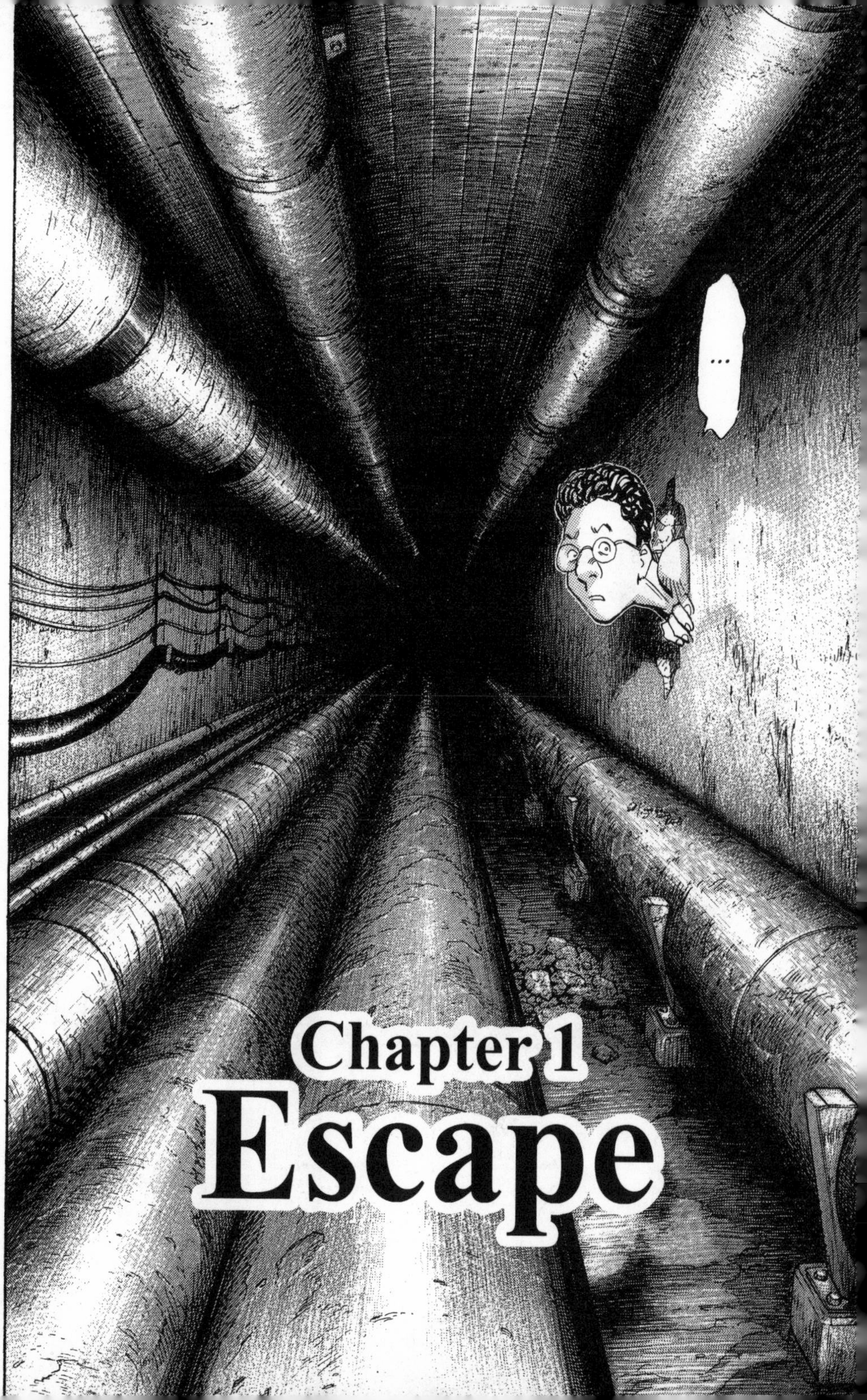
...
Chapter 1
Escape

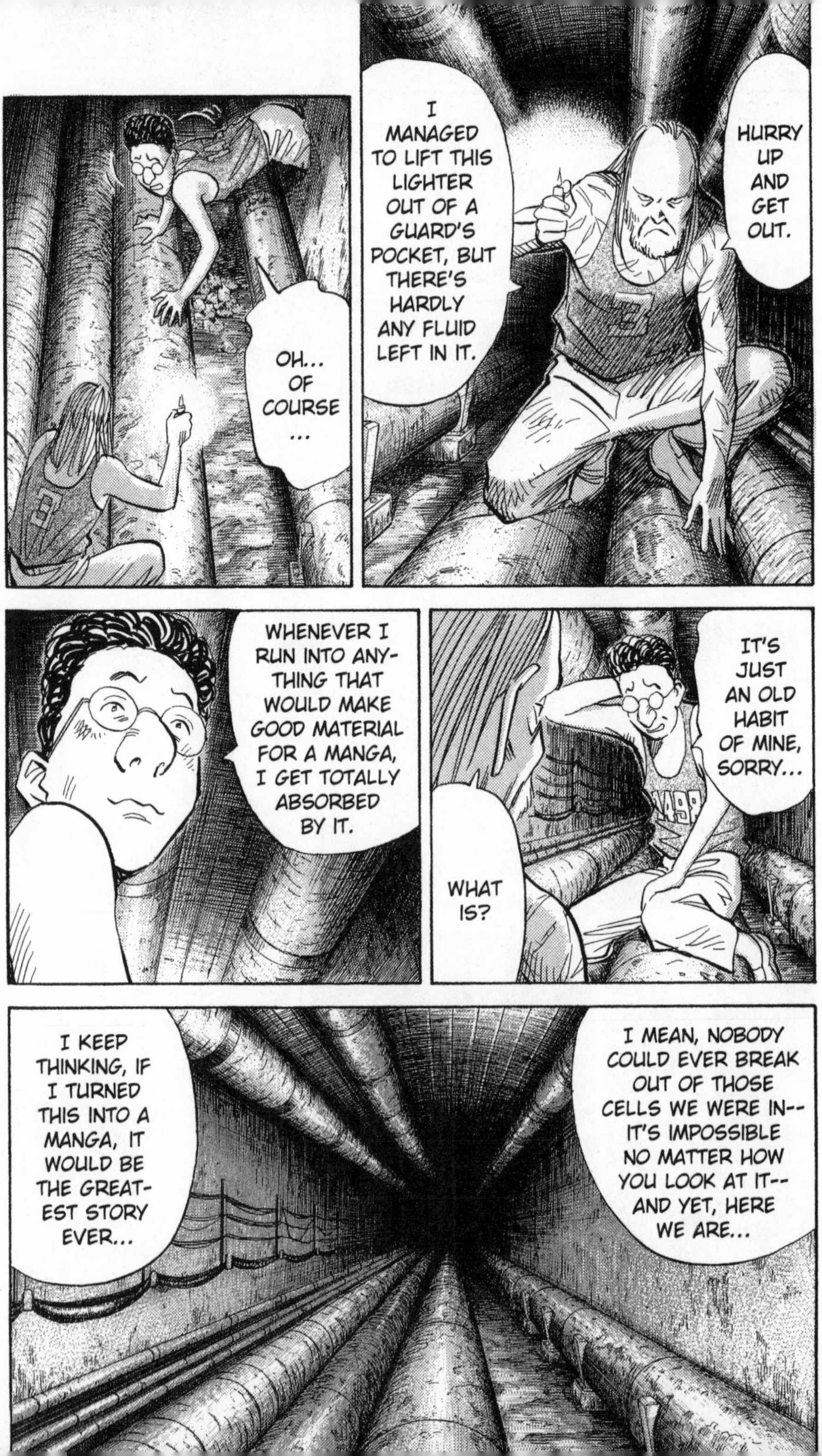
HURRY UP AND GET OUT.
I MANAGED TO LIFT THIS LIGHTER OUT OF A GUARD'S POCKET, BUT THERE'S HARDLY ANY FLUID LEFT IN IT.
OH... OF COURSE...
IT'S JUST AN OLD HABIT OF MINE, SORRY...
WHAT IS?
WHENEVER I RUN INTO ANY-THING THAT WOULD MAKE GOOD MATERIAL FOR A MANGA, I GET TOTALLY ABSORBED BY IT.
I MEAN, NOBODY COULD EVER BREAK OUT OF THOSE CELLS WE WERE IN-- IT'S IMPOSSIBLE NO MATTER HOW YOU LOOK AT IT-- AND YET, HERE WE ARE...
I KEEP THINKING, IF I TURNED THIS INTO A MANGA, IT WOULD BE THE GREAT-EST STORY EVER...

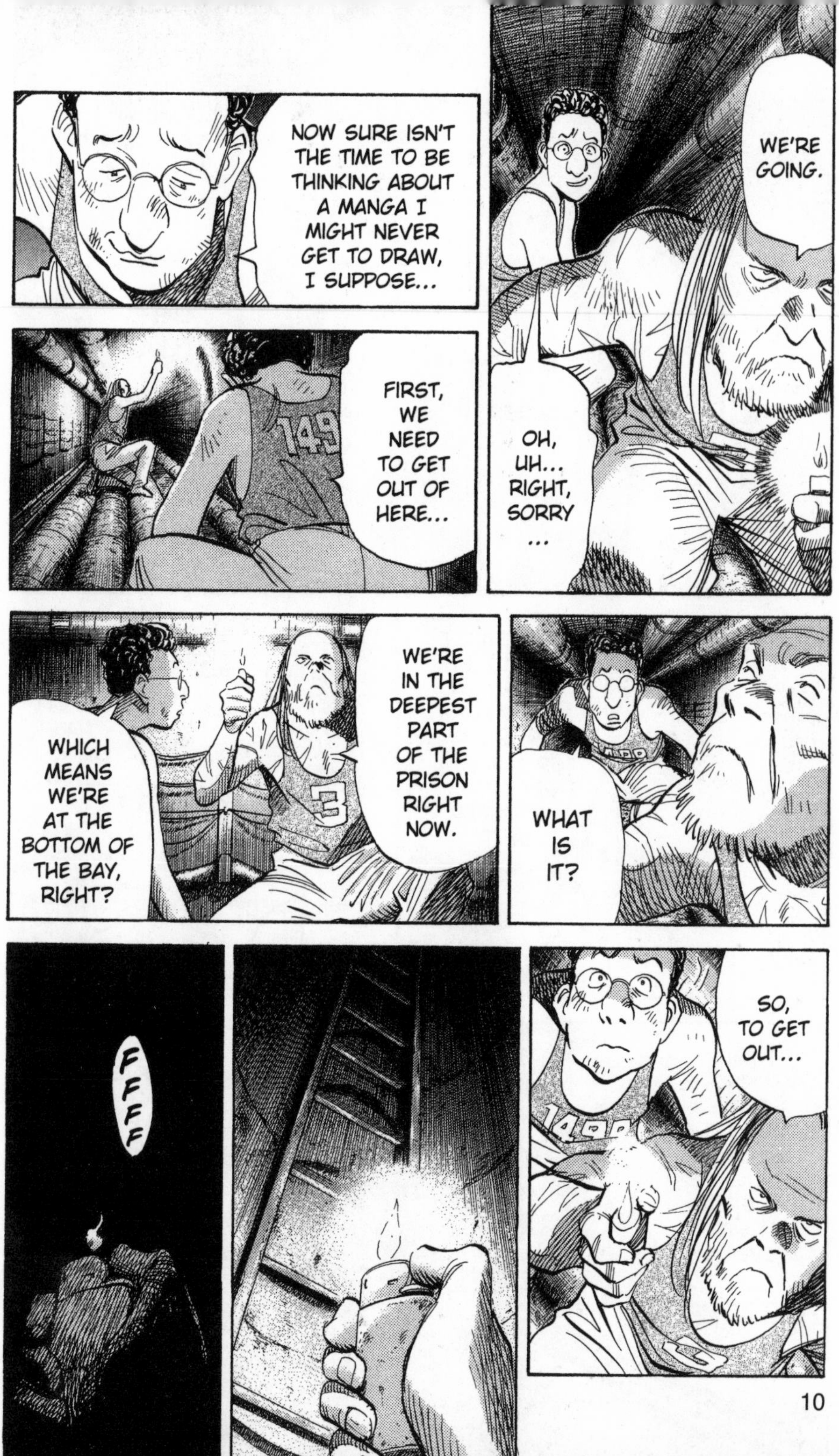
WE'RE GOING.
OH, UH... RIGHT, SORRY ...
NOW SURE ISN'T THE TIME TO BE THINKING ABOUT A MANGA I MIGHT NEVER GET TO DRAW, I SUPPOSE...
FIRST, WE NEED TO GET OUT OF HERE...
WHAT IS IT?
WE'RE IN THE DEEPEST PART OF THE PRISON RIGHT NOW.
WHICH MEANS WE'RE AT THE BOTTOM OF THE BAY, RIGHT?
SO, TO GET OUT...
FFFF

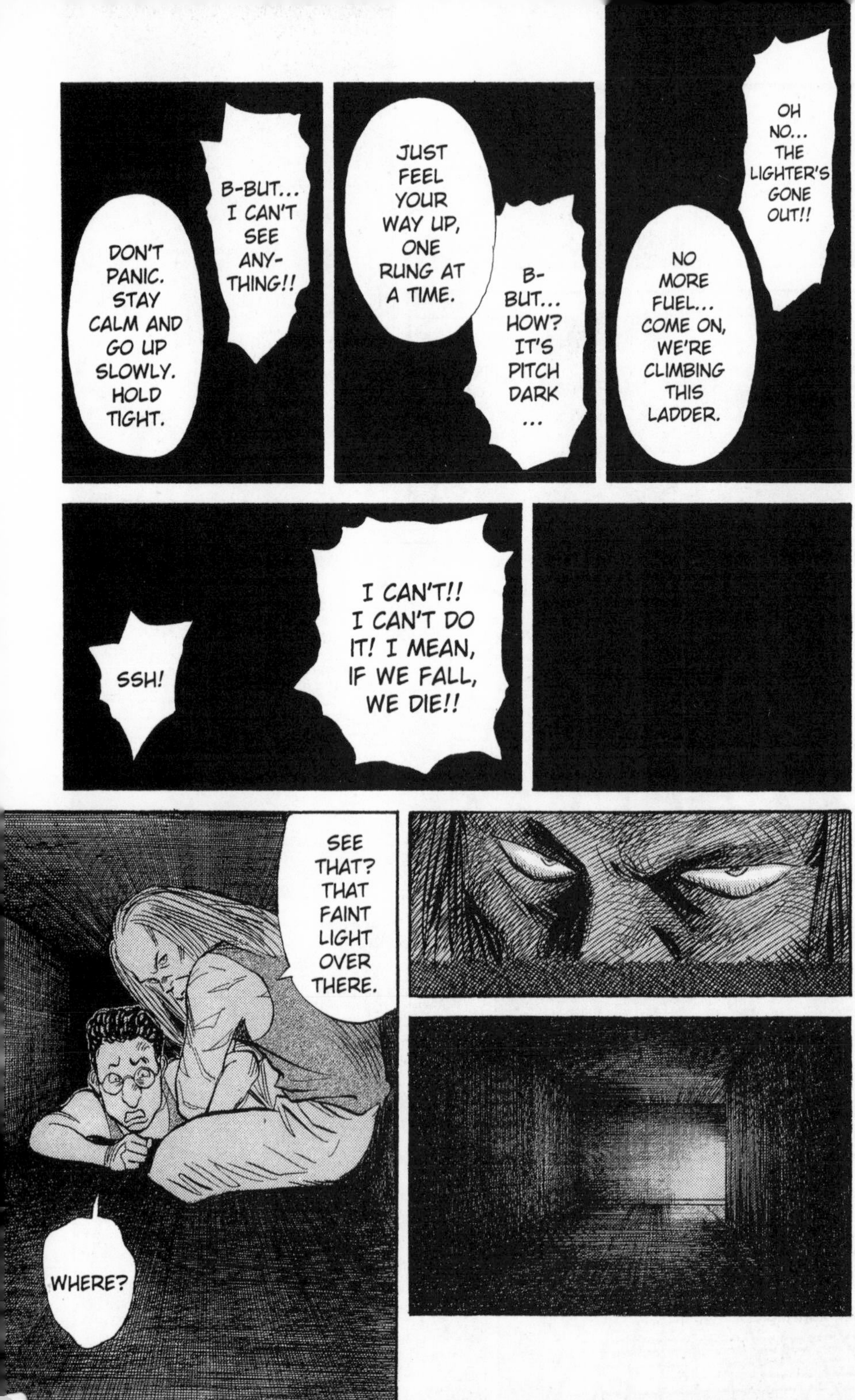

OH NO... THE LIGHTER'S GONE OUT!!
NO MORE FUEL... COME ON, WE'RE CLIMBING THIS LADDER.
JUST FEEL YOUR WAY UP, ONE RUNG AT A TIME.
B-BUT... HOW? IT'S PITCH DARK...
B-BUT... I CAN'T SEE ANY-THING!!
DON'T PANIC. STAY CALM AND GO UP SLOWLY. HOLD TIGHT.
I CAN'T!! I CAN'T DO IT! I MEAN, IF WE FALL, WE DIE!!
SSH!
SEE THAT? THAT FAINT LIGHT OVER THERE.
WHERE?

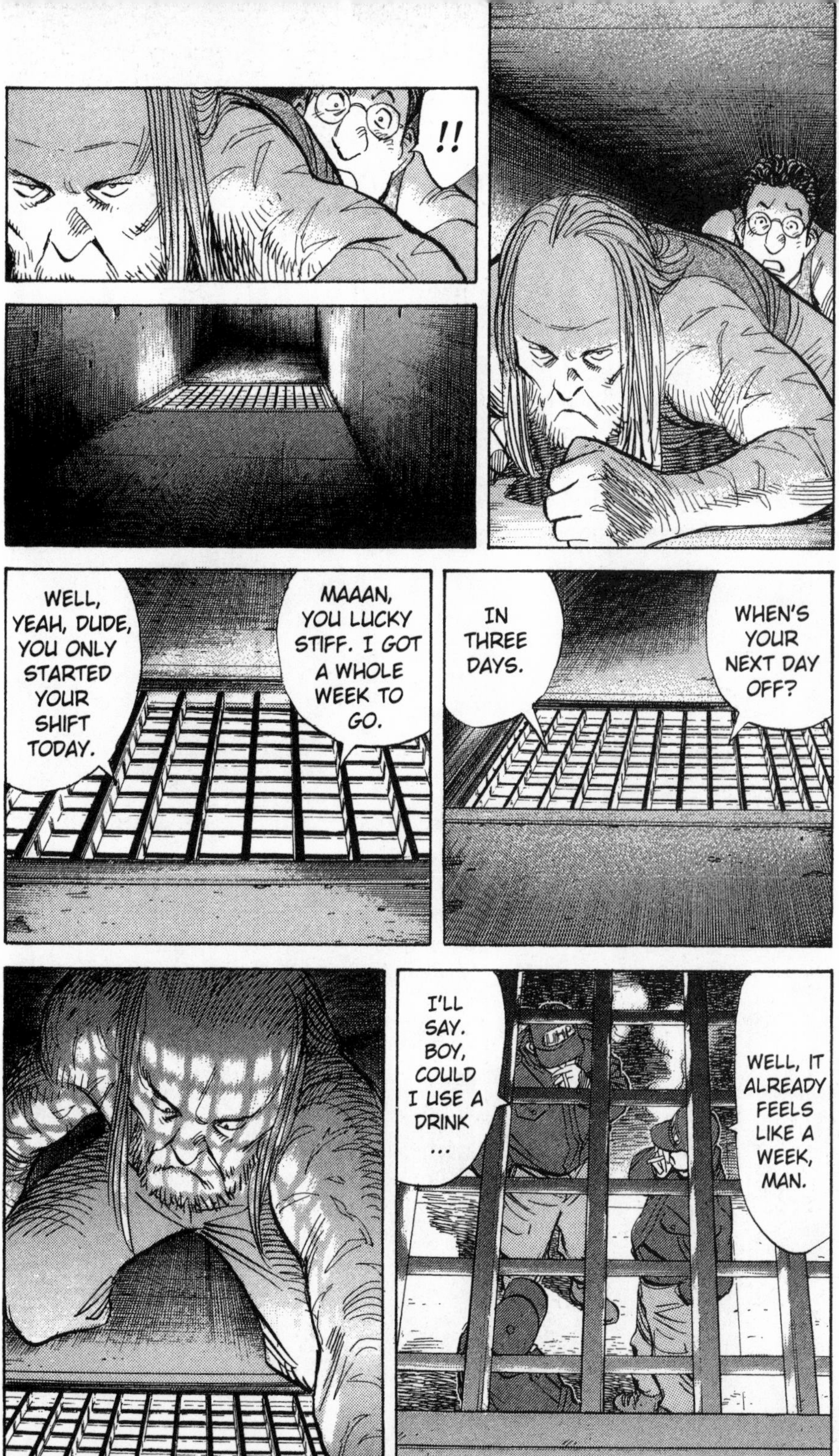
!!
WHEN'S YOUR NEXT DAY OFF?
IN THREE DAYS.
MAAAN, YOU LUCKY STIFF. I GOT A WHOLE WEEK TO GO.
WELL, YEAH, DUDE, YOU ONLY STARTED YOUR SHIFT TODAY.
WELL, IT ALREADY FEELS LIKE A WEEK, MAN.
I'LL SAY. BOY, COULD I USE A DRINK ...

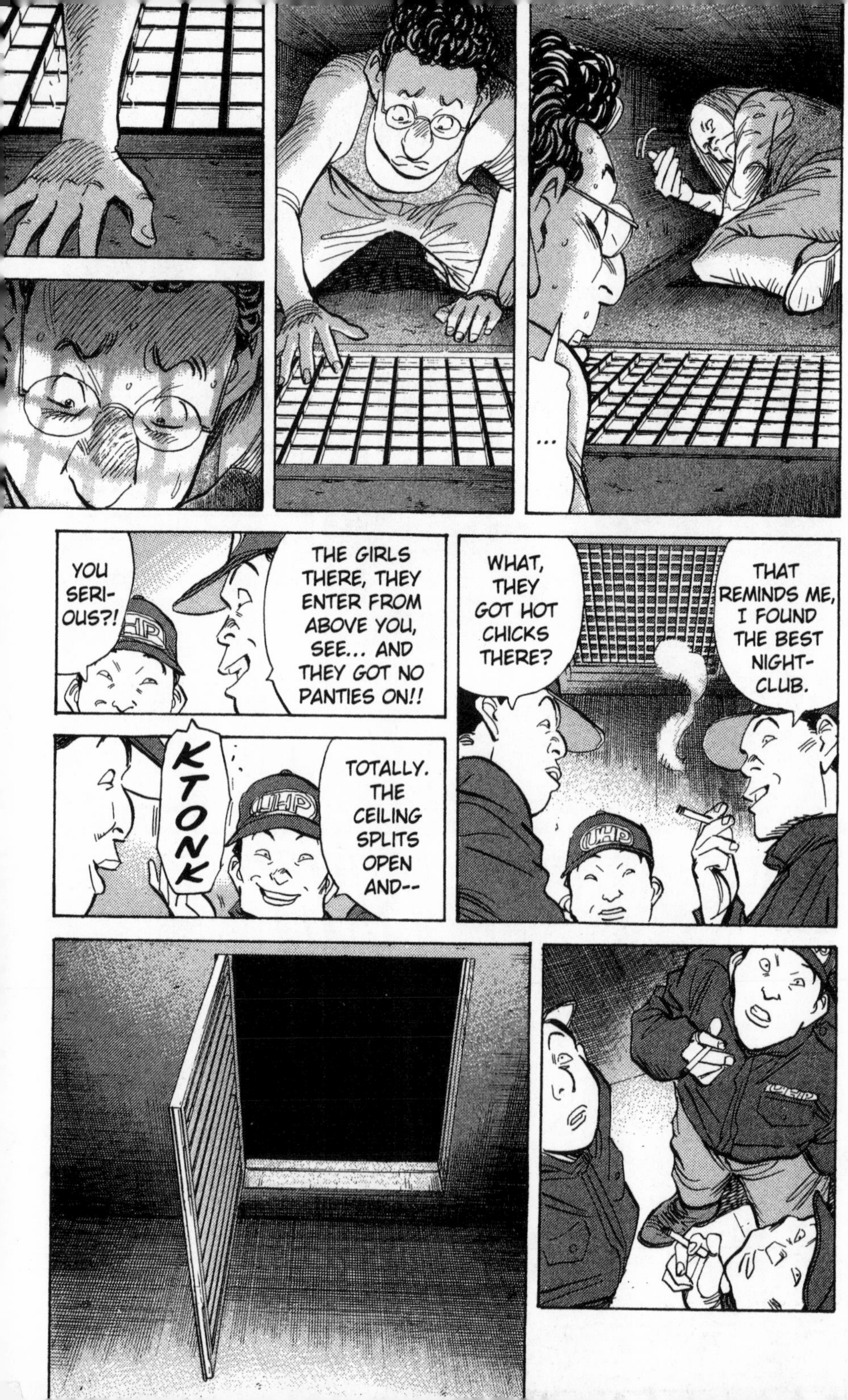
...
THAT REMINDS ME, I FOUND THE BEST NIGHT-CLUB.
WHAT, THEY GOT HOT CHICKS THERE?
THE GIRLS THERE, THEY ENTER FROM ABOVE YOU, SEE... AND THEY GOT NO PANTIES ON!!
YOU SERI-OUS?!
TOTALLY. THE CEILING SPLITS OPEN AND--
KTONK

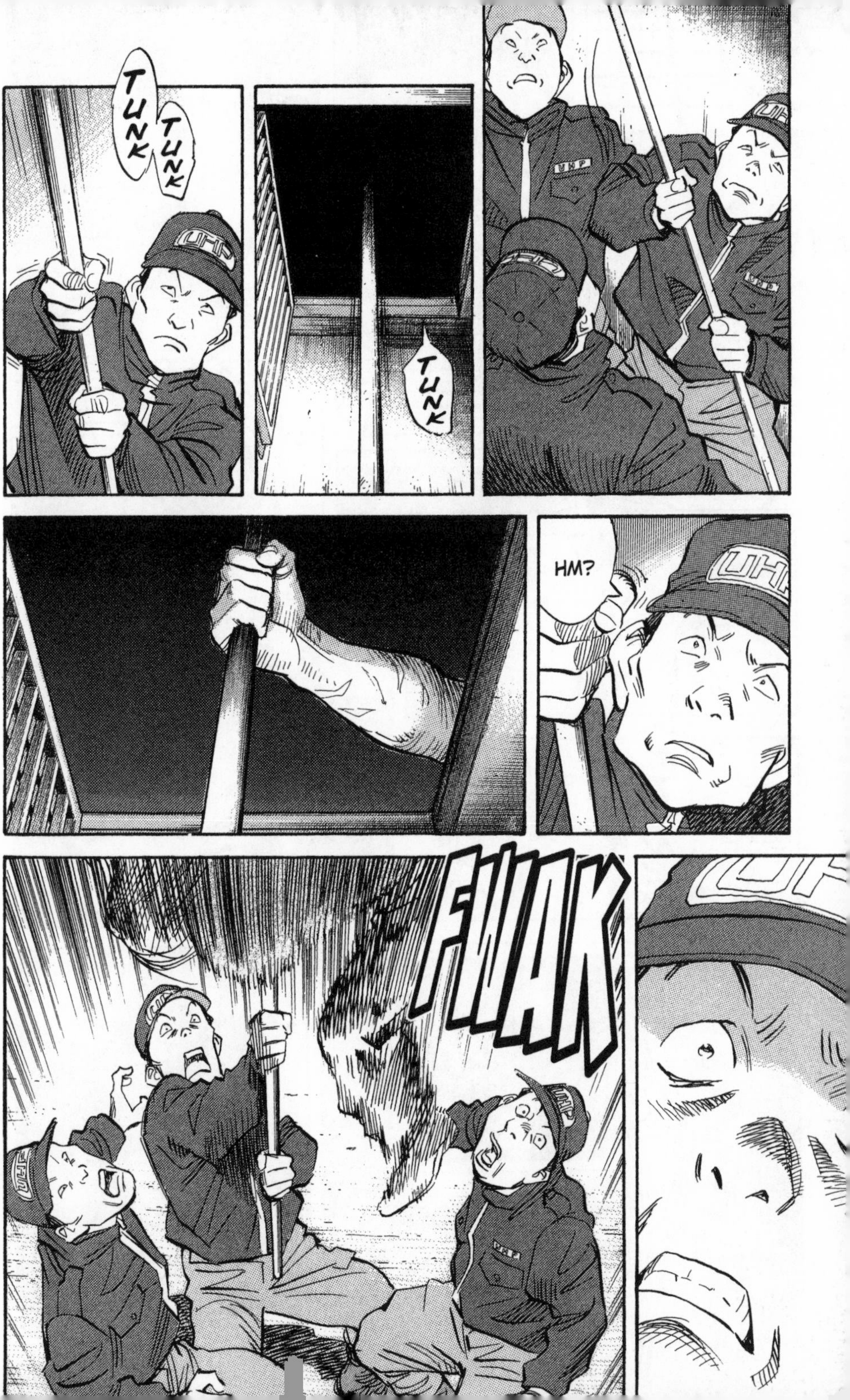
TUNK
TUNK
TUNK
HM?
FWAK

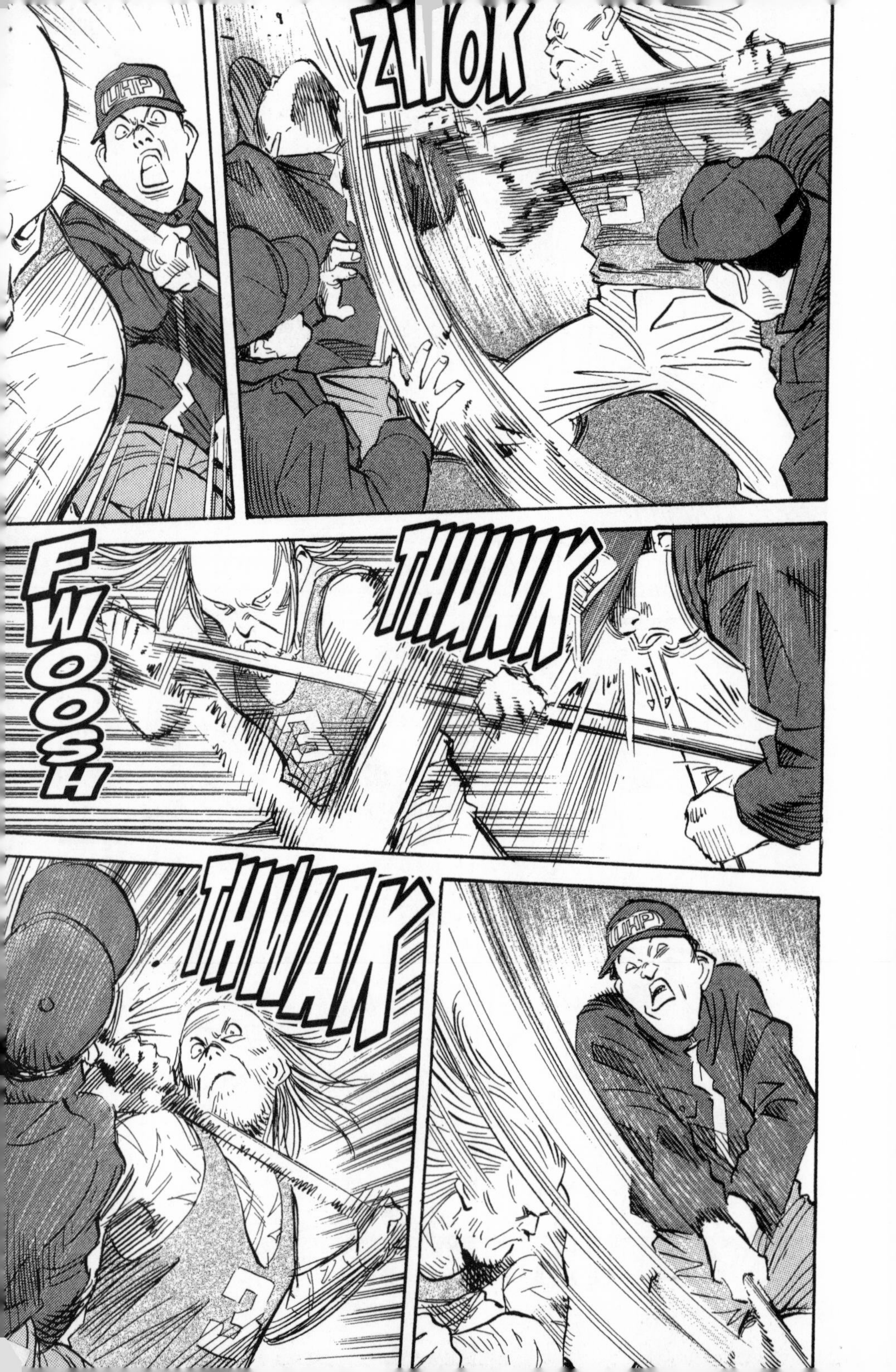
ZWOK
UHP
THUNK
FWOOSH
UHP
THWAK

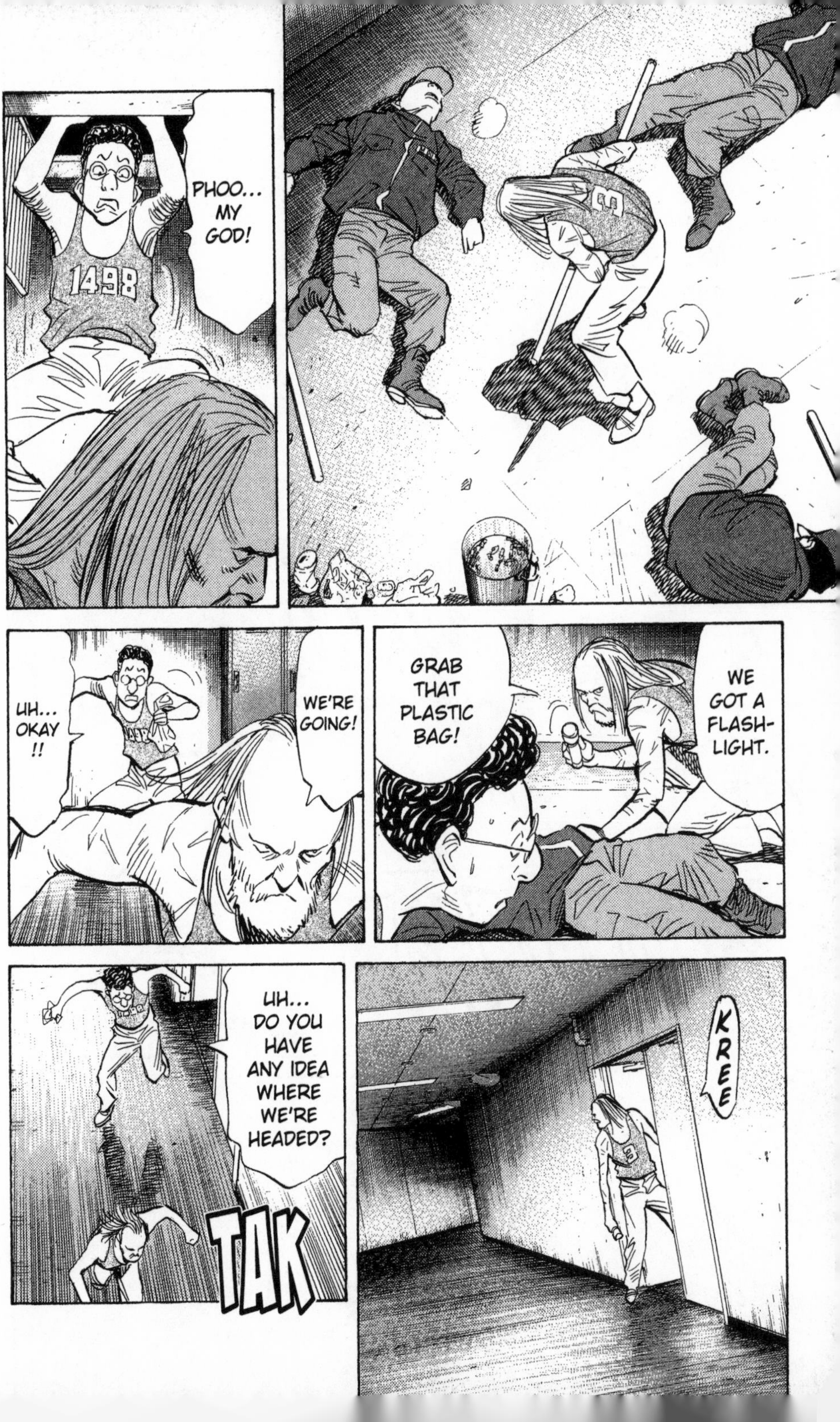
PHOO... MY GOD!
1498
WE GOT A FLASH-LIGHT.
GRAB THAT PLASTIC BAG!
WE'RE GOING!
UH... OKAY !!
KREE
UH... DO YOU HAVE ANY IDEA WHERE WE'RE HEADED?
TAK

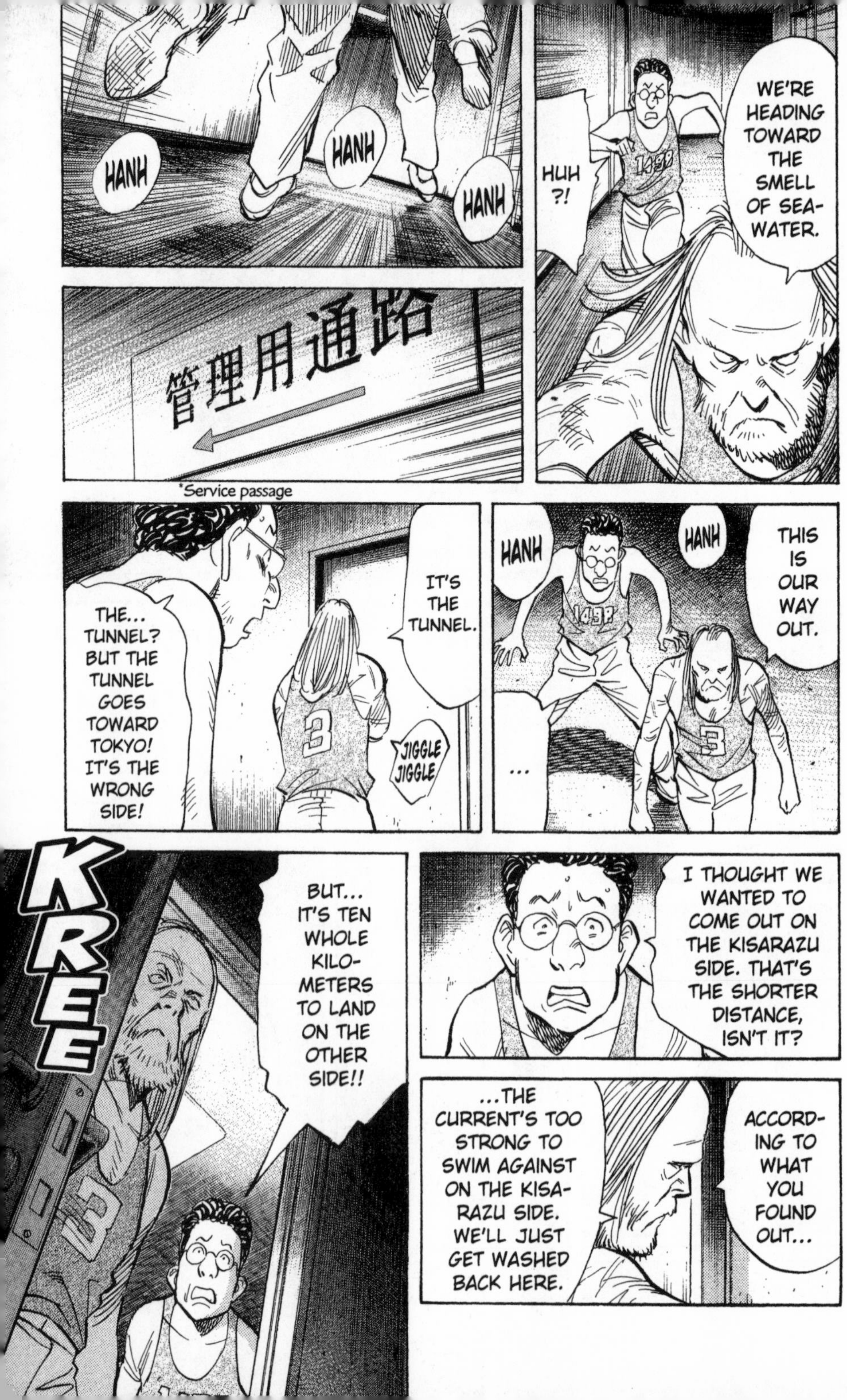

WE'RE HEADING TOWARD THE SMELL OF SEA-WATER.
HUH ?!
HANH
HANH
HANH
管理用通路
*Service passage
THIS IS OUR WAY OUT.
HANH
HANH
...
IT'S THE TUNNEL.
THE... TUNNEL? BUT THE TUNNEL GOES TOWARD TOKYO! IT'S THE WRONG SIDE!
JIGGLE JIGGLE
I THOUGHT WE WANTED TO COME OUT ON THE KISARAZU SIDE. THAT'S THE SHORTER DISTANCE, ISN'T IT?
ACCORD-ING TO WHAT YOU FOUND OUT...
...THE CURRENT'S TOO STRONG TO SWIM AGAINST ON THE KISA-RAZU SIDE. WE'LL JUST GET WASHED BACK HERE.
KREE
BUT... IT'S TEN WHOLE KILO-METERS TO LAND ON THE OTHER SIDE!!

I THOUGHT THEY SAID THE TUNNEL HAD SUNK UNDER-WATER...

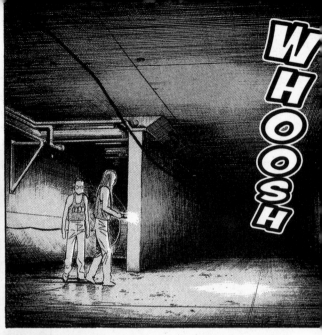

THIS IS THE SERVICE TUNNEL.

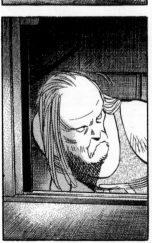

KA-SHANK

非常口
EXIT

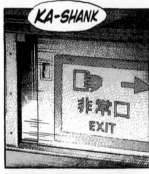

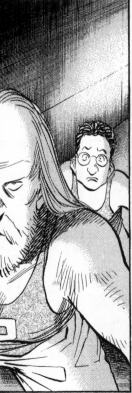

THE ROAD-WAY IS ABOVE THIS.

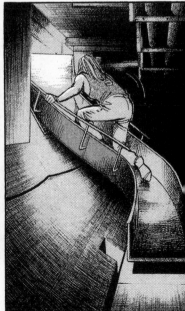

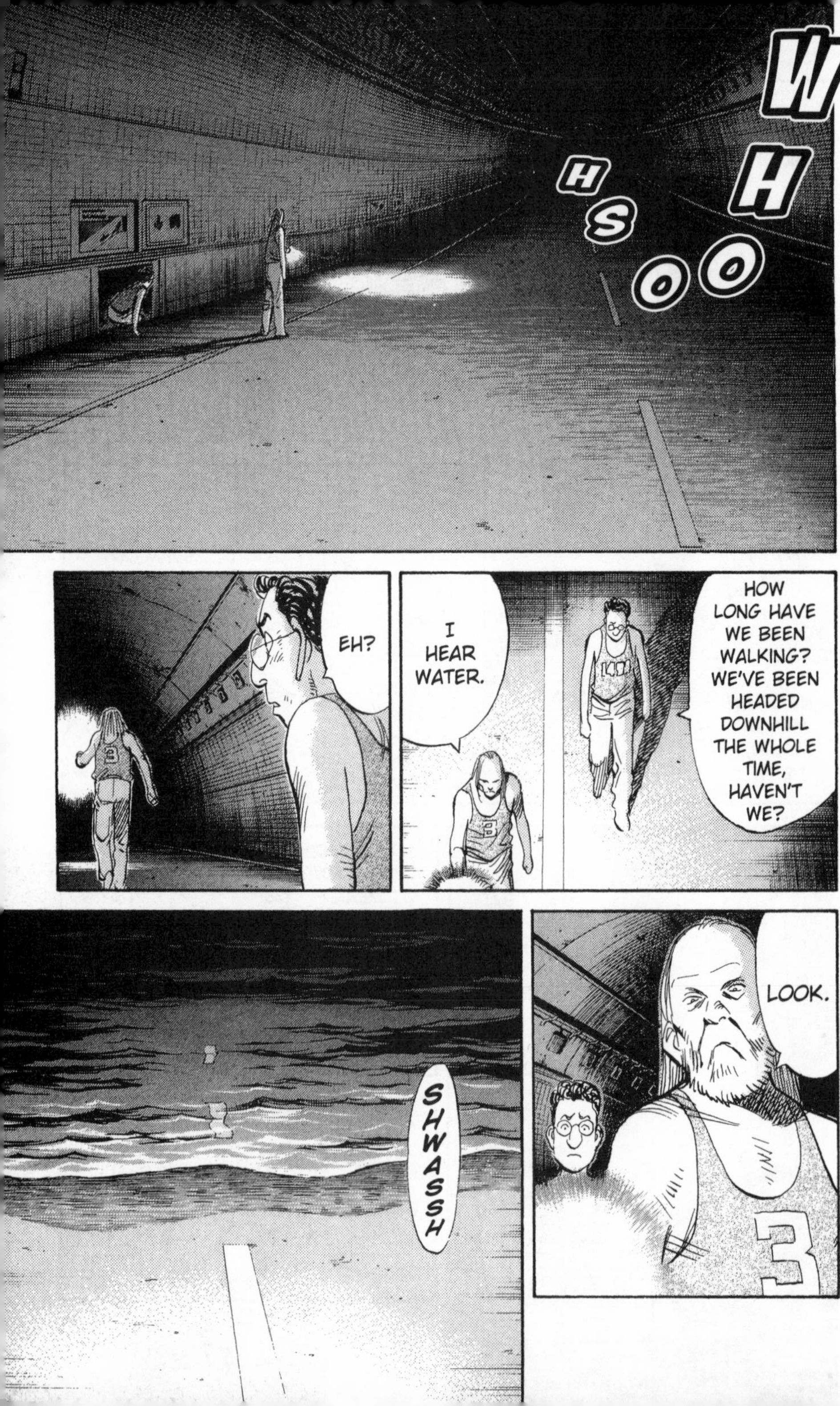
WHOOSH
HOW LONG HAVE WE BEEN WALKING? WE'VE BEEN HEADED DOWNHILL THE WHOLE TIME, HAVEN'T WE?
I HEAR WATER.
EH?
LOOK.
SHWASSH

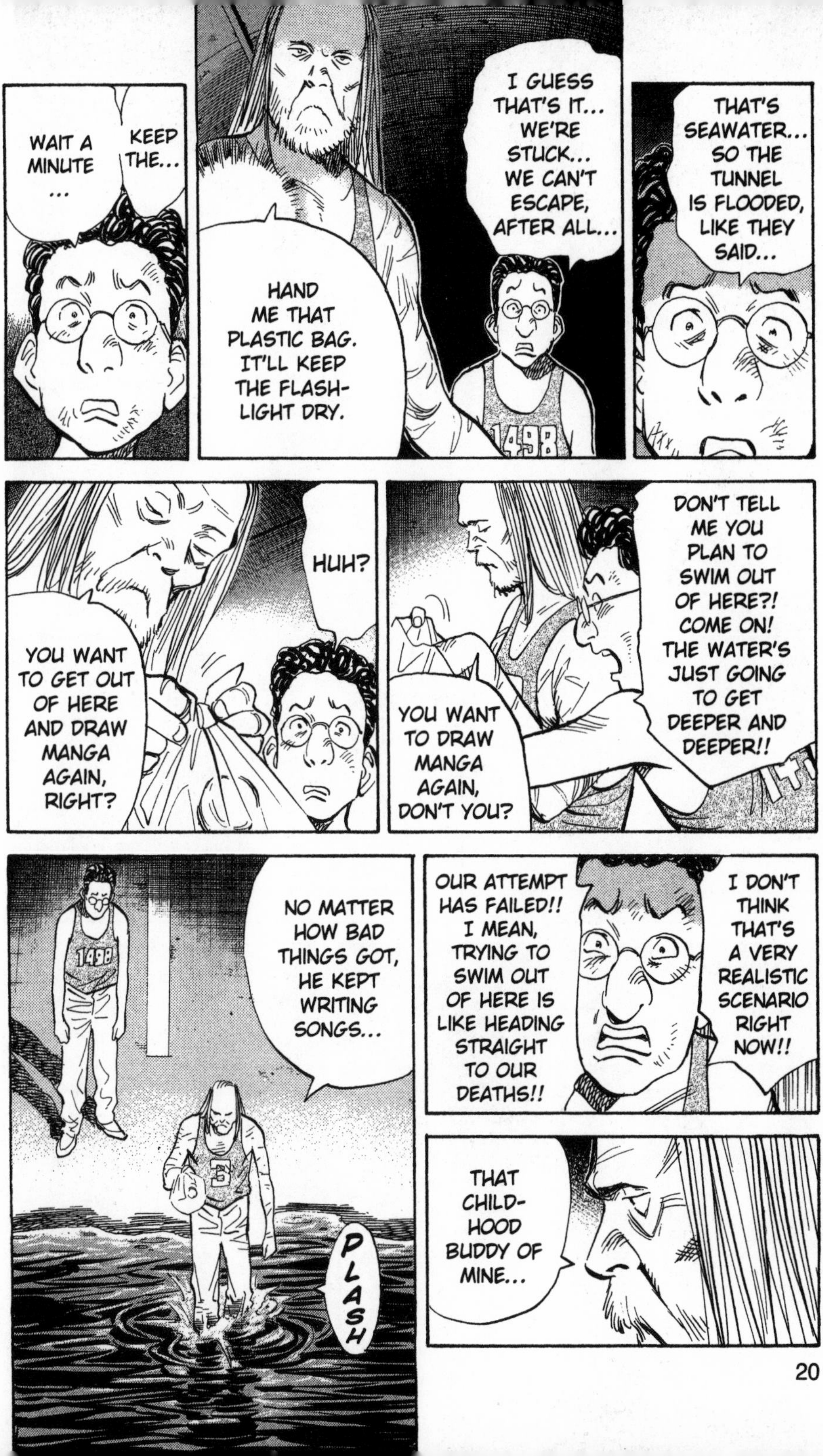
THAT'S SEAWATER... SO THE TUNNEL IS FLOODED, LIKE THEY SAID...
I GUESS THAT'S IT... WE'RE STUCK... WE CAN'T ESCAPE, AFTER ALL...
HAND ME THAT PLASTIC BAG. IT'LL KEEP THE FLASH-LIGHT DRY.
KEEP THE...
WAIT A MINUTE ...
DON'T TELL ME YOU PLAN TO SWIM OUT OF HERE?! COME ON! THE WATER'S JUST GOING TO GET DEEPER AND DEEPER!!
YOU WANT TO DRAW MANGA AGAIN, DON'T YOU?
HUH?
YOU WANT TO GET OUT OF HERE AND DRAW MANGA AGAIN, RIGHT?
I DON'T THINK THAT'S A VERY REALISTIC SCENARIO RIGHT NOW!!
OUR ATTEMPT HAS FAILED!! I MEAN, TRYING TO SWIM OUT OF HERE IS LIKE HEADING STRAIGHT TO OUR DEATHS!!
THAT CHILD-HOOD BUDDY OF MINE...
NO MATTER HOW BAD THINGS GOT, HE KEPT WRITING SONGS...
PLASH

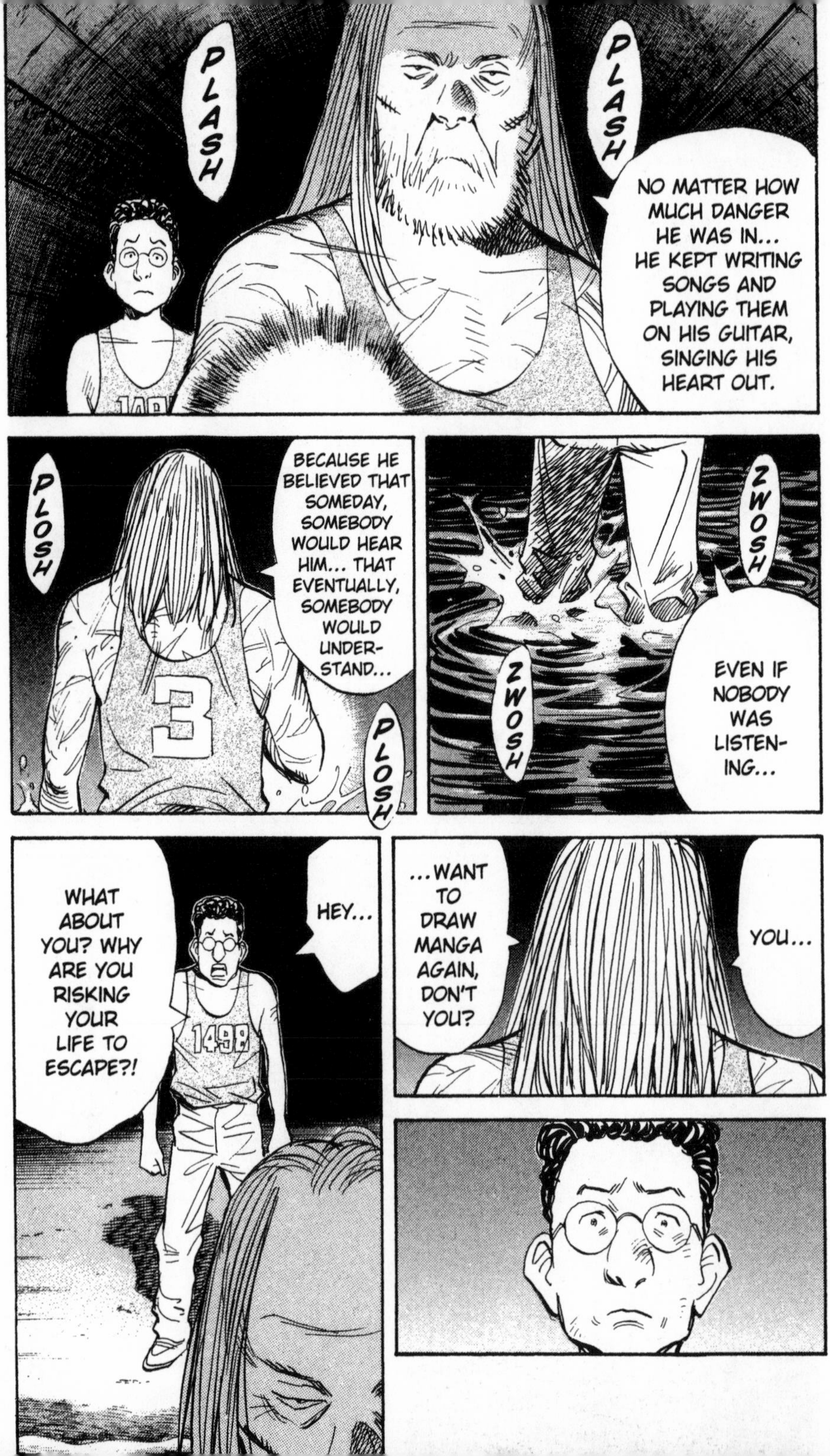
PLASH
NO MATTER HOW MUCH DANGER HE WAS IN... HE KEPT WRITING SONGS AND PLAYING THEM ON HIS GUITAR, SINGING HIS HEART OUT.
PLASH
ZWOSH
EVEN IF NOBODY WAS LISTEN-ING...
ZWOSH
PLOSH
BECAUSE HE BELIEVED THAT SOMEDAY, SOMEBODY WOULD HEAR HIM... THAT EVENTUALLY, SOMEBODY WOULD UNDER-STAND...
PLOSH
YOU...
...WANT TO DRAW MANGA AGAIN, DON'T YOU?
HEY...
WHAT ABOUT YOU? WHY ARE YOU RISKING YOUR LIFE TO ESCAPE?!

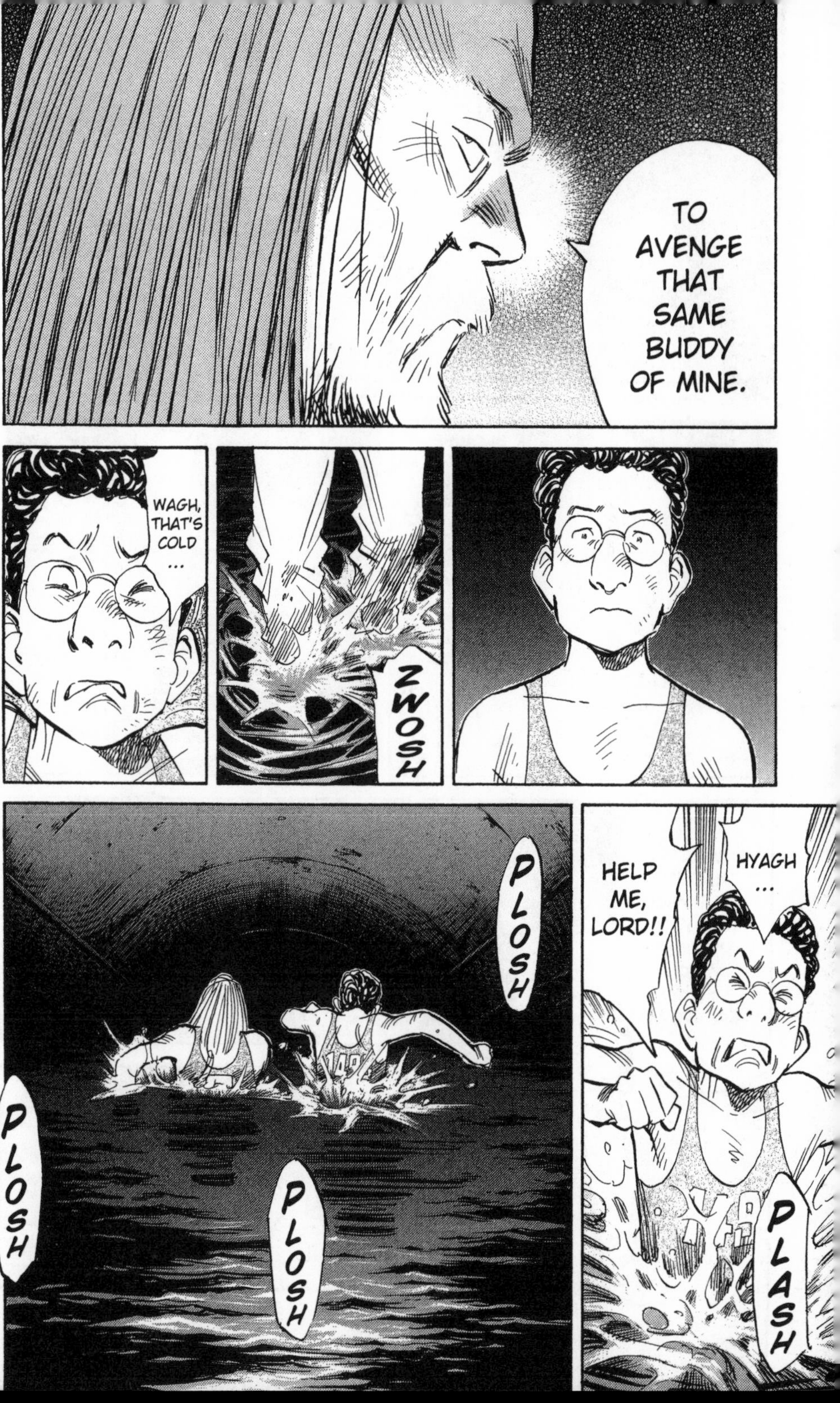
TO AVENGE THAT SAME BUDDY OF MINE.
ZWOSH
WAGH, THAT'S COLD ...
HYAGH ...
HELP ME, LORD!!
PLASH
PLOSH
PLOSH
PLOSH

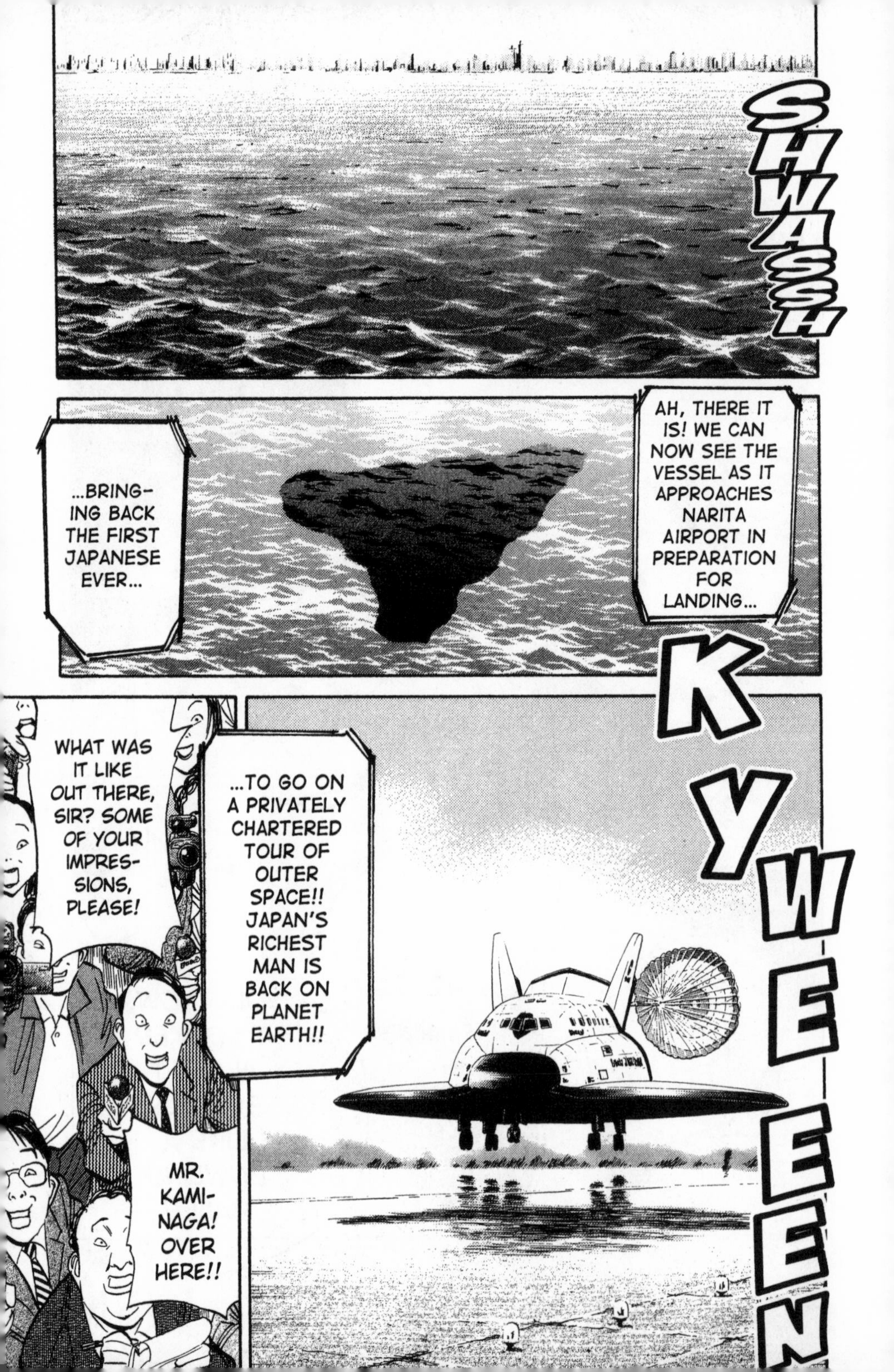
SHWASSH
AH, THERE IT IS! WE CAN NOW SEE THE VESSEL AS IT APPROACHES NARITA AIRPORT IN PREPARATION FOR LANDING...
...BRING-ING BACK THE FIRST JAPANESE EVER...
KYWEEEEN
...TO GO ON A PRIVATELY CHARTERED TOUR OF OUTER SPACE!! JAPAN'S RICHEST MAN IS BACK ON PLANET EARTH!!
WHAT WAS IT LIKE OUT THERE, SIR? SOME OF YOUR IMPRES-SIONS, PLEASE!
MR. KAMI-NAGA! OVER HERE!!

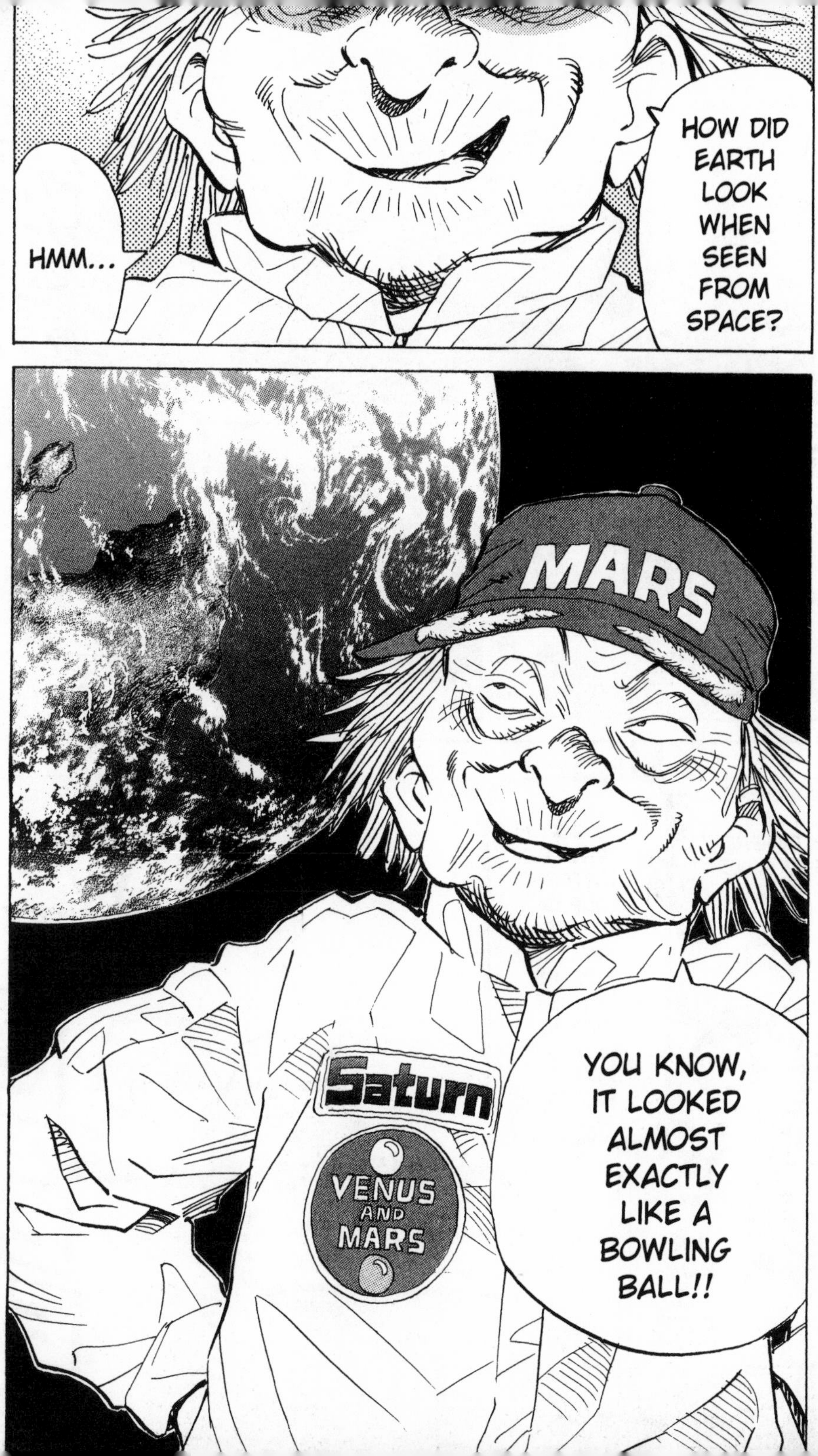
HOW DID EARTH LOOK WHEN SEEN FROM SPACE?
HMM...
MARS
YOU KNOW, IT LOOKED ALMOST EXACTLY LIKE A BOWLING BALL!!
Saturn
VENUS AND MARS

Chapter 2 Air

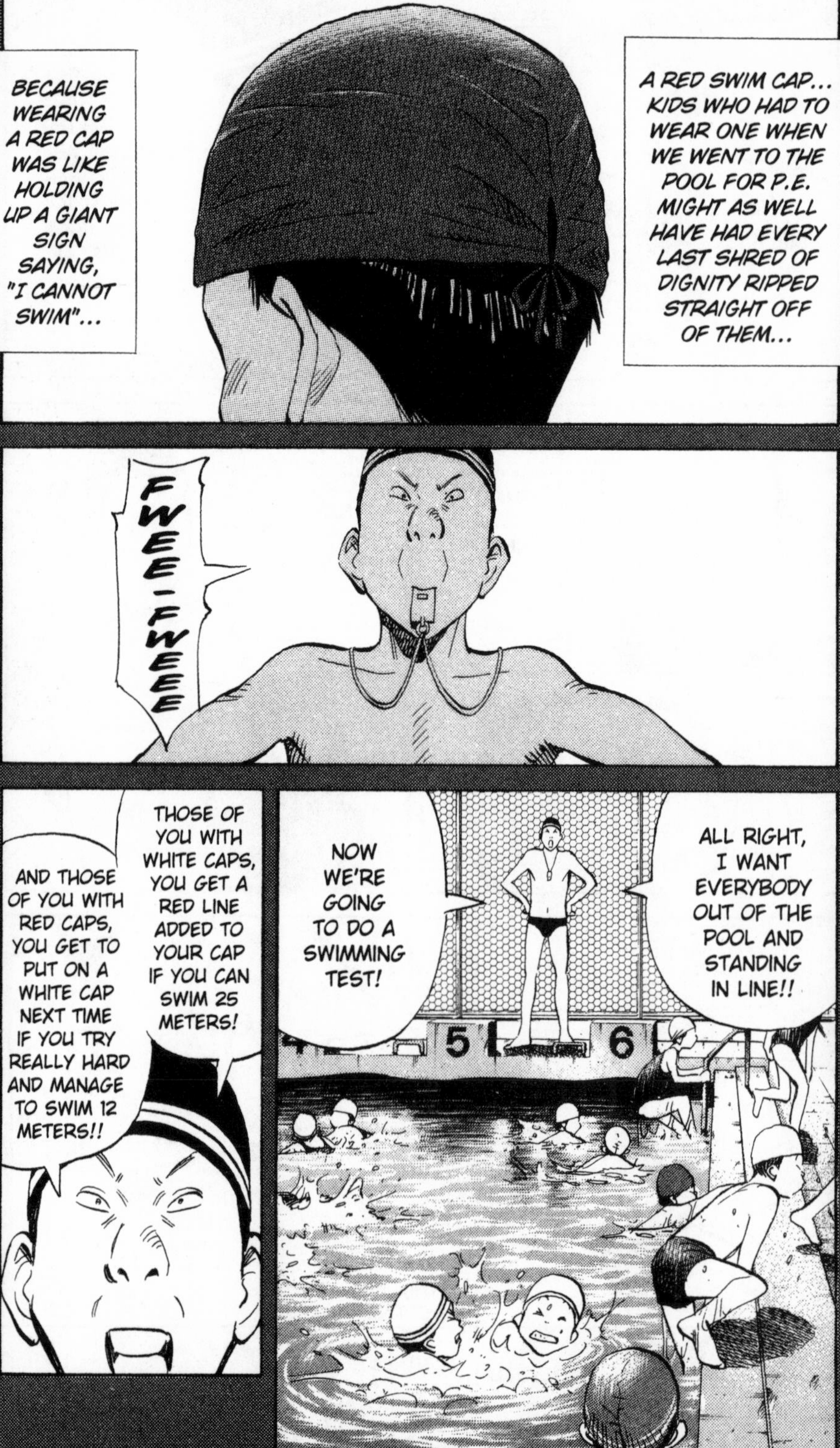
A RED SWIM CAP... KIDS WHO HAD TO WEAR ONE WHEN WE WENT TO THE POOL FOR P.E. MIGHT AS WELL HAVE HAD EVERY LAST SHRED OF DIGNITY RIPPED STRAIGHT OFF OF THEM...
BECAUSE WEARING A RED CAP WAS LIKE HOLDING UP A GIANT SIGN SAYING, "I CANNOT SWIM"...
FWEE-FWEEE
ALL RIGHT, I WANT EVERYBODY OUT OF THE POOL AND STANDING IN LINE!!
NOW WE'RE GOING TO DO A SWIMMING TEST!
THOSE OF YOU WITH WHITE CAPS, YOU GET A RED LINE ADDED TO YOUR CAP IF YOU CAN SWIM 25 METERS!
AND THOSE OF YOU WITH RED CAPS, YOU GET TO PUT ON A WHITE CAP NEXT TIME IF YOU TRY REALLY HARD AND MANAGE TO SWIM 12 METERS!!

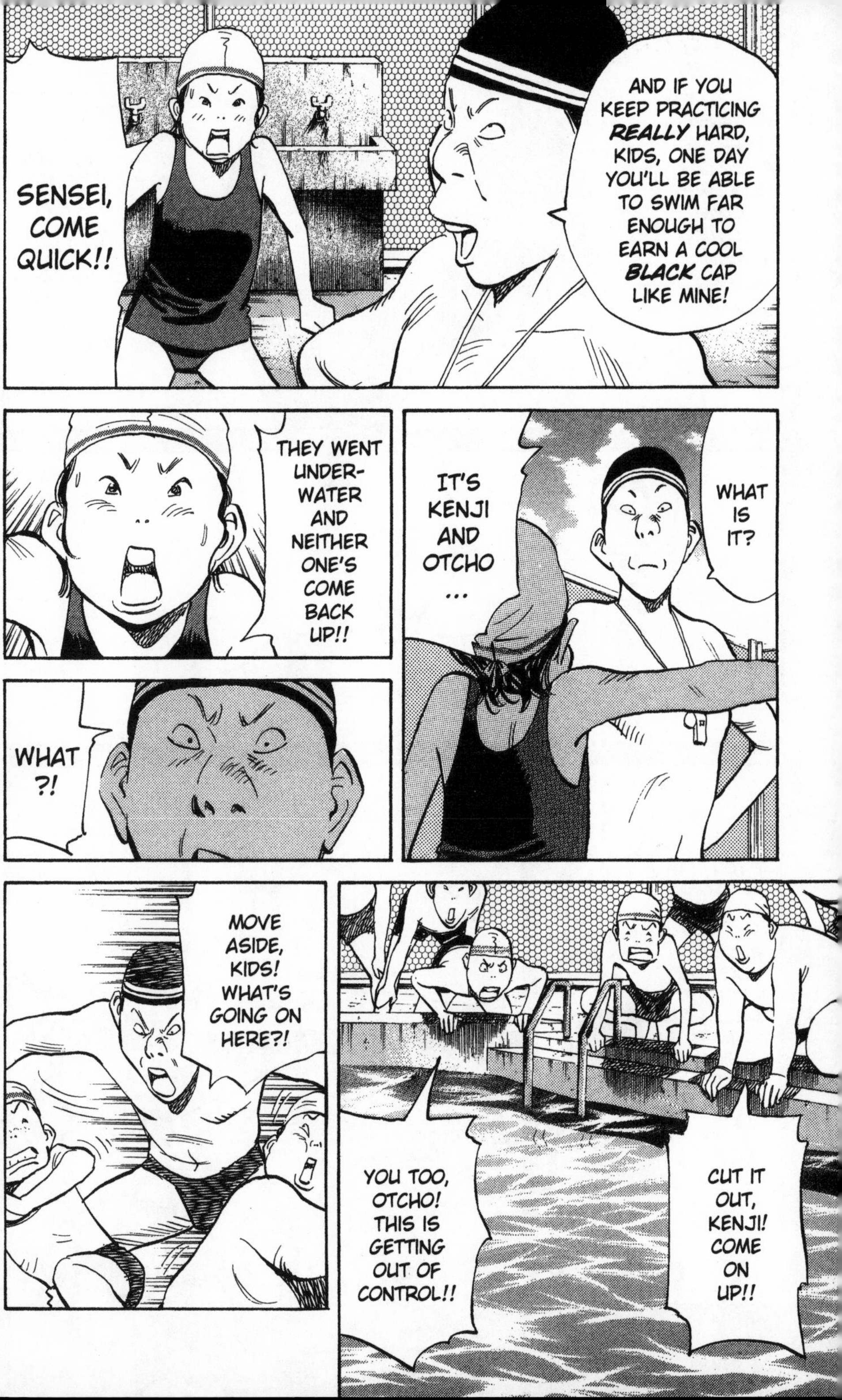
AND IF YOU KEEP PRACTICING *REALLY* HARD, KIDS, ONE DAY YOU'LL BE ABLE TO SWIM FAR ENOUGH TO EARN A COOL *BLACK* CAP LIKE MINE!
SENSEI, COME QUICK!!
WHAT IS IT?
IT'S KENJI AND OTCHO...
THEY WENT UNDER-WATER AND NEITHER ONE'S COME BACK UP!!
WHAT?!
CUT IT OUT, KENJI! COME ON UP!!
YOU TOO, OTCHO! THIS IS GETTING OUT OF CONTROL!!
MOVE ASIDE, KIDS! WHAT'S GOING ON HERE?!

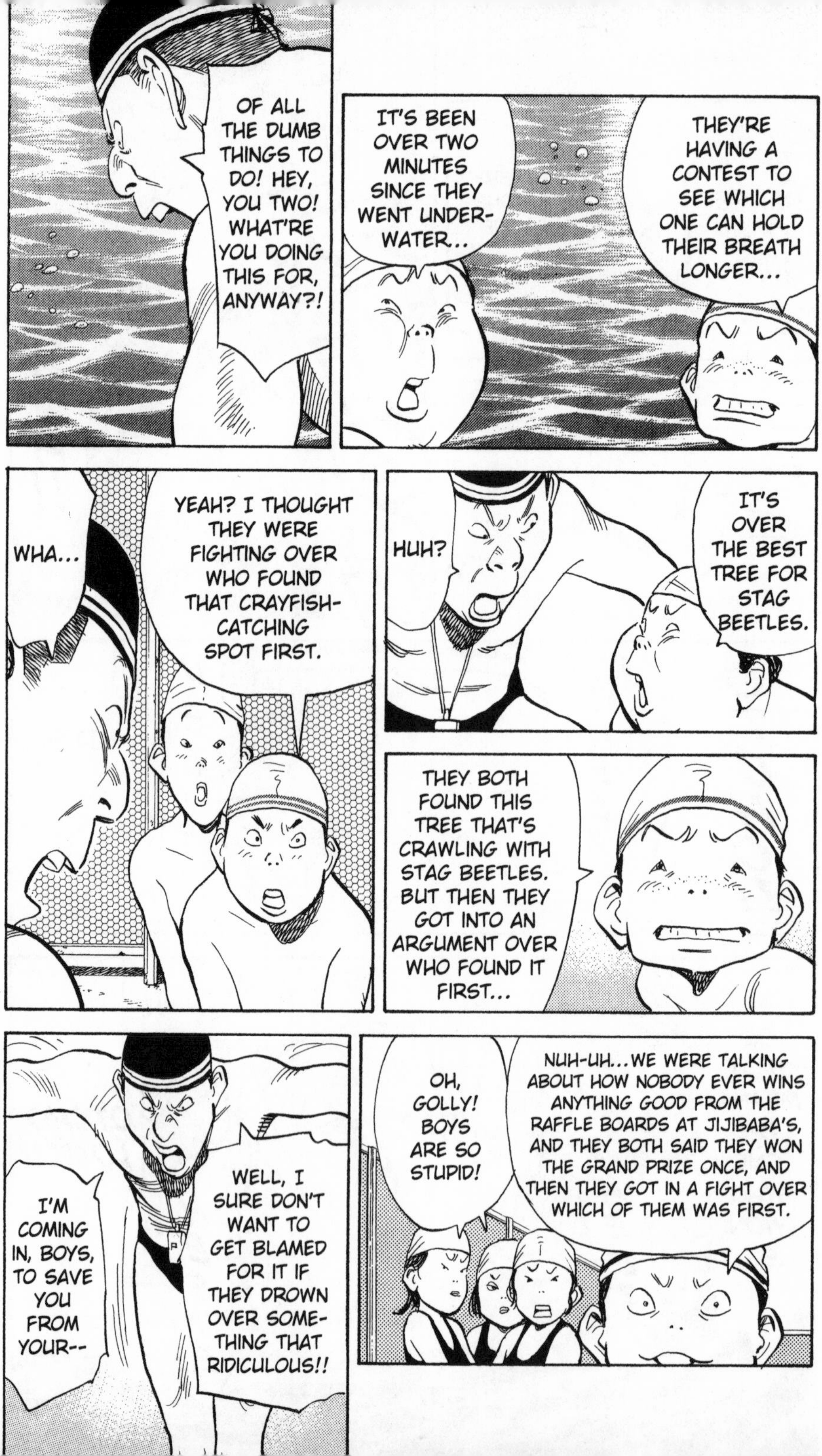
THEY'RE HAVING A CONTEST TO SEE WHICH ONE CAN HOLD THEIR BREATH LONGER...
IT'S BEEN OVER TWO MINUTES SINCE THEY WENT UNDER-WATER...
OF ALL THE DUMB THINGS TO DO! HEY, YOU TWO! WHAT'RE YOU DOING THIS FOR, ANYWAY?!
IT'S OVER THE BEST TREE FOR STAG BEETLES.
HUH?
THEY BOTH FOUND THIS TREE THAT'S CRAWLING WITH STAG BEETLES. BUT THEN THEY GOT INTO AN ARGUMENT OVER WHO FOUND IT FIRST...
YEAH? I THOUGHT THEY WERE FIGHTING OVER WHO FOUND THAT CRAYFISH-CATCHING SPOT FIRST.
WHA...
NUH-UH...WE WERE TALKING ABOUT HOW NOBODY EVER WINS ANYTHING GOOD FROM THE RAFFLE BOARDS AT JIJIBABA'S, AND THEY BOTH SAID THEY WON THE GRAND PRIZE ONCE, AND THEN THEY GOT IN A FIGHT OVER WHICH OF THEM WAS FIRST.
OH, GOLLY! BOYS ARE SO STUPID!
WELL, I SURE DON'T WANT TO GET BLAMED FOR IT IF THEY DROWN OVER SOME-THING THAT RIDICULOUS!!
I'M COMING IN, BOYS, TO SAVE YOU FROM YOUR--

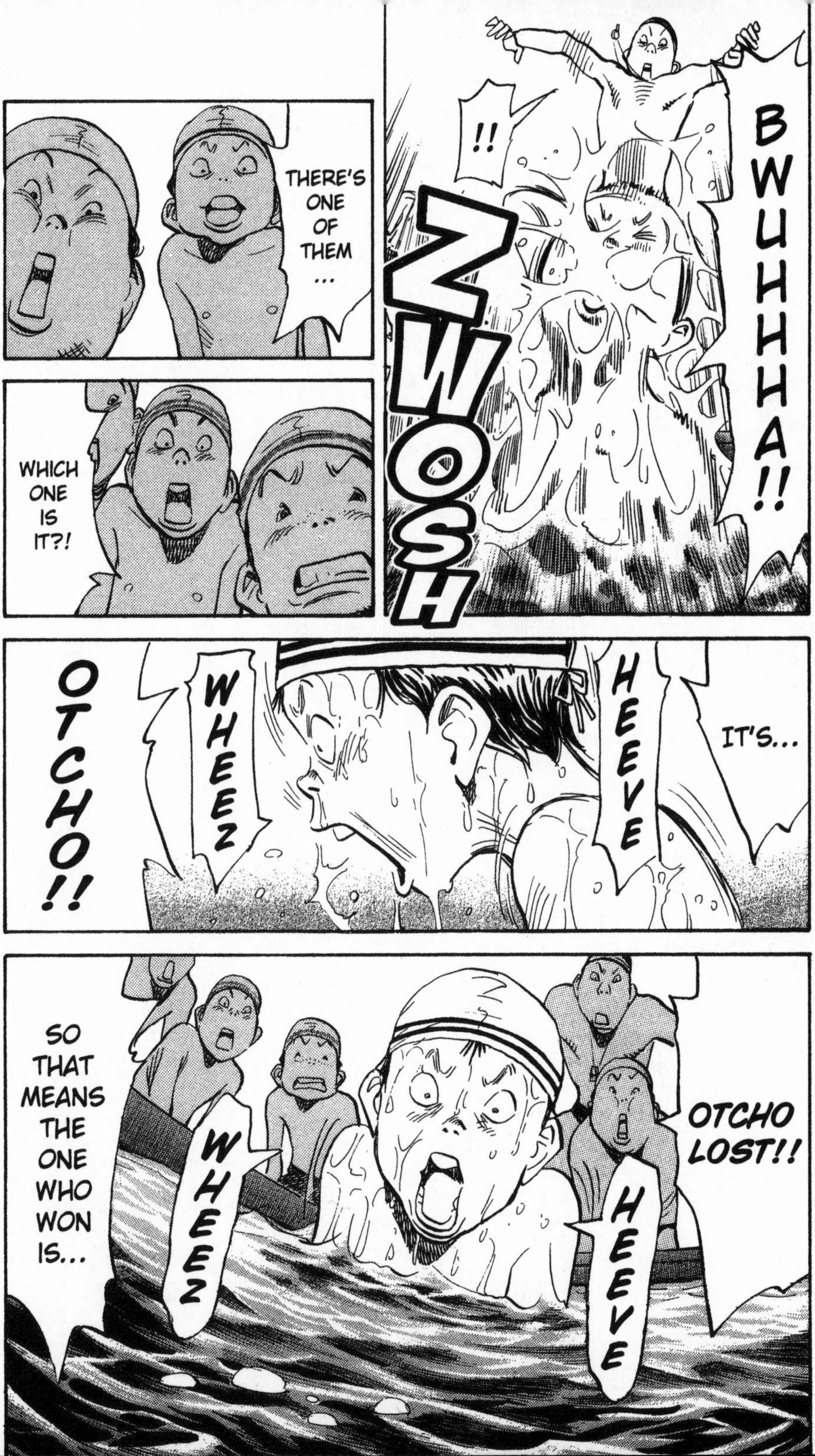
BWUHHHA!!
!!
ZWOSH
THERE'S ONE OF THEM ...
WHICH ONE IS IT?!
IT'S...
HEEVE
WHEEZ
OTCHO!!
OTCHO LOST!!
HEEVE
WHEEZ
SO THAT MEANS THE ONE WHO WON IS...

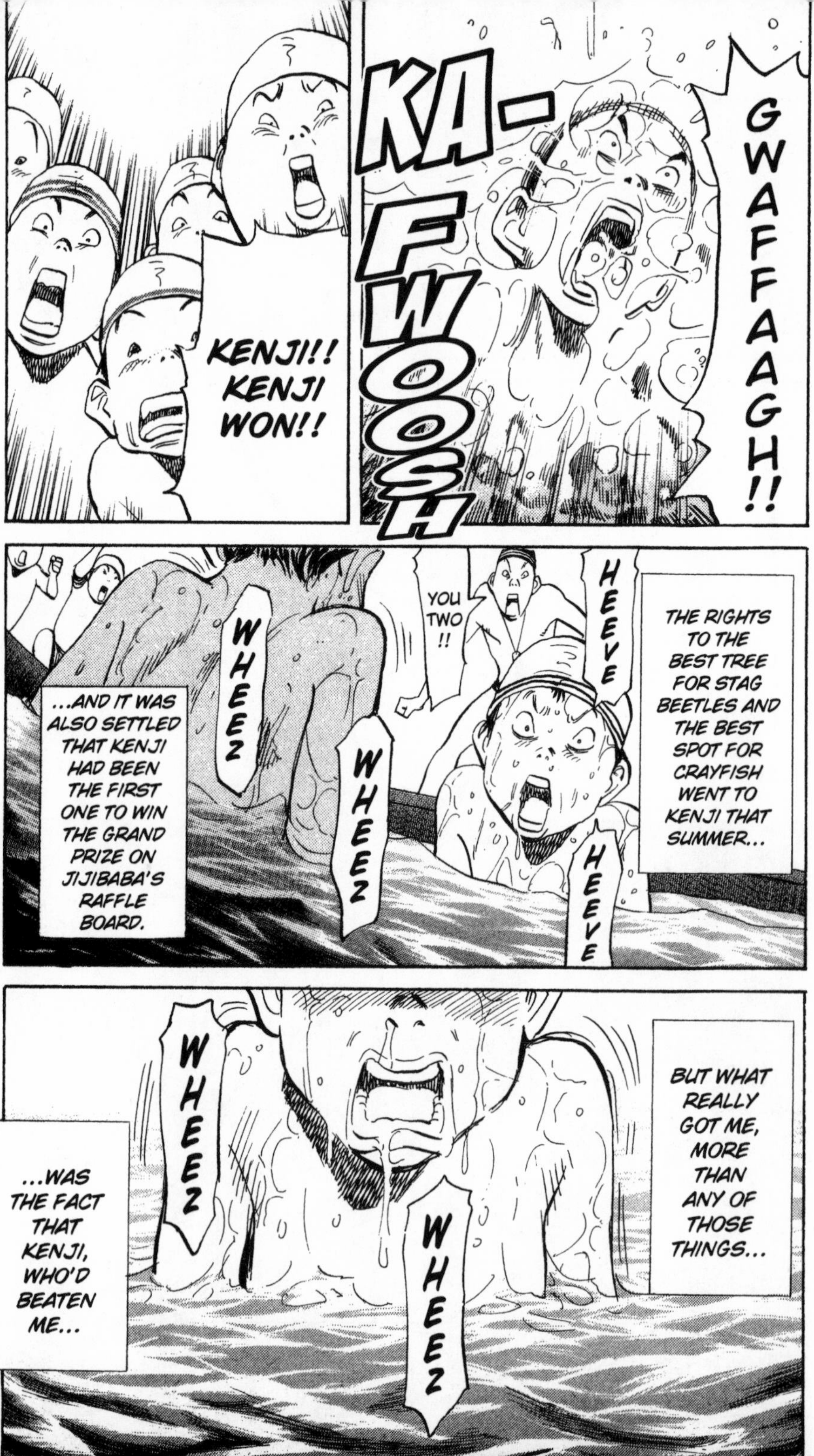
GWAFFAAGH!!
KA-FWOOSH
KENJI!! KENJI WON!!
THE RIGHTS TO THE BEST TREE FOR STAG BEETLES AND THE BEST SPOT FOR CRAYFISH WENT TO KENJI THAT SUMMER...
HEEVE
YOU TWO!!
HEEVE
WHEEZ
WHEEZ
...AND IT WAS ALSO SETTLED THAT KENJI HAD BEEN THE FIRST ONE TO WIN THE GRAND PRIZE ON JIJIBABA'S RAFFLE BOARD.
BUT WHAT REALLY GOT ME, MORE THAN ANY OF THOSE THINGS...
WHEEZ
WHEEZ
...WAS THE FACT THAT KENJI, WHO'D BEATEN ME...

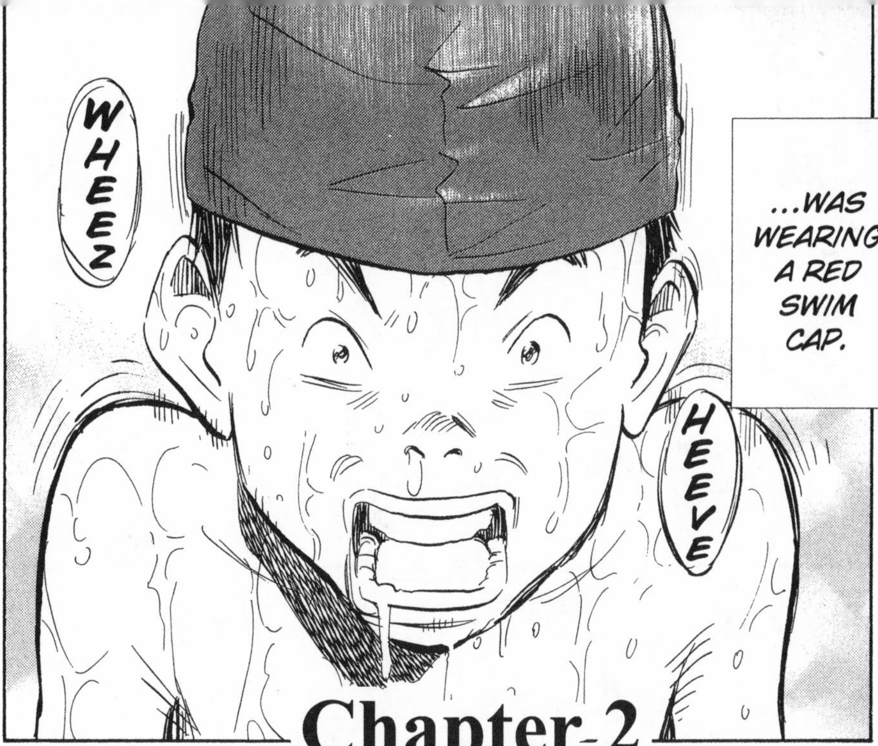
...WAS WEARING A RED SWIM CAP.
WHEEZ
HEEVE

Chapter-2
Air

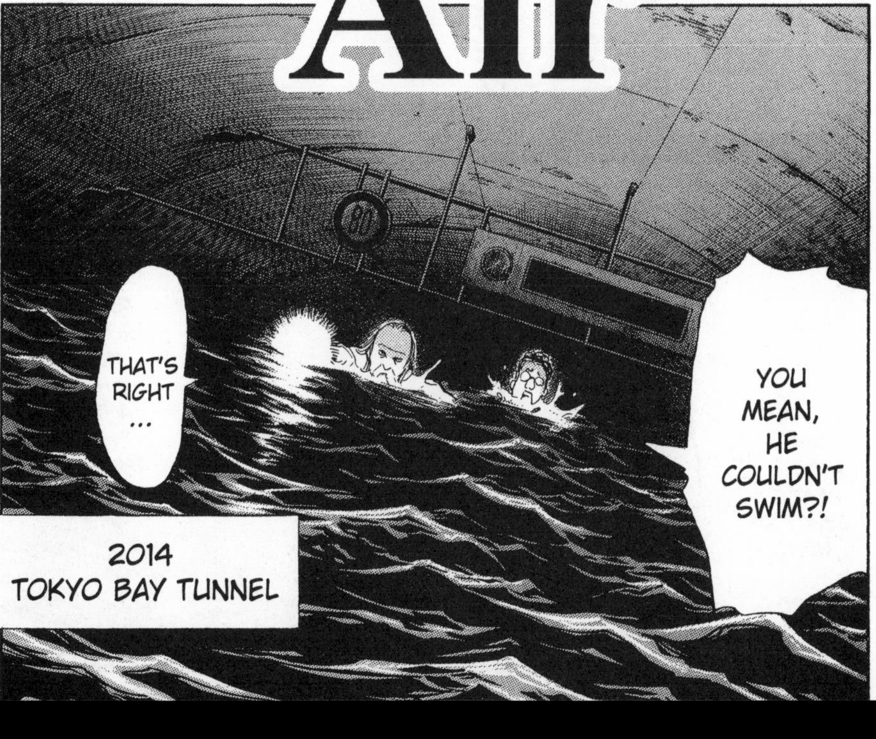
YOU MEAN, HE COULDN'T SWIM?!
THAT'S RIGHT...
2014 TOKYO BAY TUNNEL

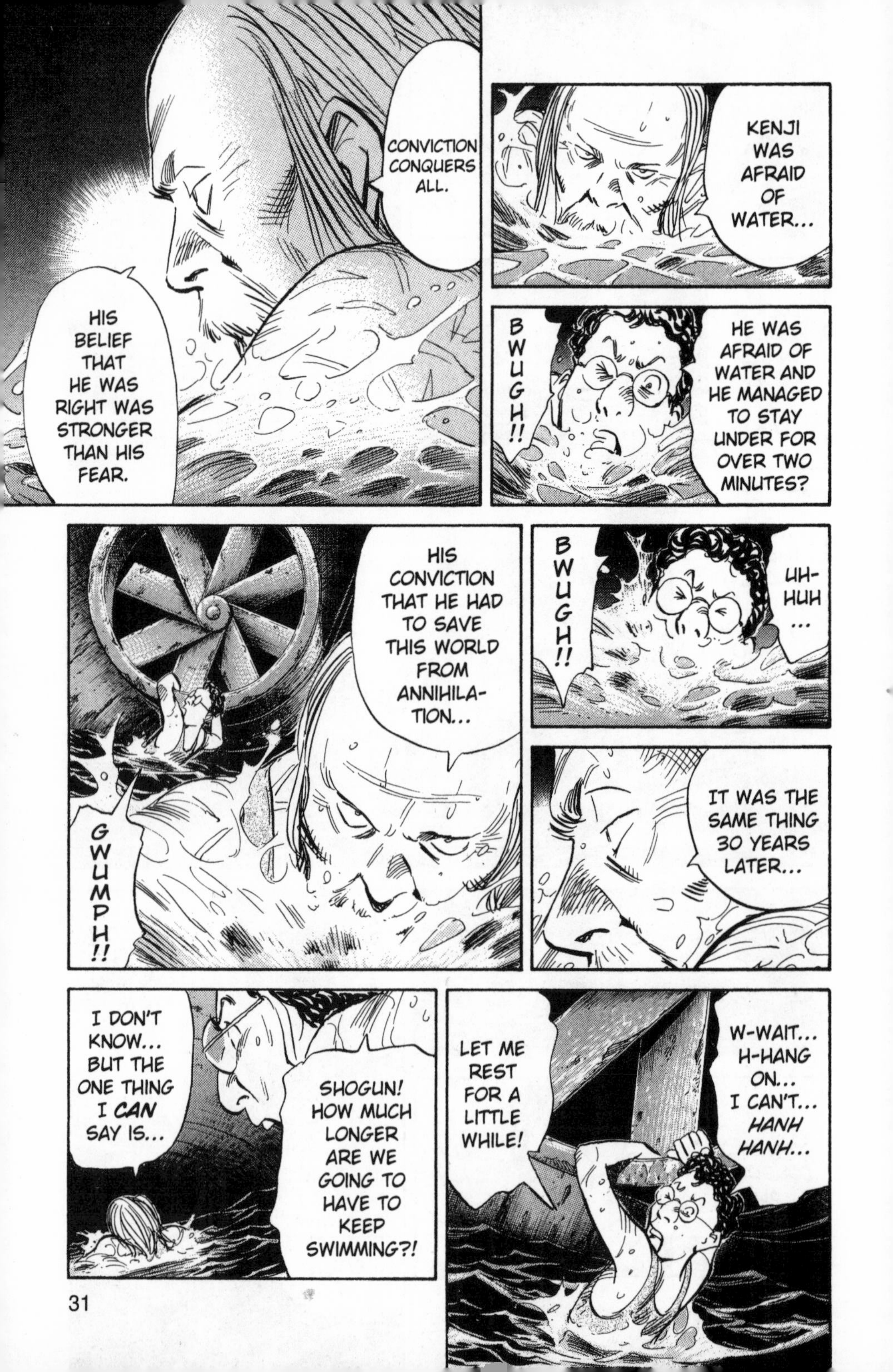
KENJI WAS AFRAID OF WATER...
HE WAS AFRAID OF WATER AND HE MANAGED TO STAY UNDER FOR OVER TWO MINUTES?
BWUGH!!
CONVICTION CONQUERS ALL.
HIS BELIEF THAT HE WAS RIGHT WAS STRONGER THAN HIS FEAR.
UH-HUH...
BWUGH!!
IT WAS THE SAME THING 30 YEARS LATER...
HIS CONVICTION THAT HE HAD TO SAVE THIS WORLD FROM ANNIHILATION...
GWUMPH!!
W-WAIT... H-HANG ON... I CAN'T... *HANH HANH*...
LET ME REST FOR A LITTLE WHILE!
SHOGUN! HOW MUCH LONGER ARE WE GOING TO HAVE TO KEEP SWIMMING?!
I DON'T KNOW... BUT THE ONE THING I *CAN* SAY IS...

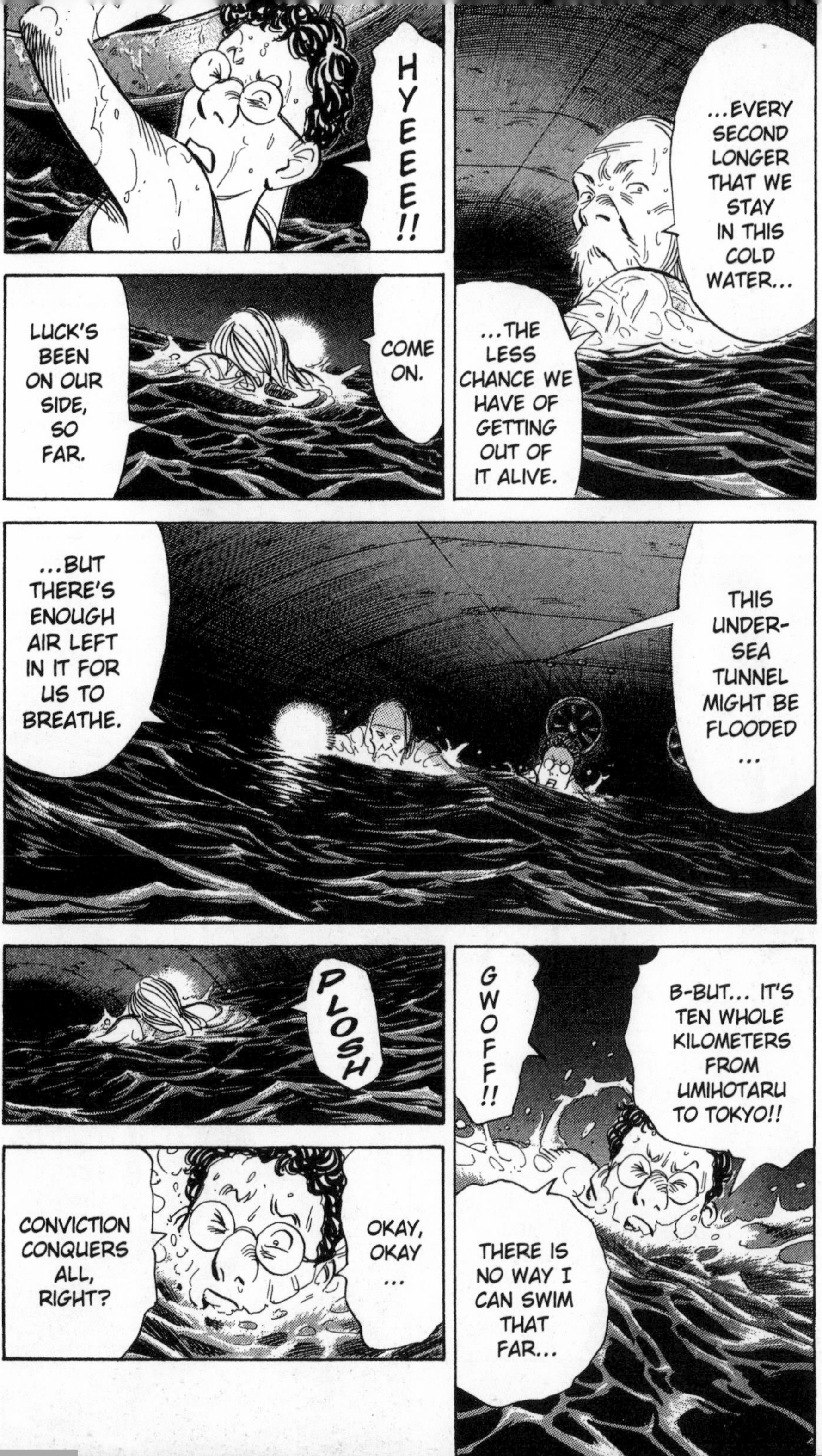
...EVERY SECOND LONGER THAT WE STAY IN THIS COLD WATER...
...THE LESS CHANCE WE HAVE OF GETTING OUT OF IT ALIVE.
HYEEE!!
COME ON.
LUCK'S BEEN ON OUR SIDE, SO FAR.
THIS UNDER-SEA TUNNEL MIGHT BE FLOODED ...
...BUT THERE'S ENOUGH AIR LEFT IN IT FOR US TO BREATHE.
GWOFF!!
B-BUT... IT'S TEN WHOLE KILOMETERS FROM UMIHOTARU TO TOKYO!!
THERE IS NO WAY I CAN SWIM THAT FAR...
PLOSH
OKAY, OKAY ...
CONVICTION CONQUERS ALL, RIGHT?

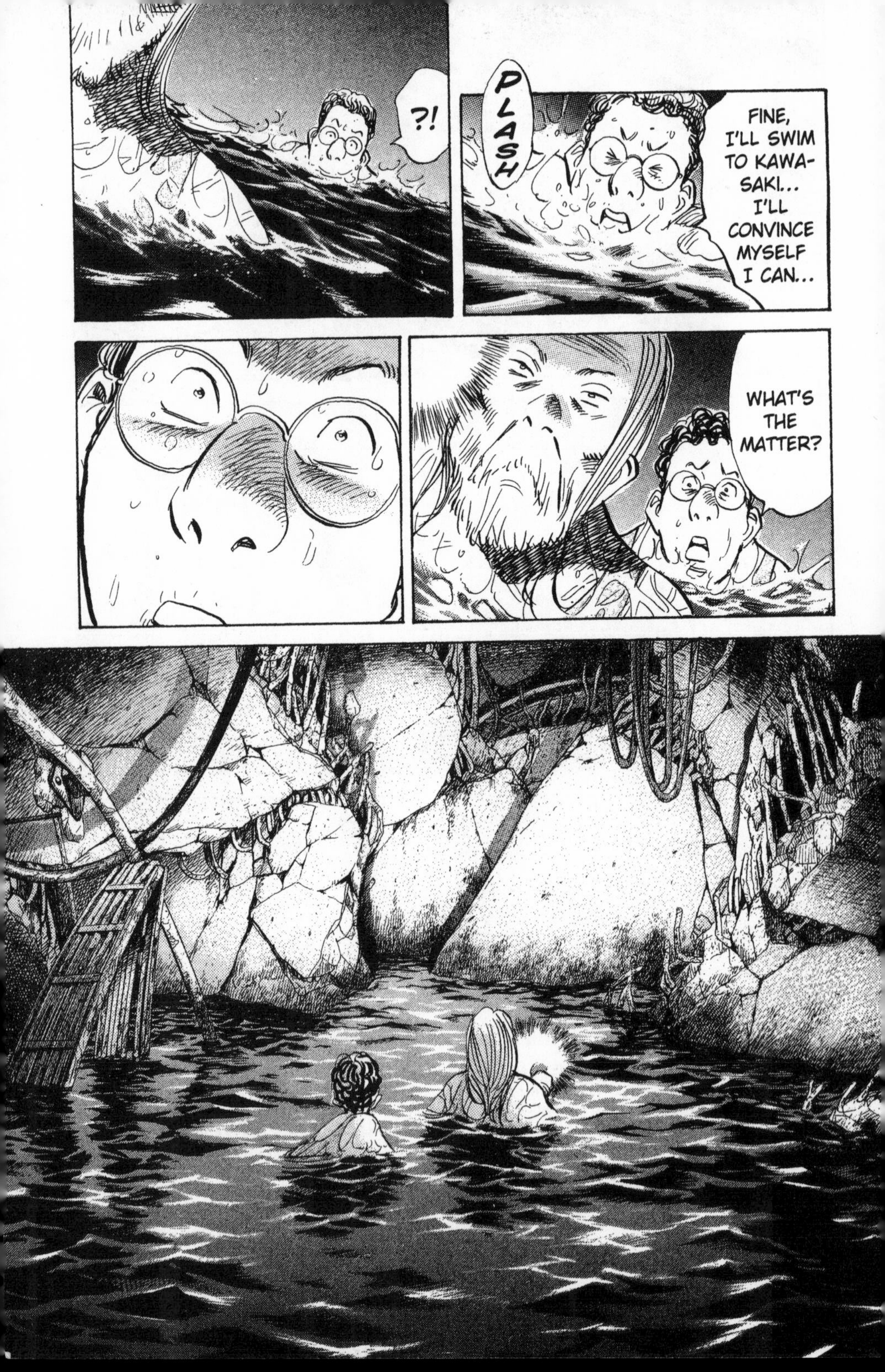
FINE, I'LL SWIM TO KAWA-SAKI... I'LL CONVINCE MYSELF I CAN...
PLASH
?!
WHAT'S THE MATTER?

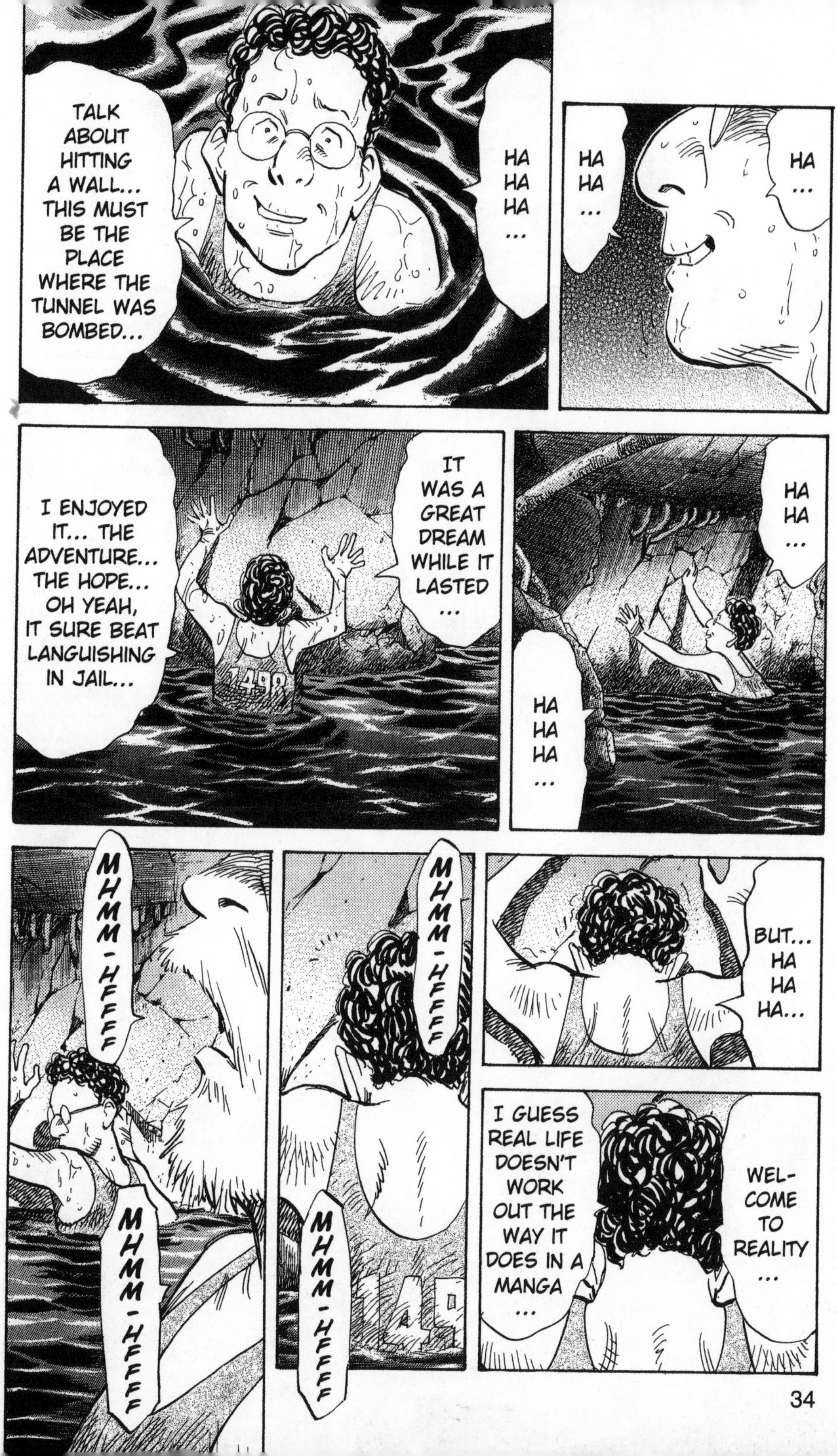
HA ...
HA HA ...
HA HA HA ...
TALK ABOUT HITTING A WALL... THIS MUST BE THE PLACE WHERE THE TUNNEL WAS BOMBED...
HA HA ...
HA HA HA ...
IT WAS A GREAT DREAM WHILE IT LASTED ...
I ENJOYED IT... THE ADVENTURE... THE HOPE... OH YEAH, IT SURE BEAT LANGUISHING IN JAIL...
BUT... HA HA HA...
WEL-COME TO REALITY ...
I GUESS REAL LIFE DOESN'T WORK OUT THE WAY IT DOES IN A MANGA ...
MHMM-HFFFF
MHMM-HFFFF
MHMM-HFFFF
MHMM-HFFFF

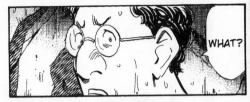

WHAT?

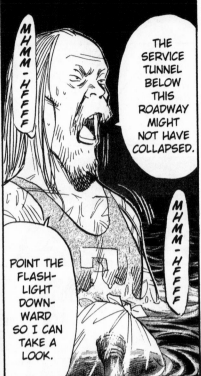

THE SERVICE TUNNEL BELOW THIS ROADWAY MIGHT NOT HAVE COLLAPSED.

MHMM-HFFFF

MHMM-HFFFF

POINT THE FLASH-LIGHT DOWN-WARD SO I CAN TAKE A LOOK.

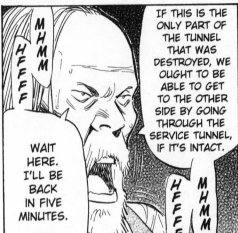

MHMM

HFFFF

IF THIS IS THE ONLY PART OF THE TUNNEL THAT WAS DESTROYED, WE OUGHT TO BE ABLE TO GET TO THE OTHER SIDE BY GOING THROUGH THE SERVICE TUNNEL, IF IT'S INTACT.

WAIT HERE. I'LL BE BACK IN FIVE MINUTES.

HFFFF

MHMM

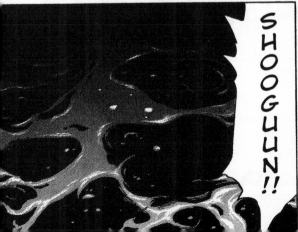

SHO-GUN!!

KA-PLOSH

YOU'RE KID-DING ME...

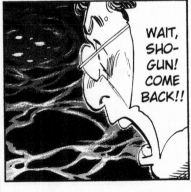

SHOOGUUN!!

WAIT, SHO-GUN! COME BACK!!

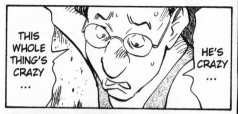

HE'S CRAZY ...
THIS WHOLE THING'S CRAZY ...
HE'S GOING TO DIE, FOR SURE ...
HOW MANY MINUTES HAS IT BEEN?
THERE'S NO WAY HE COULD HOLD HIS BREATH THIS LONG...
...
I NEED TO GO RESCUE HIM...
PWOK
THIS PLASTIC BAG...
MAYBE THE FLASH-LIGHT'S WATER-PROOF...

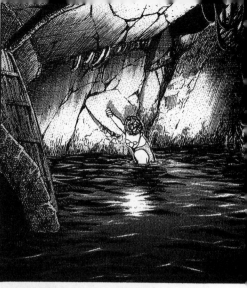

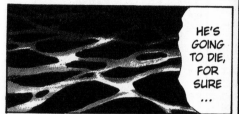

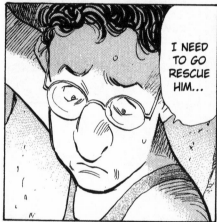

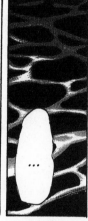

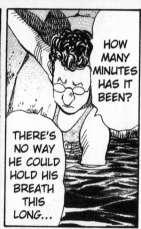

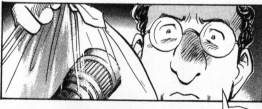

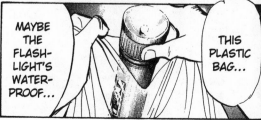

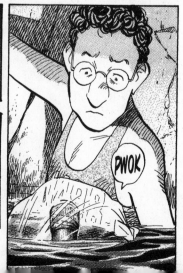

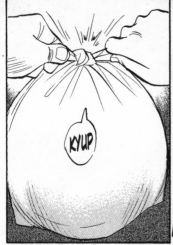

KYUP

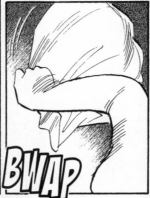

BWAP

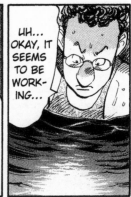

UH... OKAY, IT SEEMS TO BE WORK-ING...

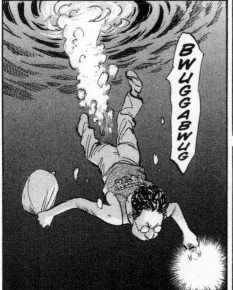

BWUGGABWUG

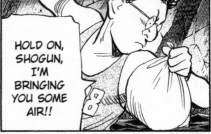

HOLD ON, SHOGUN, I'M BRINGING YOU SOME AIR!!

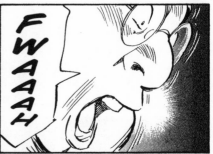

FWAAAH

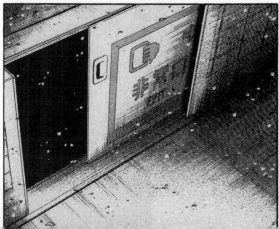

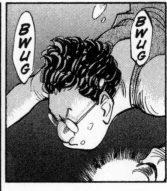

BWUG

BWUG

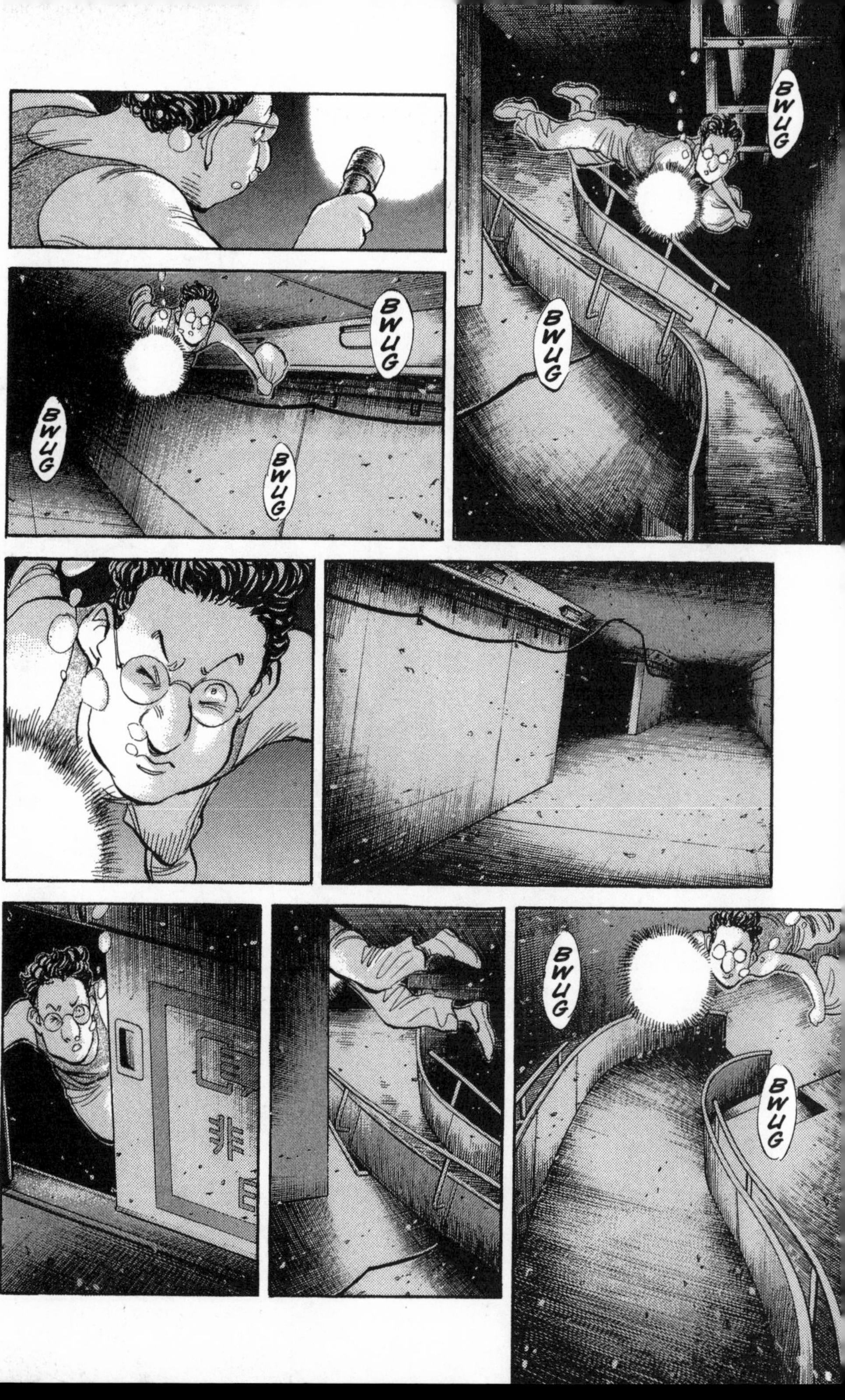
BWUG
BWUG
BWUG
BWUG
BWUG
BWUG
BWUG

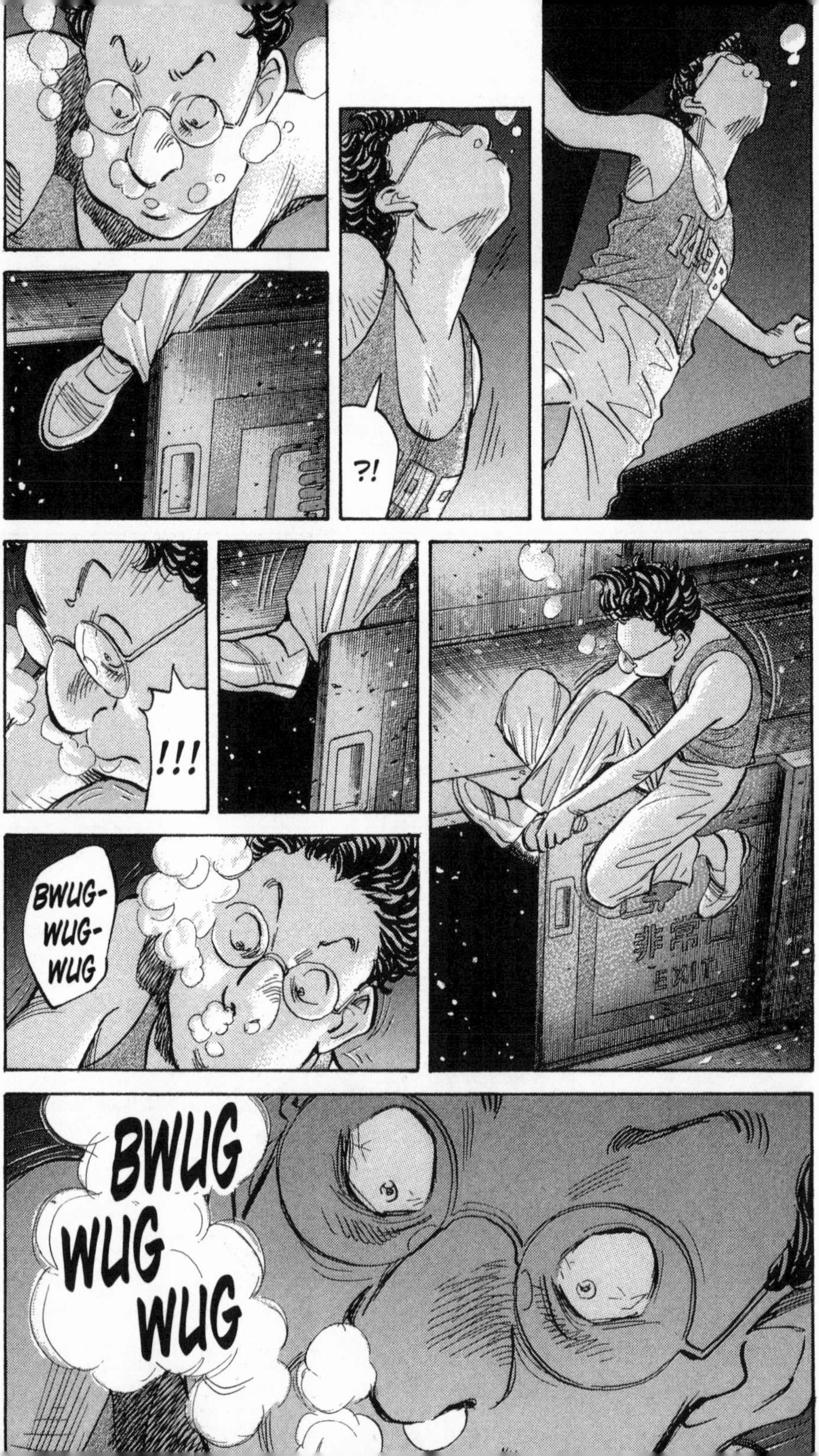
?!
非常口
EXIT
!!!
BWUG-WUG-WUG
BWUG WUG WUG

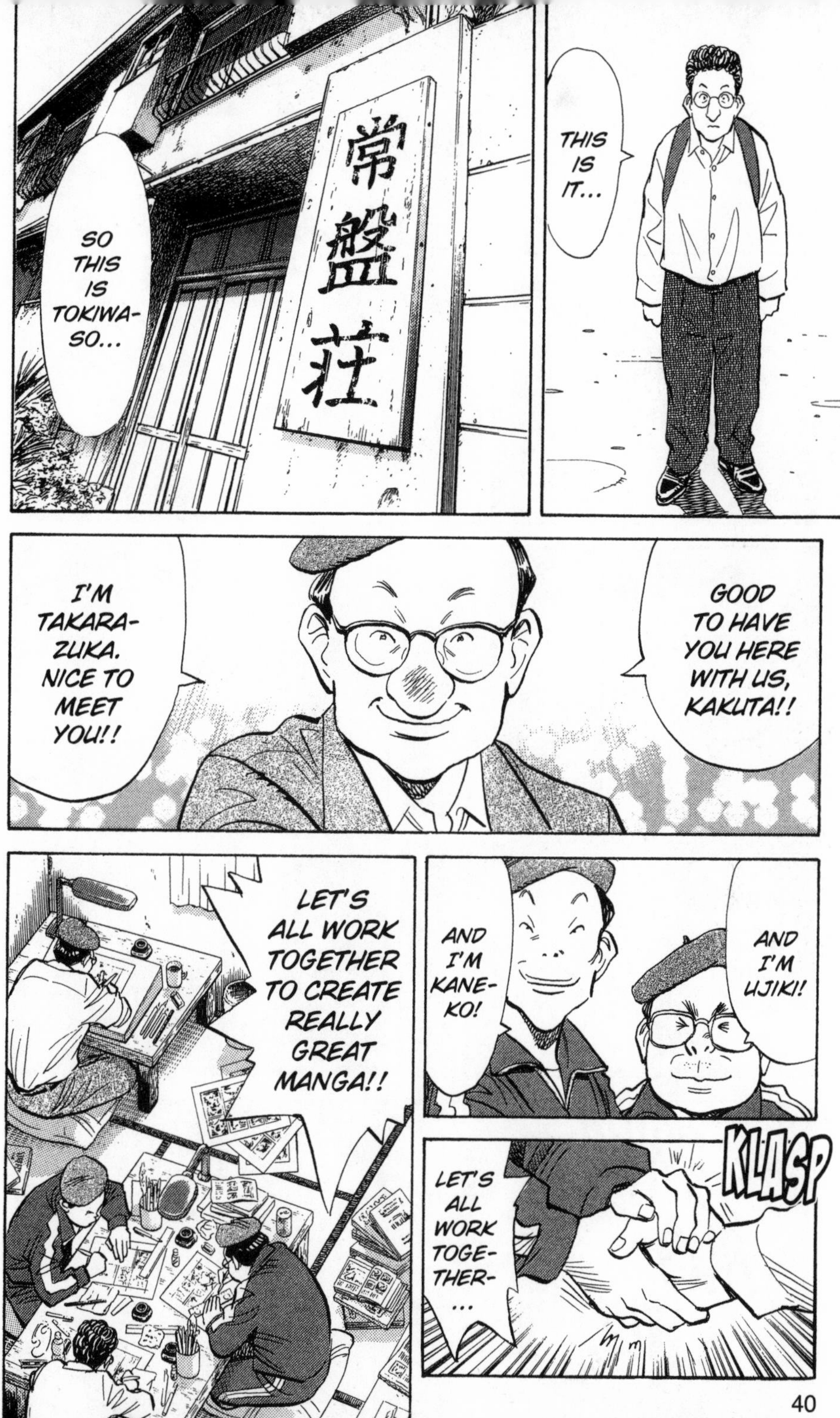
THIS IS IT...
SO THIS IS TOKIWA-SO...
常盤荘
GOOD TO HAVE YOU HERE WITH US, KAKUTA!!
I'M TAKARA-ZUKA. NICE TO MEET YOU!!
AND I'M UJIKI!
AND I'M KANE-KO!
KLASP
LET'S ALL WORK TOGE-THER-...
LET'S ALL WORK TOGETHER TO CREATE REALLY GREAT MANGA!!

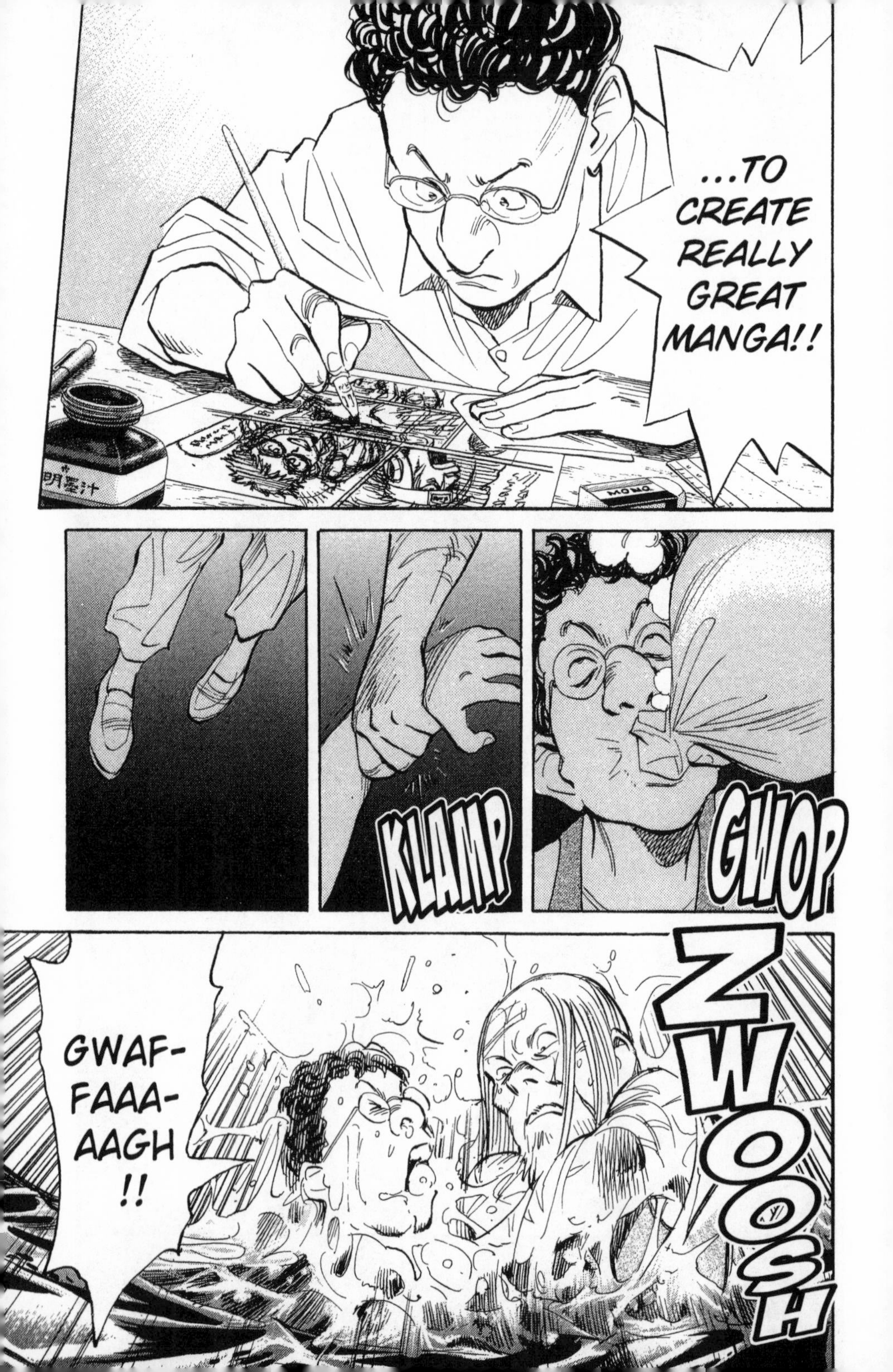
...TO CREATE REALLY GREAT MANGA!!
GWOP
KLAMP
ZWOOSH
GWAF-FAAAA-AAGH!!

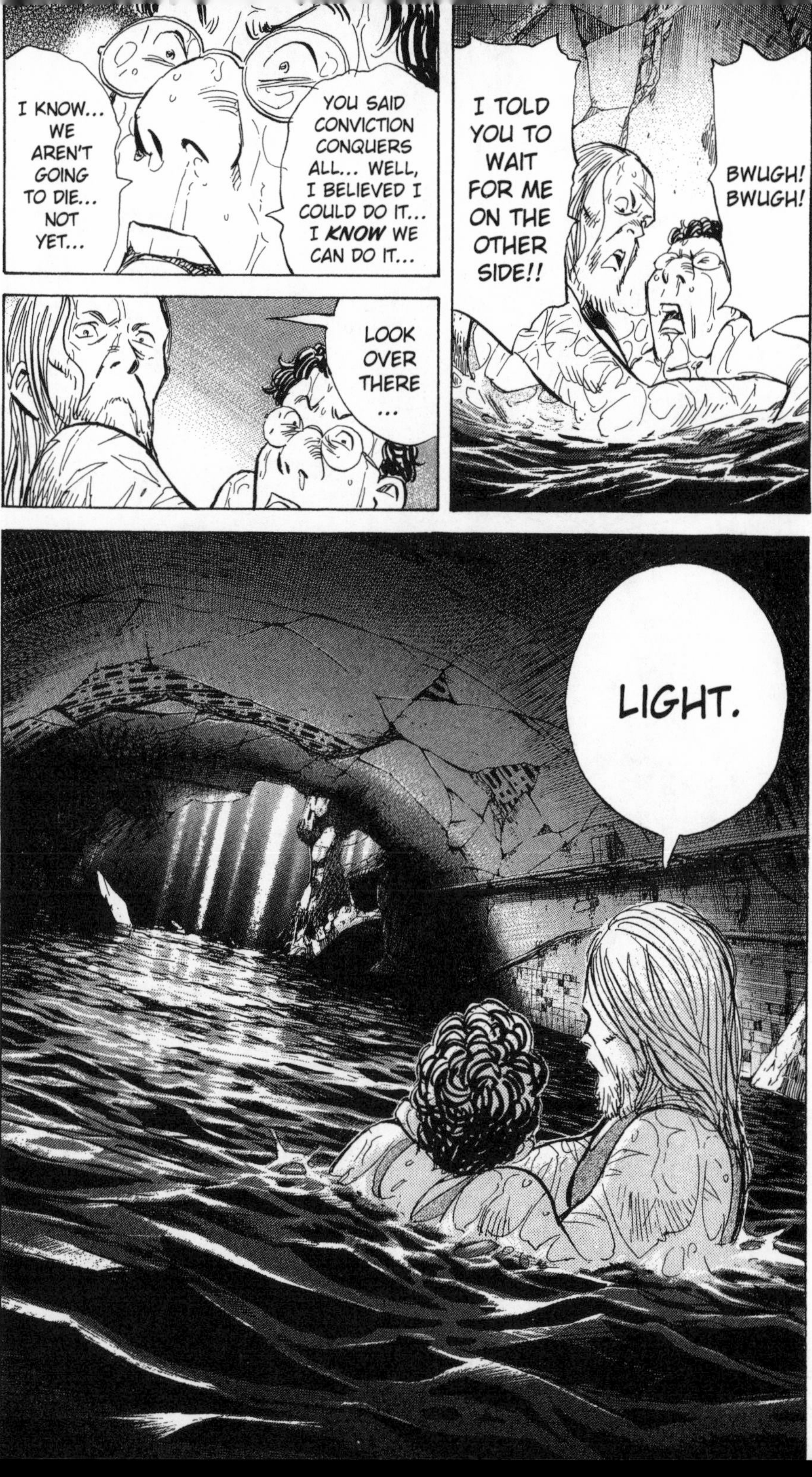
BWUGH! BWUGH!
I TOLD YOU TO WAIT FOR ME ON THE OTHER SIDE!!
YOU SAID CONVICTION CONQUERS ALL... WELL, I BELIEVED I COULD DO IT... I **KNOW** WE CAN DO IT...
I KNOW... WE AREN'T GOING TO DIE... NOT YET...
LOOK OVER THERE ...
LIGHT.

Chapter 3 Landing

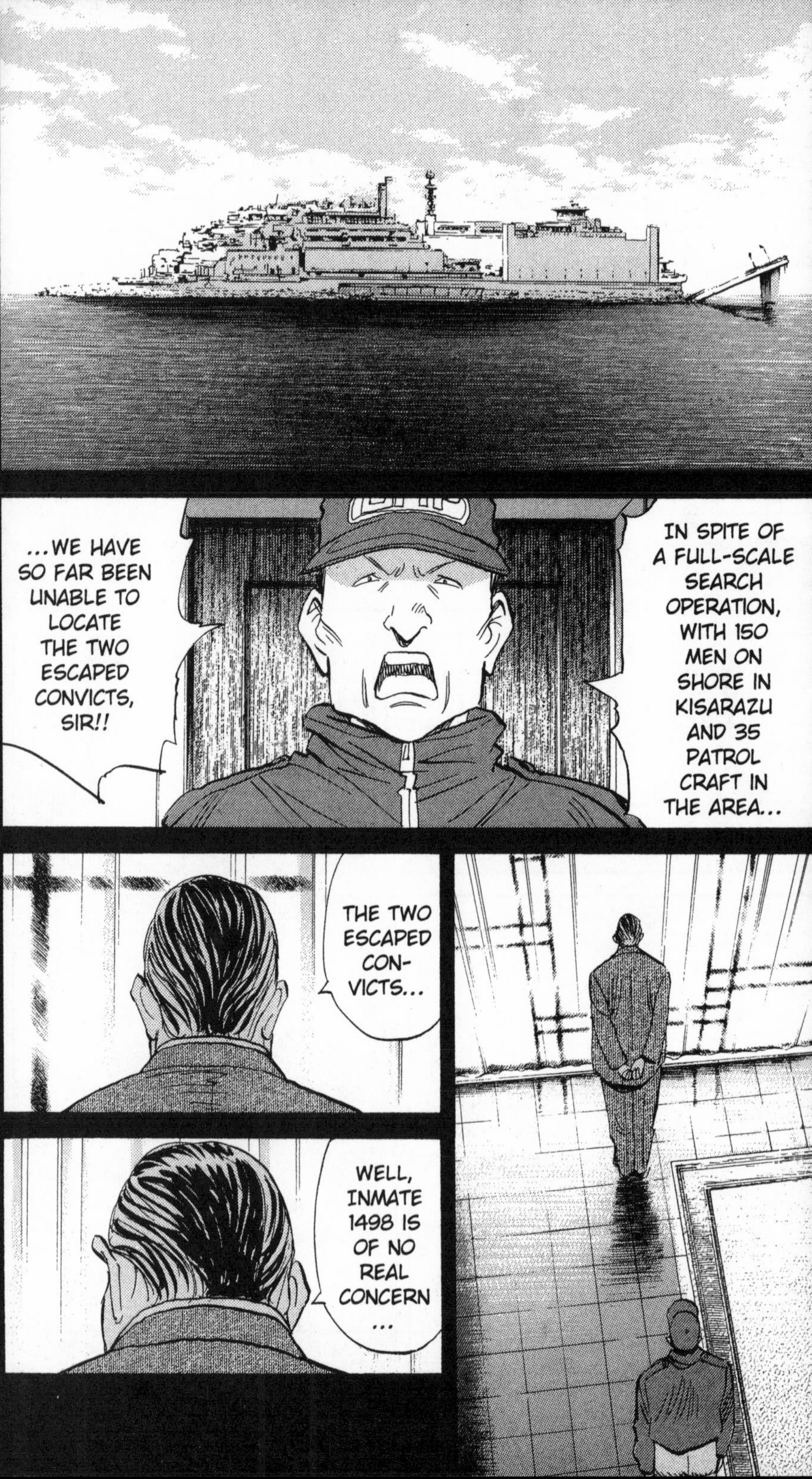
IN SPITE OF A FULL-SCALE SEARCH OPERATION, WITH 150 MEN ON SHORE IN KISARAZU AND 35 PATROL CRAFT IN THE AREA...
...WE HAVE SO FAR BEEN UNABLE TO LOCATE THE TWO ESCAPED CONVICTS, SIR!!
THE TWO ESCAPED CON-VICTS...
WELL, INMATE 1498 IS OF NO REAL CONCERN ...

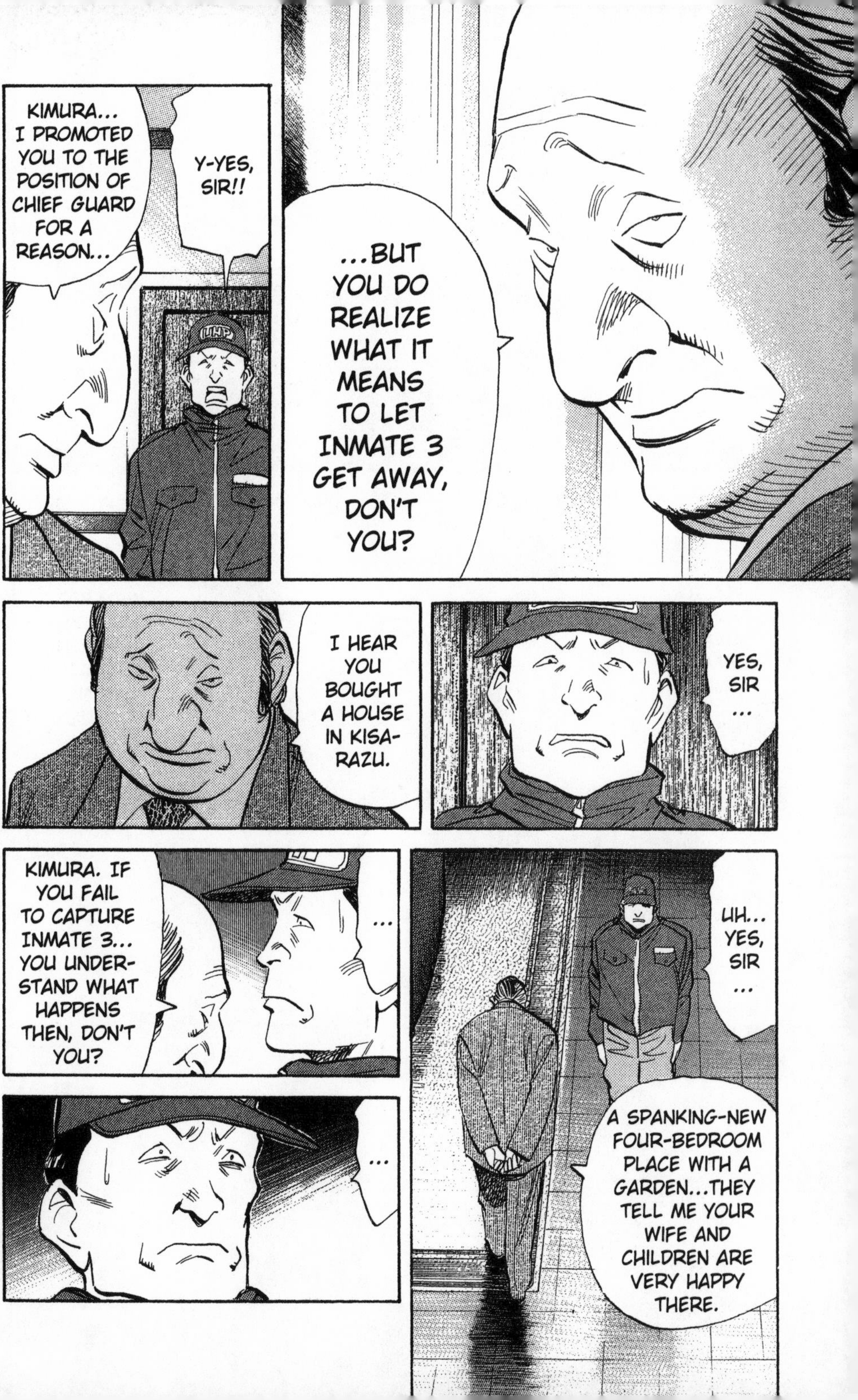
KIMURA... I PROMOTED YOU TO THE POSITION OF CHIEF GUARD FOR A REASON...
Y-YES, SIR!!
...BUT YOU DO REALIZE WHAT IT MEANS TO LET INMATE 3 GET AWAY, DON'T YOU?
I HEAR YOU BOUGHT A HOUSE IN KISA-RAZU.
YES, SIR ...
KIMURA. IF YOU FAIL TO CAPTURE INMATE 3... YOU UNDER-STAND WHAT HAPPENS THEN, DON'T YOU?
...
...
UH... YES, SIR ...
A SPANKING-NEW FOUR-BEDROOM PLACE WITH A GARDEN...THEY TELL ME YOUR WIFE AND CHILDREN ARE VERY HAPPY THERE.

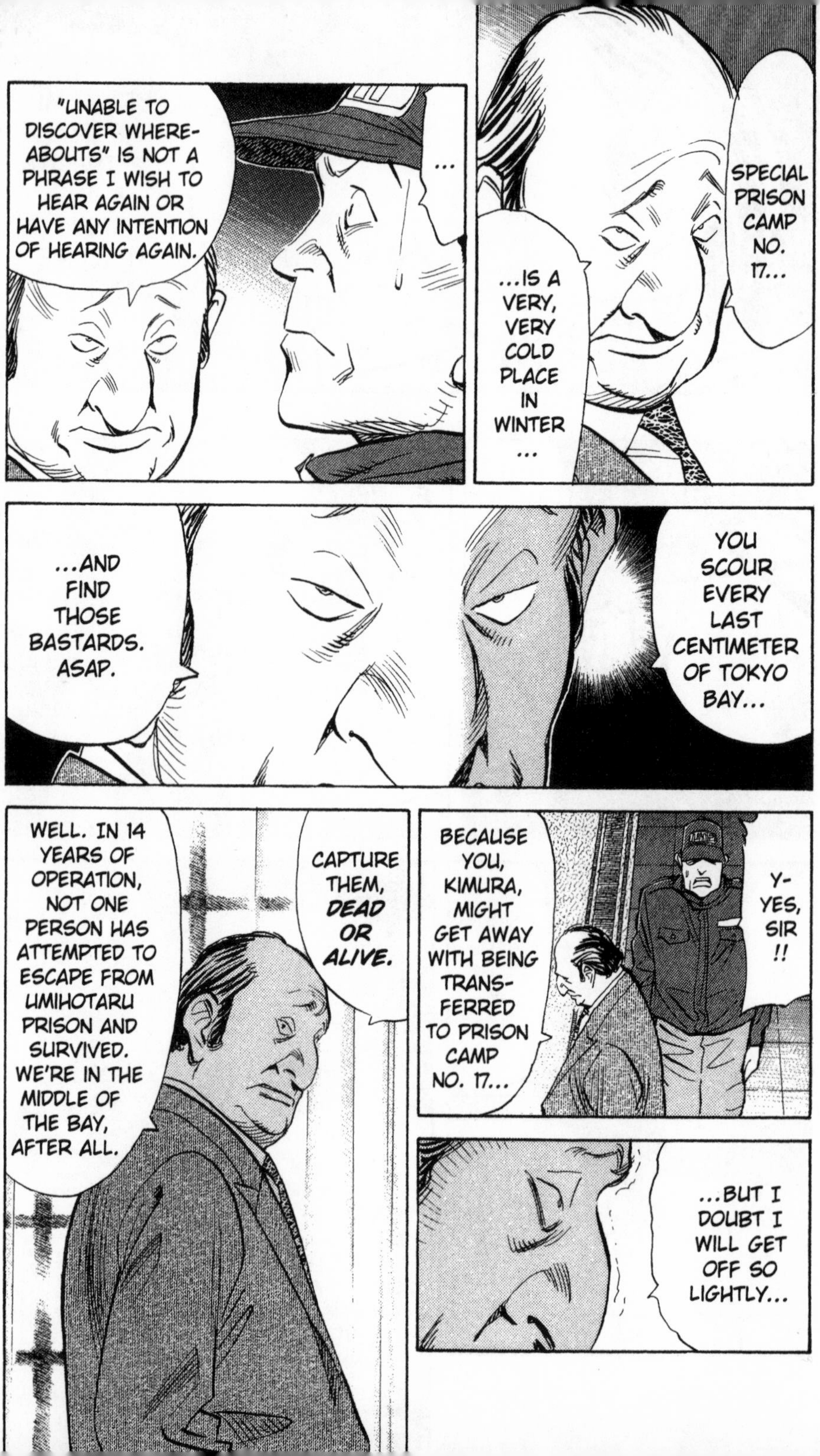
SPECIAL PRISON CAMP NO. 17...
...IS A VERY, VERY COLD PLACE IN WINTER...
"UNABLE TO DISCOVER WHEREABOUTS" IS NOT A PHRASE I WISH TO HEAR AGAIN OR HAVE ANY INTENTION OF HEARING AGAIN.
...
YOU SCOUR EVERY LAST CENTIMETER OF TOKYO BAY...
...AND FIND THOSE BASTARDS. ASAP.
Y-YES, SIR!!
BECAUSE YOU, KIMURA, MIGHT GET AWAY WITH BEING TRANSFERRED TO PRISON CAMP NO. 17...
...BUT I DOUBT I WILL GET OFF SO LIGHTLY...
CAPTURE THEM, DEAD OR ALIVE.
WELL. IN 14 YEARS OF OPERATION, NOT ONE PERSON HAS ATTEMPTED TO ESCAPE FROM UMIHOTARU PRISON AND SURVIVED. WE'RE IN THE MIDDLE OF THE BAY, AFTER ALL.

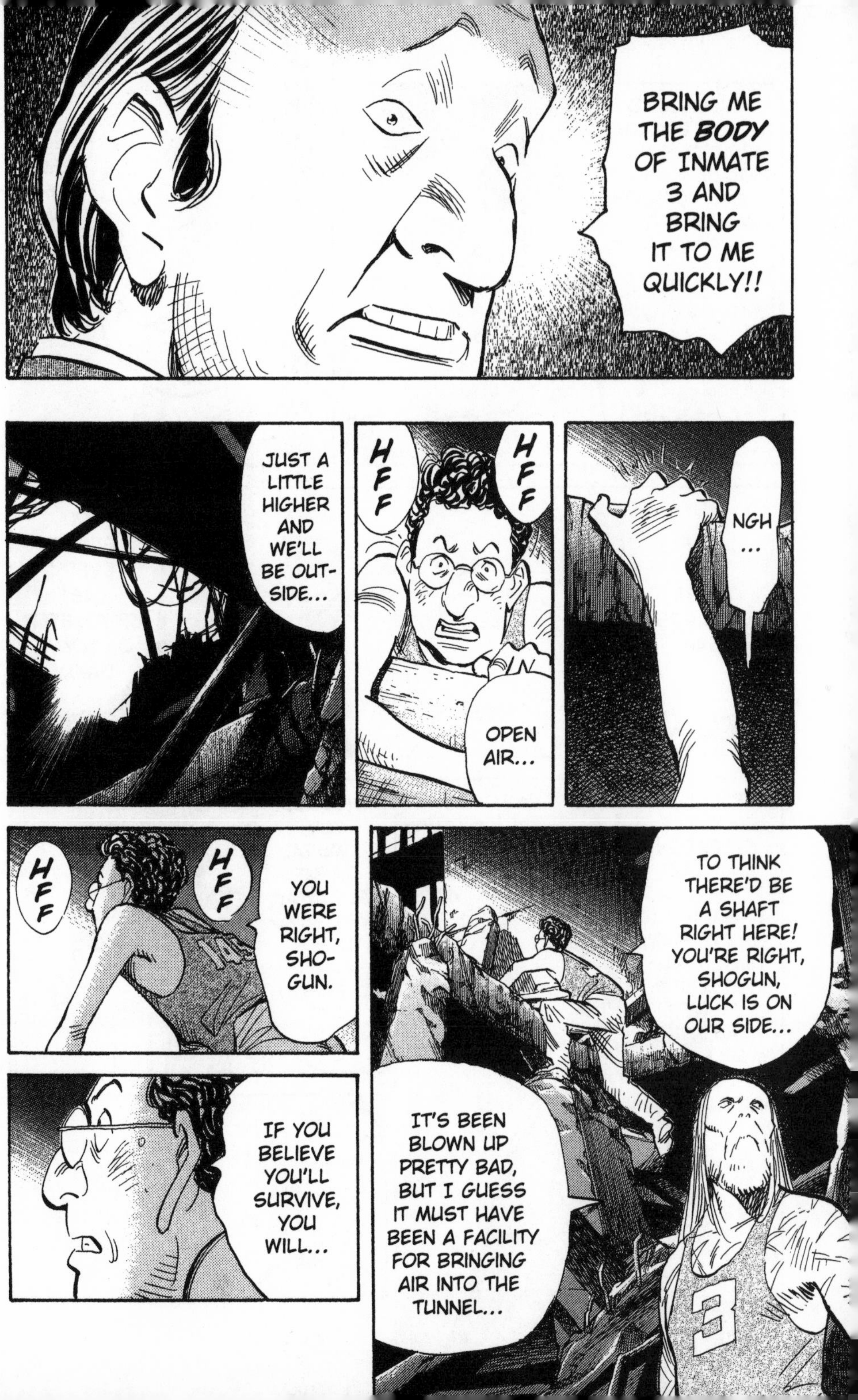
BRING ME THE *BODY* OF INMATE 3 AND BRING IT TO ME QUICKLY!!
NGH...
HFF
HFF
OPEN AIR...
JUST A LITTLE HIGHER AND WE'LL BE OUT-SIDE...
TO THINK THERE'D BE A SHAFT RIGHT HERE! YOU'RE RIGHT, SHOGUN, LUCK IS ON OUR SIDE...
IT'S BEEN BLOWN UP PRETTY BAD, BUT I GUESS IT MUST HAVE BEEN A FACILITY FOR BRINGING AIR INTO THE TUNNEL...
HFF
HFF
YOU WERE RIGHT, SHO-GUN.
IF YOU BELIEVE YOU'LL SURVIVE, YOU WILL...

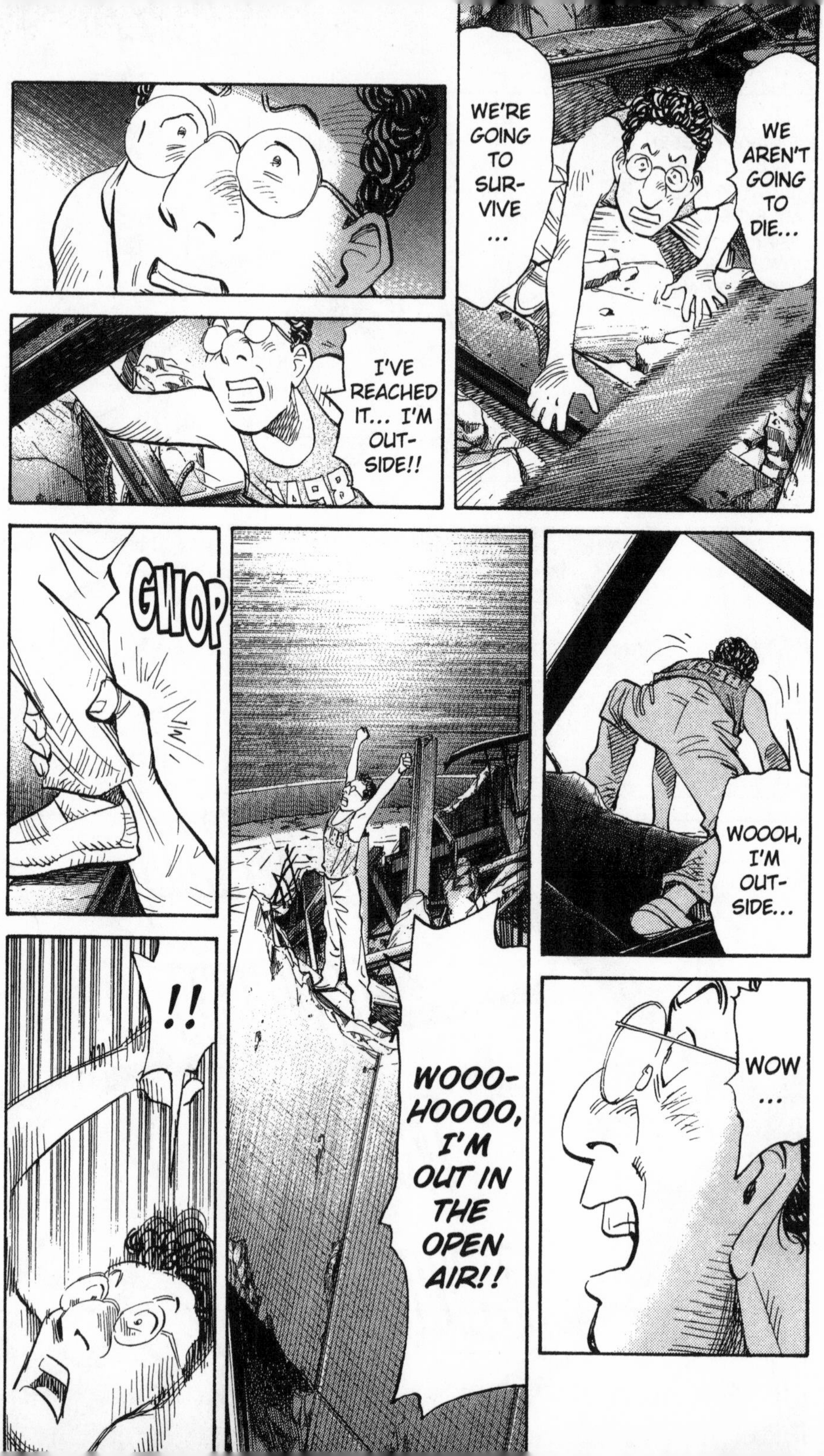
WE AREN'T GOING TO DIE...
WE'RE GOING TO SURVIVE...
I'VE REACHED IT... I'M OUTSIDE!!
WOOOH, I'M OUTSIDE...
WOW...
WOOO-HOOOO, I'M OUT IN THE OPEN AIR!!
GWOP
!!

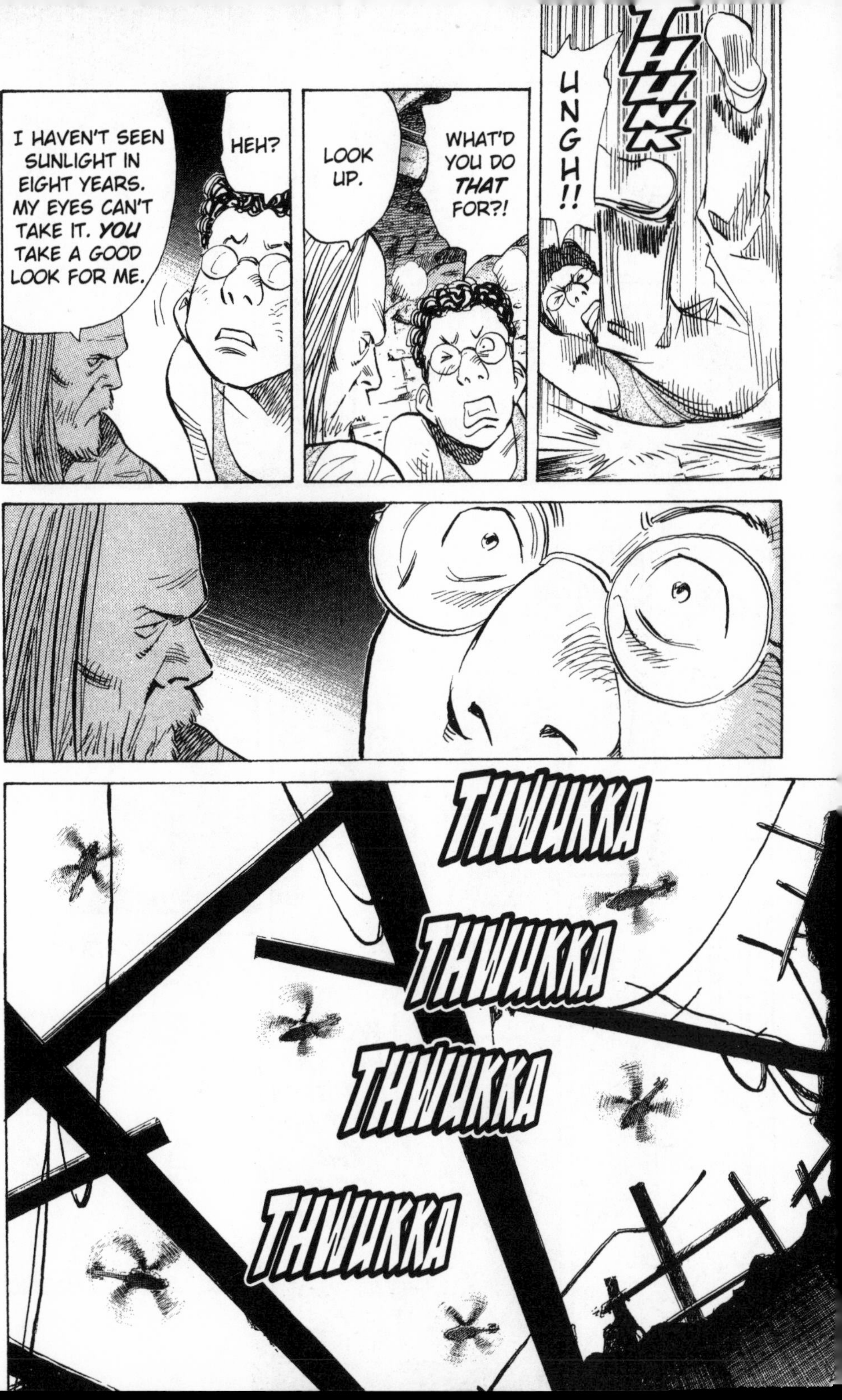
THUNK
UNGH!!
WHAT'D YOU DO THAT FOR?!
LOOK UP.
HEH?
I HAVEN'T SEEN SUNLIGHT IN EIGHT YEARS. MY EYES CAN'T TAKE IT. YOU TAKE A GOOD LOOK FOR ME.
THWUKKA
THWUKKA
THWUKKA
THWUKKA

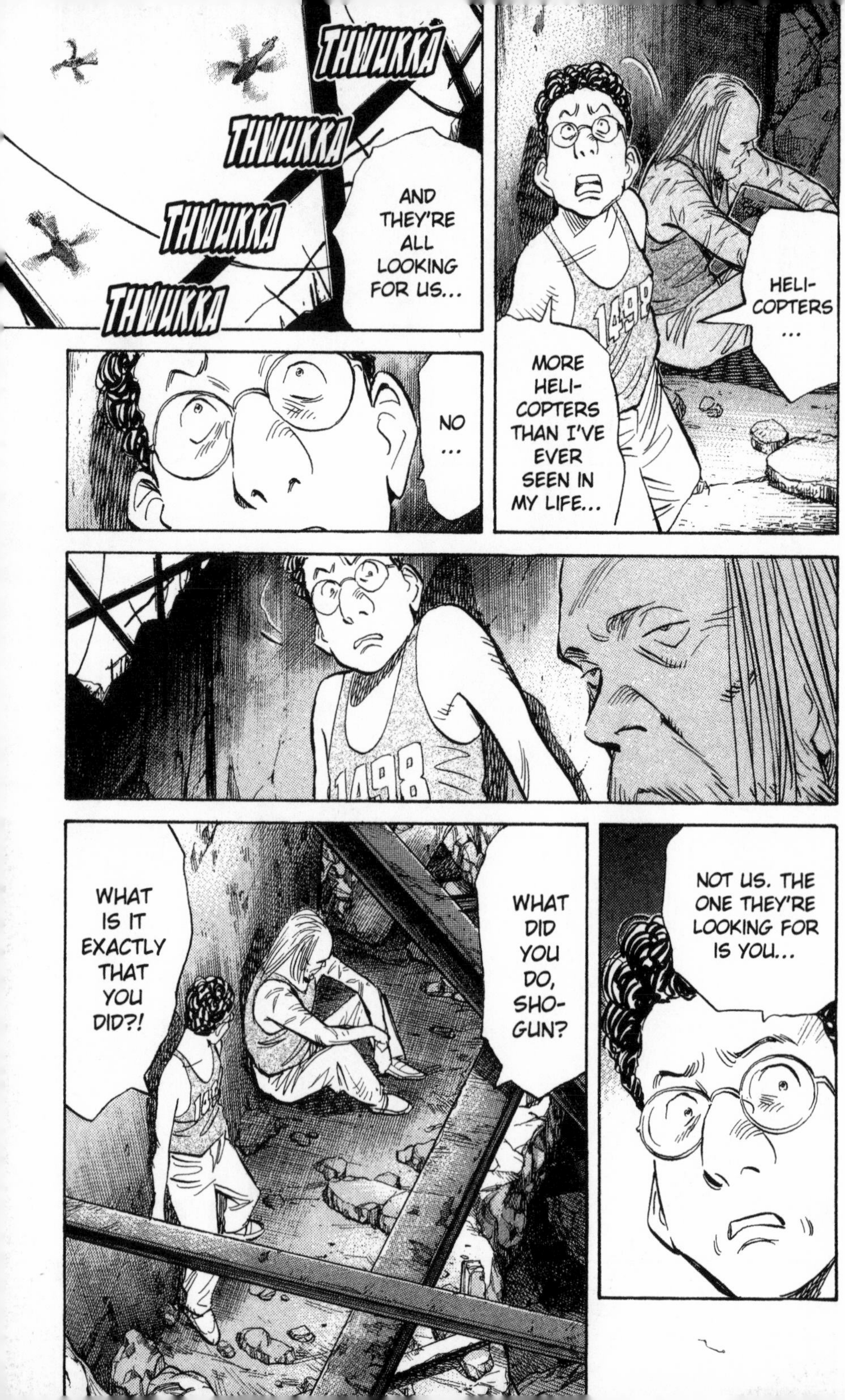
HELI-COPTERS ...
MORE HELI-COPTERS THAN I'VE EVER SEEN IN MY LIFE...
THWUKKA
THWUKKA
THWUKKA
THWUKKA
AND THEY'RE ALL LOOKING FOR US...
NO ...
NOT US. THE ONE THEY'RE LOOKING FOR IS YOU...
WHAT DID YOU DO, SHO-GUN?
WHAT IS IT EXACTLY THAT YOU DID?!

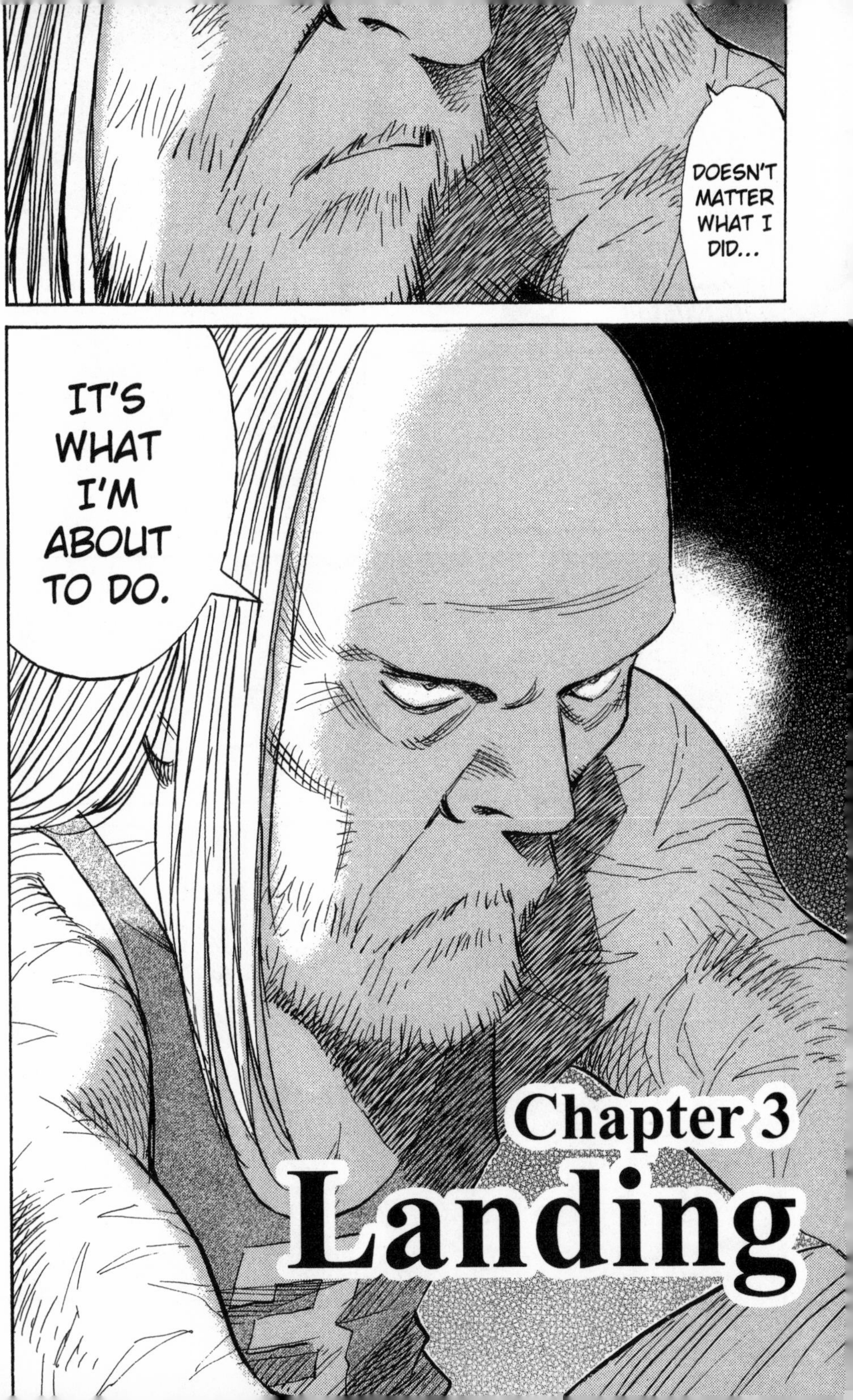
DOESN'T MATTER WHAT I DID...
IT'S WHAT I'M ABOUT TO DO.

Chapter 3 Landing

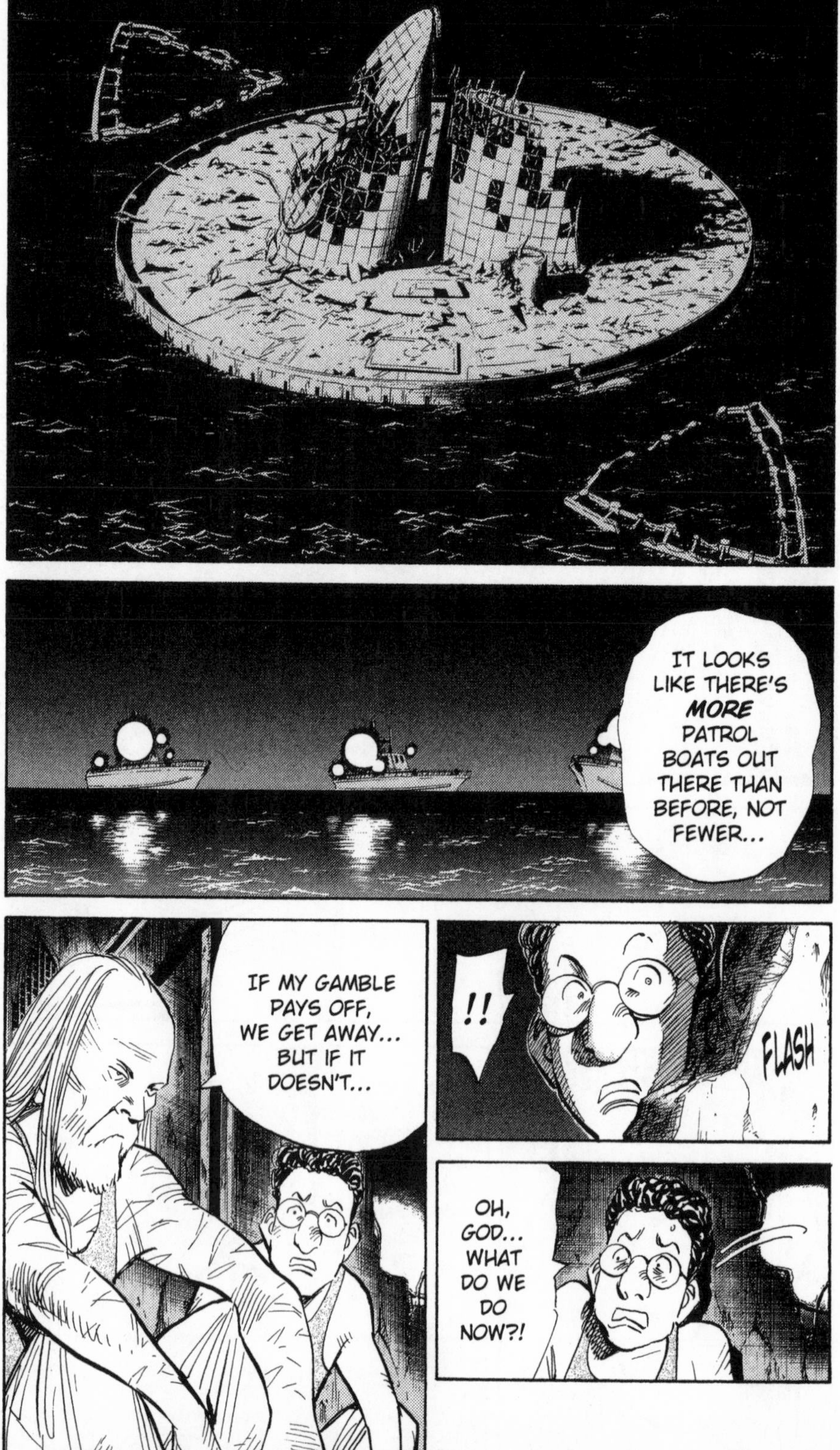
IT LOOKS LIKE THERE'S *MORE* PATROL BOATS OUT THERE THAN BEFORE, NOT FEWER...
!!
FLASH
OH, GOD... WHAT DO WE DO NOW?!
IF MY GAMBLE PAYS OFF, WE GET AWAY... BUT IF IT DOESN'T...

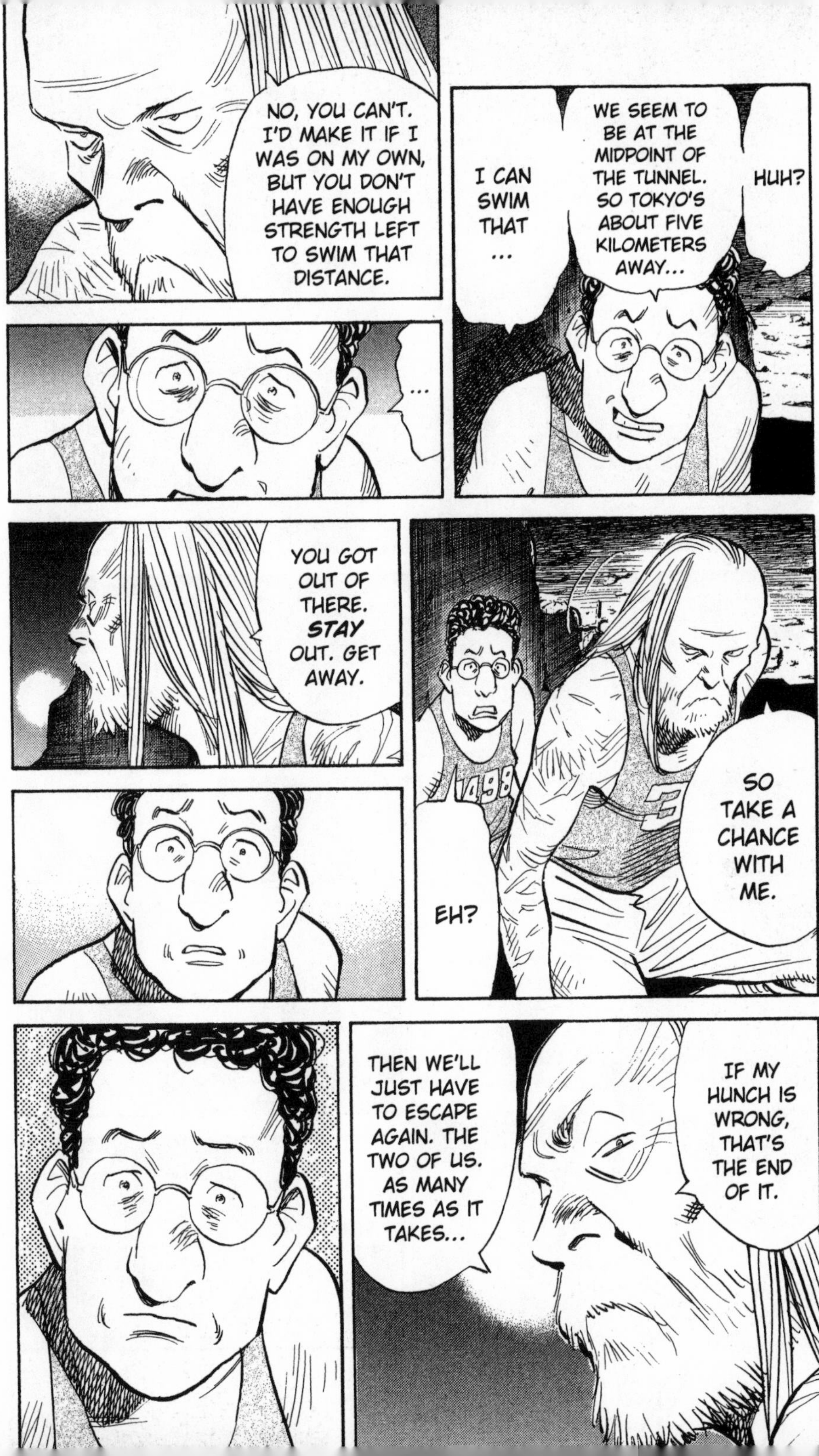
HUH?
WE SEEM TO BE AT THE MIDPOINT OF THE TUNNEL. SO TOKYO'S ABOUT FIVE KILOMETERS AWAY...
I CAN SWIM THAT ...
NO, YOU CAN'T. I'D MAKE IT IF I WAS ON MY OWN, BUT YOU DON'T HAVE ENOUGH STRENGTH LEFT TO SWIM THAT DISTANCE.
...
SO TAKE A CHANCE WITH ME.
EH?
YOU GOT OUT OF THERE. STAY OUT. GET AWAY.
IF MY HUNCH IS WRONG, THAT'S THE END OF IT.
THEN WE'LL JUST HAVE TO ESCAPE AGAIN. THE TWO OF US. AS MANY TIMES AS IT TAKES...

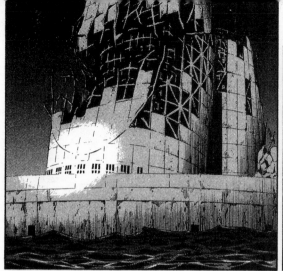

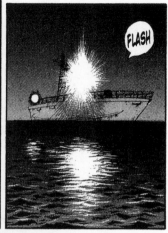

FLASH

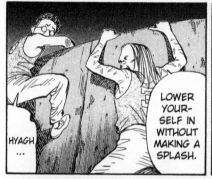

HYAGH...

LOWER YOUR-SELF IN WITHOUT MAKING A SPLASH.

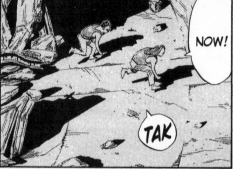

NOW!

TAK

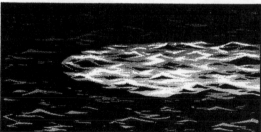

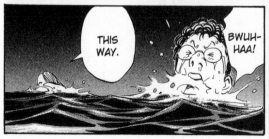

THIS WAY.

BWUH-HAA!

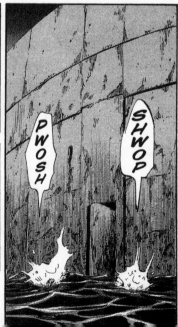

PWOSH

SHWOP

53

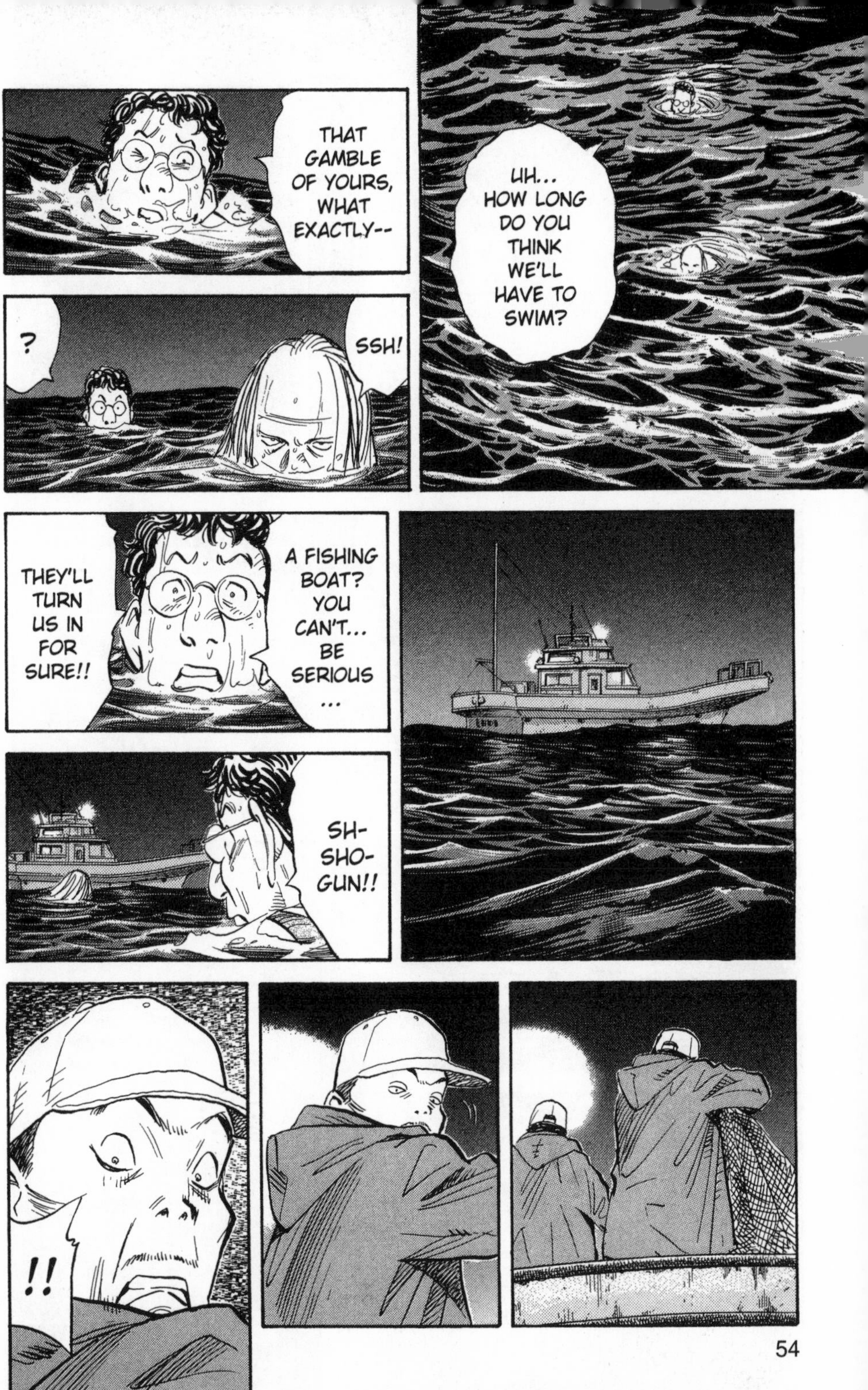
UH... HOW LONG DO YOU THINK WE'LL HAVE TO SWIM?
THAT GAMBLE OF YOURS, WHAT EXACTLY--
SSH!
?
A FISHING BOAT? YOU CAN'T... BE SERIOUS ...
THEY'LL TURN US IN FOR SURE!!
SH- SHO- GUN!!
!!

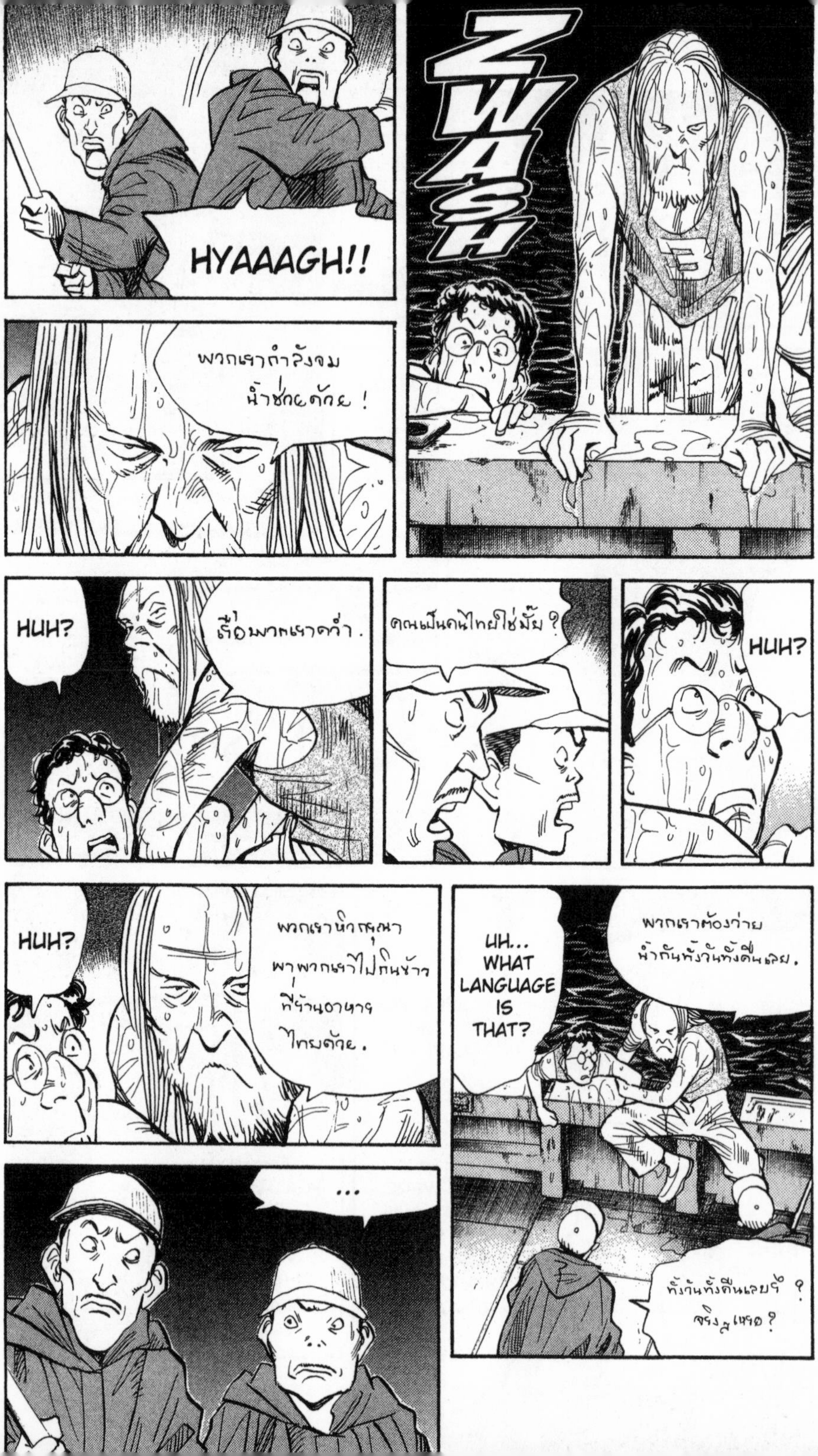
ZWASH
HYAAAGH!!
พวกเรากำลังจม น้ำช่วยด้วย!
HUH?
คุณเป็นคนไทยใช่มั้ย?
เรือพวกเราคว่ำ.
HUH?
พวกเราต้องว่าย น้ำกันทั้งวันทั้งคืนเลย.
UH... WHAT LANGUAGE IS THAT?
ทั้งวันทั้งคืนเลยหรือ? จริงๆเหรอ?
พวกเราหิว กรุณา พาพวกเราไปกินข้าว ที่ร้านอาหาร ไทยด้วย.
HUH?
...

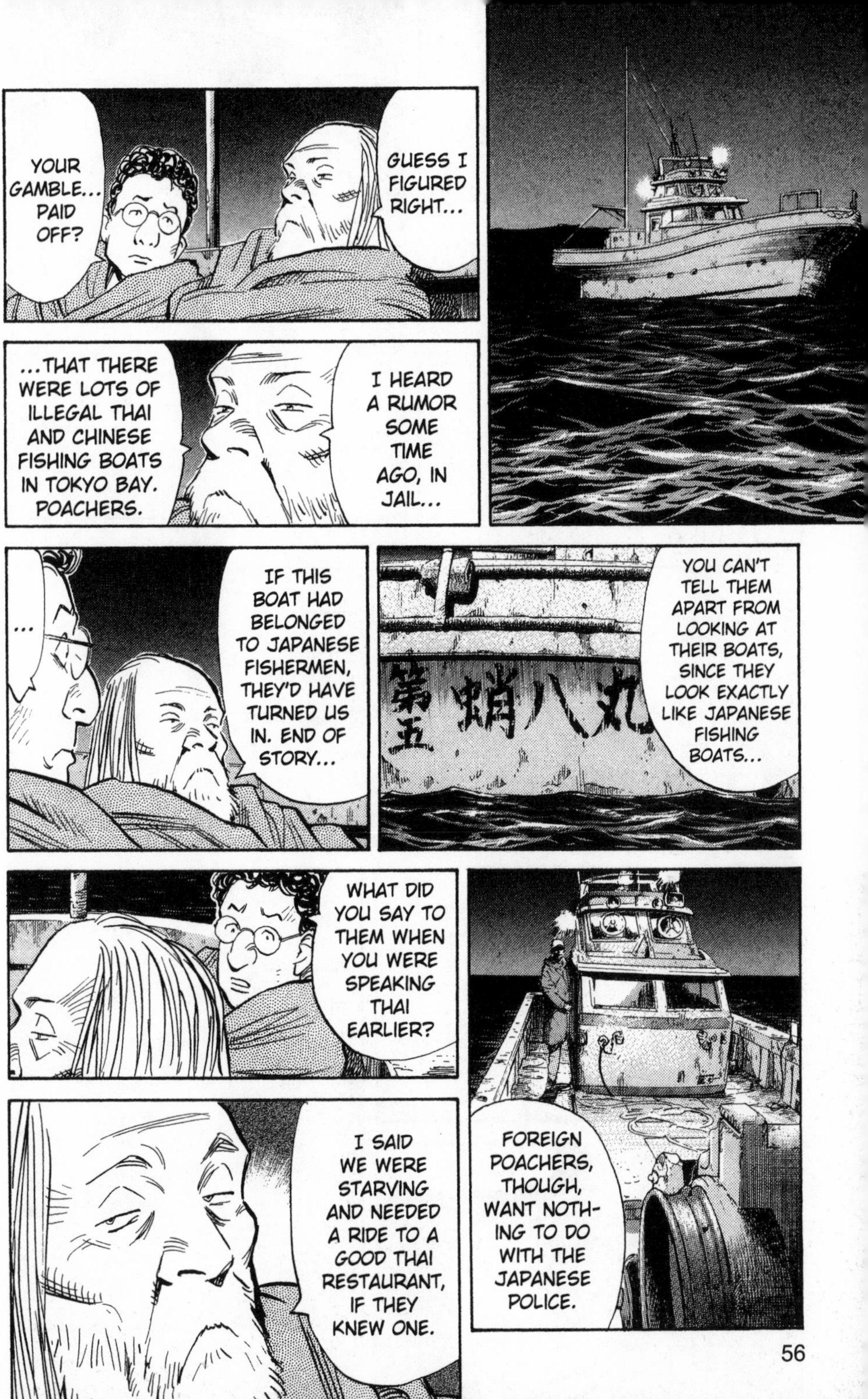
GUESS I FIGURED RIGHT...
YOUR GAMBLE... PAID OFF?
I HEARD A RUMOR SOME TIME AGO, IN JAIL...
...THAT THERE WERE LOTS OF ILLEGAL THAI AND CHINESE FISHING BOATS IN TOKYO BAY. POACHERS.
YOU CAN'T TELL THEM APART FROM LOOKING AT THEIR BOATS, SINCE THEY LOOK EXACTLY LIKE JAPANESE FISHING BOATS...
IF THIS BOAT HAD BELONGED TO JAPANESE FISHERMEN, THEY'D HAVE TURNED US IN. END OF STORY...
...
FOREIGN POACHERS, THOUGH, WANT NOTHING TO DO WITH THE JAPANESE POLICE.
WHAT DID YOU SAY TO THEM WHEN YOU WERE SPEAKING THAI EARLIER?
I SAID WE WERE STARVING AND NEEDED A RIDE TO A GOOD THAI RESTAURANT, IF THEY KNEW ONE.

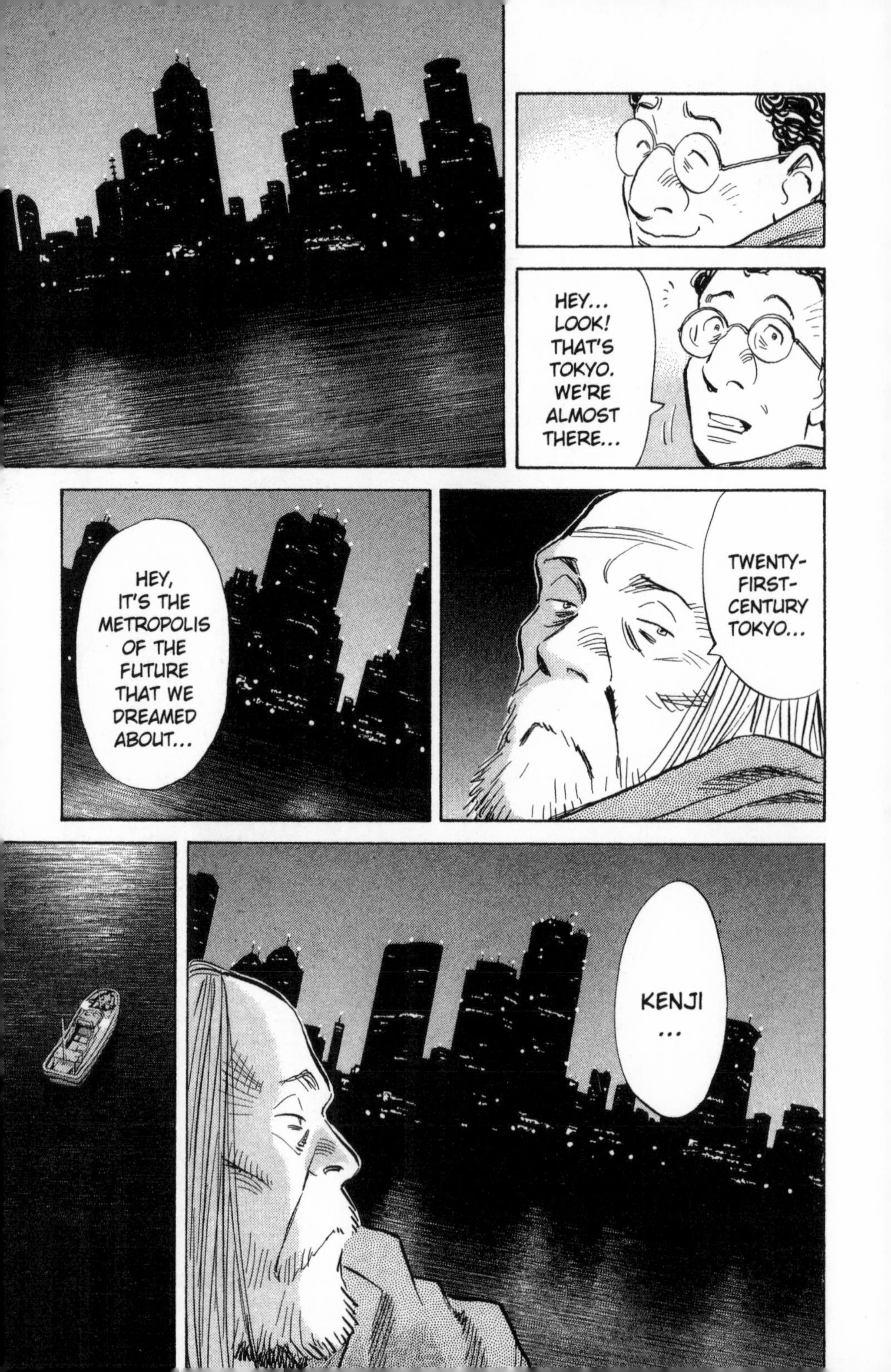
HEY... LOOK! THAT'S TOKYO. WE'RE ALMOST THERE...
TWENTY-FIRST-CENTURY TOKYO...
HEY, IT'S THE METROPOLIS OF THE FUTURE THAT WE DREAMED ABOUT...
KENJI ...

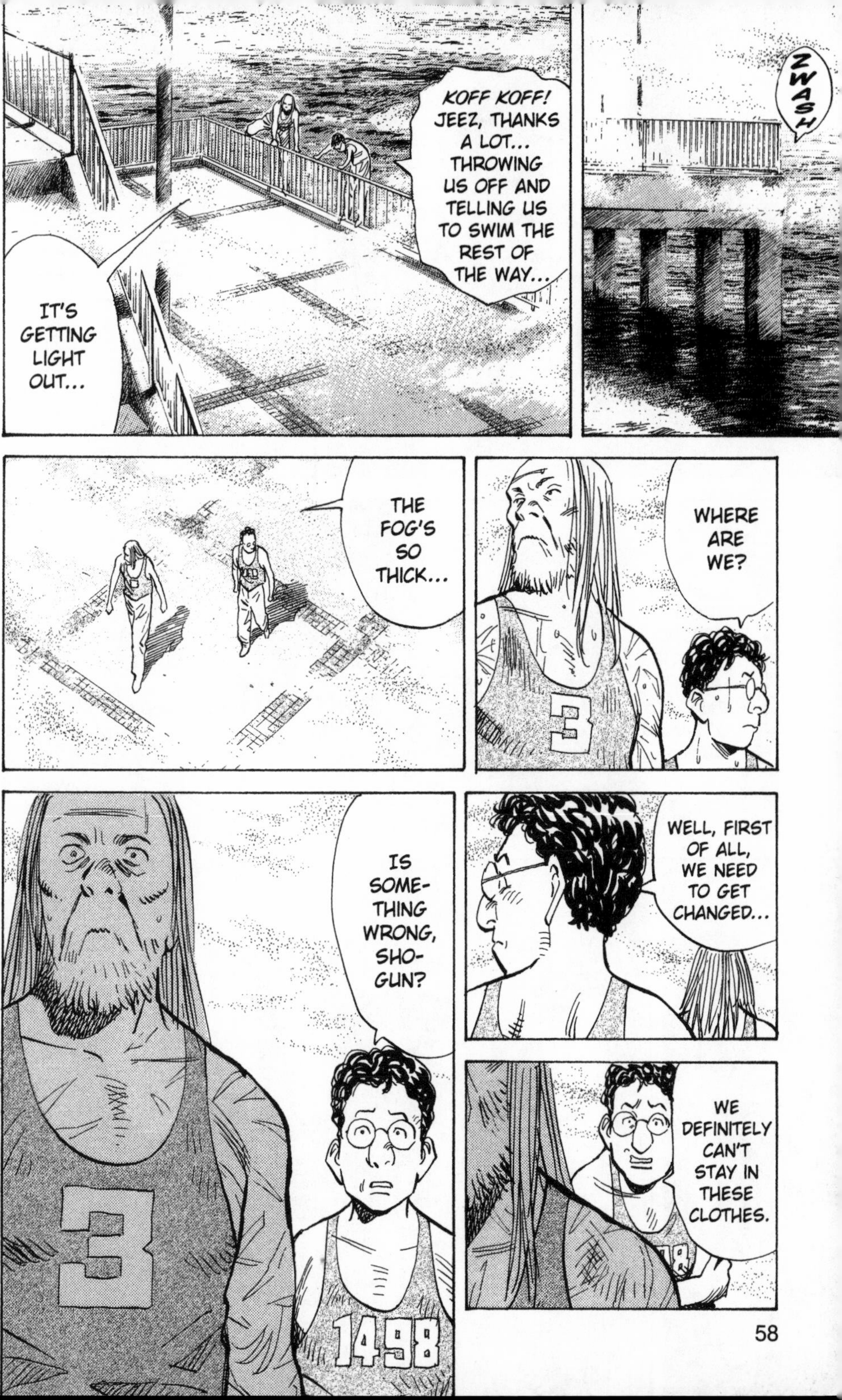
ZWASH
KOFF KOFF! JEEZ, THANKS A LOT... THROWING US OFF AND TELLING US TO SWIM THE REST OF THE WAY...
IT'S GETTING LIGHT OUT...
WHERE ARE WE?
THE FOG'S SO THICK...
WELL, FIRST OF ALL, WE NEED TO GET CHANGED...
WE DEFINITELY CAN'T STAY IN THESE CLOTHES.
IS SOME-THING WRONG, SHO-GUN?

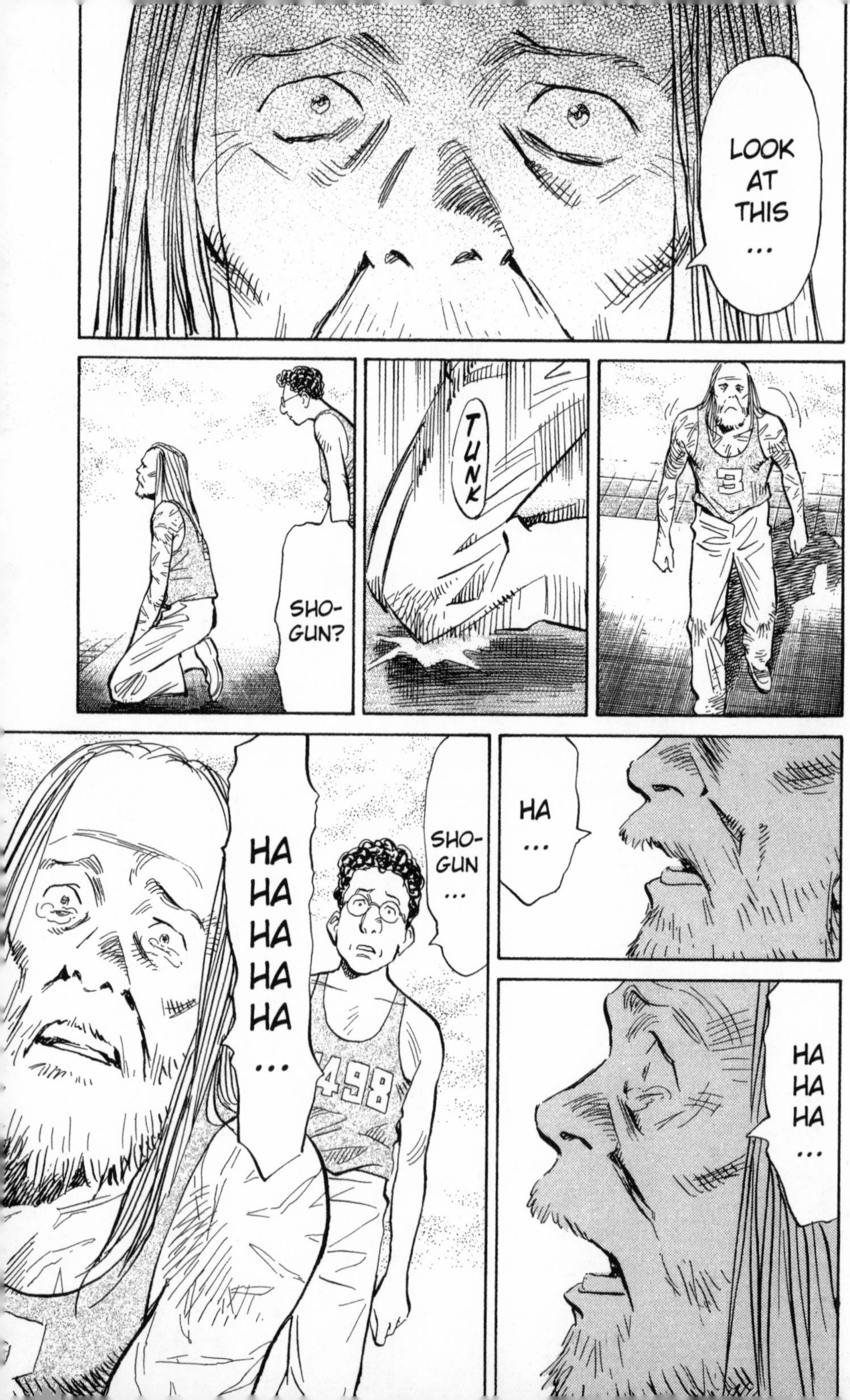
LOOK AT THIS ...
TUNK
SHO-GUN?
HA ...
HA HA HA ...
SHO-GUN ...
HA HA HA HA HA HA ...

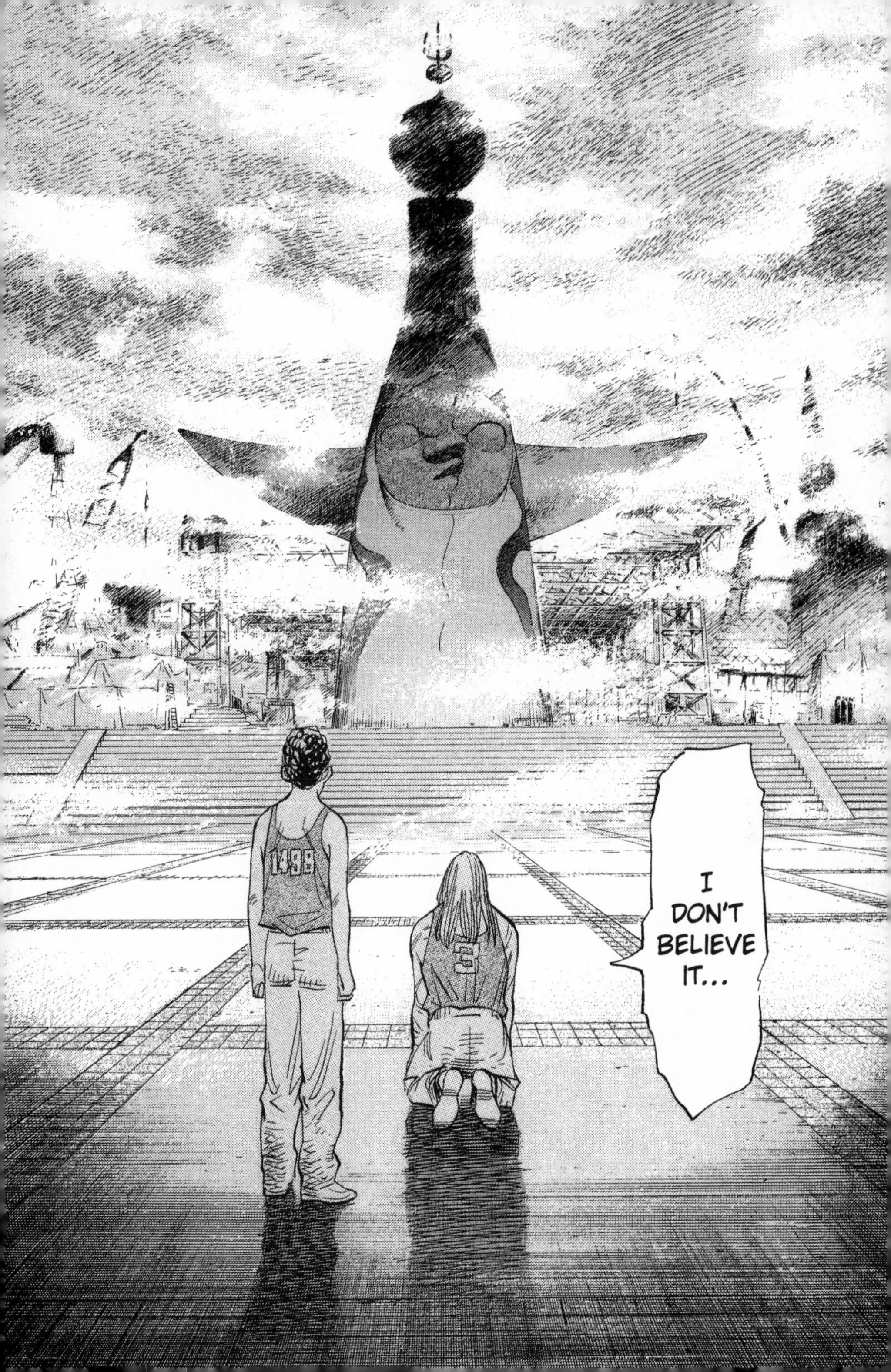
I DON'T BELIEVE IT...

Chapter 4 Expo of Dreams

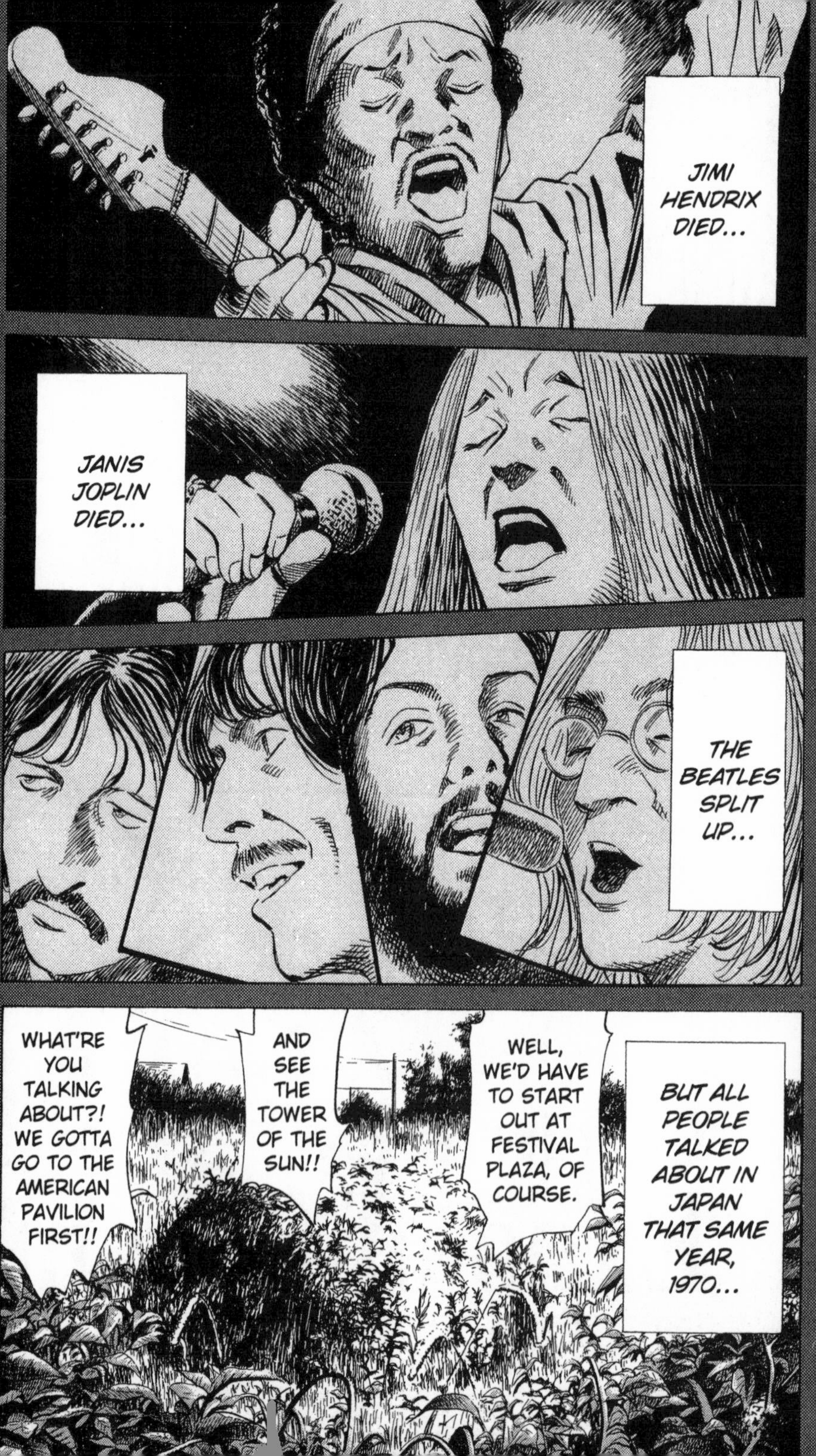

JIMI HENDRIX DIED...
JANIS JOPLIN DIED...
THE BEATLES SPLIT UP...
BUT ALL PEOPLE TALKED ABOUT IN JAPAN THAT SAME YEAR, 1970...
WELL, WE'D HAVE TO START OUT AT FESTIVAL PLAZA, OF COURSE.
AND SEE THE TOWER OF THE SUN!!
WHAT'RE YOU TALKING ABOUT?! WE GOTTA GO TO THE AMERICAN PAVILION FIRST!!

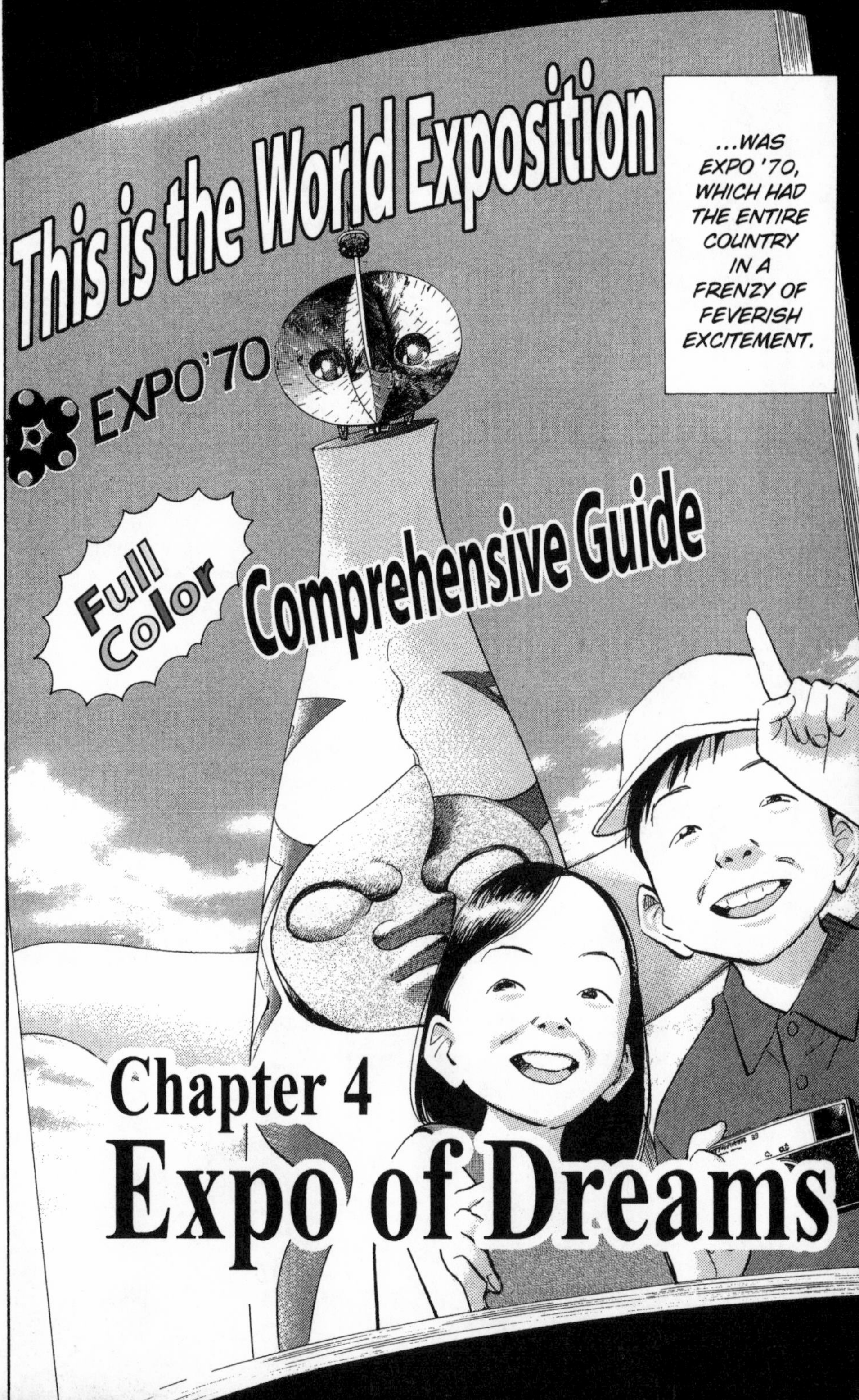
...WAS EXPO '70, WHICH HAD THE ENTIRE COUNTRY IN A FRENZY OF FEVERISH EXCITEMENT.
This is the World Exposition
EXPO'70
Full Color
Comprehensive Guide
Chapter 4
Expo of Dreams

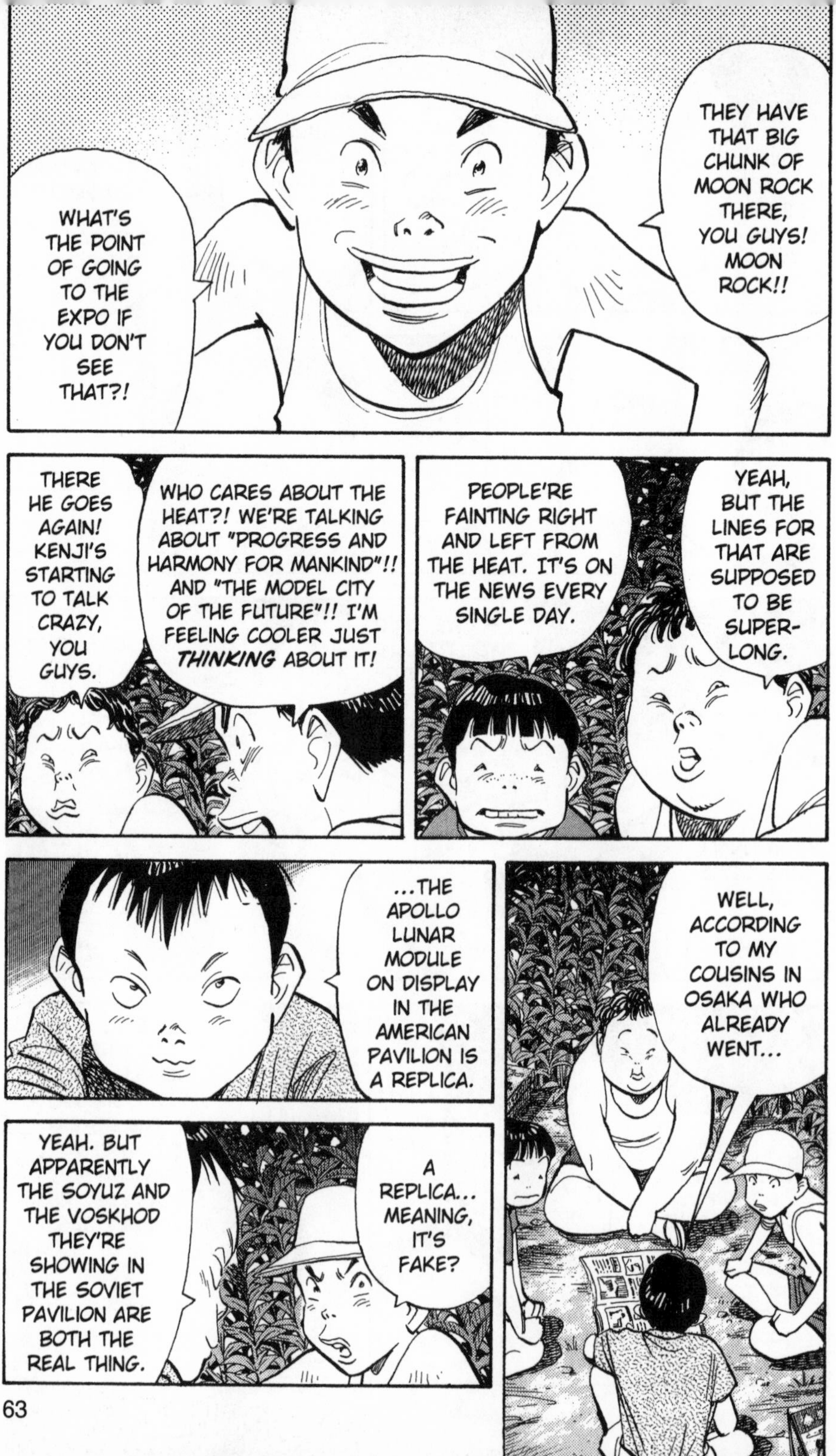
THEY HAVE THAT BIG CHUNK OF MOON ROCK THERE, YOU GUYS! MOON ROCK!!
WHAT'S THE POINT OF GOING TO THE EXPO IF YOU DON'T SEE THAT?!
YEAH, BUT THE LINES FOR THAT ARE SUPPOSED TO BE SUPER-LONG.
PEOPLE'RE FAINTING RIGHT AND LEFT FROM THE HEAT. IT'S ON THE NEWS EVERY SINGLE DAY.
WHO CARES ABOUT THE HEAT?! WE'RE TALKING ABOUT "PROGRESS AND HARMONY FOR MANKIND"!! AND "THE MODEL CITY OF THE FUTURE"!! I'M FEELING COOLER JUST *THINKING* ABOUT IT!
THERE HE GOES AGAIN! KENJI'S STARTING TO TALK CRAZY, YOU GUYS.
WELL, ACCORDING TO MY COUSINS IN OSAKA WHO ALREADY WENT...
...THE APOLLO LUNAR MODULE ON DISPLAY IN THE AMERICAN PAVILION IS A REPLICA.
A REPLICA... MEANING, IT'S FAKE?
YEAH. BUT APPARENTLY THE SOYUZ AND THE VOSKHOD THEY'RE SHOWING IN THE SOVIET PAVILION ARE BOTH THE REAL THING.

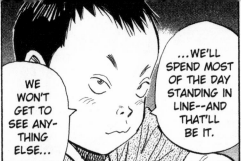

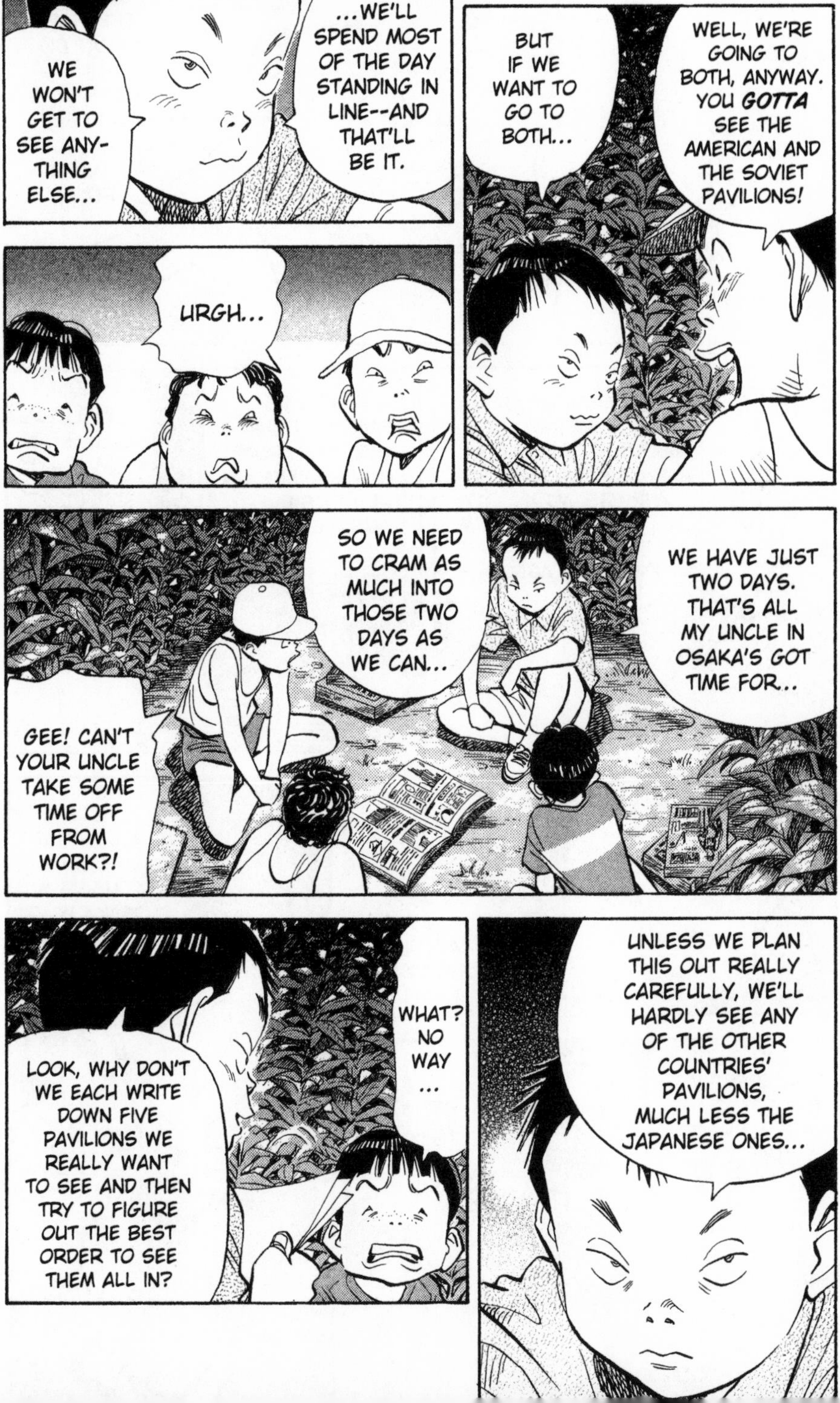
WELL, WE'RE GOING TO BOTH, ANYWAY. YOU **GOTTA** SEE THE AMERICAN AND THE SOVIET PAVILIONS!
BUT IF WE WANT TO GO TO BOTH...
...WE'LL SPEND MOST OF THE DAY STANDING IN LINE--AND THAT'LL BE IT.
WE WON'T GET TO SEE ANYTHING ELSE...
URGH...
WE HAVE JUST TWO DAYS. THAT'S ALL MY UNCLE IN OSAKA'S GOT TIME FOR...
SO WE NEED TO CRAM AS MUCH INTO THOSE TWO DAYS AS WE CAN...
GEE! CAN'T YOUR UNCLE TAKE SOME TIME OFF FROM WORK?!
UNLESS WE PLAN THIS OUT REALLY CAREFULLY, WE'LL HARDLY SEE ANY OF THE OTHER COUNTRIES' PAVILIONS, MUCH LESS THE JAPANESE ONES...
WHAT? NO WAY...
LOOK, WHY DON'T WE EACH WRITE DOWN FIVE PAVILIONS WE REALLY WANT TO SEE AND THEN TRY TO FIGURE OUT THE BEST ORDER TO SEE THEM ALL IN?

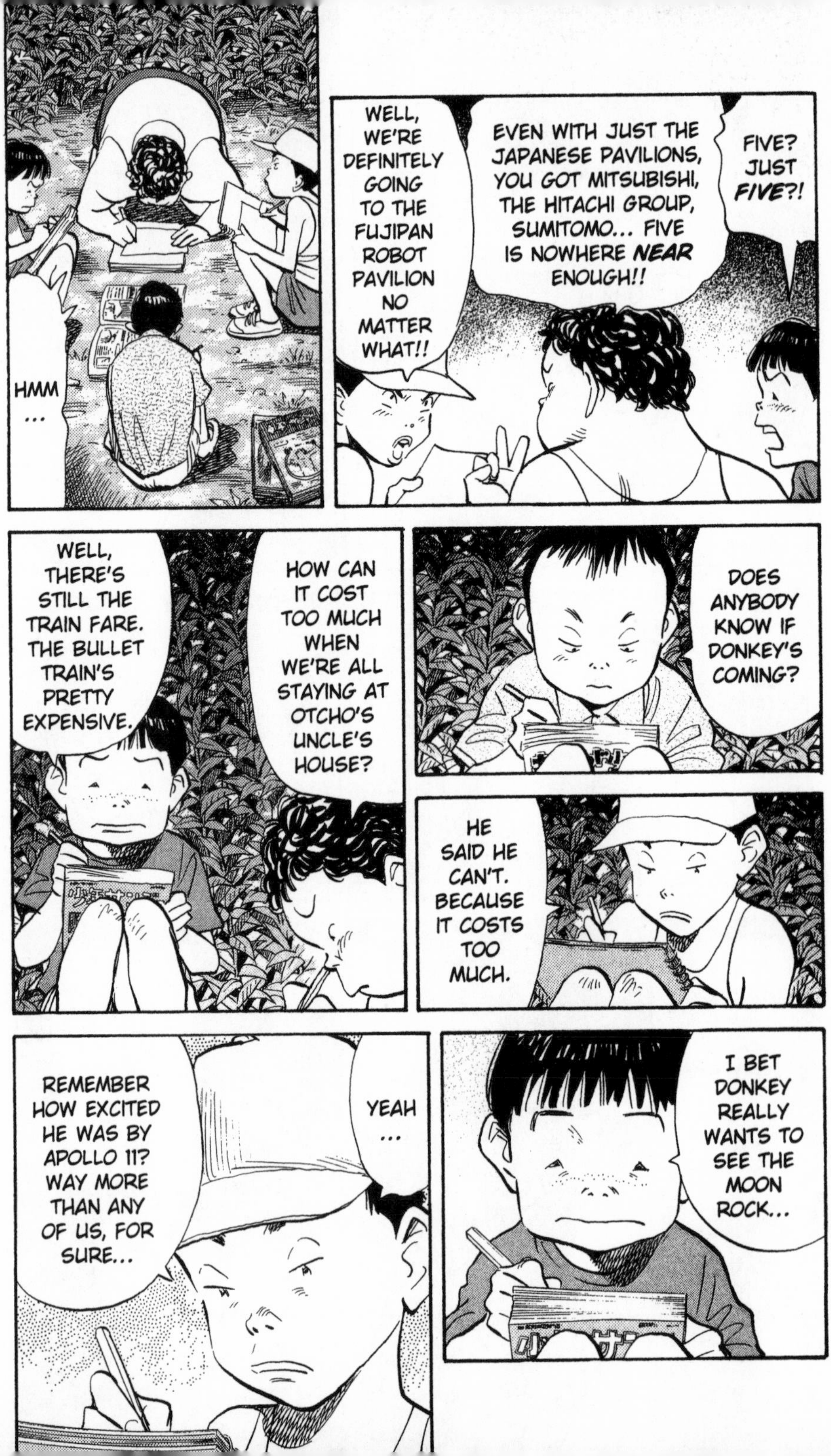
FIVE? JUST *FIVE*?!
EVEN WITH JUST THE JAPANESE PAVILIONS, YOU GOT MITSUBISHI, THE HITACHI GROUP, SUMITOMO... FIVE IS NOWHERE *NEAR* ENOUGH!!
WELL, WE'RE DEFINITELY GOING TO THE FUJIPAN ROBOT PAVILION NO MATTER WHAT!!
HMM ...
DOES ANYBODY KNOW IF DONKEY'S COMING?
HE SAID HE CAN'T. BECAUSE IT COSTS TOO MUCH.
HOW CAN IT COST TOO MUCH WHEN WE'RE ALL STAYING AT OTCHO'S UNCLE'S HOUSE?
WELL, THERE'S STILL THE TRAIN FARE. THE BULLET TRAIN'S PRETTY EXPENSIVE.
I BET DONKEY REALLY WANTS TO SEE THE MOON ROCK...
YEAH ...
REMEMBER HOW EXCITED HE WAS BY APOLLO 11? WAY MORE THAN ANY OF US, FOR SURE...

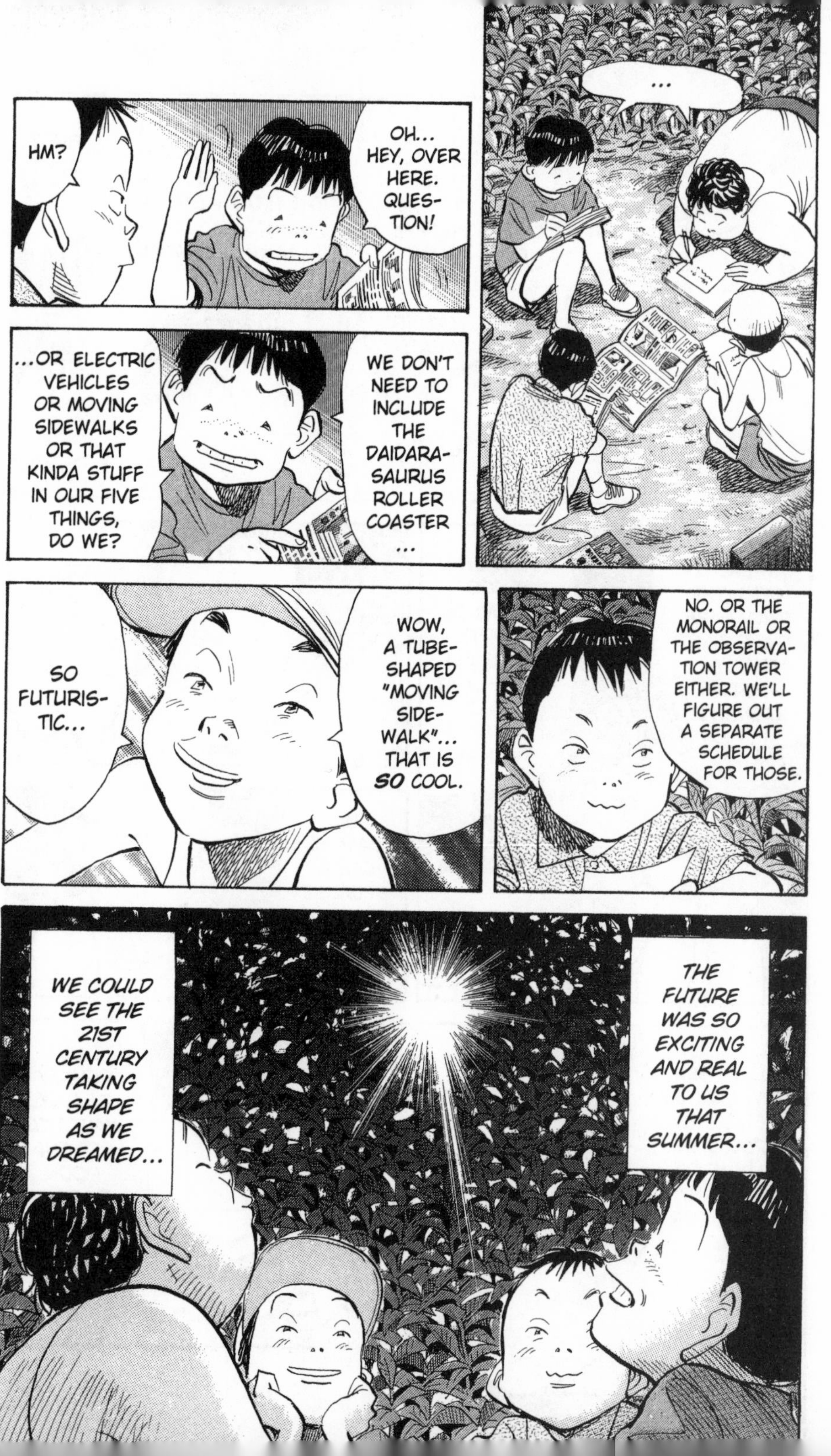
...
OH... HEY, OVER HERE. QUES-TION!
HM?
WE DON'T NEED TO INCLUDE THE DAIDARA-SAURUS ROLLER COASTER ...
...OR ELECTRIC VEHICLES OR MOVING SIDEWALKS OR THAT KINDA STUFF IN OUR FIVE THINGS, DO WE?
NO. OR THE MONORAIL OR THE OBSERVA-TION TOWER EITHER. WE'LL FIGURE OUT A SEPARATE SCHEDULE FOR THOSE.
WOW, A TUBE-SHAPED "MOVING SIDE-WALK"... THAT IS SO COOL.
SO FUTURIS-TIC...
THE FUTURE WAS SO EXCITING AND REAL TO US THAT SUMMER...
WE COULD SEE THE 21ST CENTURY TAKING SHAPE AS WE DREAMED...

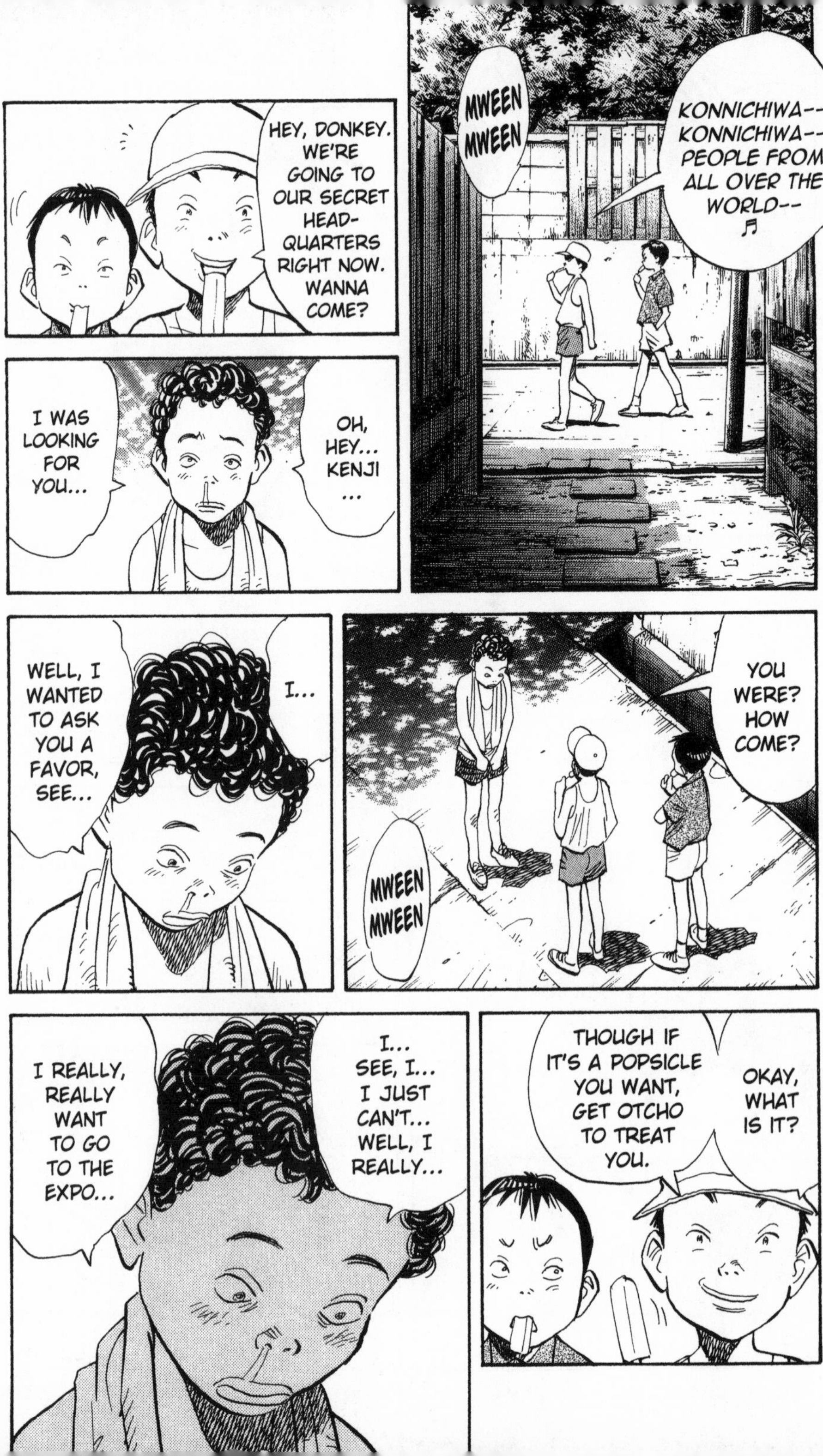
KONNICHIWA-- KONNICHIWA-- PEOPLE FROM ALL OVER THE WORLD-- ♬
MWEEN MWEEN
HEY, DONKEY. WE'RE GOING TO OUR SECRET HEAD-QUARTERS RIGHT NOW. WANNA COME?
OH, HEY... KENJI...
I WAS LOOKING FOR YOU...
YOU WERE? HOW COME?
MWEEN MWEEN
I...
WELL, I WANTED TO ASK YOU A FAVOR, SEE...
OKAY, WHAT IS IT?
THOUGH IF IT'S A POPSICLE YOU WANT, GET OTCHO TO TREAT YOU.
I... SEE, I... I JUST CAN'T... WELL, I REALLY...
I REALLY, REALLY WANT TO GO TO THE EXPO...

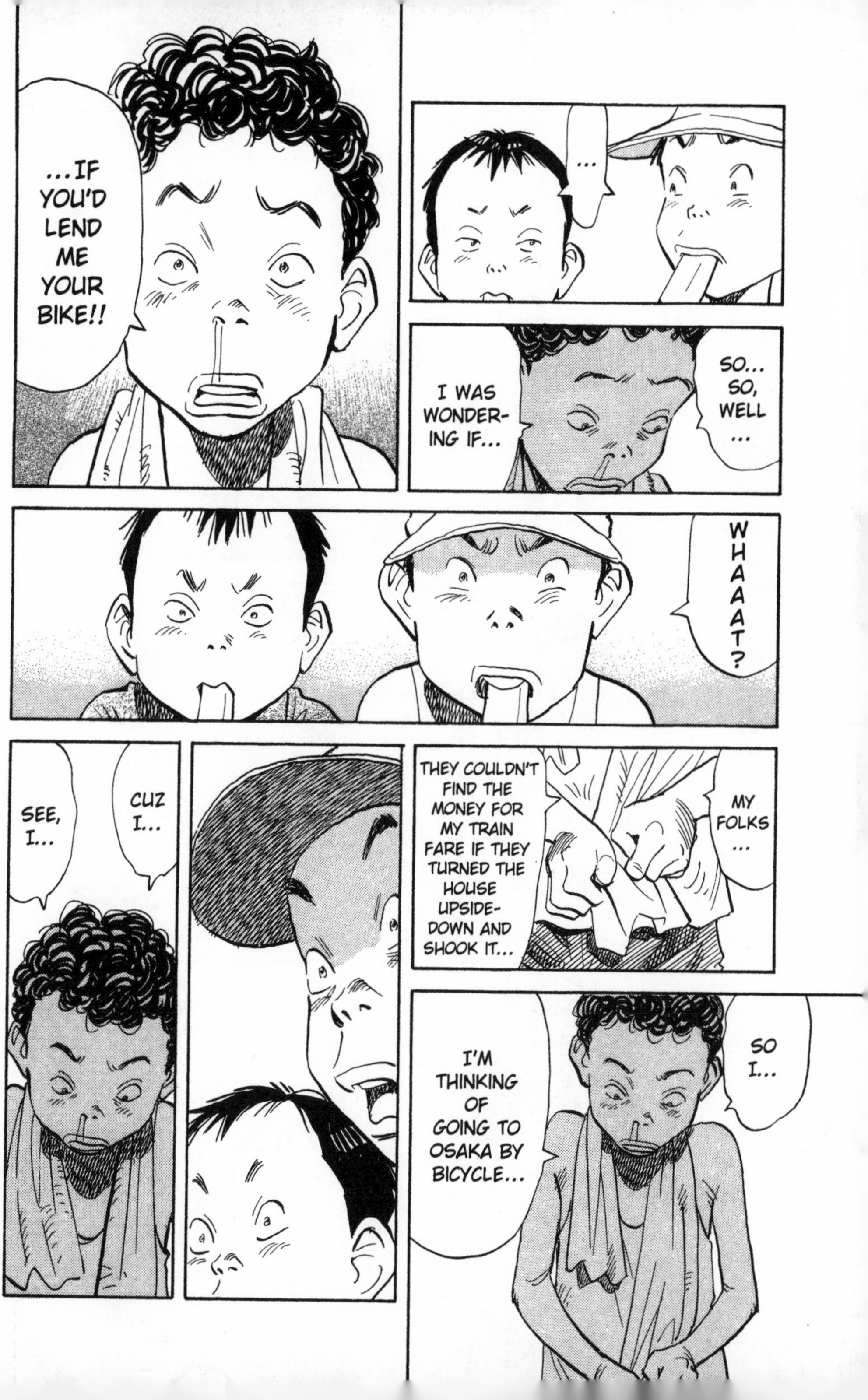
...
SO... SO, WELL ...
I WAS WONDER-ING IF...
...IF YOU'D LEND ME YOUR BIKE!!
WHAAAAT?
MY FOLKS ...
THEY COULDN'T FIND THE MONEY FOR MY TRAIN FARE IF THEY TURNED THE HOUSE UPSIDE-DOWN AND SHOOK IT...
SO I...
I'M THINKING OF GOING TO OSAKA BY BICYCLE...
CUZ I...
SEE, I...

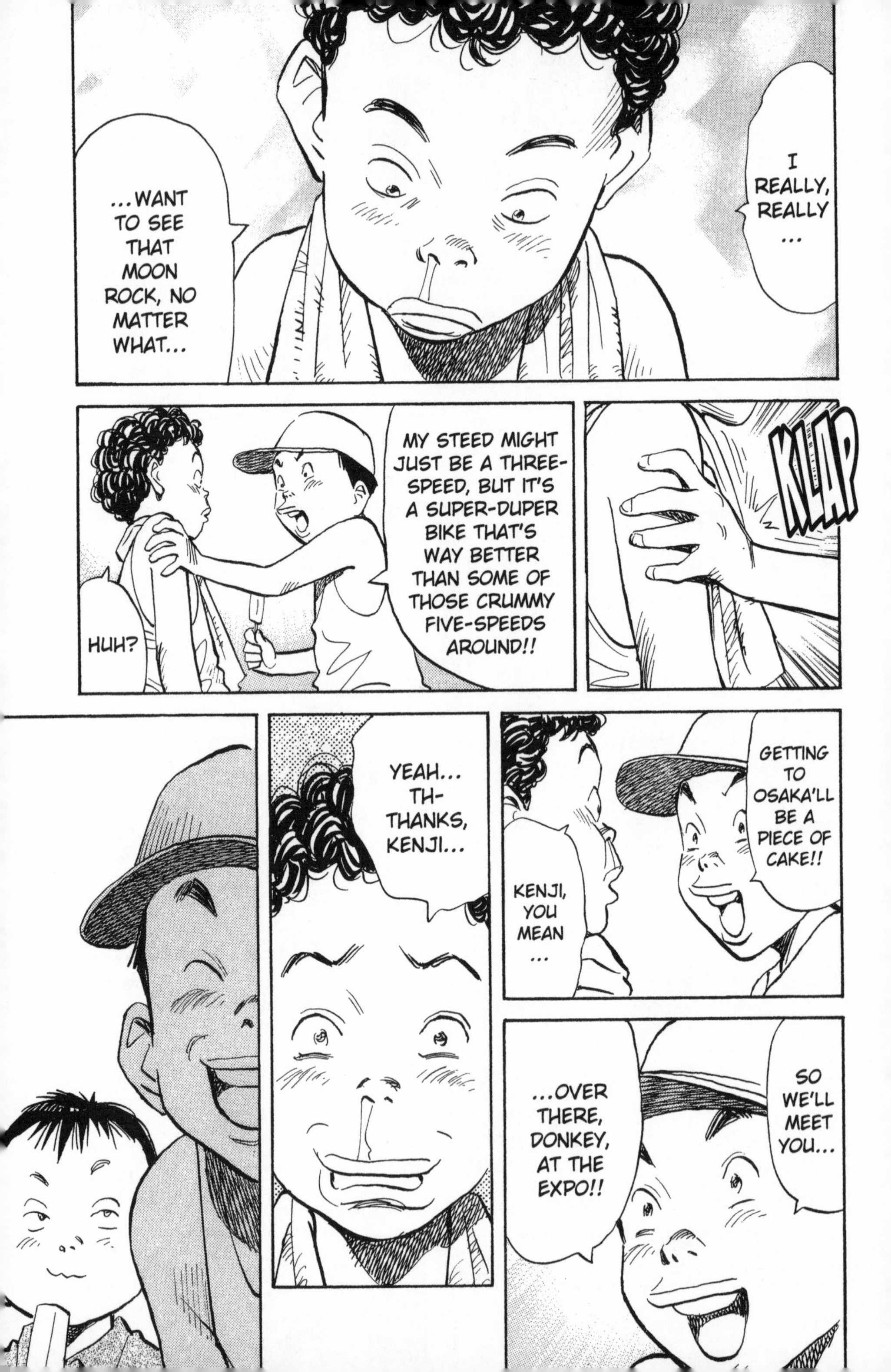
I REALLY, REALLY ...
...WANT TO SEE THAT MOON ROCK, NO MATTER WHAT...
KLAP
MY STEED MIGHT JUST BE A THREE-SPEED, BUT IT'S A SUPER-DUPER BIKE THAT'S WAY BETTER THAN SOME OF THOSE CRUMMY FIVE-SPEEDS AROUND!!
HUH?
GETTING TO OSAKA'LL BE A PIECE OF CAKE!!
KENJI, YOU MEAN ...
SO WE'LL MEET YOU...
...OVER THERE, DONKEY, AT THE EXPO!!
YEAH... TH-THANKS, KENJI...

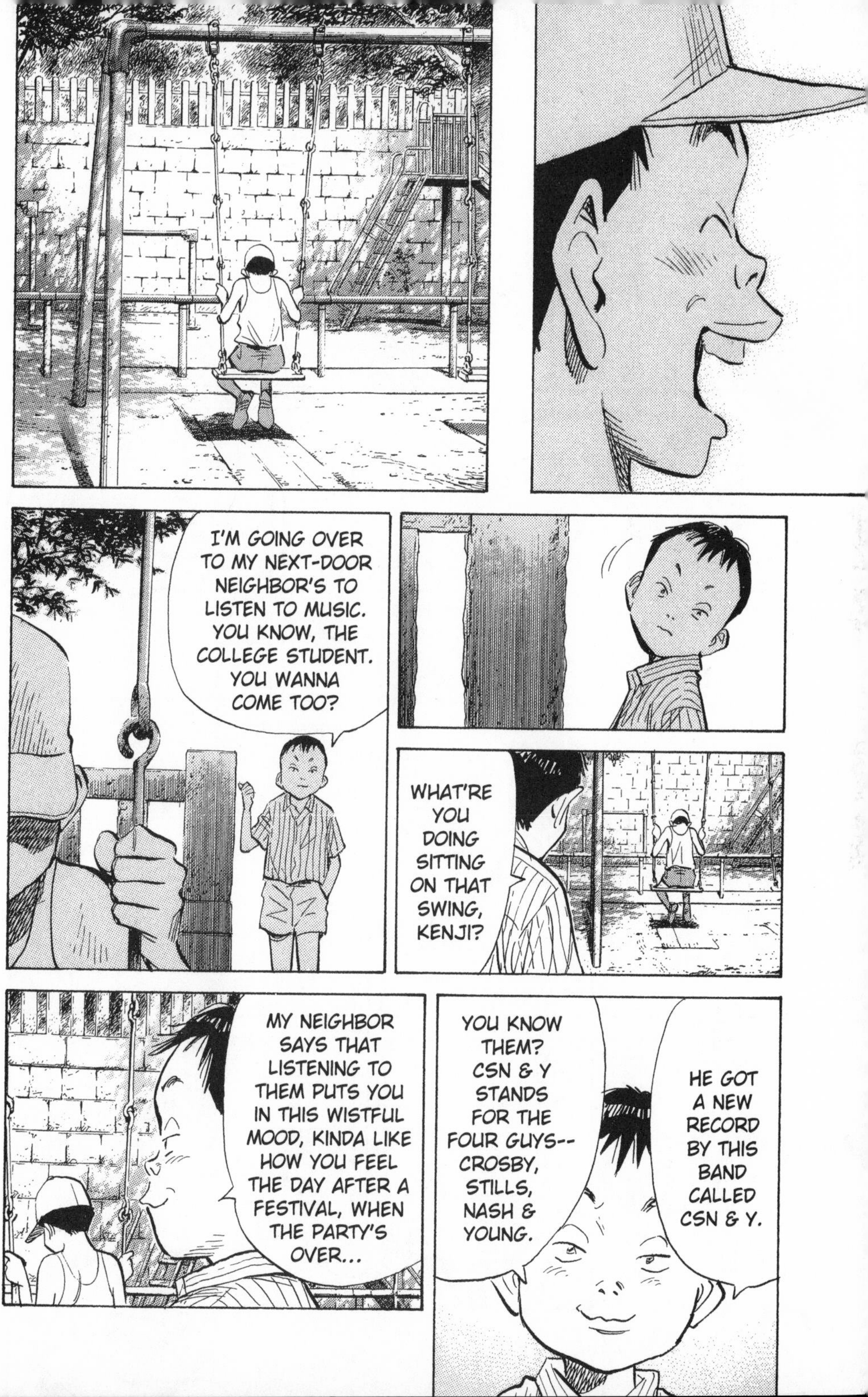
WHAT'RE YOU DOING SITTING ON THAT SWING, KENJI?
I'M GOING OVER TO MY NEXT-DOOR NEIGHBOR'S TO LISTEN TO MUSIC. YOU KNOW, THE COLLEGE STUDENT. YOU WANNA COME TOO?
HE GOT A NEW RECORD BY THIS BAND CALLED CSN & Y.
YOU KNOW THEM? CSN & Y STANDS FOR THE FOUR GUYS-- CROSBY, STILLS, NASH & YOUNG.
MY NEIGHBOR SAYS THAT LISTENING TO THEM PUTS YOU IN THIS WISTFUL MOOD, KINDA LIKE HOW YOU FEEL THE DAY AFTER A FESTIVAL, WHEN THE PARTY'S OVER...

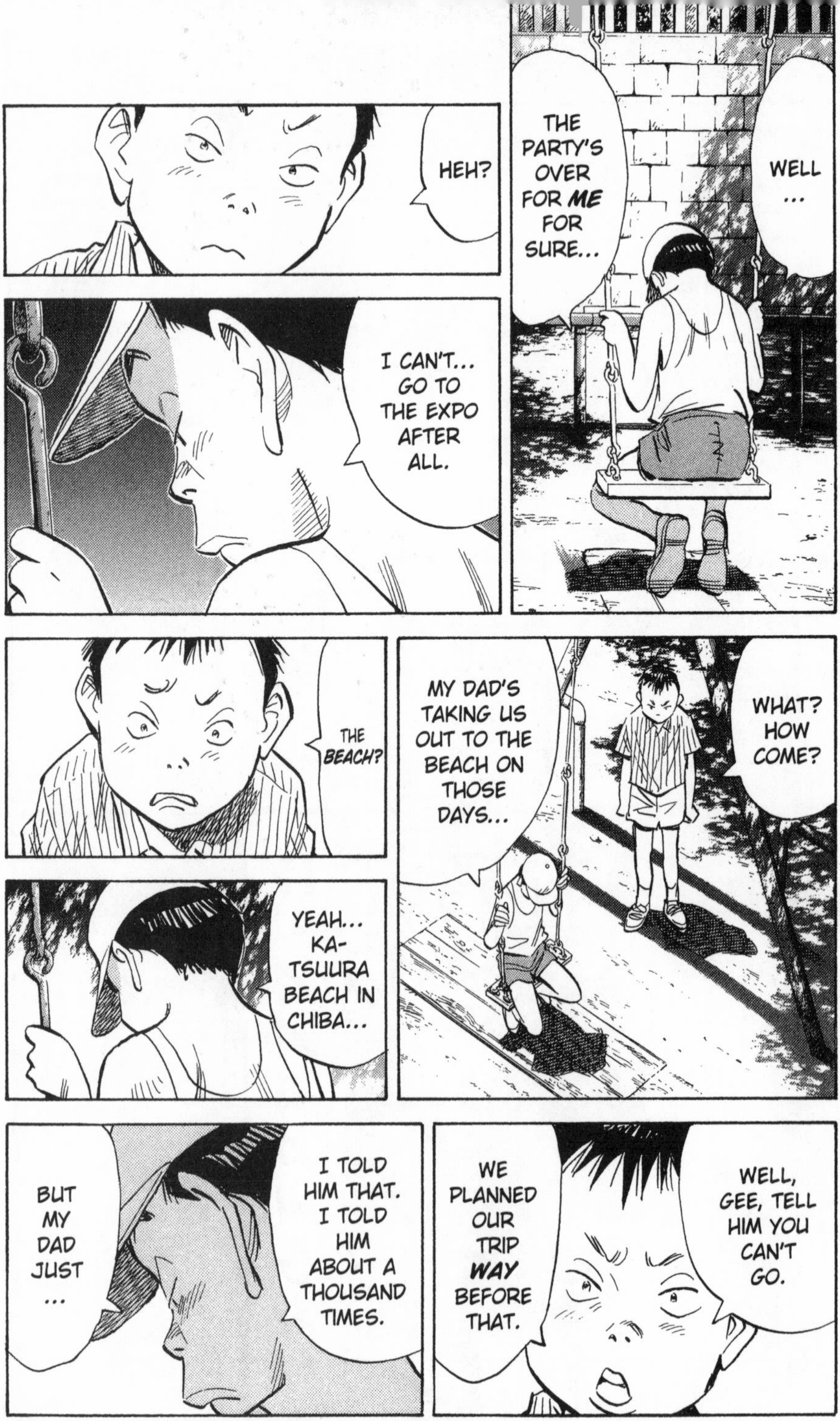
WELL ...
THE PARTY'S OVER FOR **ME** FOR SURE...
HEH?
I CAN'T... GO TO THE EXPO AFTER ALL.
WHAT? HOW COME?
MY DAD'S TAKING US OUT TO THE BEACH ON THOSE DAYS...
THE *BEACH?*
YEAH... KA-TSUURA BEACH IN CHIBA...
WELL, GEE, TELL HIM YOU CAN'T GO.
WE PLANNED OUR TRIP **WAY** BEFORE THAT.
I TOLD HIM THAT. I TOLD HIM ABOUT A THOUSAND TIMES.
BUT MY DAD JUST ...

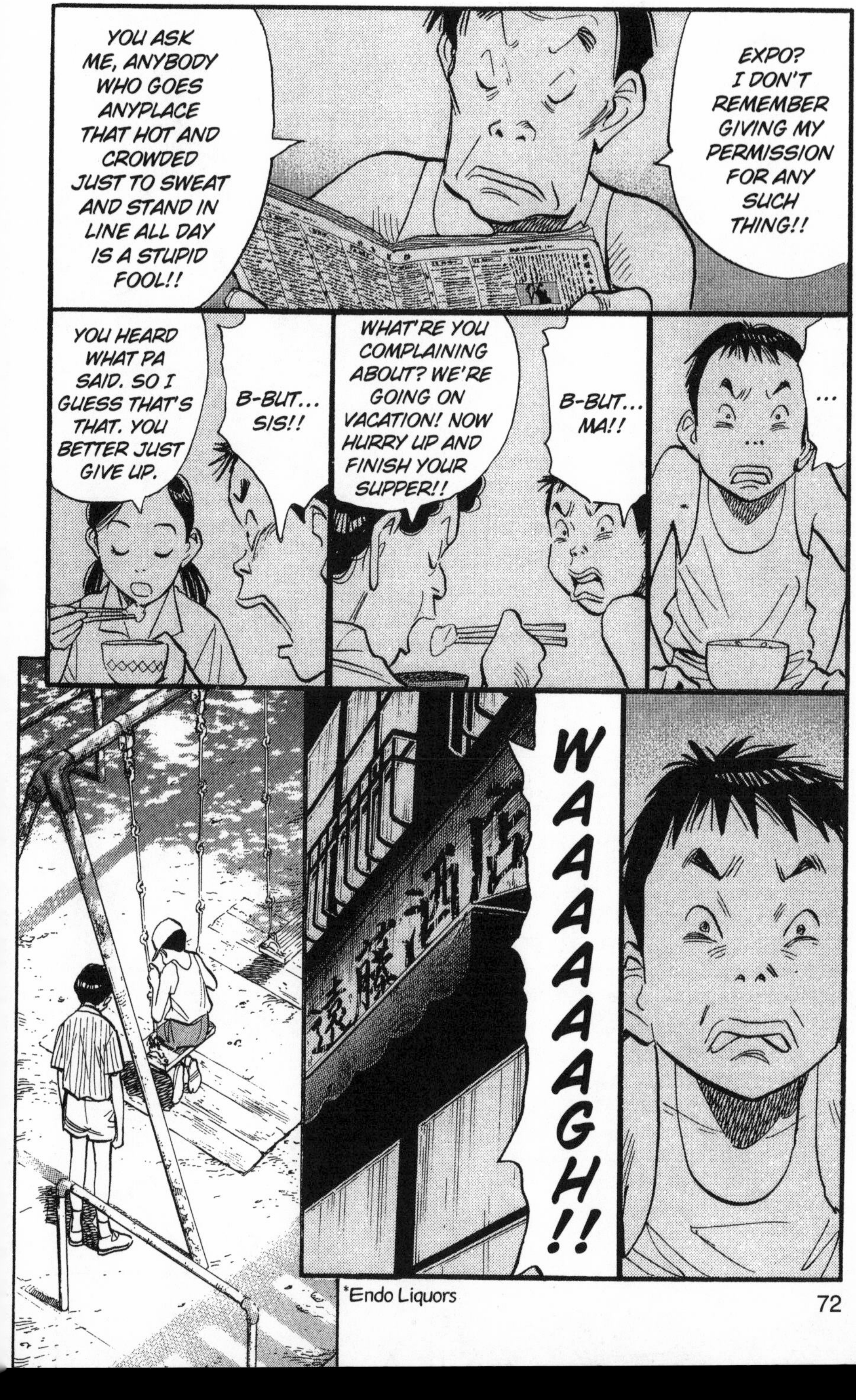
EXPO? I DON'T REMEMBER GIVING MY PERMISSION FOR ANY SUCH THING!!
YOU ASK ME, ANYBODY WHO GOES ANYPLACE THAT HOT AND CROWDED JUST TO SWEAT AND STAND IN LINE ALL DAY IS A STUPID FOOL!!
...
B-BUT... MA!!
WHAT'RE YOU COMPLAINING ABOUT? WE'RE GOING ON VACATION! NOW HURRY UP AND FINISH YOUR SUPPER!!
B-BUT... SIS!!
YOU HEARD WHAT PA SAID. SO I GUESS THAT'S THAT. YOU BETTER JUST GIVE UP.
WAAAAAAAAGH!!
遠藤酒店

*Endo Liquors

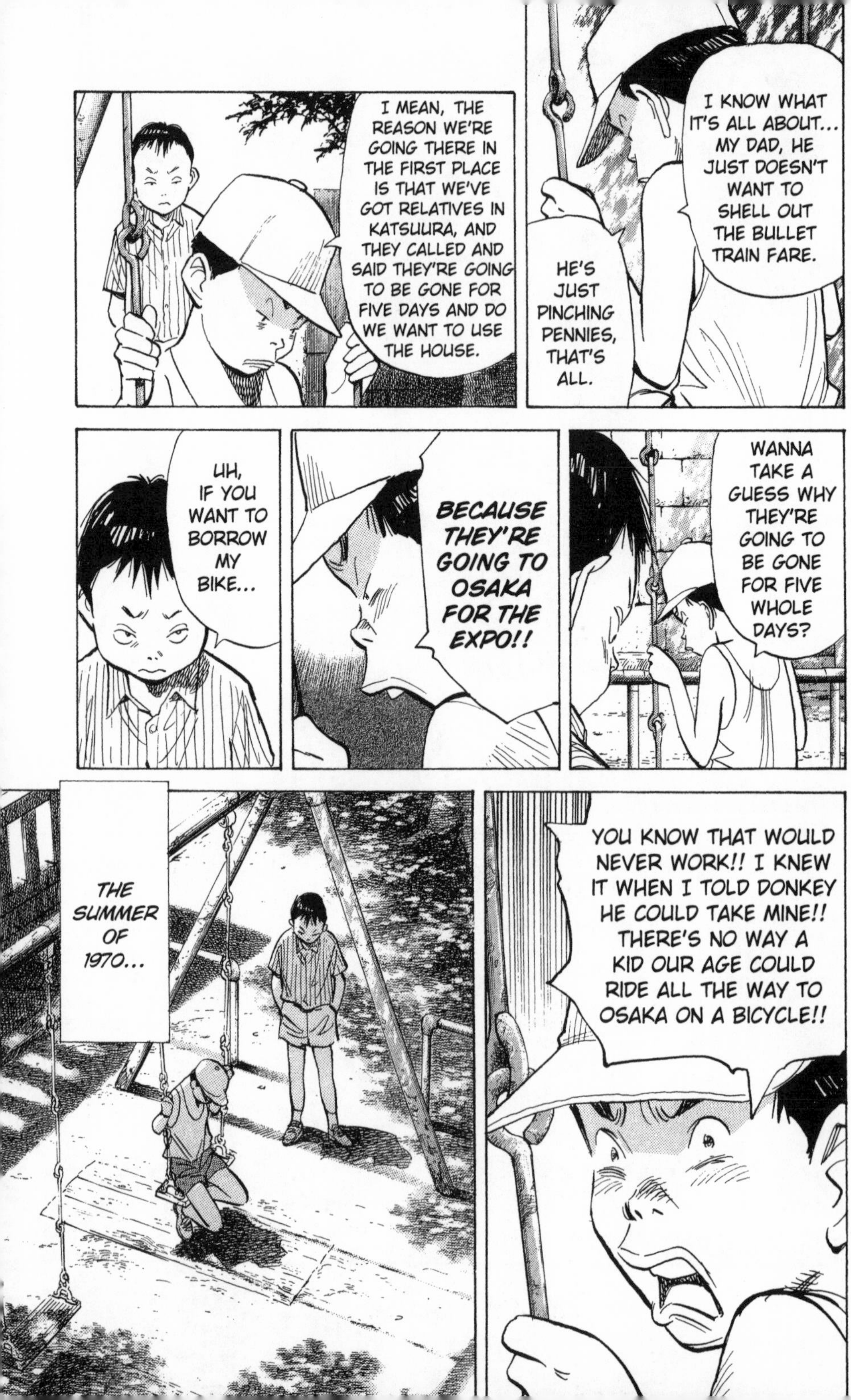
I KNOW WHAT IT'S ALL ABOUT... MY DAD, HE JUST DOESN'T WANT TO SHELL OUT THE BULLET TRAIN FARE.
HE'S JUST PINCHING PENNIES, THAT'S ALL.
I MEAN, THE REASON WE'RE GOING THERE IN THE FIRST PLACE IS THAT WE'VE GOT RELATIVES IN KATSUURA, AND THEY CALLED AND SAID THEY'RE GOING TO BE GONE FOR FIVE DAYS AND DO WE WANT TO USE THE HOUSE.
WANNA TAKE A GUESS WHY THEY'RE GOING TO BE GONE FOR FIVE WHOLE DAYS?
BECAUSE THEY'RE GOING TO OSAKA FOR THE EXPO!!
UH, IF YOU WANT TO BORROW MY BIKE...
YOU KNOW THAT WOULD NEVER WORK!! I KNEW IT WHEN I TOLD DONKEY HE COULD TAKE MINE!! THERE'S NO WAY A KID OUR AGE COULD RIDE ALL THE WAY TO OSAKA ON A BICYCLE!!
THE SUMMER OF 1970...

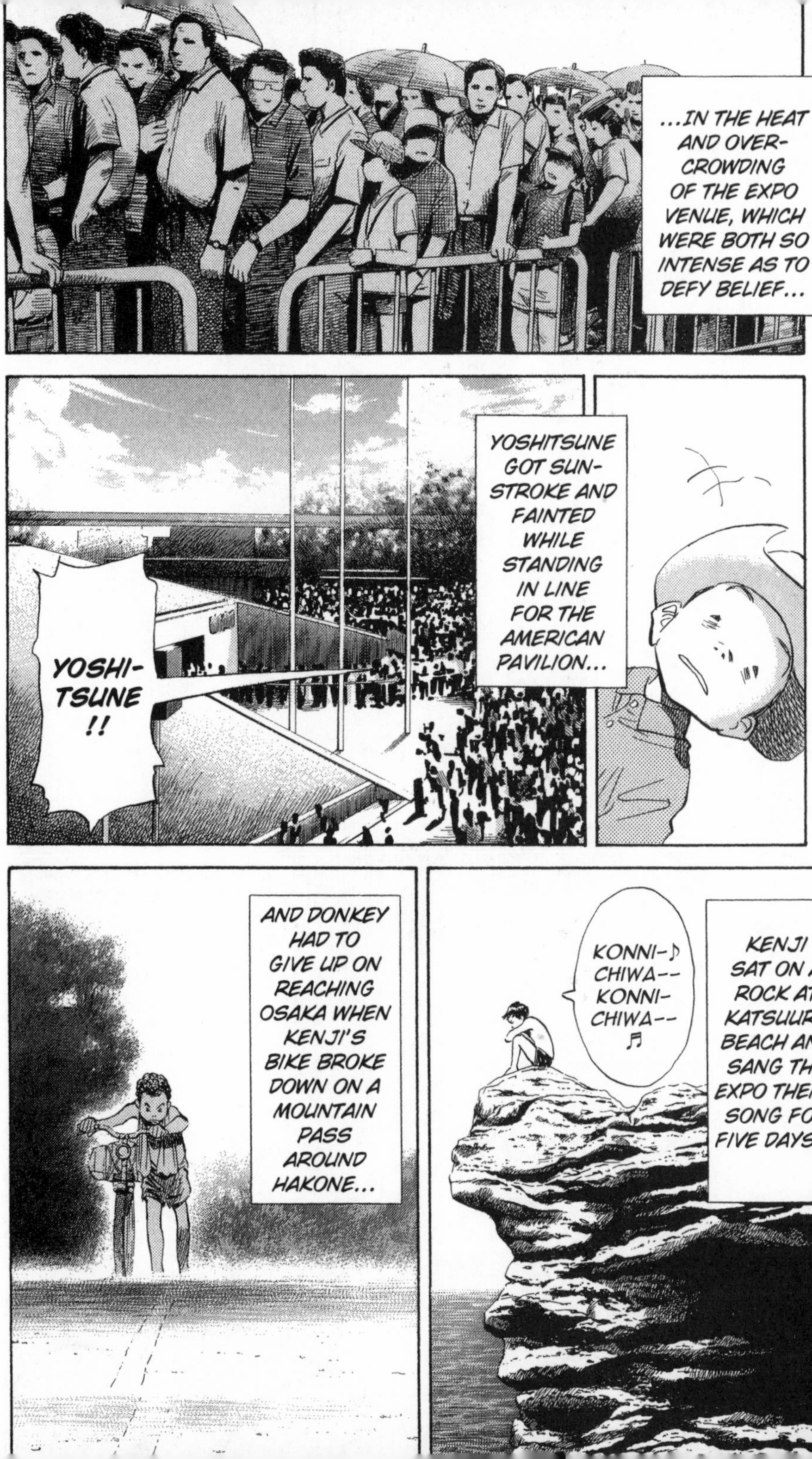

...IN THE HEAT AND OVER-CROWDING OF THE EXPO VENUE, WHICH WERE BOTH SO INTENSE AS TO DEFY BELIEF...
YOSHITSUNE GOT SUN-STROKE AND FAINTED WHILE STANDING IN LINE FOR THE AMERICAN PAVILION...
YOSHI-TSUNE !!
KENJI SAT ON A ROCK AT KATSUURA BEACH AND SANG THE EXPO THEME SONG FOR FIVE DAYS...
KONNI-♪ CHIWA-- KONNI-CHIWA-- ♬
AND DONKEY HAD TO GIVE UP ON REACHING OSAKA WHEN KENJI'S BIKE BROKE DOWN ON A MOUNTAIN PASS AROUND HAKONE...

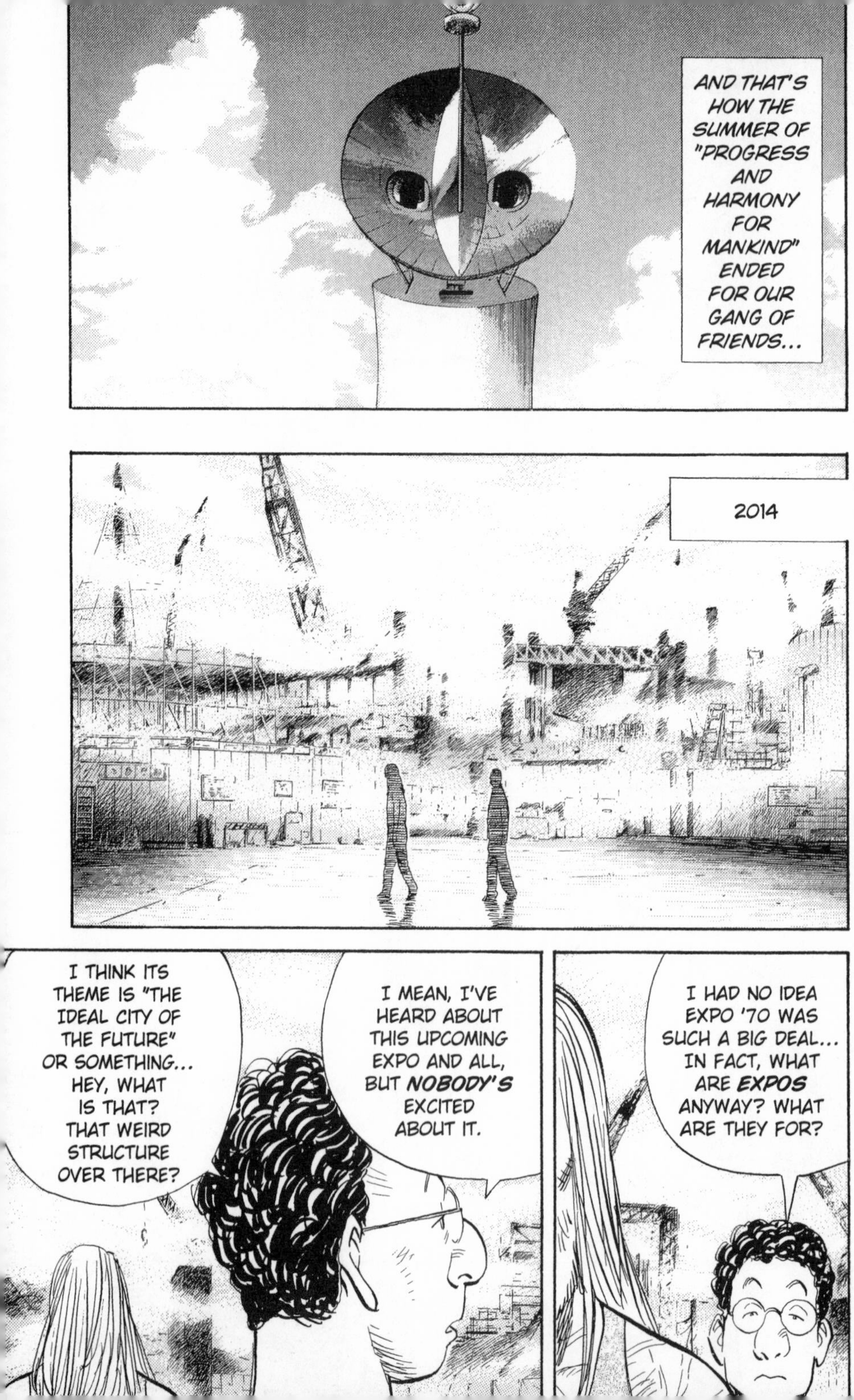
AND THAT'S HOW THE SUMMER OF "PROGRESS AND HARMONY FOR MANKIND" ENDED FOR OUR GANG OF FRIENDS...
2014
I HAD NO IDEA EXPO '70 WAS SUCH A BIG DEAL... IN FACT, WHAT ARE EXPOS ANYWAY? WHAT ARE THEY FOR?
I MEAN, I'VE HEARD ABOUT THIS UPCOMING EXPO AND ALL, BUT NOBODY'S EXCITED ABOUT IT.
I THINK ITS THEME IS "THE IDEAL CITY OF THE FUTURE" OR SOMETHING... HEY, WHAT IS THAT? THAT WEIRD STRUCTURE OVER THERE?

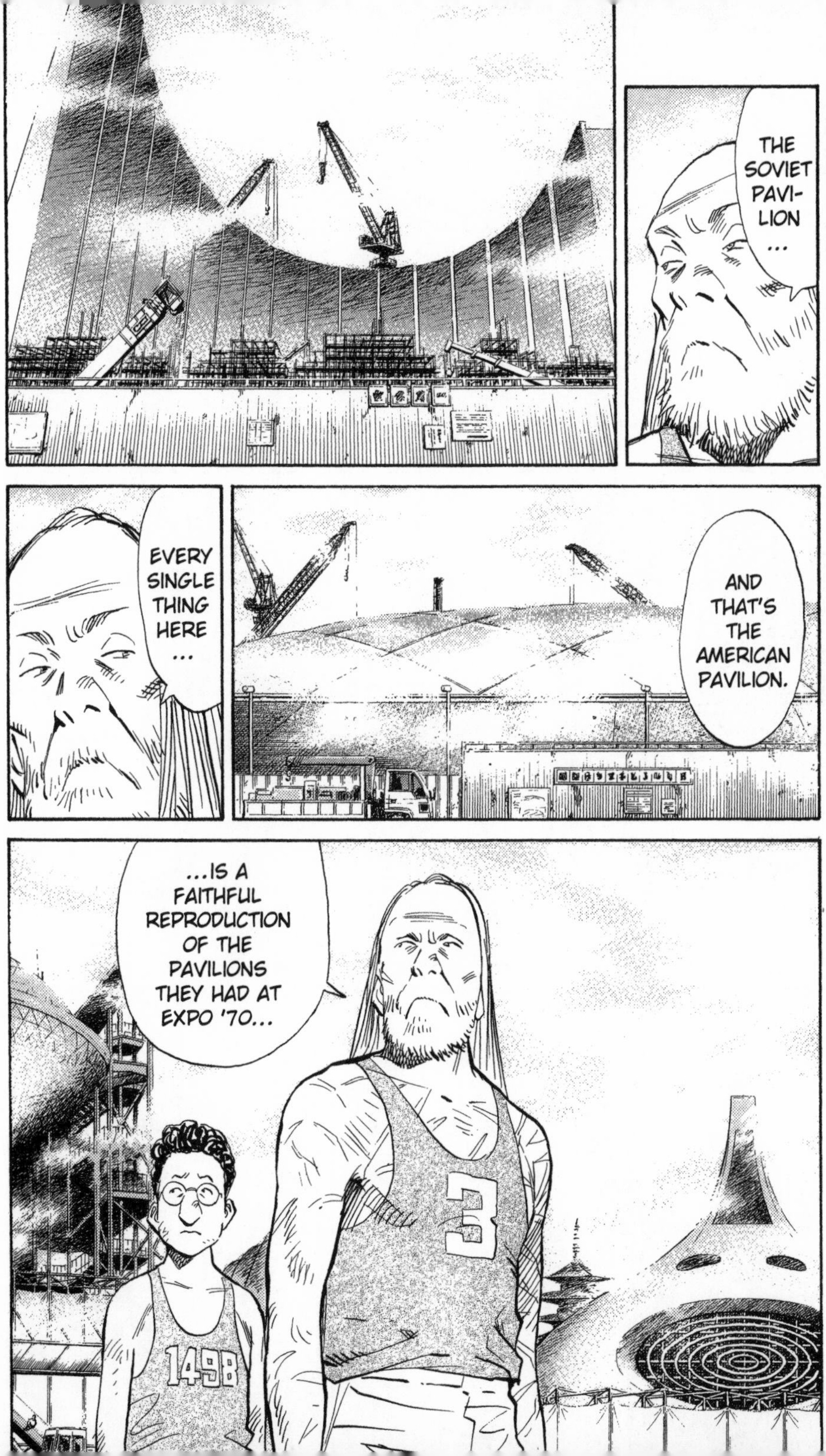
THE SOVIET PAVI-LION ...
AND THAT'S THE AMERICAN PAVILION.
EVERY SINGLE THING HERE ...
...IS A FAITHFUL REPRODUCTION OF THE PAVILIONS THEY HAD AT EXPO '70...

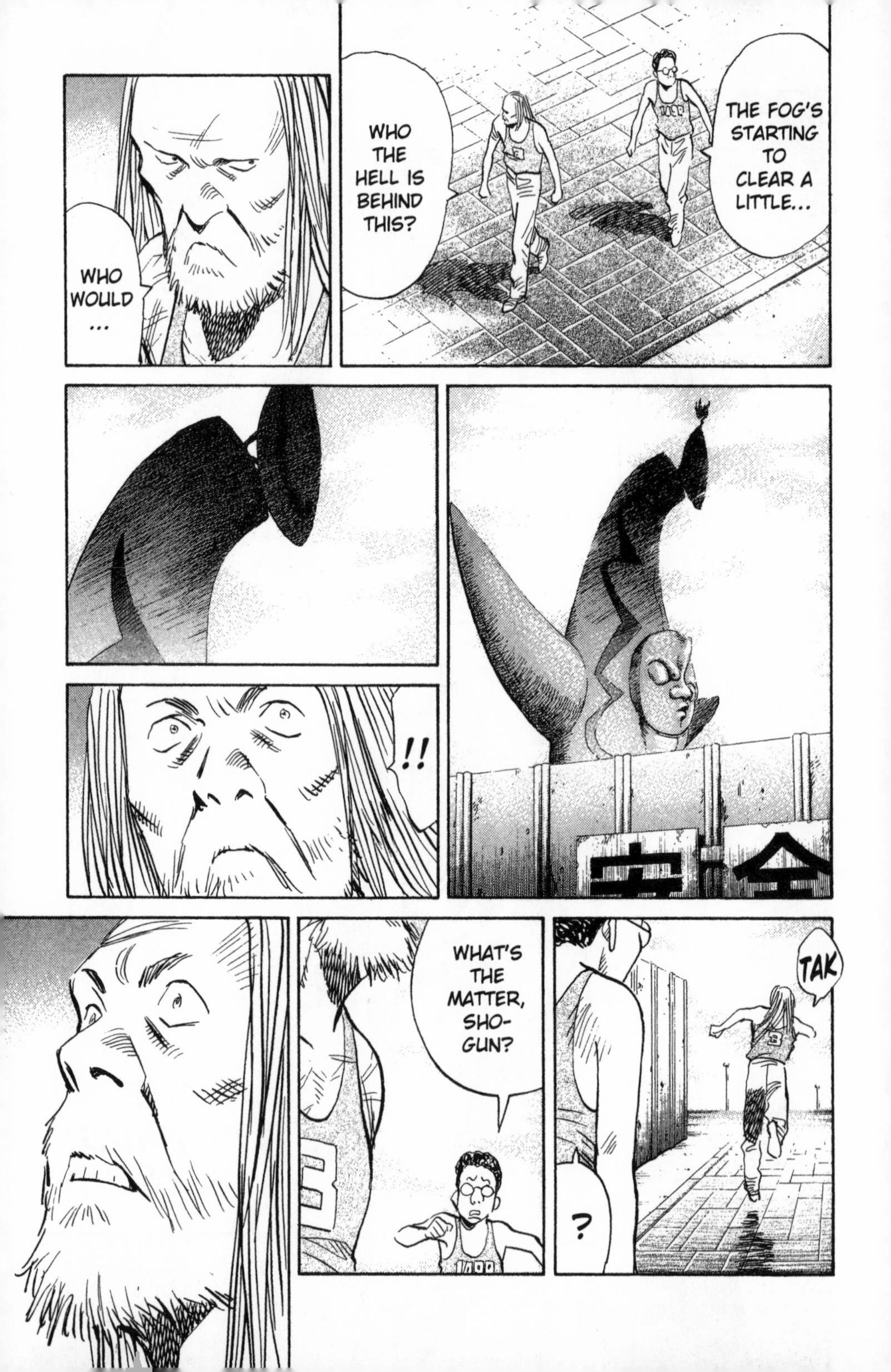
THE FOG'S STARTING TO CLEAR A LITTLE...
WHO THE HELL IS BEHIND THIS?
WHO WOULD ...
安全
!!
TAK
?
WHAT'S THE MATTER, SHO-GUN?

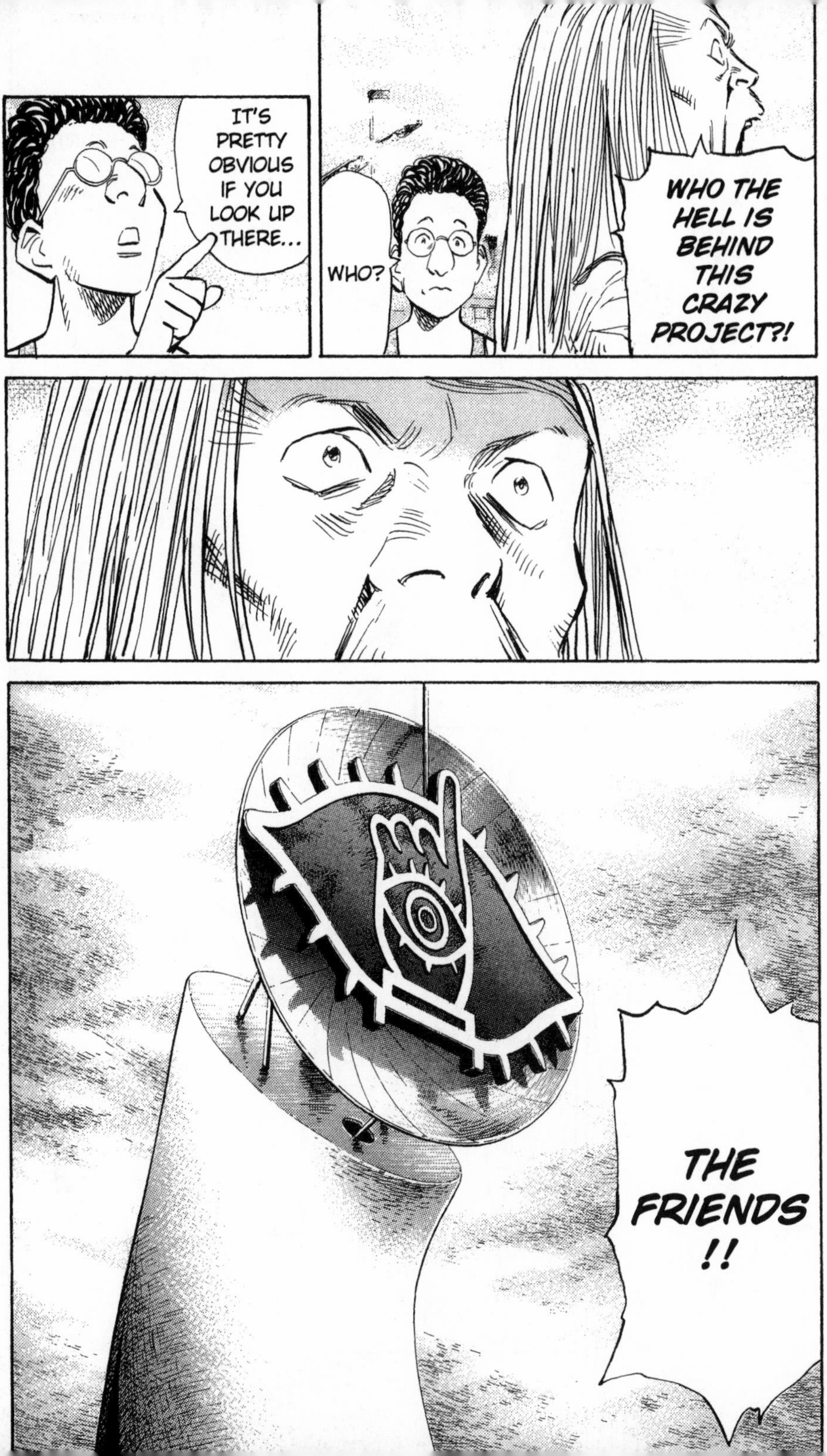
WHO THE HELL IS BEHIND THIS CRAZY PROJECT?!
WHO?
IT'S PRETTY OBVIOUS IF YOU LOOK UP THERE...
THE FRIENDS!!

Chapter 5 Koizumi

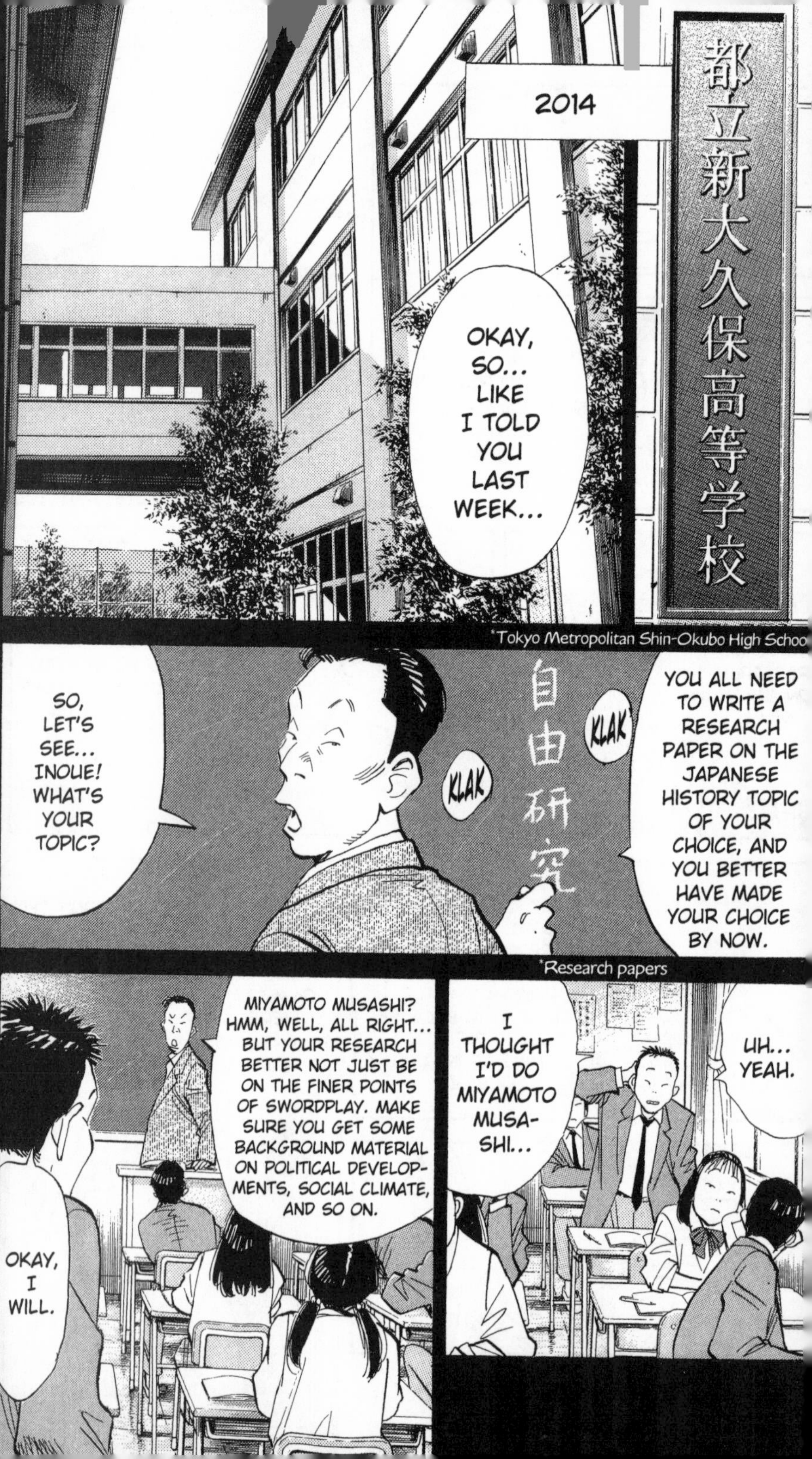
2014
都立新大久保高等学校
OKAY, SO... LIKE I TOLD YOU LAST WEEK...
*Tokyo Metropolitan Shin-Okubo High School
自由研究
YOU ALL NEED TO WRITE A RESEARCH PAPER ON THE JAPANESE HISTORY TOPIC OF YOUR CHOICE, AND YOU BETTER HAVE MADE YOUR CHOICE BY NOW.
KLAK
KLAK
SO, LET'S SEE... INOUE! WHAT'S YOUR TOPIC?
*Research papers
UH... YEAH.
I THOUGHT I'D DO MIYAMOTO MUSASHI...
MIYAMOTO MUSASHI? HMM, WELL, ALL RIGHT... BUT YOUR RESEARCH BETTER NOT JUST BE ON THE FINER POINTS OF SWORDPLAY. MAKE SURE YOU GET SOME BACKGROUND MATERIAL ON POLITICAL DEVELOPMENTS, SOCIAL CLIMATE, AND SO ON.
OKAY, I WILL.

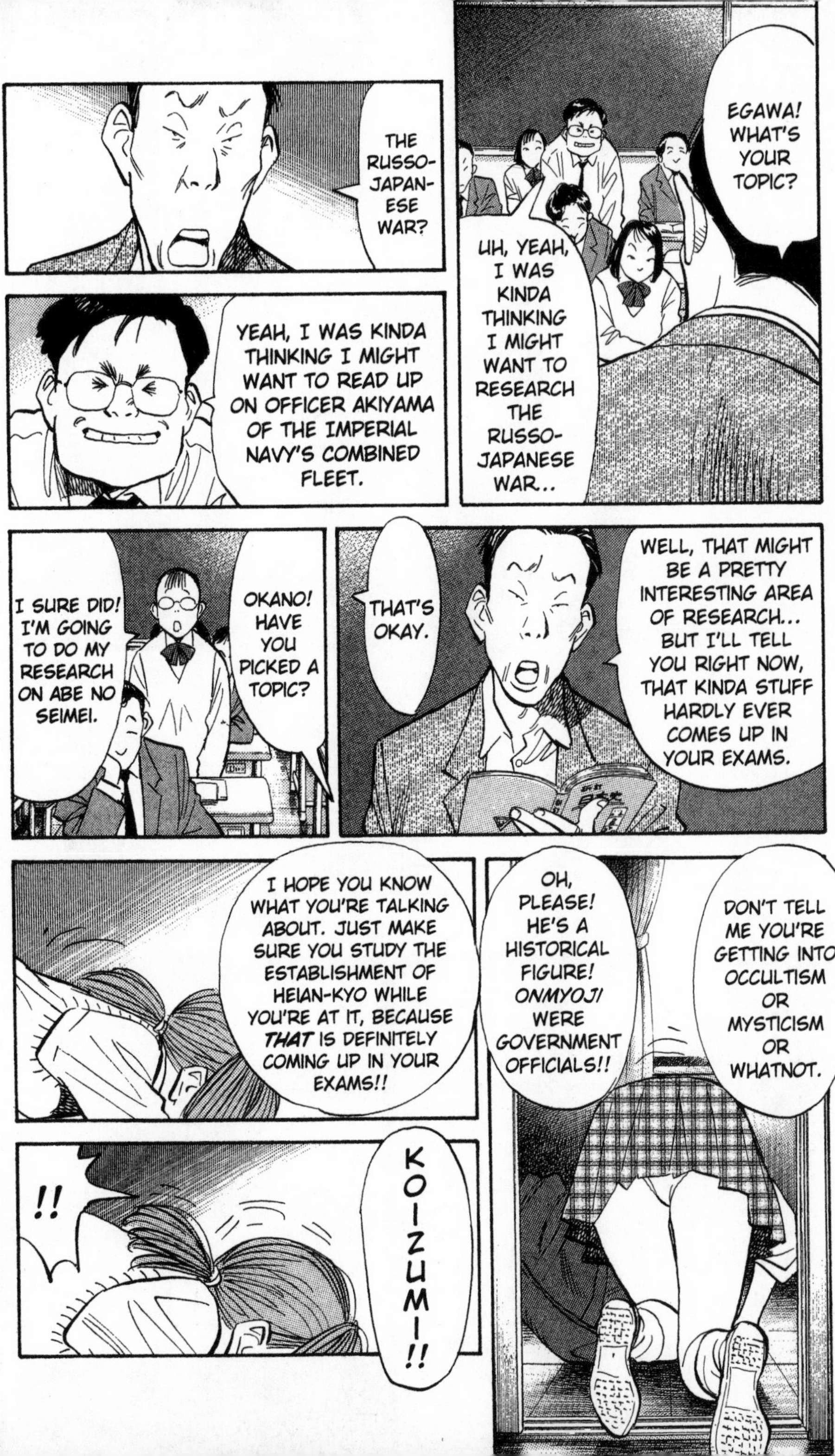
EGAWA! WHAT'S YOUR TOPIC?
UH, YEAH, I WAS KINDA THINKING I MIGHT WANT TO RESEARCH THE RUSSO-JAPANESE WAR...
THE RUSSO-JAPAN-ESE WAR?
YEAH, I WAS KINDA THINKING I MIGHT WANT TO READ UP ON OFFICER AKIYAMA OF THE IMPERIAL NAVY'S COMBINED FLEET.
WELL, THAT MIGHT BE A PRETTY INTERESTING AREA OF RESEARCH... BUT I'LL TELL YOU RIGHT NOW, THAT KINDA STUFF HARDLY EVER COMES UP IN YOUR EXAMS.
THAT'S OKAY.
OKANO! HAVE YOU PICKED A TOPIC?
I SURE DID! I'M GOING TO DO MY RESEARCH ON ABE NO SEIMEI.
DON'T TELL ME YOU'RE GETTING INTO OCCULTISM OR MYSTICISM OR WHATNOT.
OH, PLEASE! HE'S A HISTORICAL FIGURE! *ONMYOJI* WERE GOVERNMENT OFFICIALS!!
I HOPE YOU KNOW WHAT YOU'RE TALKING ABOUT. JUST MAKE SURE YOU STUDY THE ESTABLISHMENT OF HEIAN-KYO WHILE YOU'RE AT IT, BECAUSE ***THAT*** IS DEFINITELY COMING UP IN YOUR EXAMS!!
KOIZUMI!!
!!

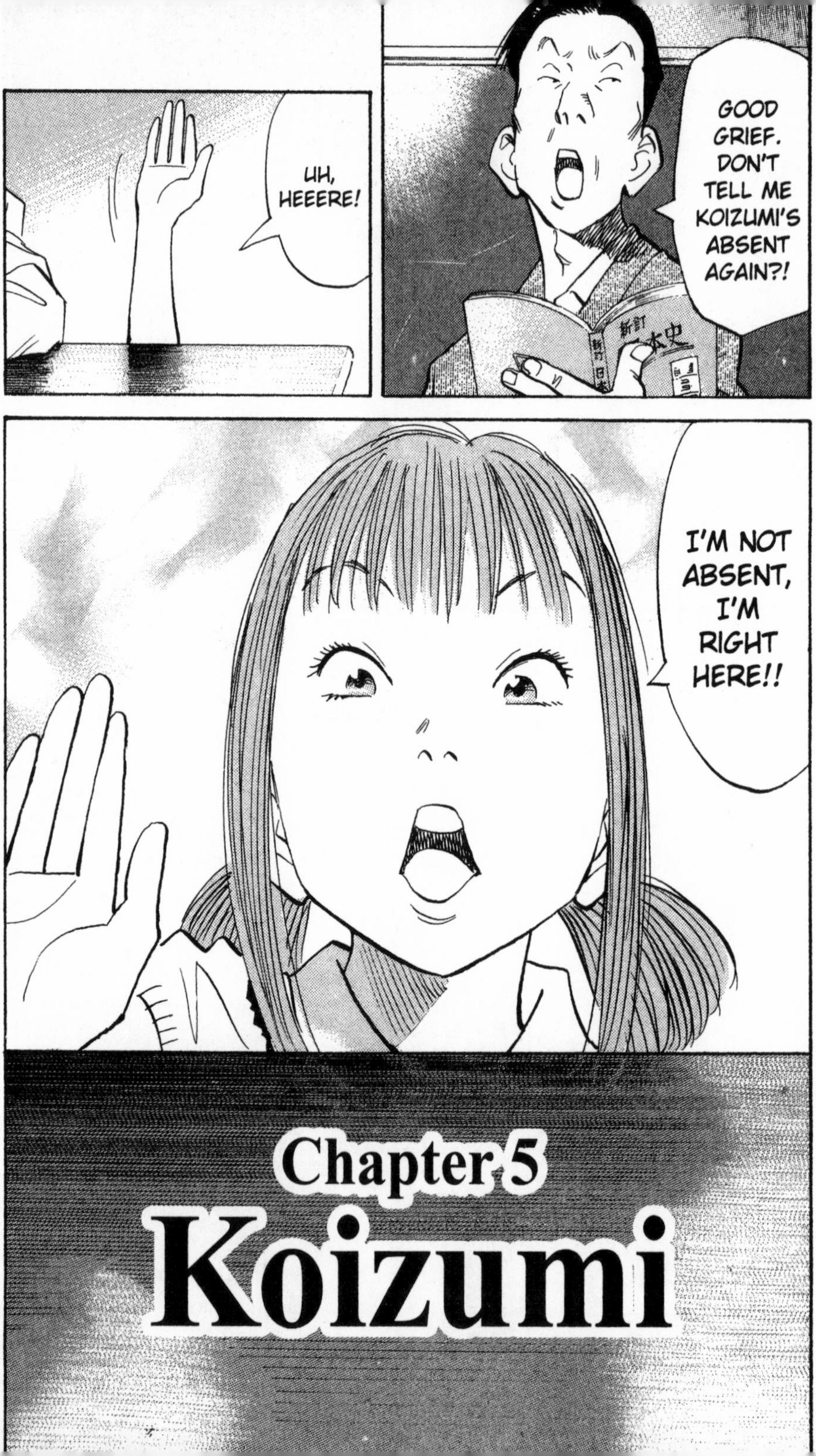
GOOD GRIEF. DON'T TELL ME KOIZUMI'S ABSENT AGAIN?!
UH, HEEERE!
I'M NOT ABSENT, I'M RIGHT HERE!!

Chapter 5
Koizumi

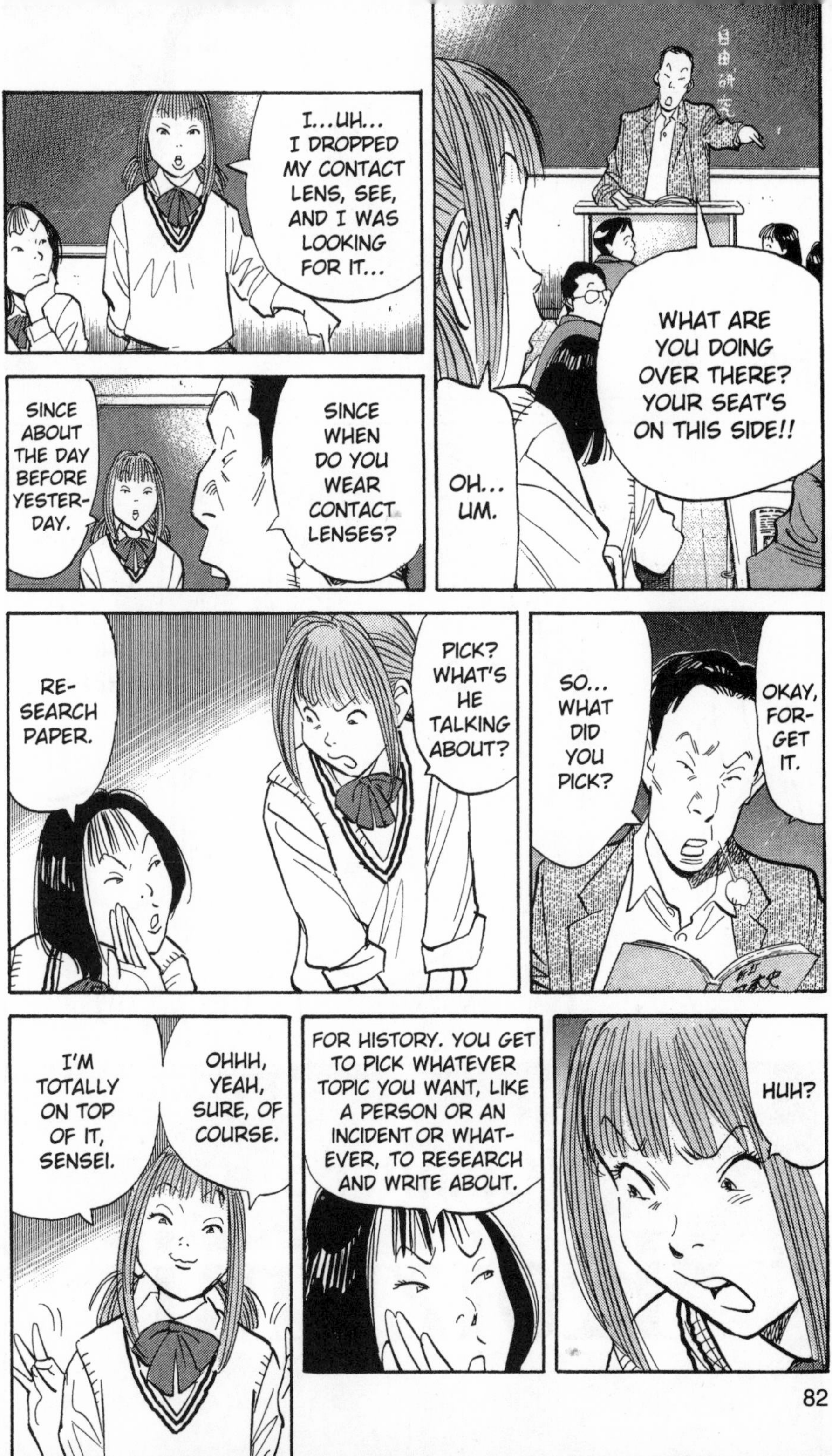
WHAT ARE YOU DOING OVER THERE? YOUR SEAT'S ON THIS SIDE!!
OH... UM.
I...UH... I DROPPED MY CONTACT LENS, SEE, AND I WAS LOOKING FOR IT...
SINCE WHEN DO YOU WEAR CONTACT LENSES?
SINCE ABOUT THE DAY BEFORE YESTER-DAY.
OKAY, FOR-GET IT.
SO... WHAT DID YOU PICK?
PICK? WHAT'S HE TALKING ABOUT?
RE-SEARCH PAPER.
HUH?
FOR HISTORY. YOU GET TO PICK WHATEVER TOPIC YOU WANT, LIKE A PERSON OR AN INCIDENT OR WHAT-EVER, TO RESEARCH AND WRITE ABOUT.
OHHH, YEAH, SURE, OF COURSE.
I'M TOTALLY ON TOP OF IT, SENSEI.

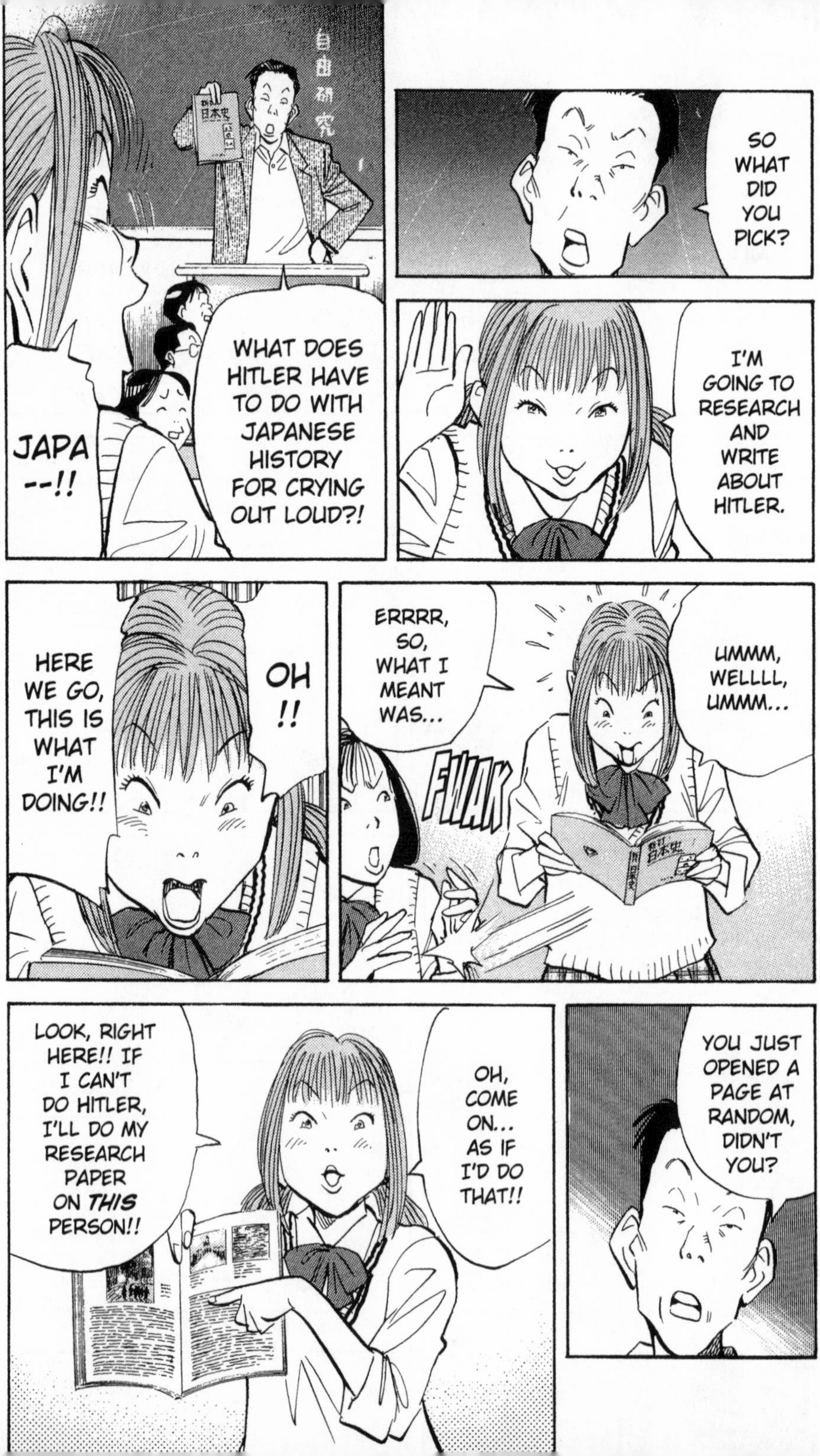
SO WHAT DID YOU PICK?
I'M GOING TO RESEARCH AND WRITE ABOUT HITLER.
自由研究
WHAT DOES HITLER HAVE TO DO WITH JAPANESE HISTORY FOR CRYING OUT LOUD?!
JAPA --!!
UMMM, WELLLL, UMMM...
ERRRR, SO, WHAT I MEANT WAS...
FWAK
OH !!
HERE WE GO, THIS IS WHAT I'M DOING!!
YOU JUST OPENED A PAGE AT RANDOM, DIDN'T YOU?
OH, COME ON... AS IF I'D DO THAT!!
LOOK, RIGHT HERE!! IF I CAN'T DO HITLER, I'LL DO MY RESEARCH PAPER ON *THIS* PERSON!!

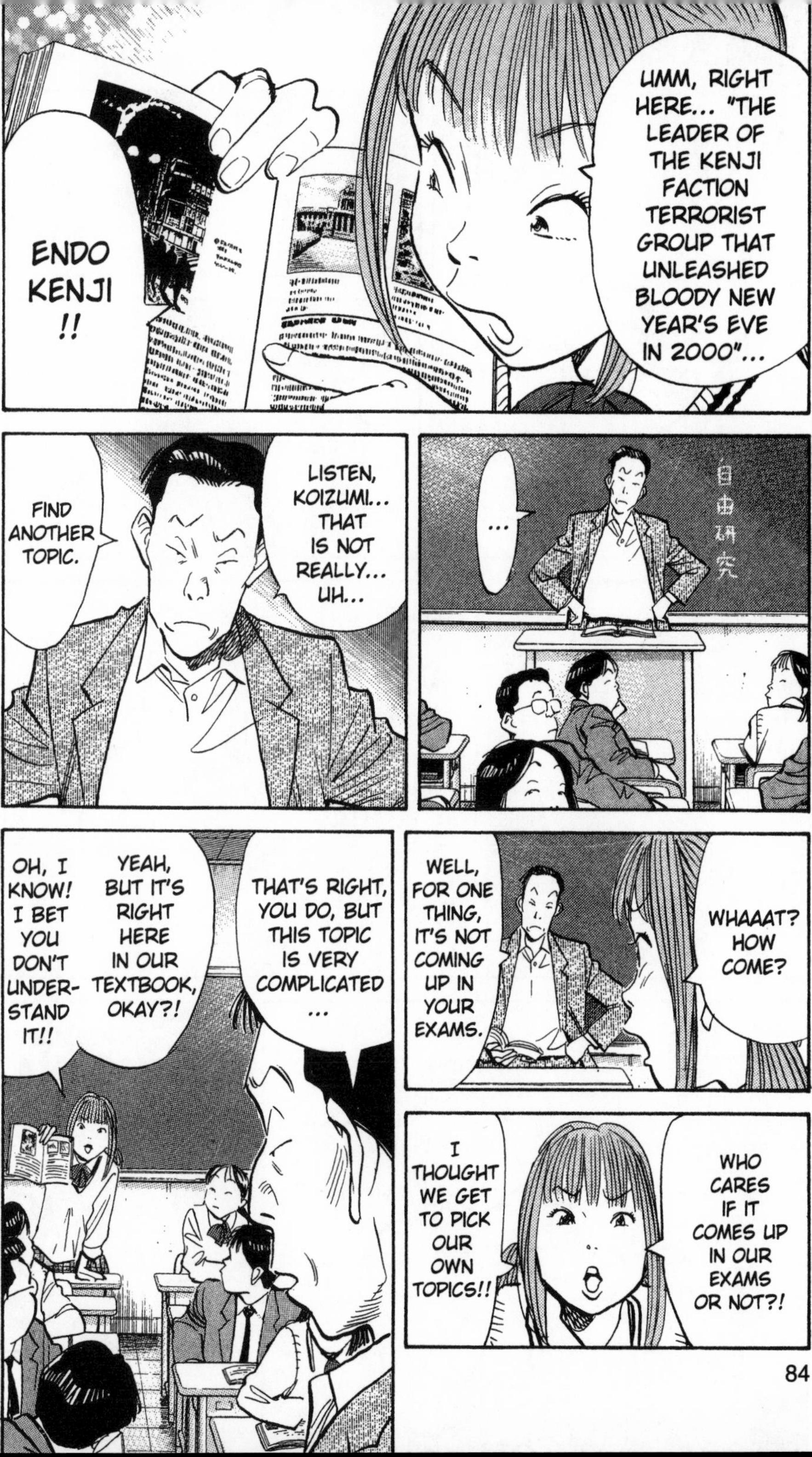
UMM, RIGHT HERE... "THE LEADER OF THE KENJI FACTION TERRORIST GROUP THAT UNLEASHED BLOODY NEW YEAR'S EVE IN 2000"...
ENDO KENJI !!
自由研究
...
LISTEN, KOIZUMI... THAT IS NOT REALLY... UH...
FIND ANOTHER TOPIC.
WHAAAT? HOW COME?
WELL, FOR ONE THING, IT'S NOT COMING UP IN YOUR EXAMS.
WHO CARES IF IT COMES UP IN OUR EXAMS OR NOT?!
I THOUGHT WE GET TO PICK OUR OWN TOPICS!!
THAT'S RIGHT, YOU DO, BUT THIS TOPIC IS VERY COMPLICATED ...
YEAH, BUT IT'S RIGHT HERE IN OUR TEXTBOOK, OKAY?!
OH, I KNOW! I BET YOU DON'T UNDER-STAND IT!!

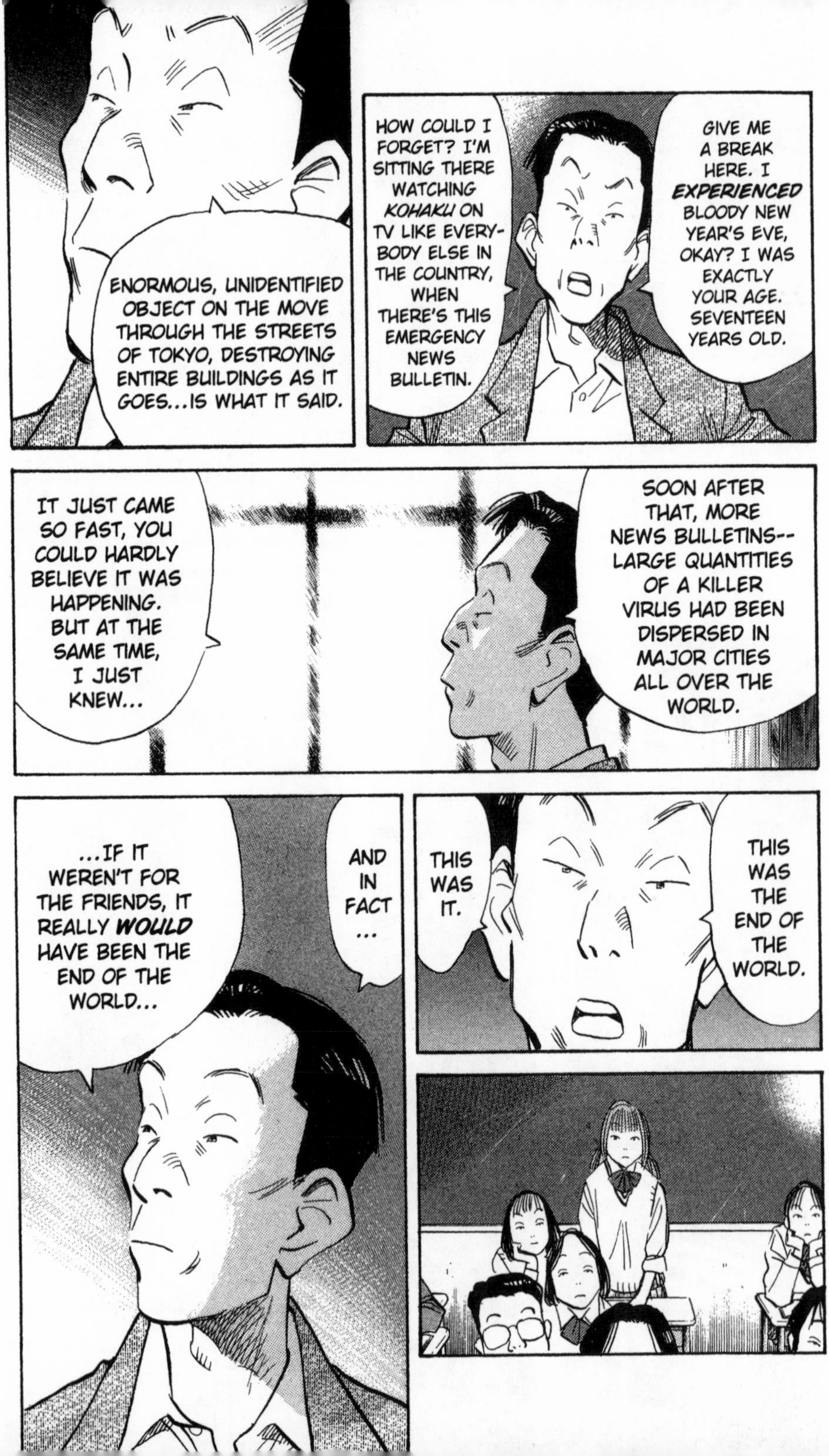
GIVE ME A BREAK HERE. I **EXPERIENCED** BLOODY NEW YEAR'S EVE, OKAY? I WAS EXACTLY YOUR AGE. SEVENTEEN YEARS OLD.
HOW COULD I FORGET? I'M SITTING THERE WATCHING *KOHAKU* ON TV LIKE EVERYBODY ELSE IN THE COUNTRY, WHEN THERE'S THIS EMERGENCY NEWS BULLETIN.
ENORMOUS, UNIDENTIFIED OBJECT ON THE MOVE THROUGH THE STREETS OF TOKYO, DESTROYING ENTIRE BUILDINGS AS IT GOES...IS WHAT IT SAID.
SOON AFTER THAT, MORE NEWS BULLETINS--LARGE QUANTITIES OF A KILLER VIRUS HAD BEEN DISPERSED IN MAJOR CITIES ALL OVER THE WORLD.
IT JUST CAME SO FAST, YOU COULD HARDLY BELIEVE IT WAS HAPPENING. BUT AT THE SAME TIME, I JUST KNEW...
THIS WAS THE END OF THE WORLD.
THIS WAS IT.
AND IN FACT...
...IF IT WEREN'T FOR THE FRIENDS, IT REALLY **WOULD** HAVE BEEN THE END OF THE WORLD...

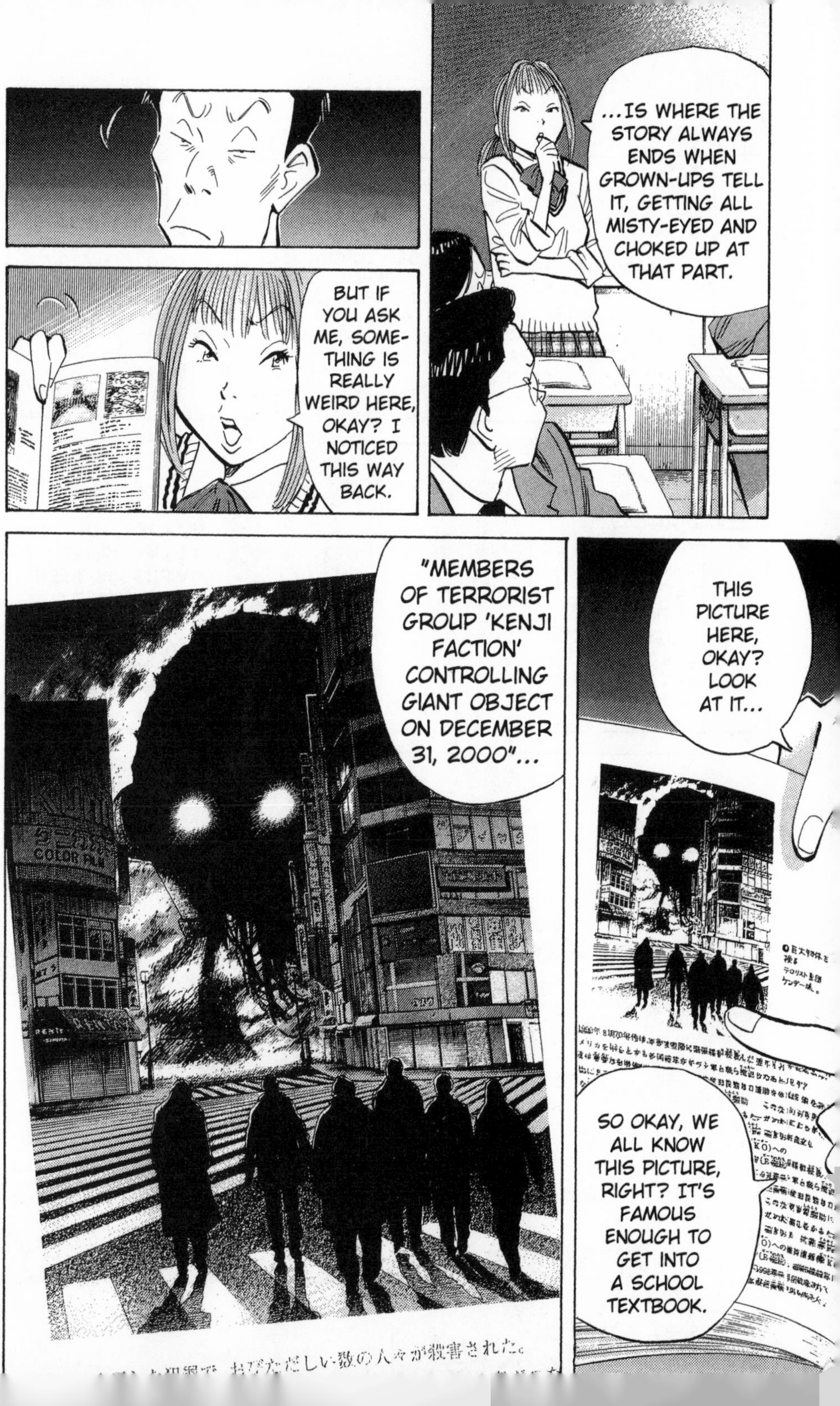
...IS WHERE THE STORY ALWAYS ENDS WHEN GROWN-UPS TELL IT, GETTING ALL MISTY-EYED AND CHOKED UP AT THAT PART.
BUT IF YOU ASK ME, SOMETHING IS REALLY WEIRD HERE, OKAY? I NOTICED THIS WAY BACK.
THIS PICTURE HERE, OKAY? LOOK AT IT...
SO OKAY, WE ALL KNOW THIS PICTURE, RIGHT? IT'S FAMOUS ENOUGH TO GET INTO A SCHOOL TEXTBOOK.
"MEMBERS OF TERRORIST GROUP 'KENJI FACTION' CONTROLLING GIANT OBJECT ON DECEMBER 31, 2000"...
COLOR FILM
おびただしい数の人々が殺害された。

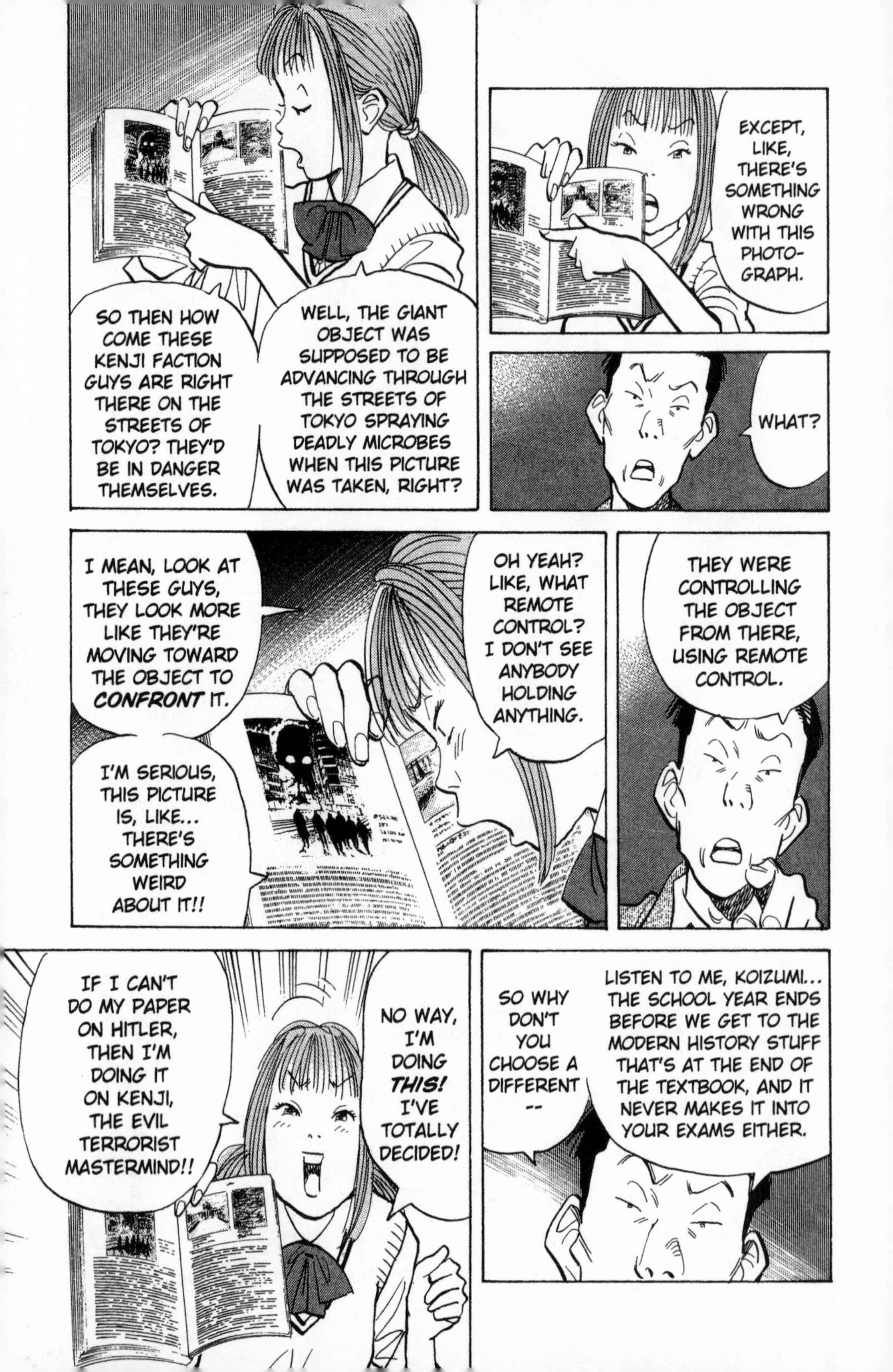
EXCEPT, LIKE, THERE'S SOMETHING WRONG WITH THIS PHOTO-GRAPH.
WHAT?
WELL, THE GIANT OBJECT WAS SUPPOSED TO BE ADVANCING THROUGH THE STREETS OF TOKYO SPRAYING DEADLY MICROBES WHEN THIS PICTURE WAS TAKEN, RIGHT?
SO THEN HOW COME THESE KENJI FACTION GUYS ARE RIGHT THERE ON THE STREETS OF TOKYO? THEY'D BE IN DANGER THEMSELVES.
THEY WERE CONTROLLING THE OBJECT FROM THERE, USING REMOTE CONTROL.
OH YEAH? LIKE, WHAT REMOTE CONTROL? I DON'T SEE ANYBODY HOLDING ANYTHING.
I MEAN, LOOK AT THESE GUYS, THEY LOOK MORE LIKE THEY'RE MOVING TOWARD THE OBJECT TO ***CONFRONT*** IT.
I'M SERIOUS, THIS PICTURE IS, LIKE... THERE'S SOMETHING WEIRD ABOUT IT!!
LISTEN TO ME, KOIZUMI... THE SCHOOL YEAR ENDS BEFORE WE GET TO THE MODERN HISTORY STUFF THAT'S AT THE END OF THE TEXTBOOK, AND IT NEVER MAKES IT INTO YOUR EXAMS EITHER.
SO WHY DON'T YOU CHOOSE A DIFFERENT --
NO WAY, I'M DOING ***THIS!*** I'VE TOTALLY DECIDED!
IF I CAN'T DO MY PAPER ON HITLER, THEN I'M DOING IT ON KENJI, THE EVIL TERRORIST MASTERMIND!!

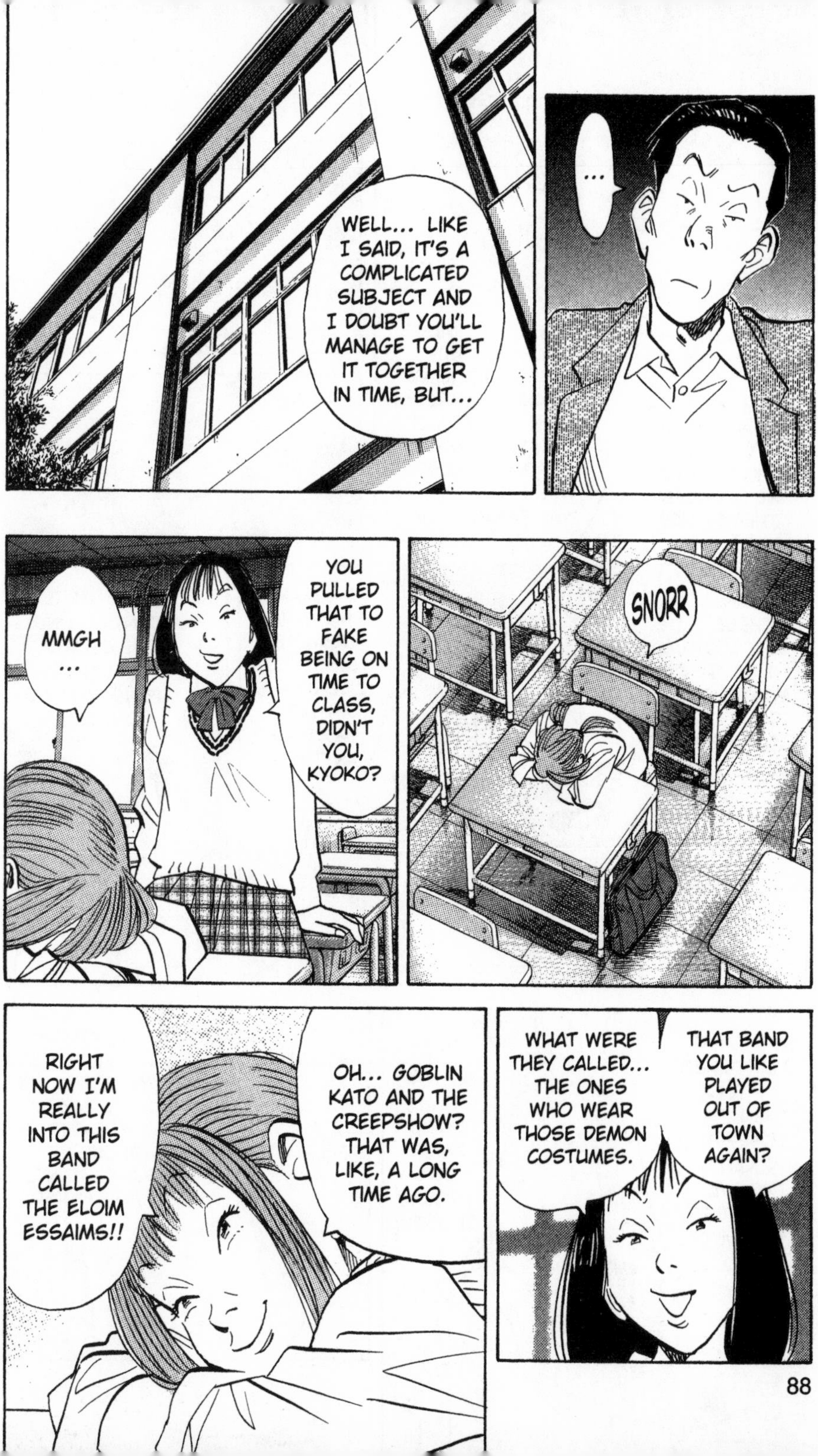
...
WELL... LIKE I SAID, IT'S A COMPLICATED SUBJECT AND I DOUBT YOU'LL MANAGE TO GET IT TOGETHER IN TIME, BUT...
SNORR
YOU PULLED THAT TO FAKE BEING ON TIME TO CLASS, DIDN'T YOU, KYOKO?
MMGH ...
THAT BAND YOU LIKE PLAYED OUT OF TOWN AGAIN?
WHAT WERE THEY CALLED... THE ONES WHO WEAR THOSE DEMON COSTUMES.
OH... GOBLIN KATO AND THE CREEPSHOW? THAT WAS, LIKE, A LONG TIME AGO.
RIGHT NOW I'M REALLY INTO THIS BAND CALLED THE ELOIM ESSAIMS!!

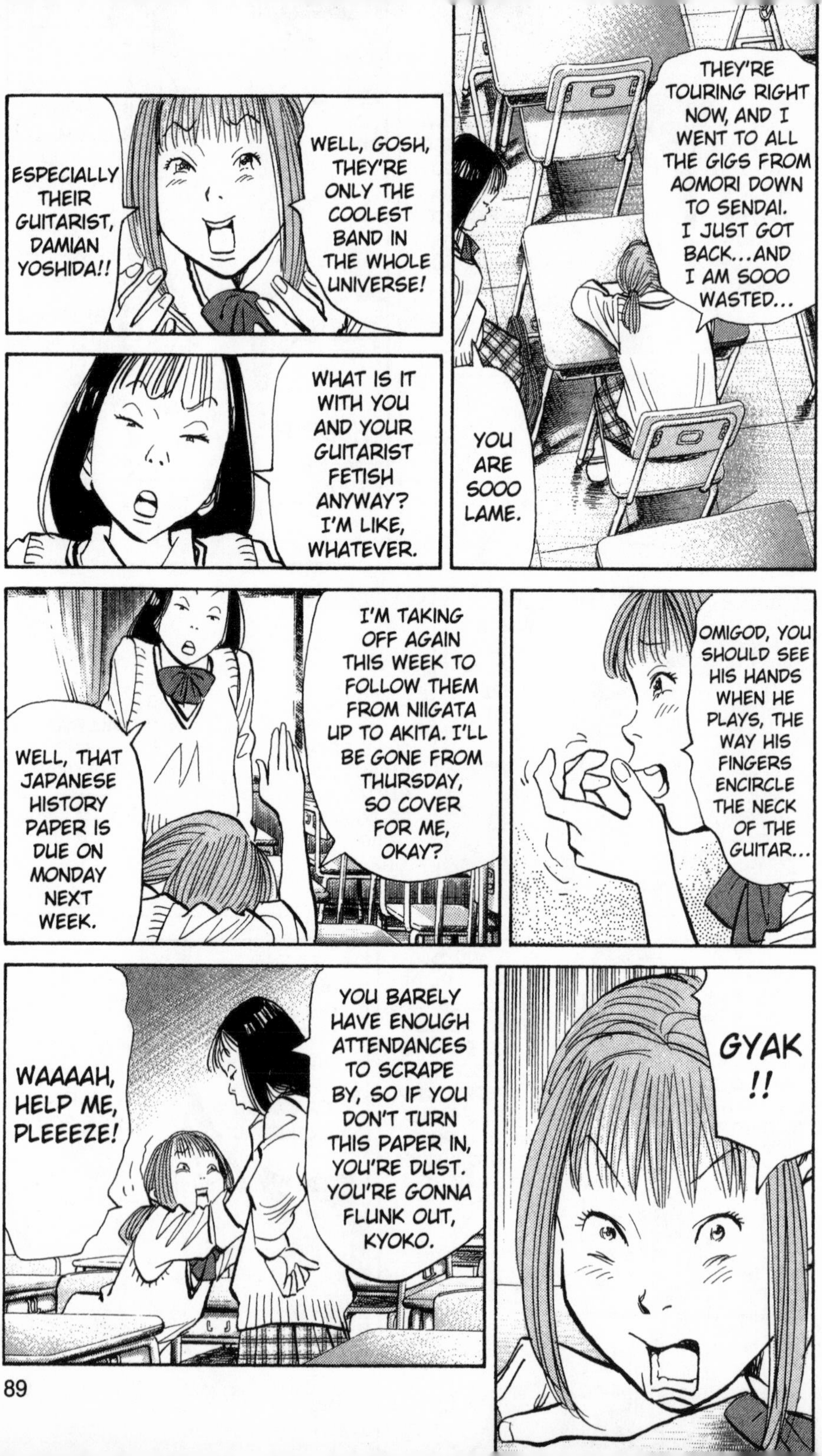
THEY'RE TOURING RIGHT NOW, AND I WENT TO ALL THE GIGS FROM AOMORI DOWN TO SENDAI. I JUST GOT BACK...AND I AM SOOO WASTED...
YOU ARE SOOO LAME.
WELL, GOSH, THEY'RE ONLY THE COOLEST BAND IN THE WHOLE UNIVERSE!
ESPECIALLY THEIR GUITARIST, DAMIAN YOSHIDA!!
WHAT IS IT WITH YOU AND YOUR GUITARIST FETISH ANYWAY? I'M LIKE, WHATEVER.
OMIGOD, YOU SHOULD SEE HIS HANDS WHEN HE PLAYS, THE WAY HIS FINGERS ENCIRCLE THE NECK OF THE GUITAR...
I'M TAKING OFF AGAIN THIS WEEK TO FOLLOW THEM FROM NIIGATA UP TO AKITA. I'LL BE GONE FROM THURSDAY, SO COVER FOR ME, OKAY?
WELL, THAT JAPANESE HISTORY PAPER IS DUE ON MONDAY NEXT WEEK.
GYAK !!
YOU BARELY HAVE ENOUGH ATTENDANCES TO SCRAPE BY, SO IF YOU DON'T TURN THIS PAPER IN, YOU'RE DUST. YOU'RE GONNA FLUNK OUT, KYOKO.
WAAAAH, HELP ME, PLEEEZE!

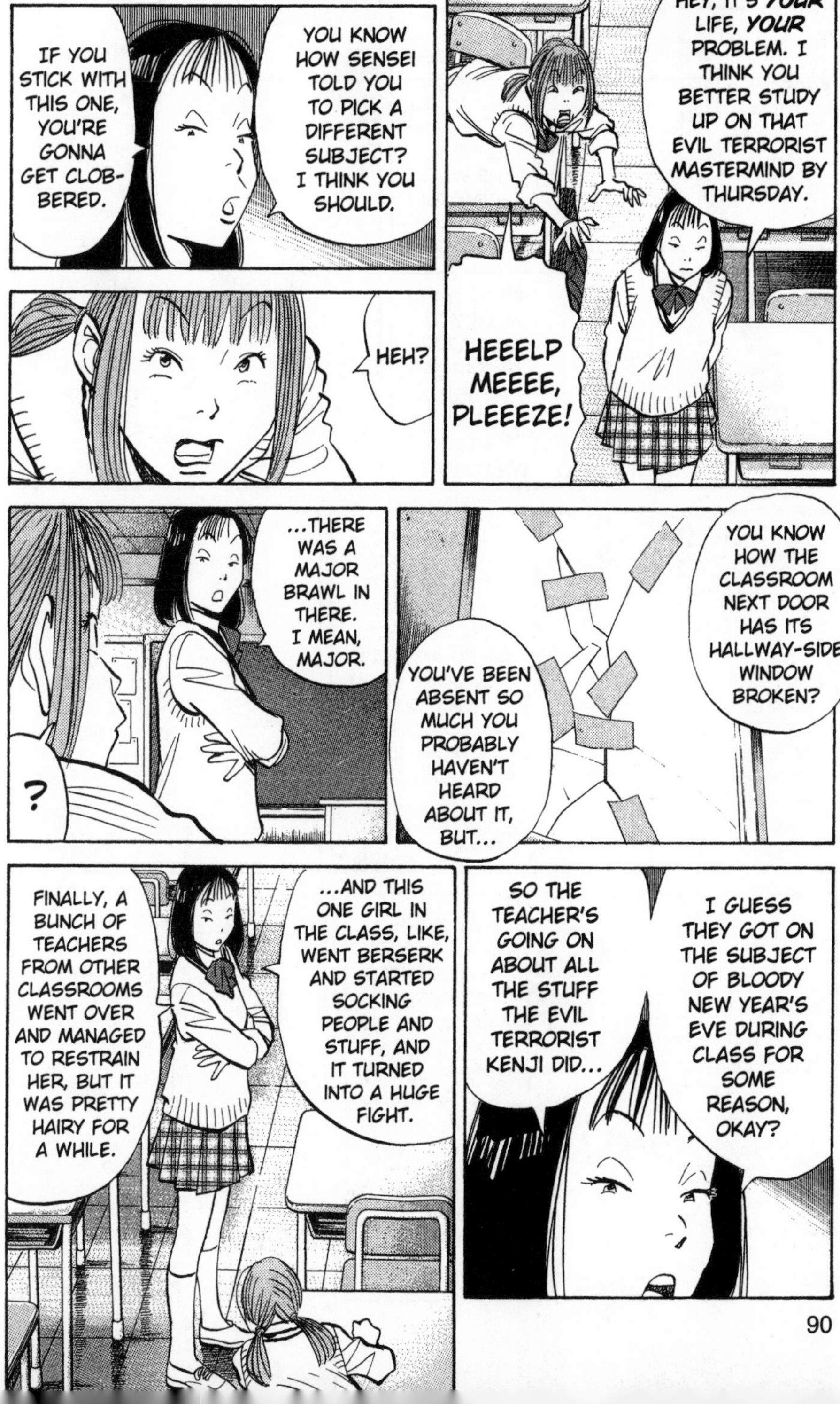
HEY, IT'S ***YOUR*** LIFE, ***YOUR*** PROBLEM. I THINK YOU BETTER STUDY UP ON THAT EVIL TERRORIST MASTERMIND BY THURSDAY.
HEEELP MEEEE, PLEEEZE!
YOU KNOW HOW SENSEI TOLD YOU TO PICK A DIFFERENT SUBJECT? I THINK YOU SHOULD.
IF YOU STICK WITH THIS ONE, YOU'RE GONNA GET CLOB-BERED.
HEH?
YOU KNOW HOW THE CLASSROOM NEXT DOOR HAS ITS HALLWAY-SIDE WINDOW BROKEN?
YOU'VE BEEN ABSENT SO MUCH YOU PROBABLY HAVEN'T HEARD ABOUT IT, BUT...
...THERE WAS A MAJOR BRAWL IN THERE. I MEAN, MAJOR.
?
I GUESS THEY GOT ON THE SUBJECT OF BLOODY NEW YEAR'S EVE DURING CLASS FOR SOME REASON, OKAY?
SO THE TEACHER'S GOING ON ABOUT ALL THE STUFF THE EVIL TERRORIST KENJI DID...
...AND THIS ONE GIRL IN THE CLASS, LIKE, WENT BERSERK AND STARTED SOCKING PEOPLE AND STUFF, AND IT TURNED INTO A HUGE FIGHT.
FINALLY, A BUNCH OF TEACHERS FROM OTHER CLASSROOMS WENT OVER AND MANAGED TO RESTRAIN HER, BUT IT WAS PRETTY HAIRY FOR A WHILE.

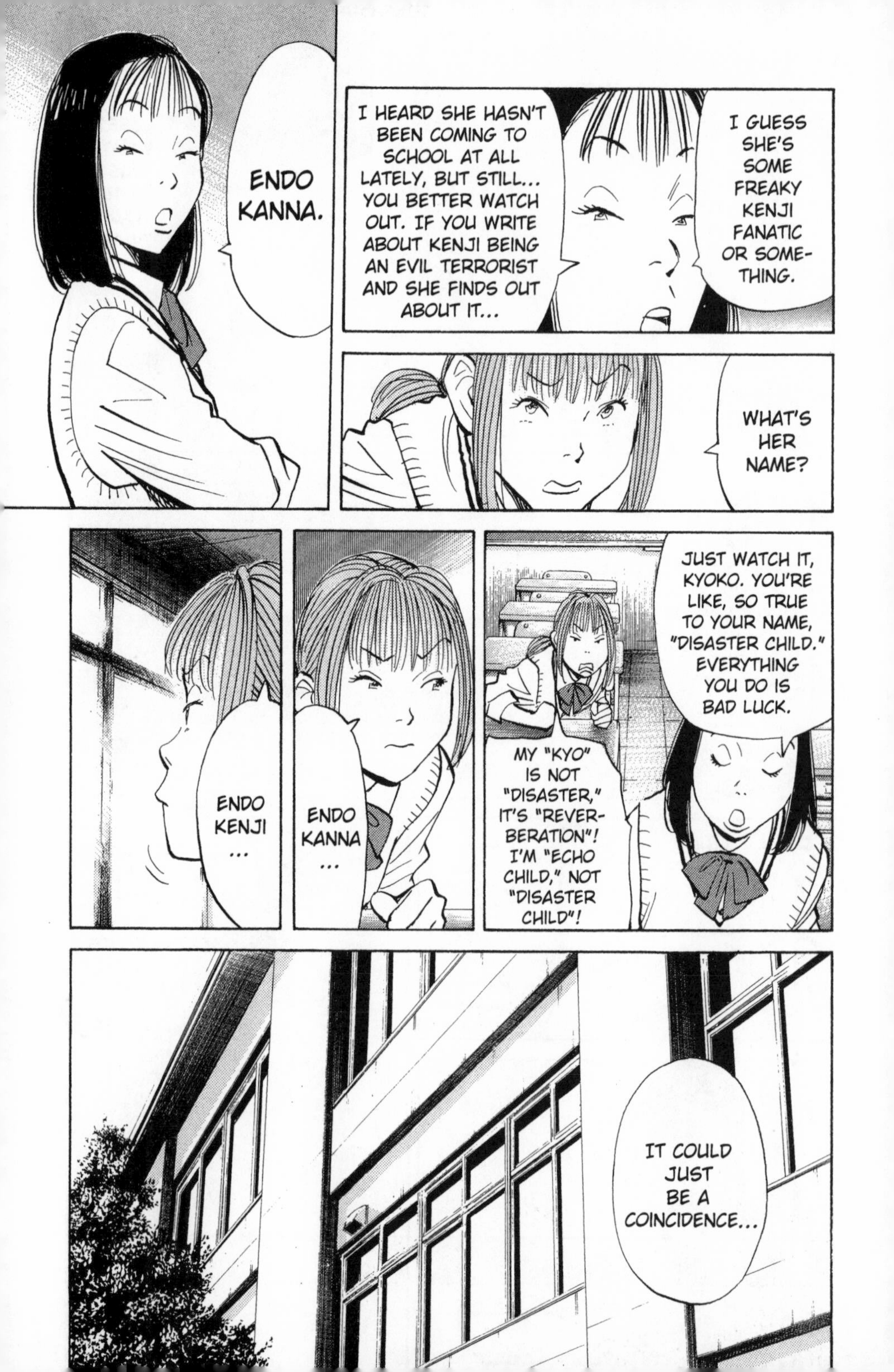
I GUESS SHE'S SOME FREAKY KENJI FANATIC OR SOME-THING.
I HEARD SHE HASN'T BEEN COMING TO SCHOOL AT ALL LATELY, BUT STILL... YOU BETTER WATCH OUT. IF YOU WRITE ABOUT KENJI BEING AN EVIL TERRORIST AND SHE FINDS OUT ABOUT IT...
WHAT'S HER NAME?
ENDO KANNA.
JUST WATCH IT, KYOKO. YOU'RE LIKE, SO TRUE TO YOUR NAME, "DISASTER CHILD." EVERYTHING YOU DO IS BAD LUCK.
MY "KYO" IS NOT "DISASTER," IT'S "REVER-BERATION"! I'M "ECHO CHILD," NOT "DISASTER CHILD"!
ENDO KANNA ...
ENDO KENJI ...
IT COULD JUST BE A COINCIDENCE...

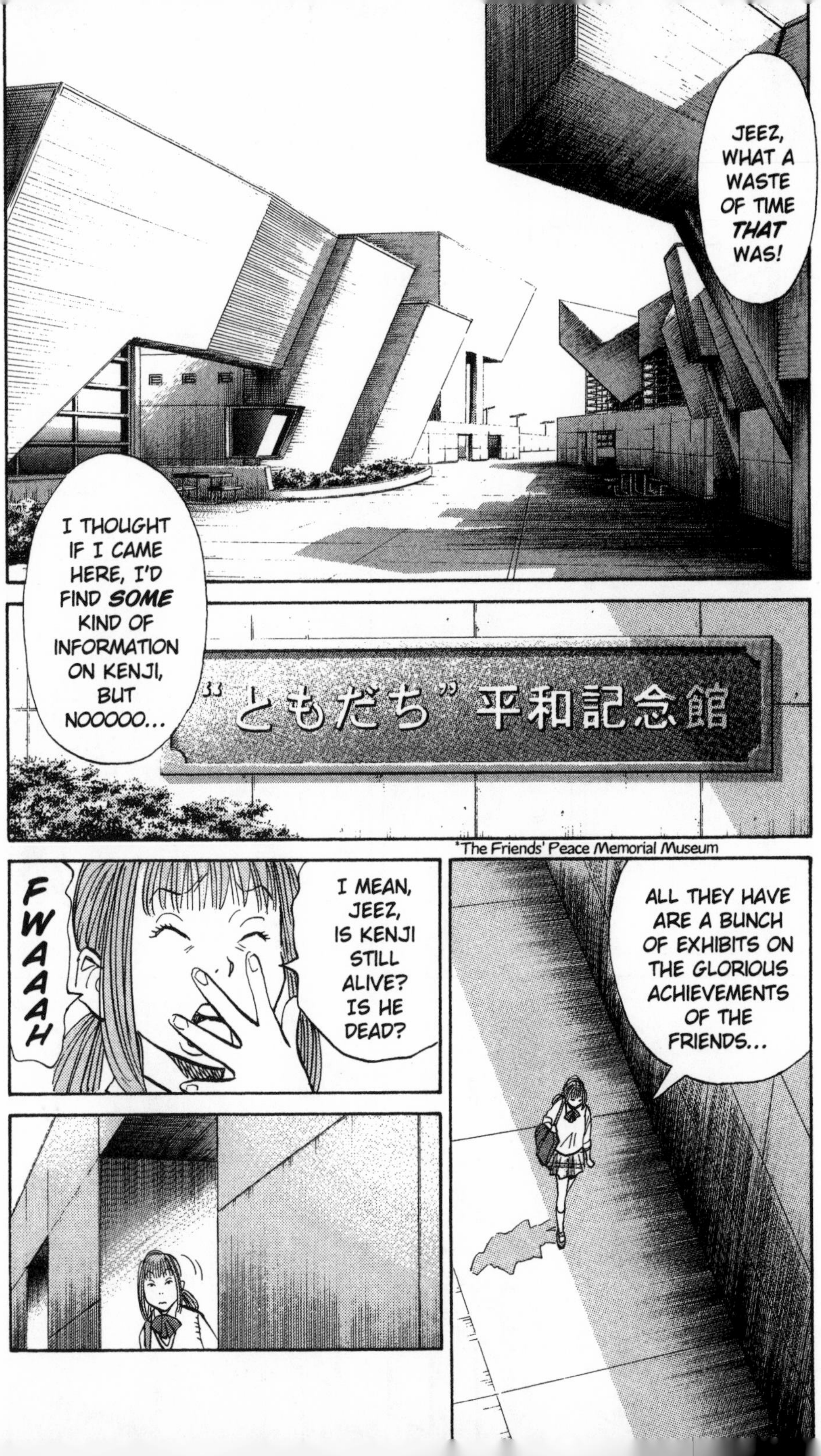
JEEZ, WHAT A WASTE OF TIME THAT WAS!
I THOUGHT IF I CAME HERE, I'D FIND SOME KIND OF INFORMATION ON KENJI, BUT NOOOOO...
“ともだち”平和記念館
'The Friends' Peace Memorial Museum
ALL THEY HAVE ARE A BUNCH OF EXHIBITS ON THE GLORIOUS ACHIEVEMENTS OF THE FRIENDS...
I MEAN, JEEZ, IS KENJI STILL ALIVE? IS HE DEAD?
FWAAAAH

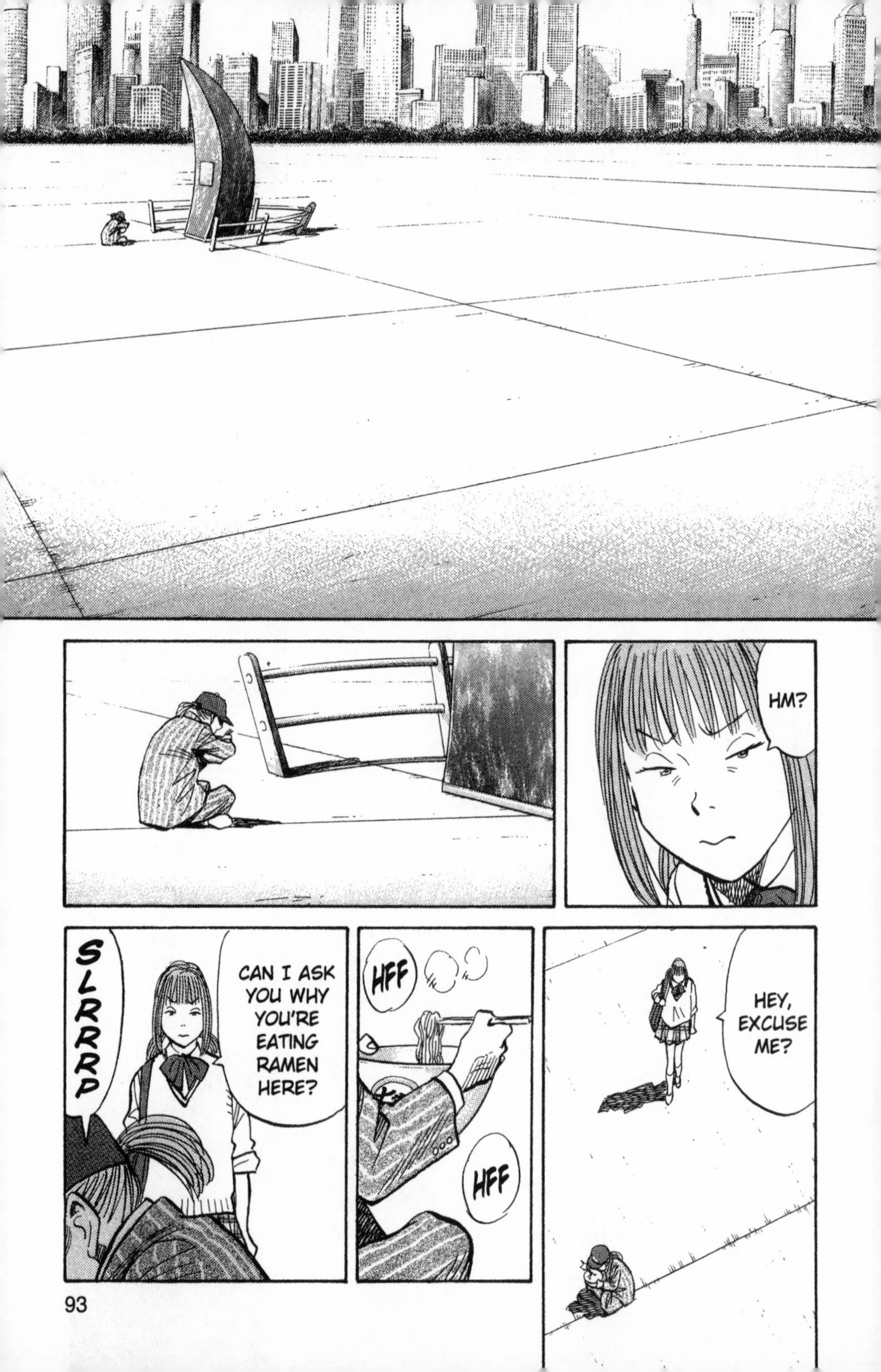
HM?
HEY, EXCUSE ME?
HFF
HFF
CAN I ASK YOU WHY YOU'RE EATING RAMEN HERE?
SLRRRP

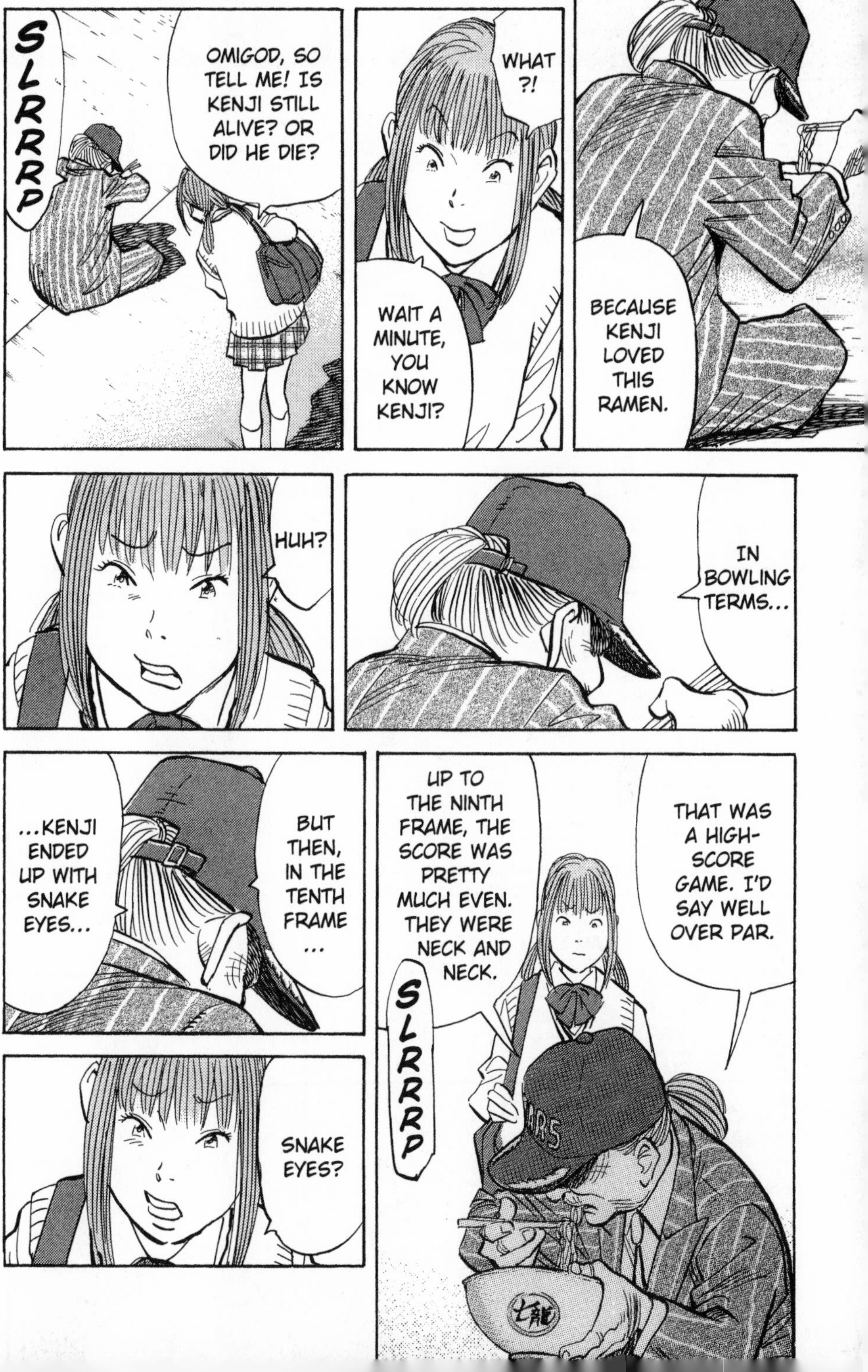
BECAUSE KENJI LOVED THIS RAMEN.
WHAT?!
WAIT A MINUTE, YOU KNOW KENJI?
OMIGOD, SO TELL ME! IS KENJI STILL ALIVE? OR DID HE DIE?
SLRRRP
IN BOWLING TERMS...
HUH?
THAT WAS A HIGH-SCORE GAME. I'D SAY WELL OVER PAR.
UP TO THE NINTH FRAME, THE SCORE WAS PRETTY MUCH EVEN. THEY WERE NECK AND NECK.
SLRRRP
BUT THEN, IN THE TENTH FRAME...
...KENJI ENDED UP WITH SNAKE EYES...
SNAKE EYES?

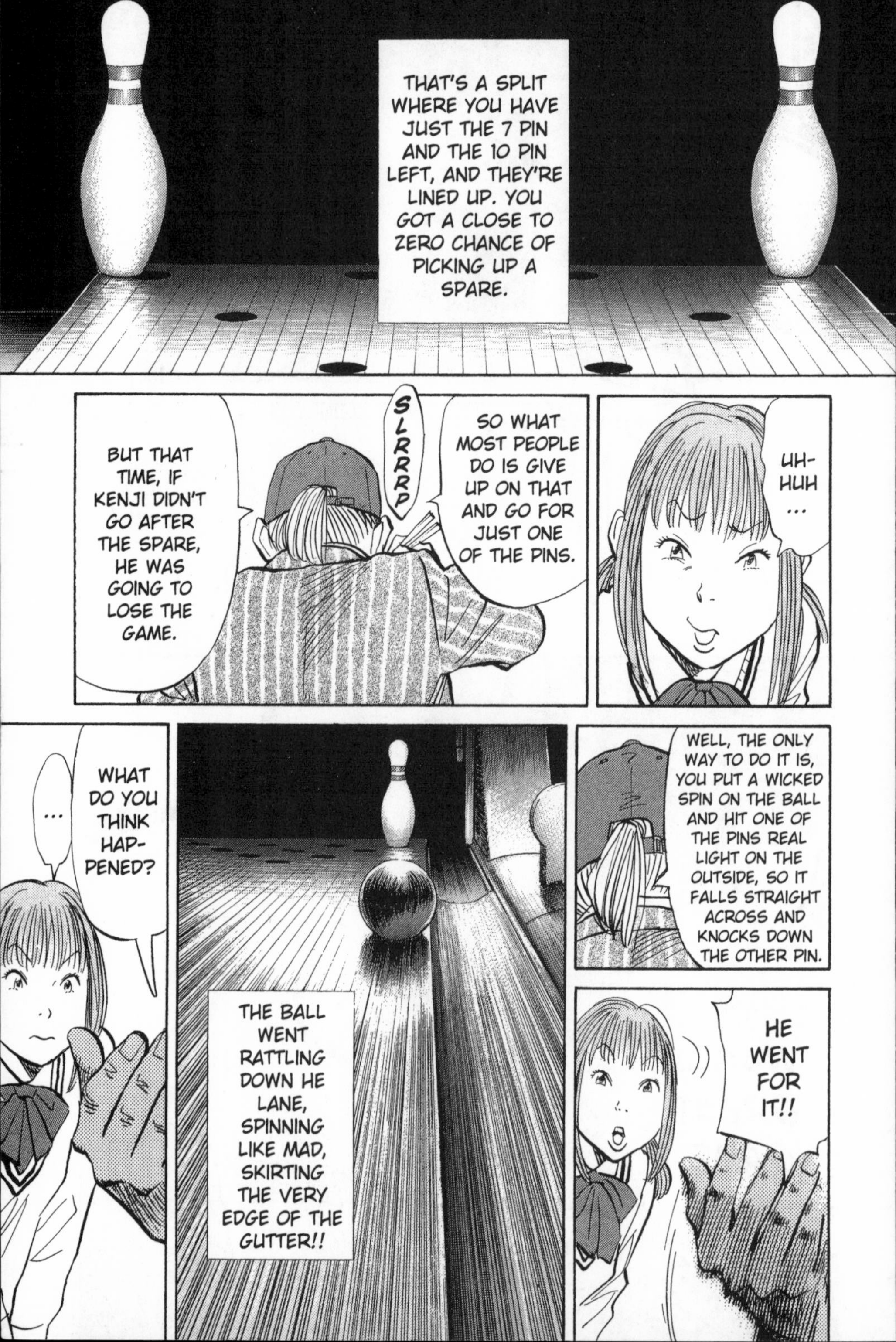
THAT'S A SPLIT WHERE YOU HAVE JUST THE 7 PIN AND THE 10 PIN LEFT, AND THEY'RE LINED UP. YOU GOT A CLOSE TO ZERO CHANCE OF PICKING UP A SPARE.
UH-HUH ...
SO WHAT MOST PEOPLE DO IS GIVE UP ON THAT AND GO FOR JUST ONE OF THE PINS.
SLRRRP
BUT THAT TIME, IF KENJI DIDN'T GO AFTER THE SPARE, HE WAS GOING TO LOSE THE GAME.
WELL, THE ONLY WAY TO DO IT IS, YOU PUT A WICKED SPIN ON THE BALL AND HIT ONE OF THE PINS REAL LIGHT ON THE OUTSIDE, SO IT FALLS STRAIGHT ACROSS AND KNOCKS DOWN THE OTHER PIN.
HE WENT FOR IT!!
THE BALL WENT RATTLING DOWN HE LANE, SPINNING LIKE MAD, SKIRTING THE VERY EDGE OF THE GUTTER!!
WHAT DO YOU THINK HAP-PENED?
...

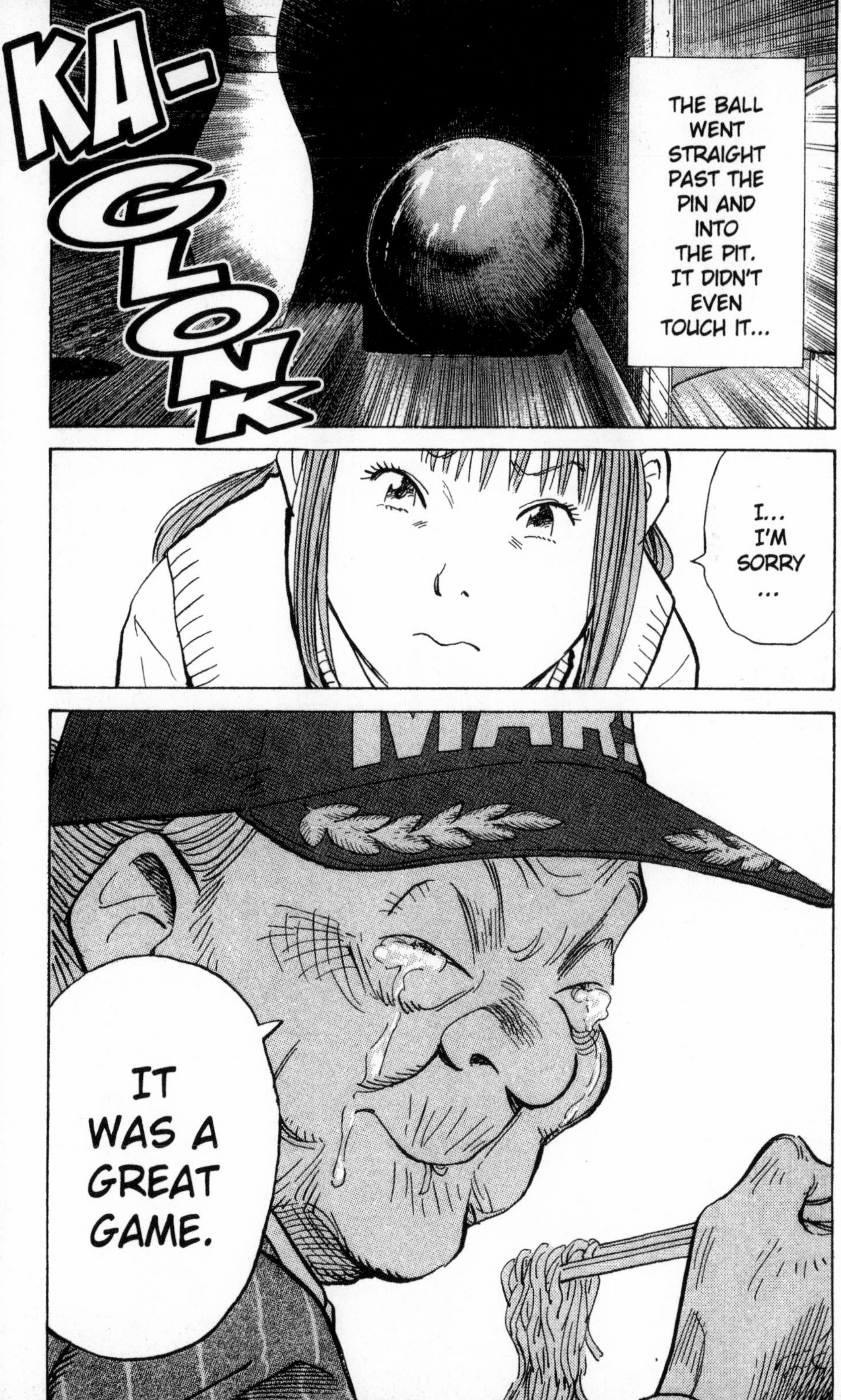
THE BALL WENT STRAIGHT PAST THE PIN AND INTO THE PIT. IT DIDN'T EVEN TOUCH IT...
KA-GLONK
I... I'M SORRY...
MAR
IT WAS A GREAT GAME.

Chapter 6 Kamisama's Autograph

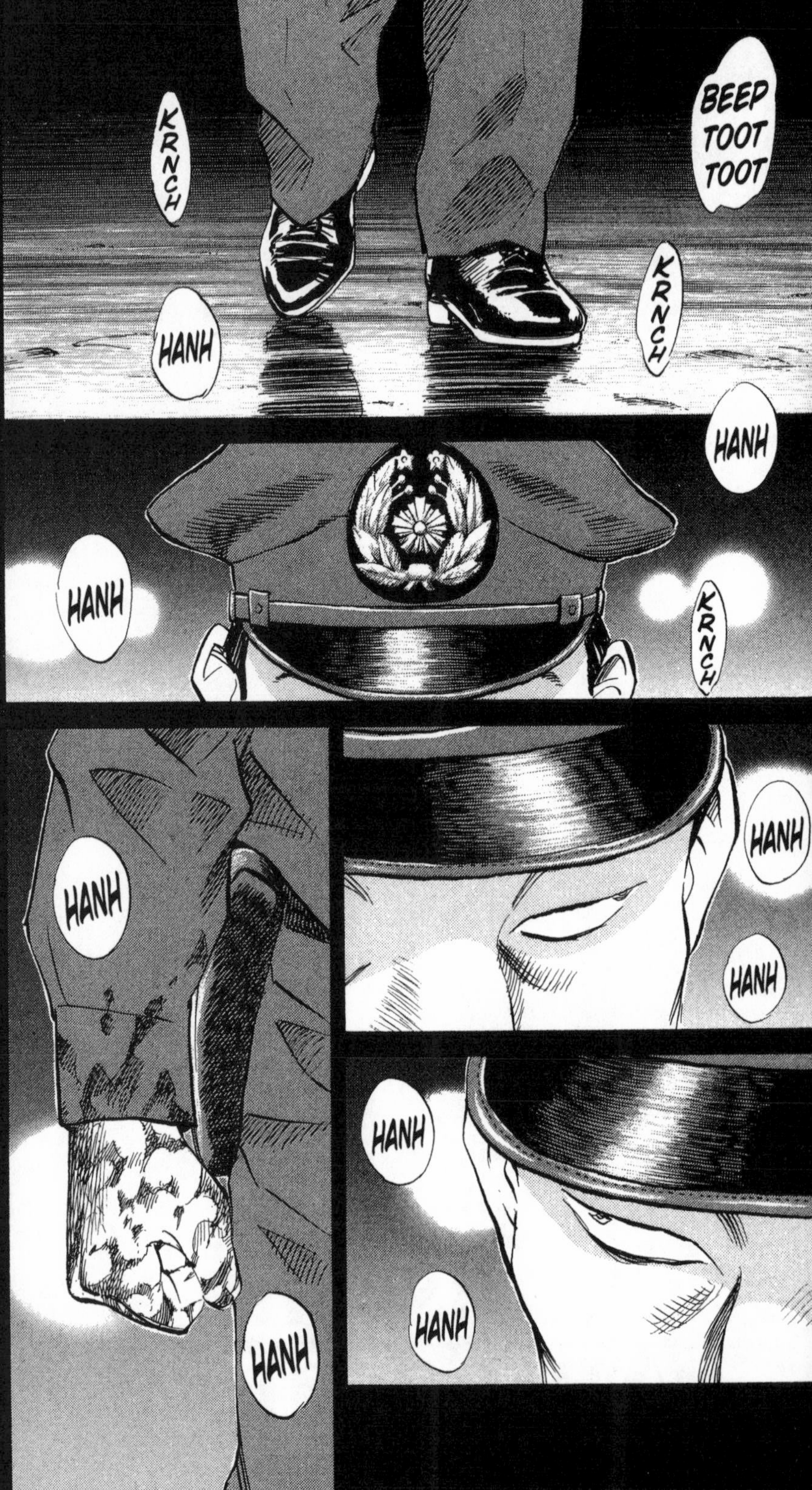
BEEP TOOT TOOT
KRNCH
KRNCH
HANH
HANH
KRNCH
HANH
HANH
HANH
HANH
HANH
HANH
HANH

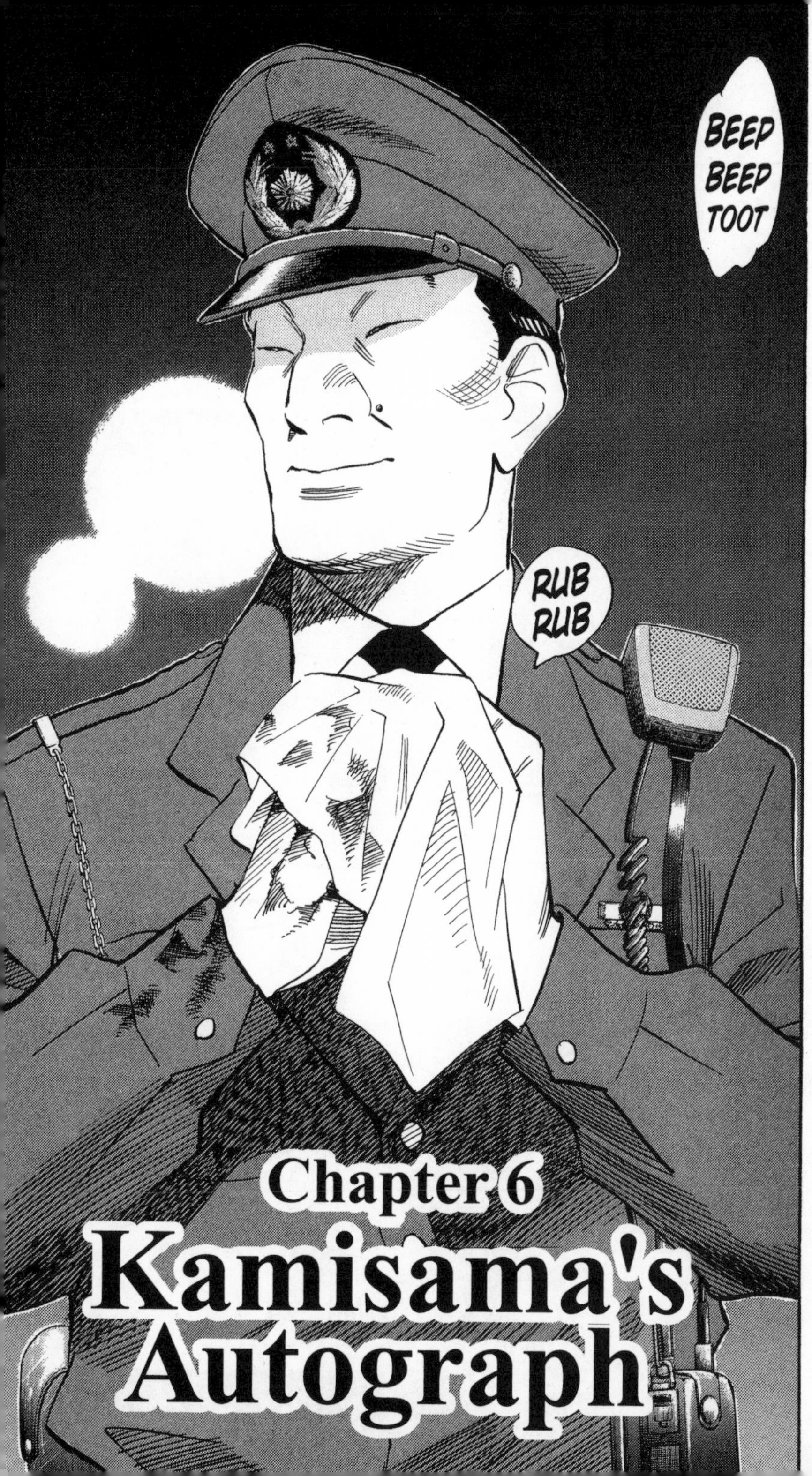

Chapter 6
Kamisama's Autograph

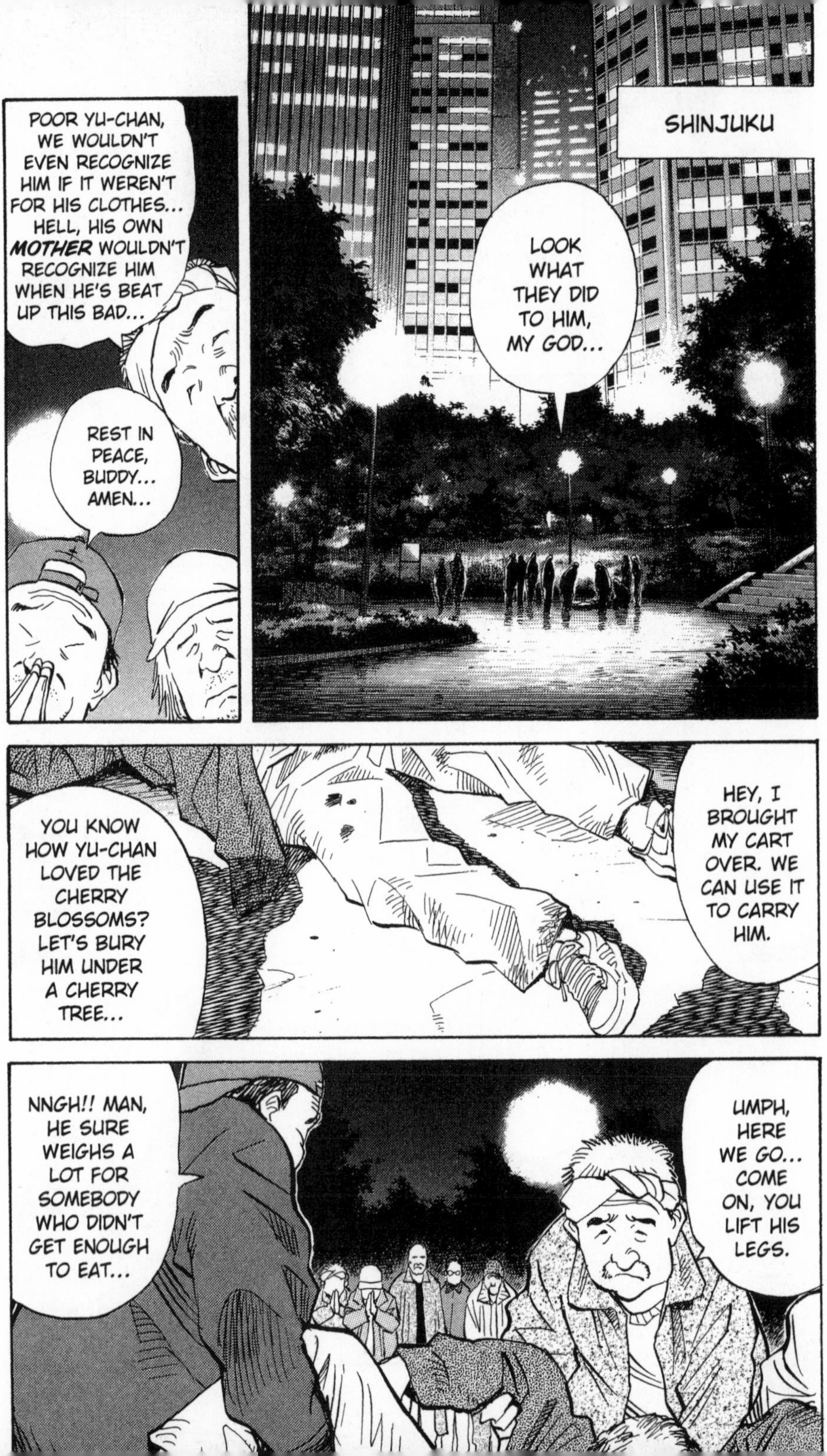
SHINJUKU
LOOK WHAT THEY DID TO HIM, MY GOD...
POOR YU-CHAN, WE WOULDN'T EVEN RECOGNIZE HIM IF IT WEREN'T FOR HIS CLOTHES... HELL, HIS OWN *MOTHER* WOULDN'T RECOGNIZE HIM WHEN HE'S BEAT UP THIS BAD...
REST IN PEACE, BUDDY... AMEN...
HEY, I BROUGHT MY CART OVER. WE CAN USE IT TO CARRY HIM.
YOU KNOW HOW YU-CHAN LOVED THE CHERRY BLOSSOMS? LET'S BURY HIM UNDER A CHERRY TREE...
UMPH, HERE WE GO... COME ON, YOU LIFT HIS LEGS.
NNGH!! MAN, HE SURE WEIGHS A LOT FOR SOMEBODY WHO DIDN'T GET ENOUGH TO EAT...

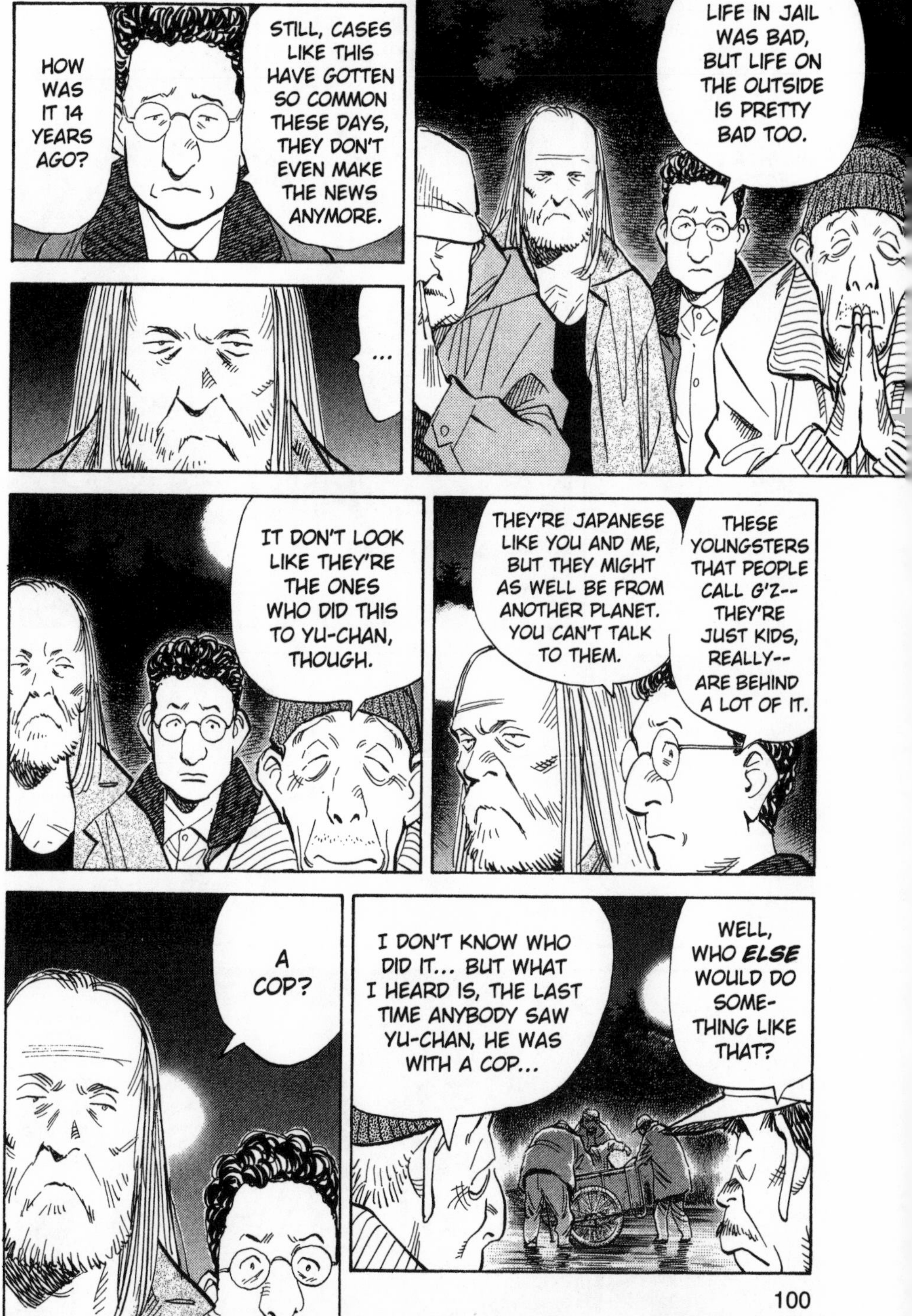
LIFE IN JAIL WAS BAD, BUT LIFE ON THE OUTSIDE IS PRETTY BAD TOO.
STILL, CASES LIKE THIS HAVE GOTTEN SO COMMON THESE DAYS, THEY DON'T EVEN MAKE THE NEWS ANYMORE.
HOW WAS IT 14 YEARS AGO?
...
THESE YOUNGSTERS THAT PEOPLE CALL G'Z-- THEY'RE JUST KIDS, REALLY-- ARE BEHIND A LOT OF IT.
THEY'RE JAPANESE LIKE YOU AND ME, BUT THEY MIGHT AS WELL BE FROM ANOTHER PLANET. YOU CAN'T TALK TO THEM.
IT DON'T LOOK LIKE THEY'RE THE ONES WHO DID THIS TO YU-CHAN, THOUGH.
WELL, WHO *ELSE* WOULD DO SOME-THING LIKE THAT?
I DON'T KNOW WHO DID IT... BUT WHAT I HEARD IS, THE LAST TIME ANYBODY SAW YU-CHAN, HE WAS WITH A COP...
A COP?

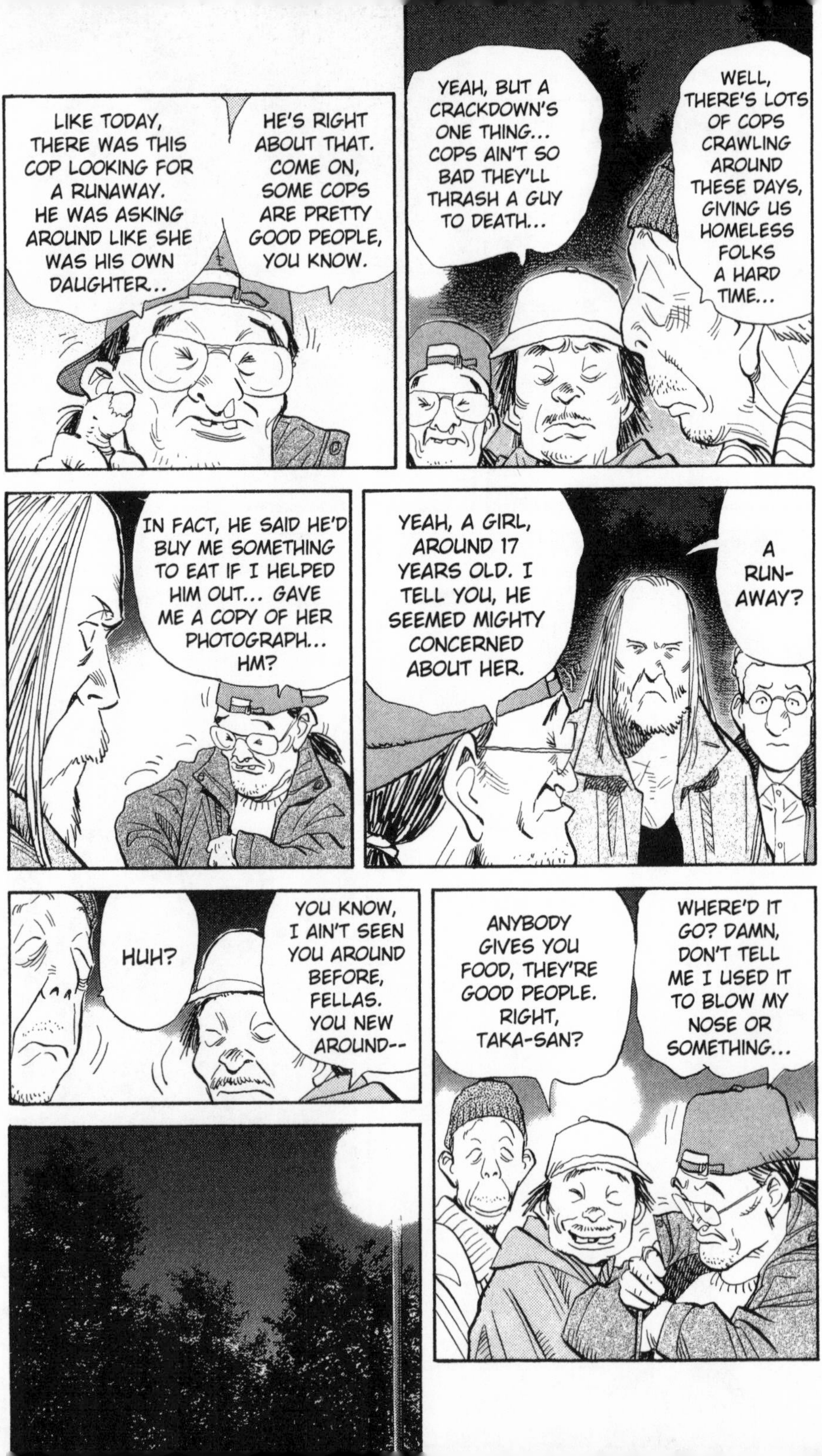
WELL, THERE'S LOTS OF COPS CRAWLING AROUND THESE DAYS, GIVING US HOMELESS FOLKS A HARD TIME...
YEAH, BUT A CRACKDOWN'S ONE THING... COPS AIN'T SO BAD THEY'LL THRASH A GUY TO DEATH...
HE'S RIGHT ABOUT THAT. COME ON, SOME COPS ARE PRETTY GOOD PEOPLE, YOU KNOW.
LIKE TODAY, THERE WAS THIS COP LOOKING FOR A RUNAWAY. HE WAS ASKING AROUND LIKE SHE WAS HIS OWN DAUGHTER...
A RUN-AWAY?
YEAH, A GIRL, AROUND 17 YEARS OLD. I TELL YOU, HE SEEMED MIGHTY CONCERNED ABOUT HER.
IN FACT, HE SAID HE'D BUY ME SOMETHING TO EAT IF I HELPED HIM OUT... GAVE ME A COPY OF HER PHOTOGRAPH... HM?
WHERE'D IT GO? DAMN, DON'T TELL ME I USED IT TO BLOW MY NOSE OR SOMETHING...
ANYBODY GIVES YOU FOOD, THEY'RE GOOD PEOPLE. RIGHT, TAKA-SAN?
YOU KNOW, I AIN'T SEEN YOU AROUND BEFORE, FELLAS. YOU NEW AROUND--
HUH?

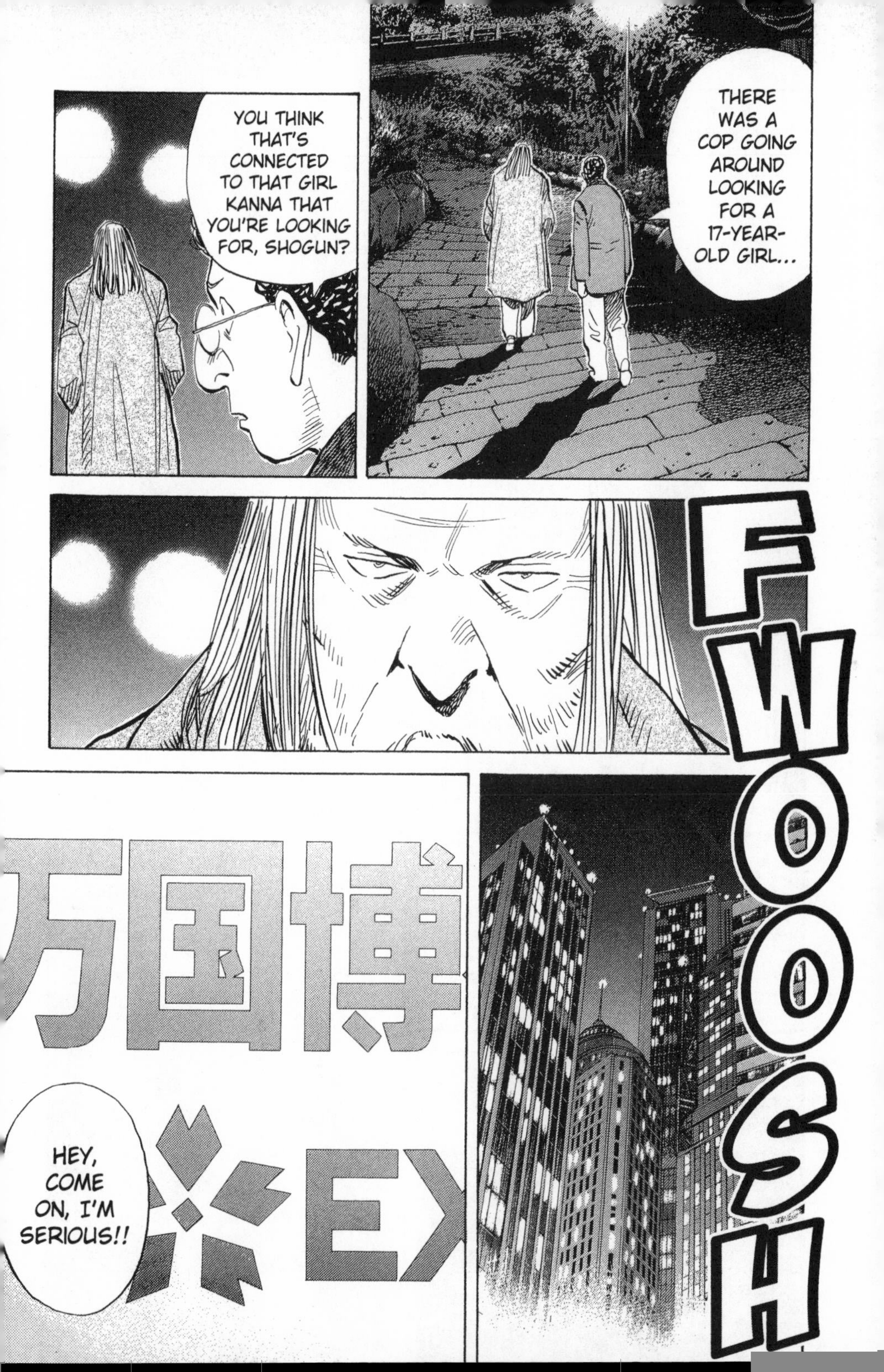
THERE WAS A COP GOING AROUND LOOKING FOR A 17-YEAR-OLD GIRL...
YOU THINK THAT'S CONNECTED TO THAT GIRL KANNA THAT YOU'RE LOOKING FOR, SHOGUN?
FWOOSH
万国博
EX
HEY, COME ON, I'M SERIOUS!!

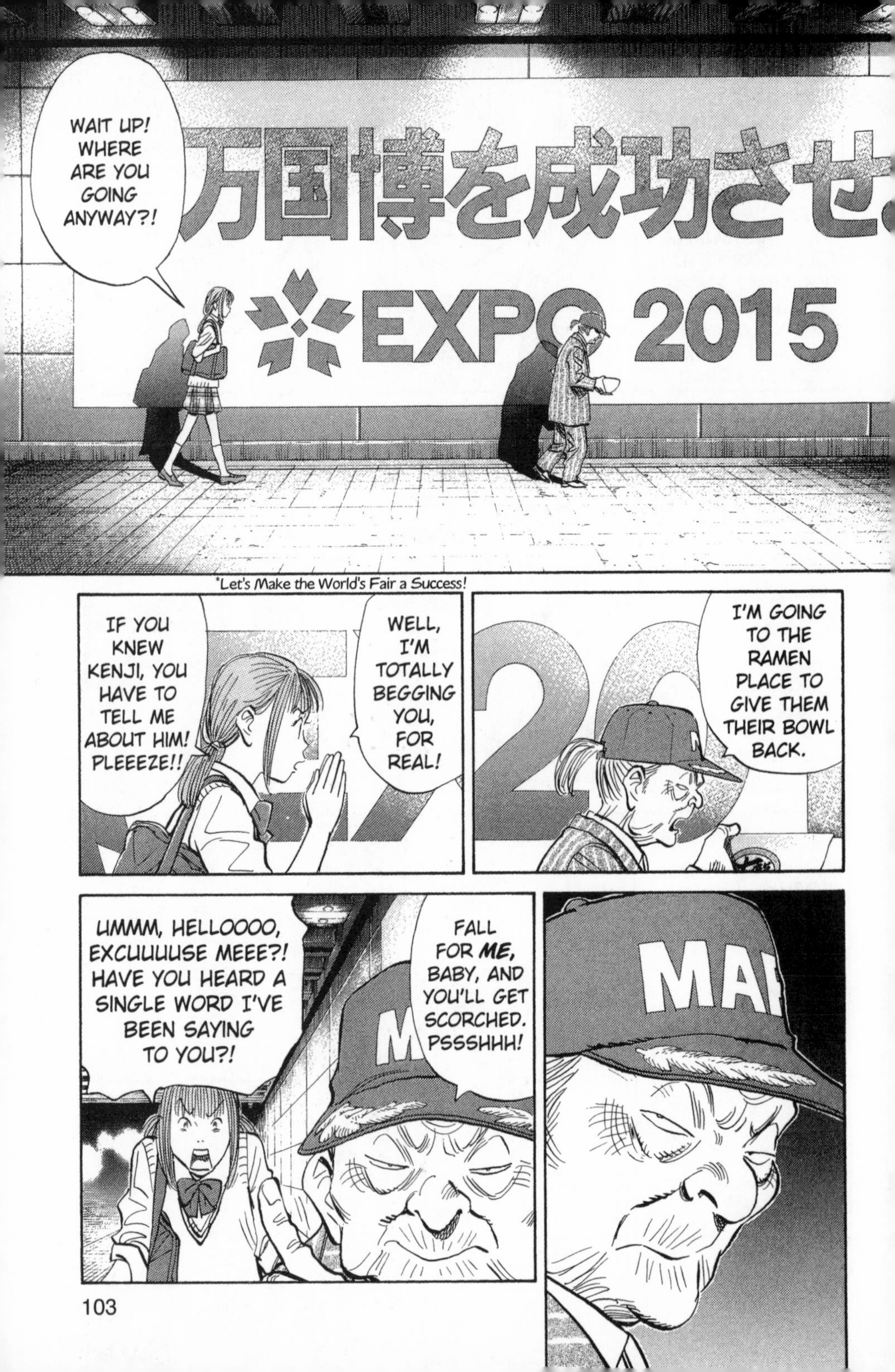
WAIT UP! WHERE ARE YOU GOING ANYWAY?!
万国博を成功させ
EXPO 2015
I'M GOING TO THE RAMEN PLACE TO GIVE THEM THEIR BOWL BACK.
WELL, I'M TOTALLY BEGGING YOU, FOR REAL!
IF YOU KNEW KENJI, YOU HAVE TO TELL ME ABOUT HIM! PLEEEZE!!
FALL FOR **ME,** BABY, AND YOU'LL GET SCORCHED. PSSSHHH!
UMMM, HELLOOOO, EXCUUUUSE MEEE?! HAVE YOU HEARD A SINGLE WORD I'VE BEEN SAYING TO YOU?!

*Let's Make the World's Fair a Success!

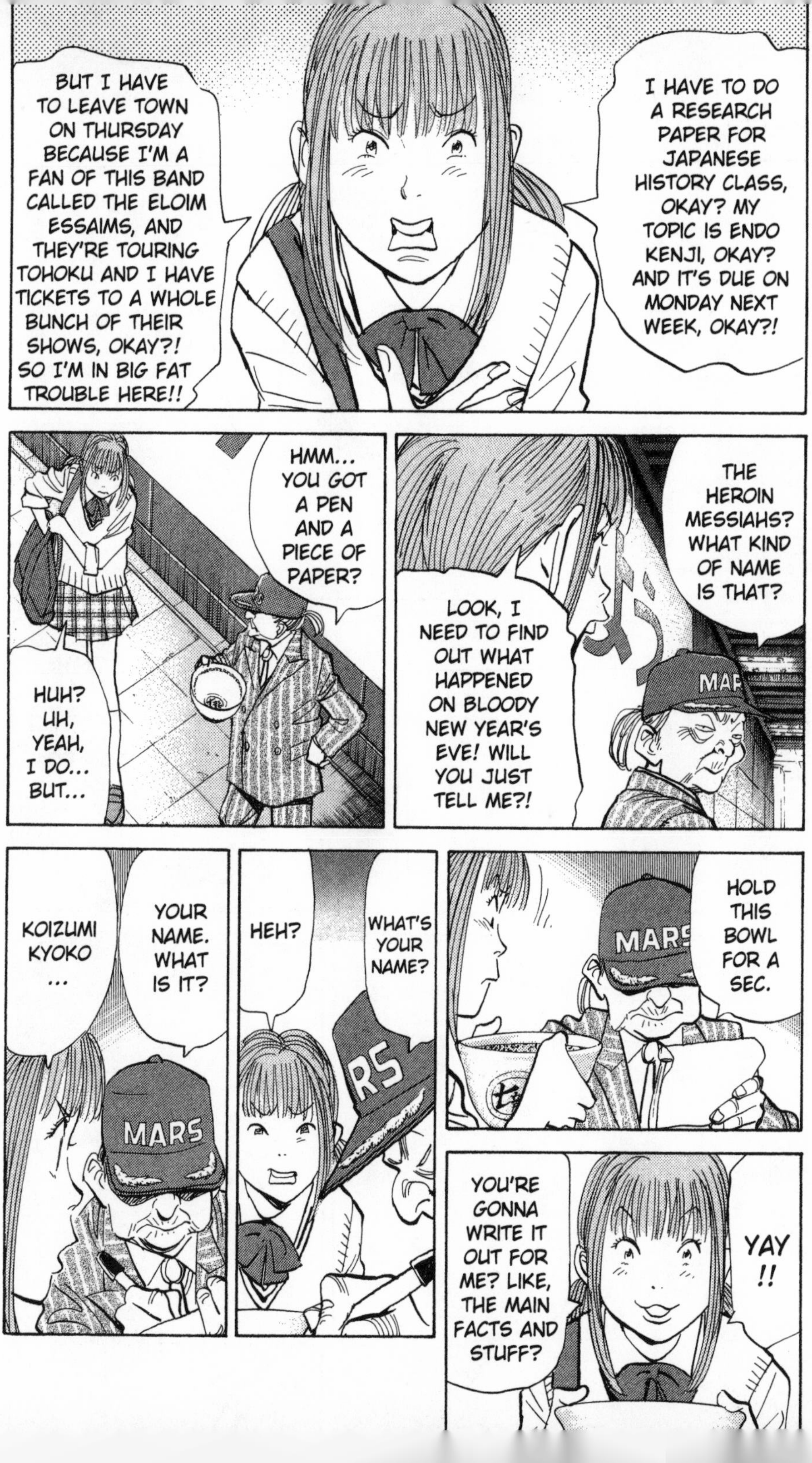
I HAVE TO DO A RESEARCH PAPER FOR JAPANESE HISTORY CLASS, OKAY? MY TOPIC IS ENDO KENJI, OKAY? AND IT'S DUE ON MONDAY NEXT WEEK, OKAY?!
BUT I HAVE TO LEAVE TOWN ON THURSDAY BECAUSE I'M A FAN OF THIS BAND CALLED THE ELOIM ESSAIMS, AND THEY'RE TOURING TOHOKU AND I HAVE TICKETS TO A WHOLE BUNCH OF THEIR SHOWS, OKAY?! SO I'M IN BIG FAT TROUBLE HERE!!
THE HEROIN MESSIAHS? WHAT KIND OF NAME IS THAT?
LOOK, I NEED TO FIND OUT WHAT HAPPENED ON BLOODY NEW YEAR'S EVE! WILL YOU JUST TELL ME?!
MARS
HMM... YOU GOT A PEN AND A PIECE OF PAPER?
HUH? UH, YEAH, I DO... BUT...
HOLD THIS BOWL FOR A SEC.
MARS
YAY!!
YOU'RE GONNA WRITE IT OUT FOR ME? LIKE, THE MAIN FACTS AND STUFF?
WHAT'S YOUR NAME?
HEH?
RS
YOUR NAME. WHAT IS IT?
KOIZUMI KYOKO...
MARS

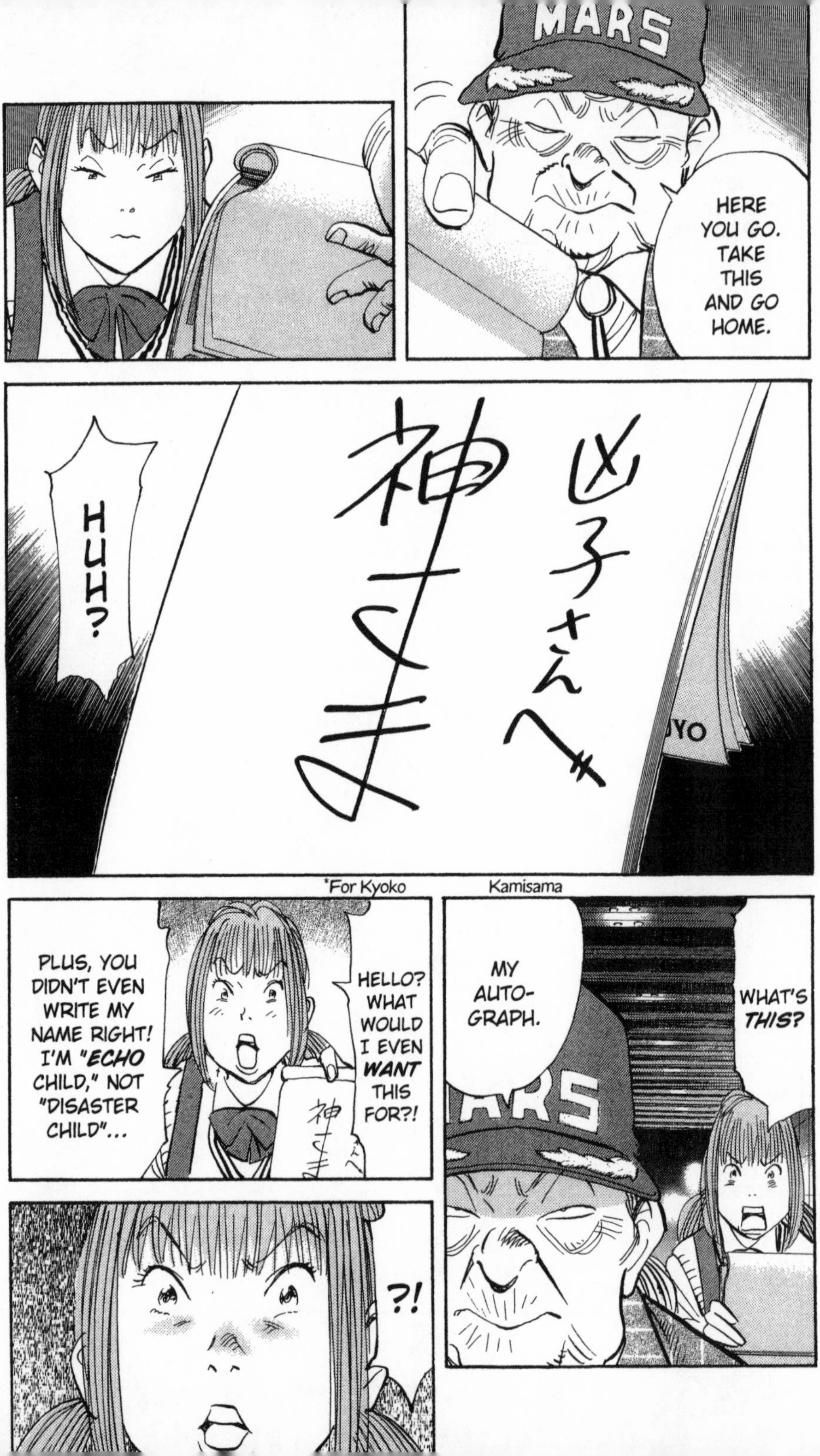
HERE YOU GO. TAKE THIS AND GO HOME.
凶子さんへ
神さま
JYO
HUH?
WHAT'S *THIS?*
MY AUTO-GRAPH.
HELLO? WHAT WOULD I EVEN *WANT* THIS FOR?!
PLUS, YOU DIDN'T EVEN WRITE MY NAME RIGHT! I'M "*ECHO* CHILD," NOT "DISASTER CHILD"...
?!
*For Kyoko Kamisama

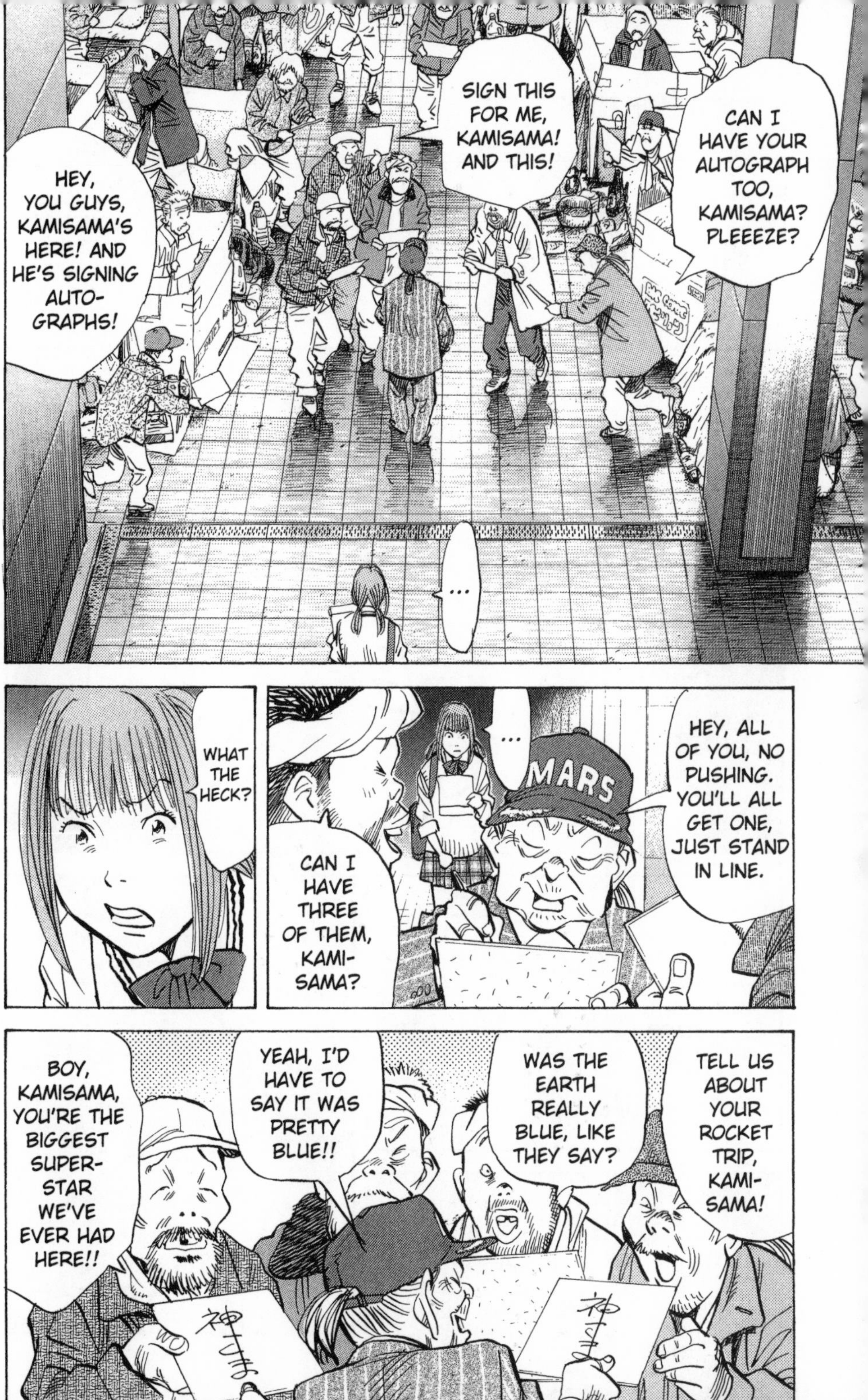
CAN I HAVE YOUR AUTOGRAPH TOO, KAMISAMA? PLEEEZE?
SIGN THIS FOR ME, KAMISAMA! AND THIS!
HEY, YOU GUYS, KAMISAMA'S HERE! AND HE'S SIGNING AUTO-GRAPHS!
...
HEY, ALL OF YOU, NO PUSHING. YOU'LL ALL GET ONE, JUST STAND IN LINE.
MARS
...
CAN I HAVE THREE OF THEM, KAMI-SAMA?
WHAT THE HECK?
TELL US ABOUT YOUR ROCKET TRIP, KAMI-SAMA!
WAS THE EARTH REALLY BLUE, LIKE THEY SAY?
YEAH, I'D HAVE TO SAY IT WAS PRETTY BLUE!!
BOY, KAMISAMA, YOU'RE THE BIGGEST SUPER-STAR WE'VE EVER HAD HERE!!

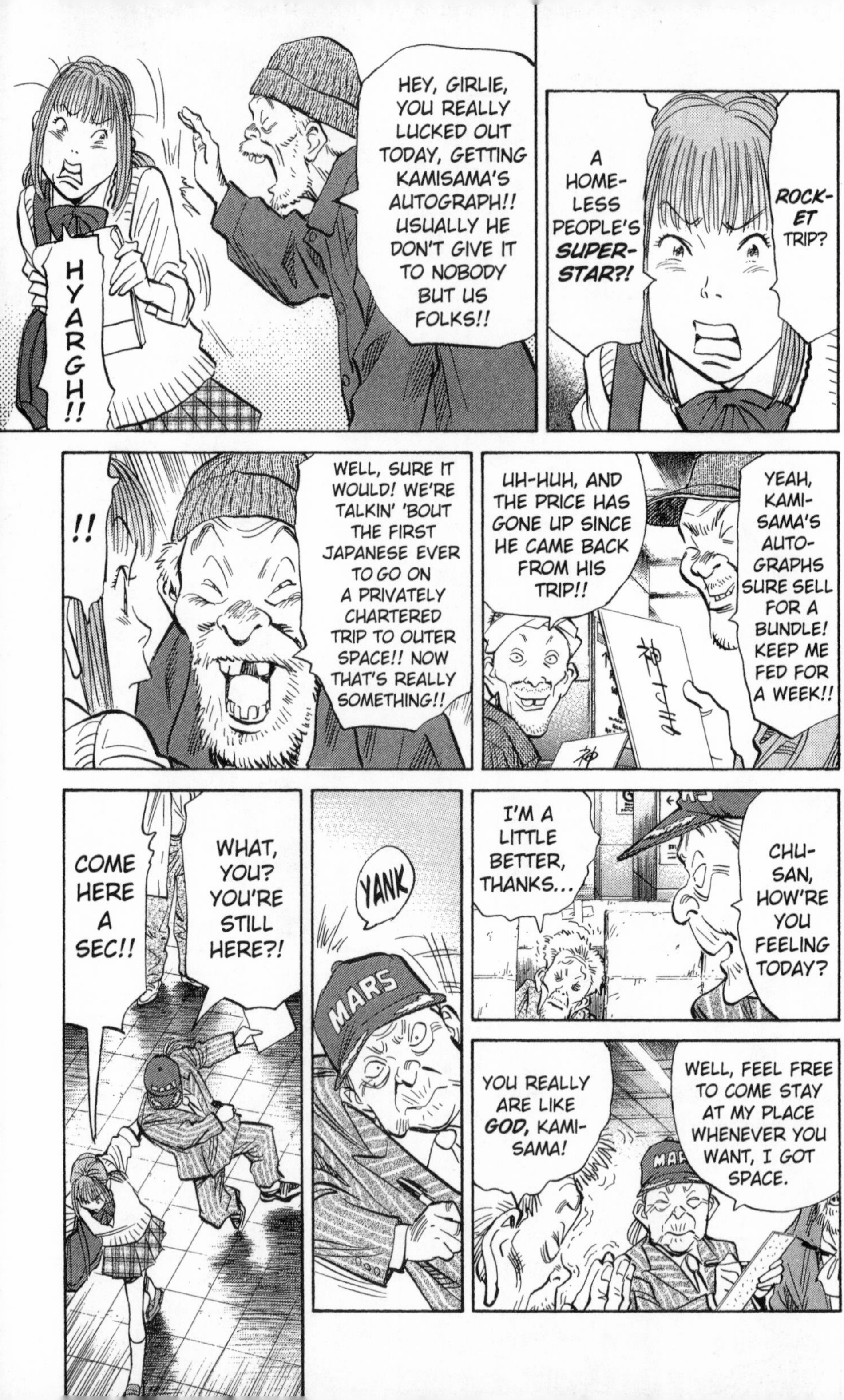
ROCKET TRIP?
A HOMELESS PEOPLE'S SUPERSTAR?!
HEY, GIRLIE, YOU REALLY LUCKED OUT TODAY, GETTING KAMISAMA'S AUTOGRAPH!! USUALLY HE DON'T GIVE IT TO NOBODY BUT US FOLKS!!
HYARGH!!
YEAH, KAMISAMA'S AUTOGRAPHS SURE SELL FOR A BUNDLE! KEEP ME FED FOR A WEEK!!
UH-HUH, AND THE PRICE HAS GONE UP SINCE HE CAME BACK FROM HIS TRIP!!
WELL, SURE IT WOULD! WE'RE TALKIN' 'BOUT THE FIRST JAPANESE EVER TO GO ON A PRIVATELY CHARTERED TRIP TO OUTER SPACE!! NOW THAT'S REALLY SOMETHING!!
!!
CHU-SAN, HOW'RE YOU FEELING TODAY?
I'M A LITTLE BETTER, THANKS...
WELL, FEEL FREE TO COME STAY AT MY PLACE WHENEVER YOU WANT, I GOT SPACE.
YOU REALLY ARE LIKE GOD, KAMISAMA!
YANK
MARS
WHAT, YOU? YOU'RE STILL HERE?!
COME HERE A SEC!!

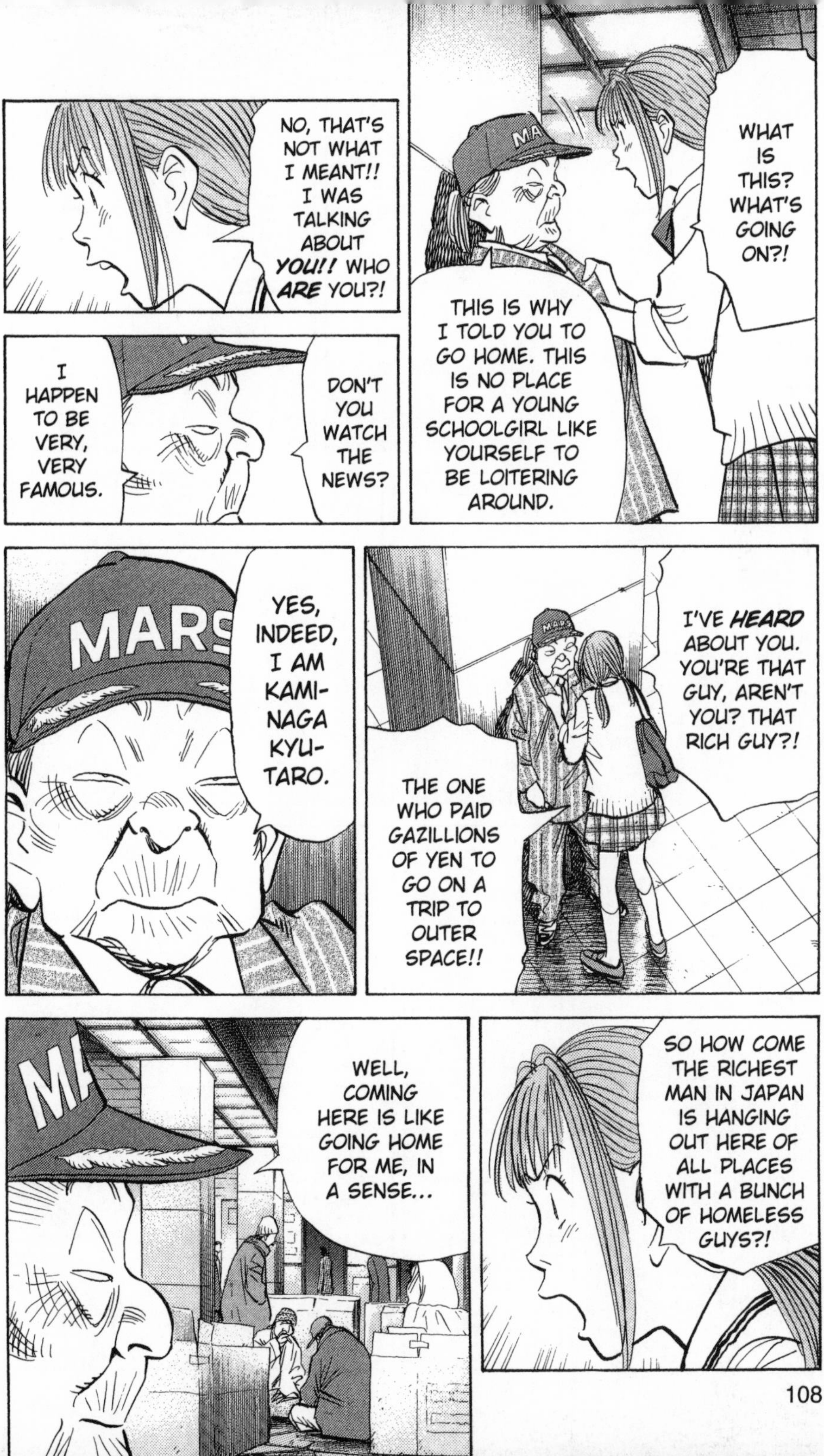
WHAT IS THIS? WHAT'S GOING ON?!
THIS IS WHY I TOLD YOU TO GO HOME. THIS IS NO PLACE FOR A YOUNG SCHOOLGIRL LIKE YOURSELF TO BE LOITERING AROUND.
NO, THAT'S NOT WHAT I MEANT!! I WAS TALKING ABOUT ***YOU!!*** WHO ***ARE*** YOU?!
DON'T YOU WATCH THE NEWS?
I HAPPEN TO BE VERY, VERY FAMOUS.
I'VE ***HEARD*** ABOUT YOU. YOU'RE THAT GUY, AREN'T YOU? THAT RICH GUY?!
THE ONE WHO PAID GAZILLIONS OF YEN TO GO ON A TRIP TO OUTER SPACE!!
YES, INDEED, I AM KAMI-NAGA KYU-TARO.
SO HOW COME THE RICHEST MAN IN JAPAN IS HANGING OUT HERE OF ALL PLACES WITH A BUNCH OF HOMELESS GUYS?!
WELL, COMING HERE IS LIKE GOING HOME FOR ME, IN A SENSE...

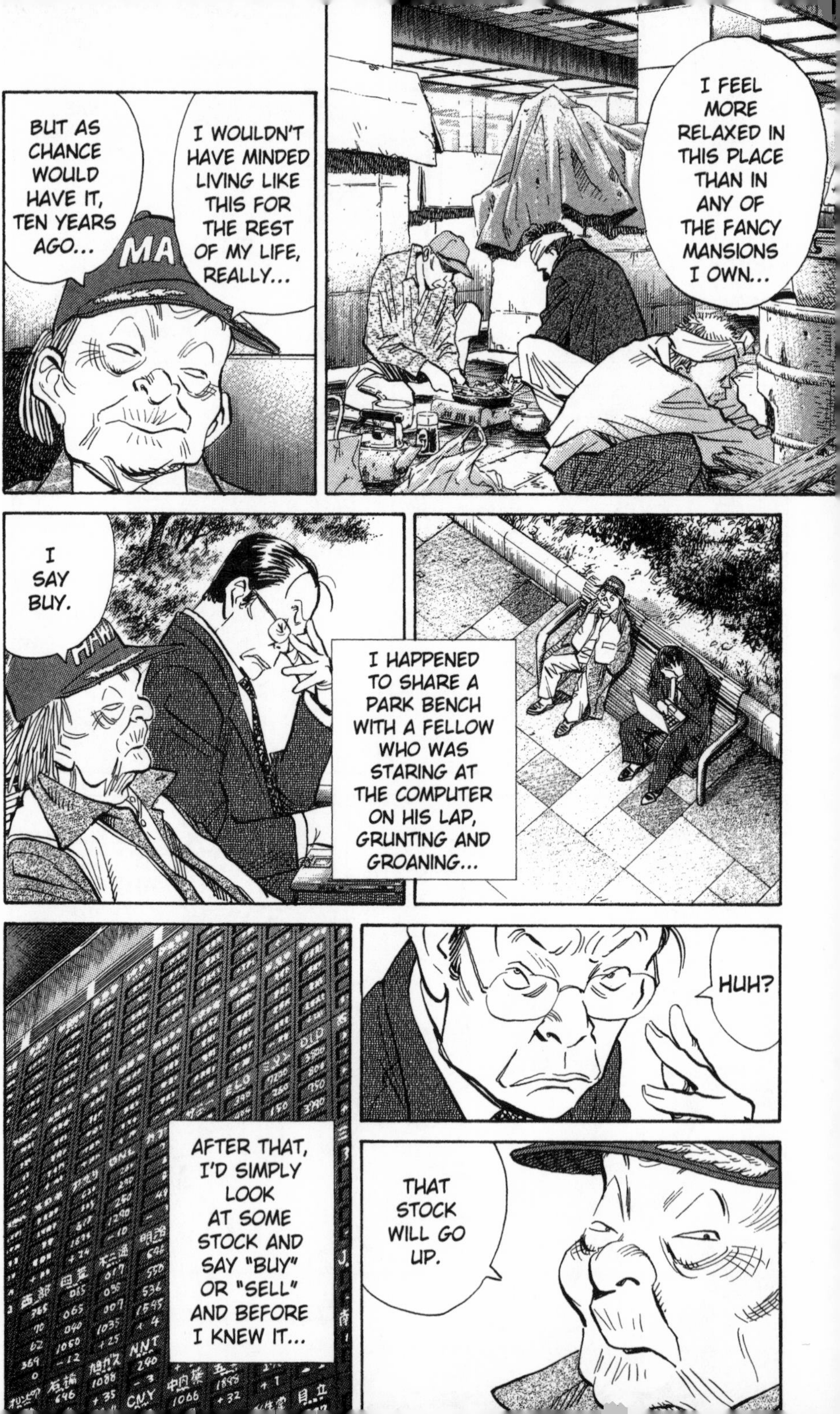
I FEEL MORE RELAXED IN THIS PLACE THAN IN ANY OF THE FANCY MANSIONS I OWN...
I WOULDN'T HAVE MINDED LIVING LIKE THIS FOR THE REST OF MY LIFE, REALLY...
BUT AS CHANCE WOULD HAVE IT, TEN YEARS AGO...
MA
I HAPPENED TO SHARE A PARK BENCH WITH A FELLOW WHO WAS STARING AT THE COMPUTER ON HIS LAP, GRUNTING AND GROANING...
I SAY BUY.
HUH?
THAT STOCK WILL GO UP.
AFTER THAT, I'D SIMPLY LOOK AT SOME STOCK AND SAY "BUY" OR "SELL" AND BEFORE I KNEW IT...

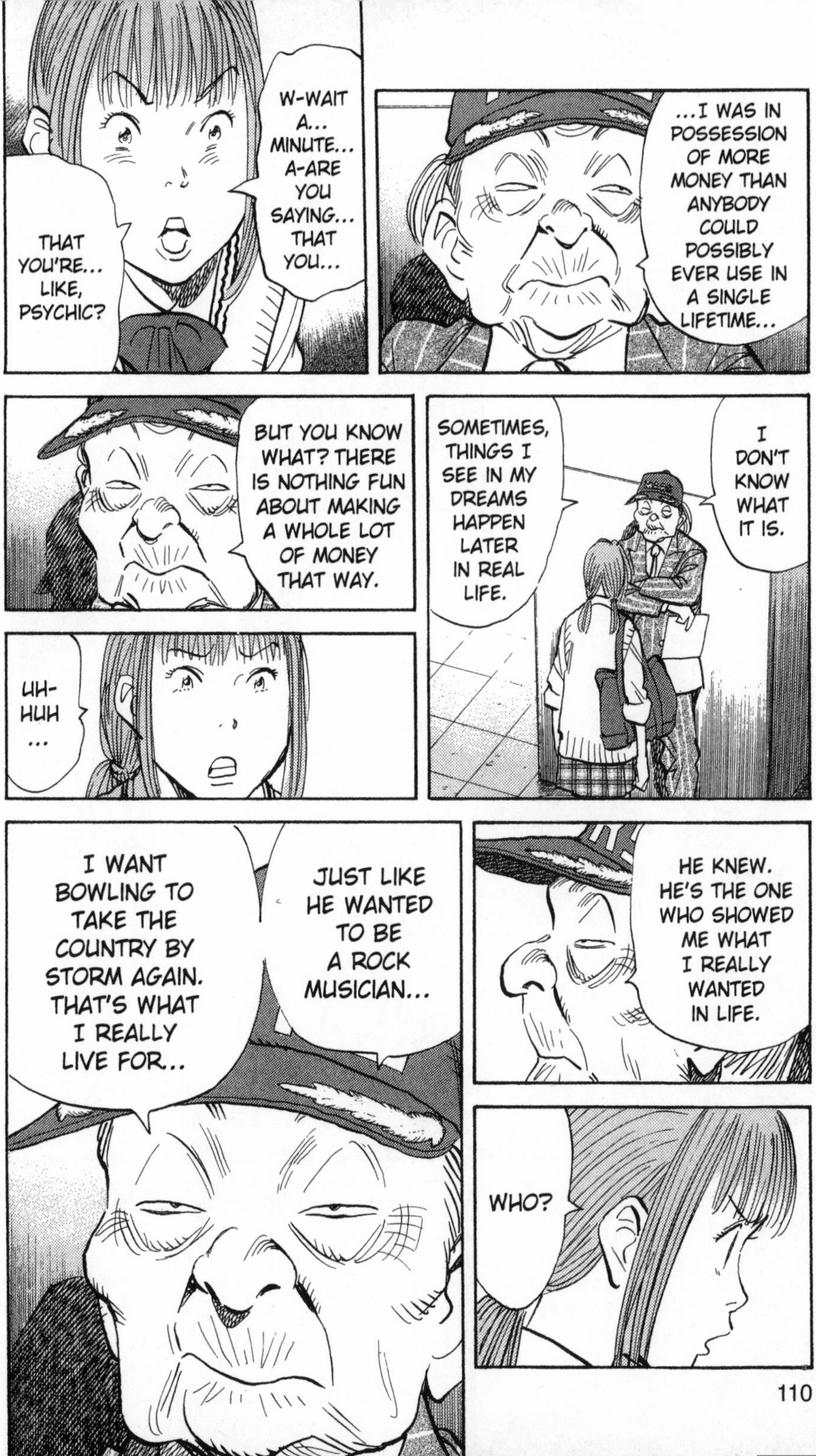
...I WAS IN POSSESSION OF MORE MONEY THAN ANYBODY COULD POSSIBLY EVER USE IN A SINGLE LIFETIME...
W-WAIT A... MINUTE... A-ARE YOU SAYING... THAT YOU...
THAT YOU'RE... LIKE, PSYCHIC?
I DON'T KNOW WHAT IT IS.
SOMETIMES, THINGS I SEE IN MY DREAMS HAPPEN LATER IN REAL LIFE.
BUT YOU KNOW WHAT? THERE IS NOTHING FUN ABOUT MAKING A WHOLE LOT OF MONEY THAT WAY.
UH-HUH ...
HE KNEW. HE'S THE ONE WHO SHOWED ME WHAT I REALLY WANTED IN LIFE.
WHO?
JUST LIKE HE WANTED TO BE A ROCK MUSICIAN...
I WANT BOWLING TO TAKE THE COUNTRY BY STORM AGAIN. THAT'S WHAT I REALLY LIVE FOR...

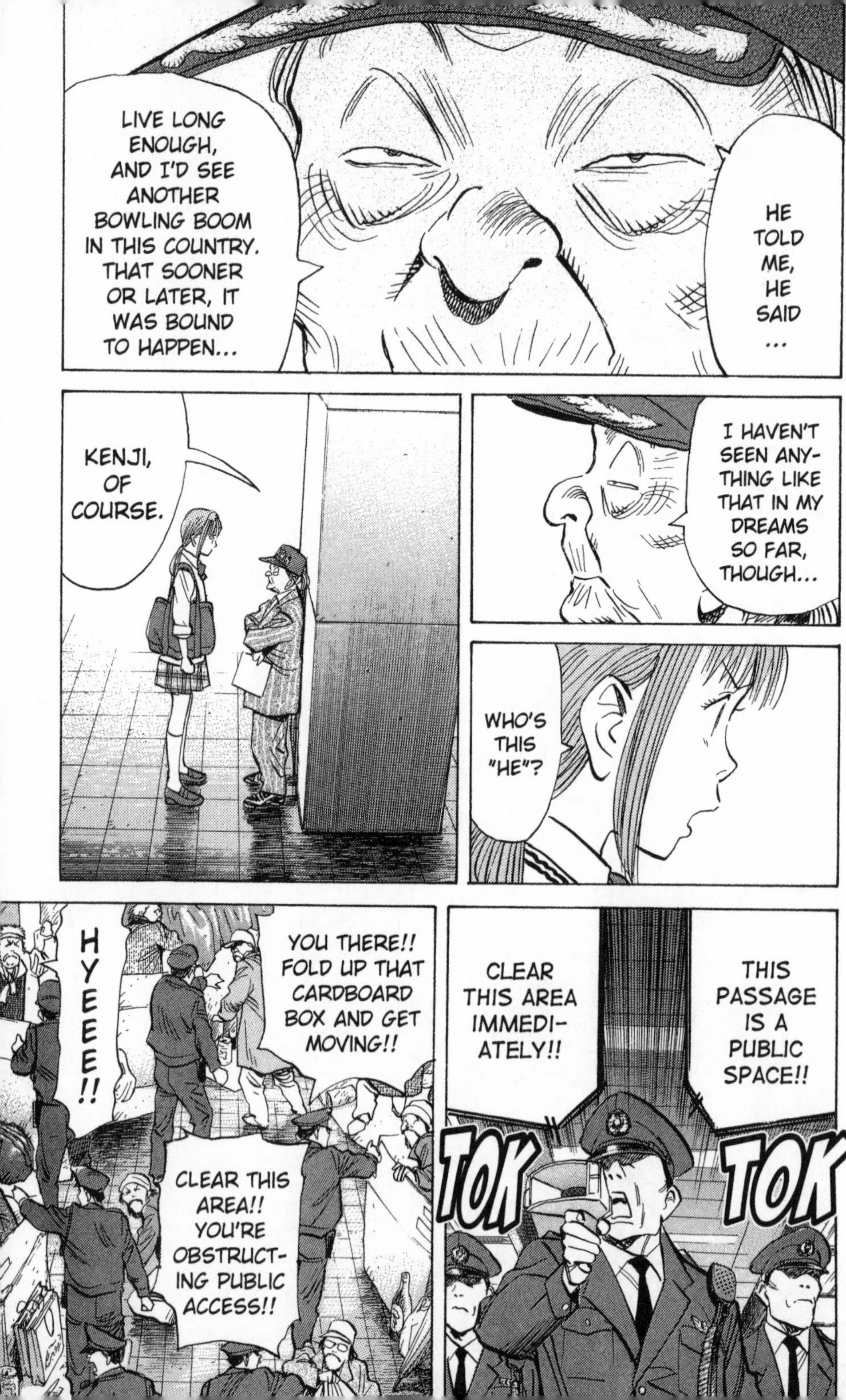
HE TOLD ME, HE SAID ...
LIVE LONG ENOUGH, AND I'D SEE ANOTHER BOWLING BOOM IN THIS COUNTRY. THAT SOONER OR LATER, IT WAS BOUND TO HAPPEN...
I HAVEN'T SEEN ANYTHING LIKE THAT IN MY DREAMS SO FAR, THOUGH...
WHO'S THIS "HE"?
KENJI, OF COURSE.
THIS PASSAGE IS A PUBLIC SPACE!!
CLEAR THIS AREA IMMEDIATELY!!
TOK TOK
YOU THERE!! FOLD UP THAT CARDBOARD BOX AND GET MOVING!!
HYEEEE!!
CLEAR THIS AREA!! YOU'RE OBSTRUCTING PUBLIC ACCESS!!

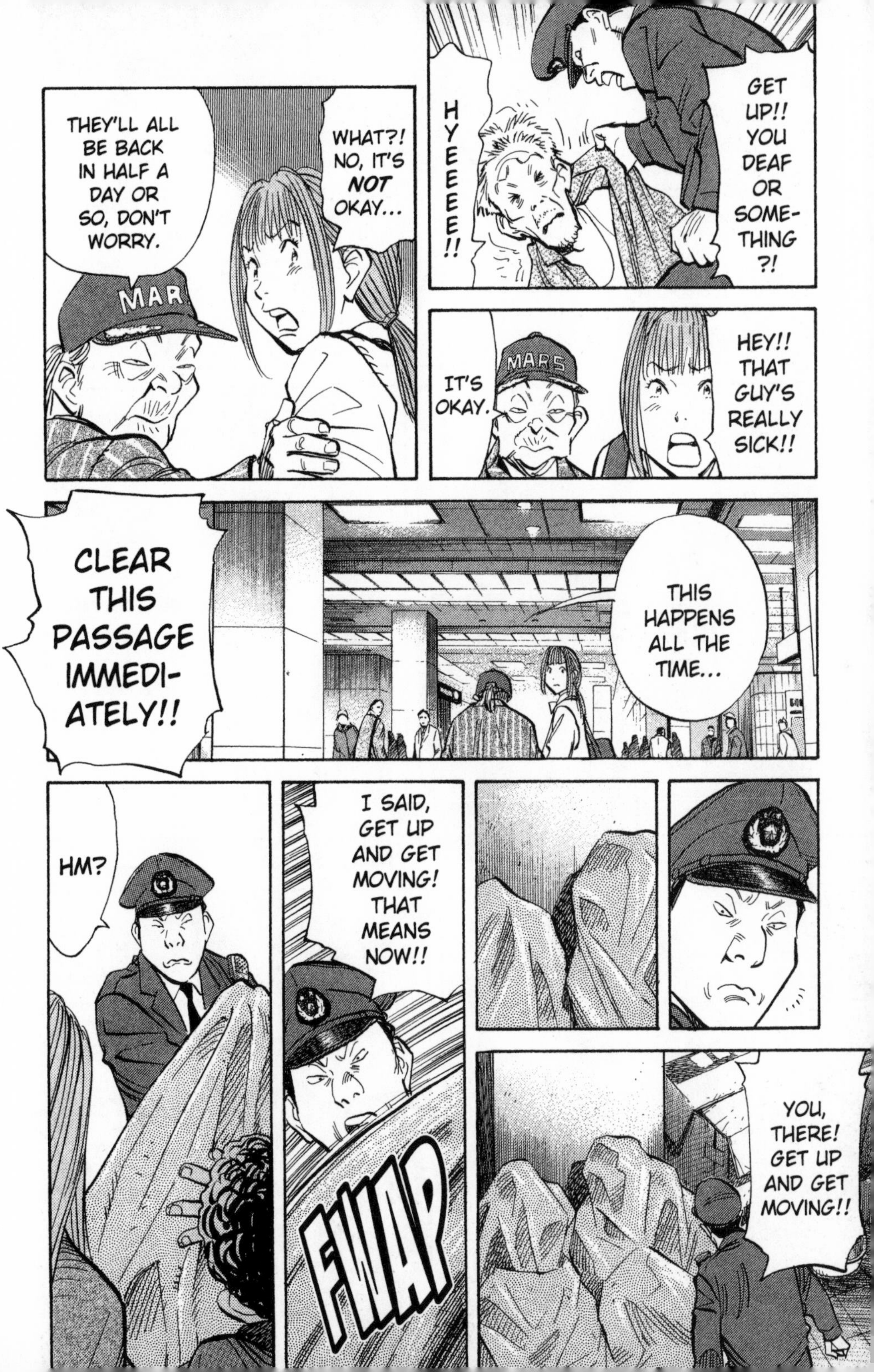
GET UP!! YOU DEAF OR SOMETHING?!
HYEEEEE!!
HEY!! THAT GUY'S REALLY SICK!!
MARS
IT'S OKAY.
WHAT?! NO, IT'S NOT OKAY...
THEY'LL ALL BE BACK IN HALF A DAY OR SO, DON'T WORRY.
MAR
THIS HAPPENS ALL THE TIME...
CLEAR THIS PASSAGE IMMEDIATELY!!
YOU, THERE! GET UP AND GET MOVING!!
I SAID, GET UP AND GET MOVING! THAT MEANS NOW!!
FWAP
HM?

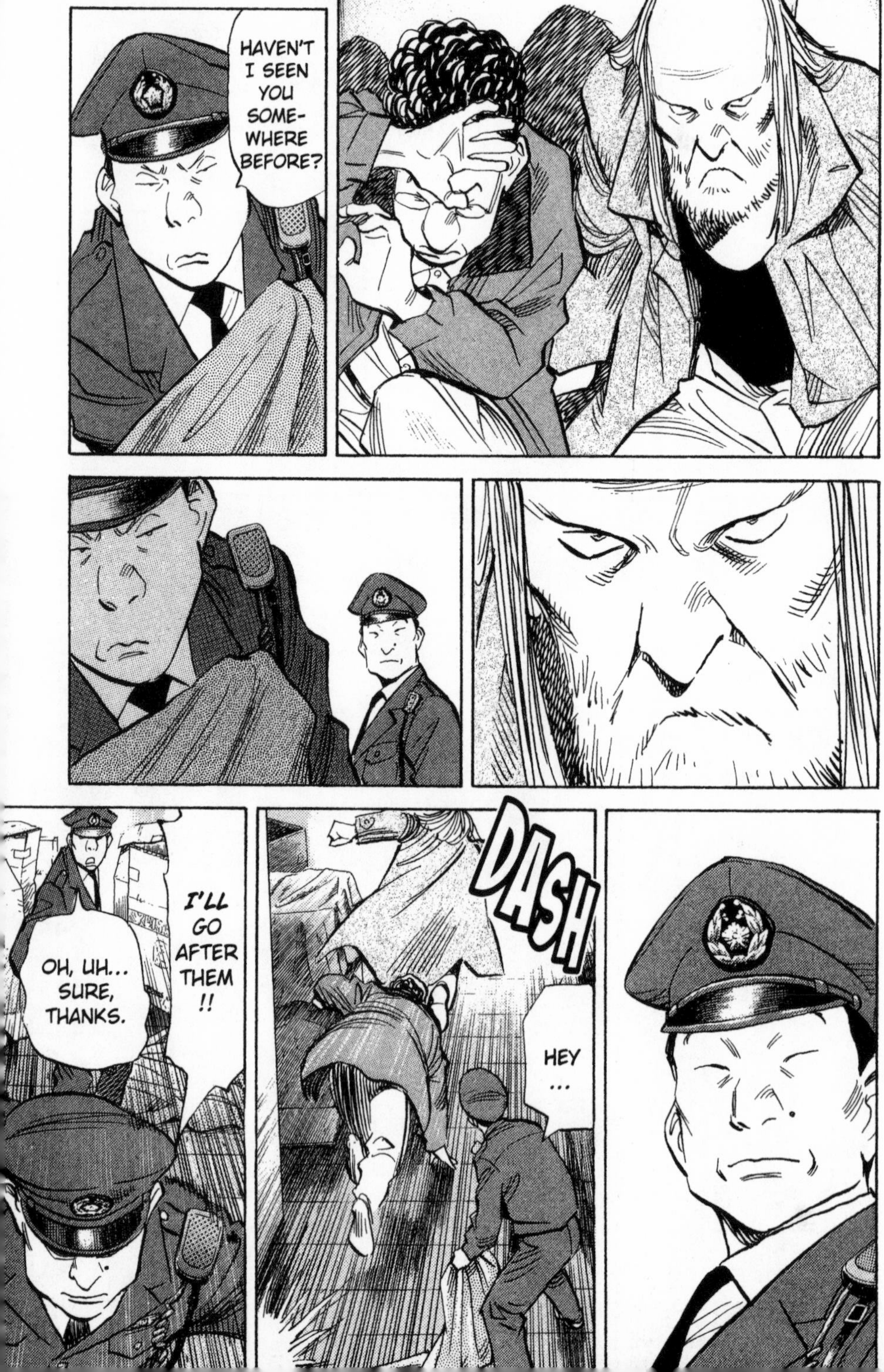
HAVEN'T I SEEN YOU SOME-WHERE BEFORE?
DASH
HEY ...
I'LL GO AFTER THEM !!
OH, UH... SURE, THANKS.

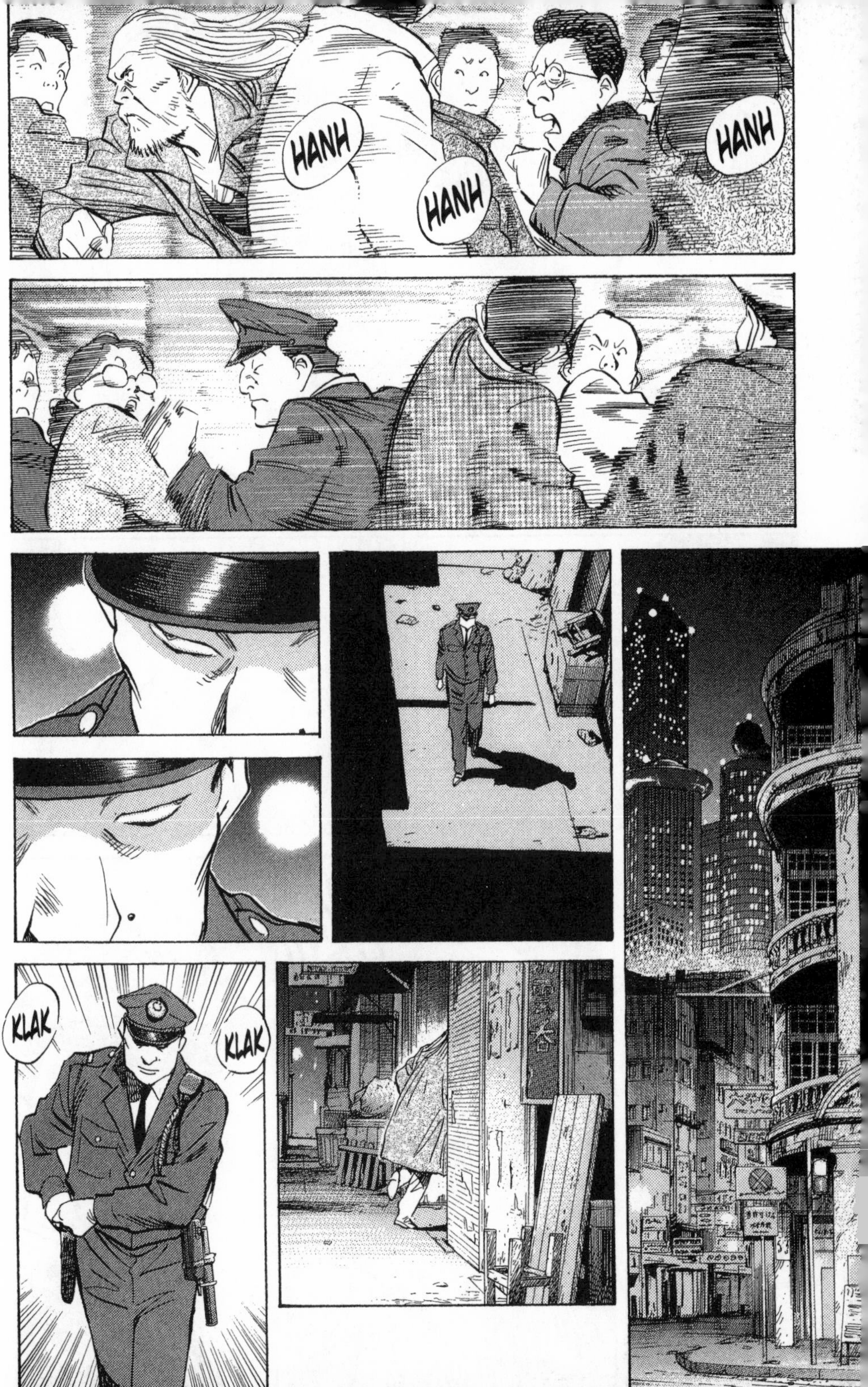
HANH
HANH
HANH
KLAK
KLAK

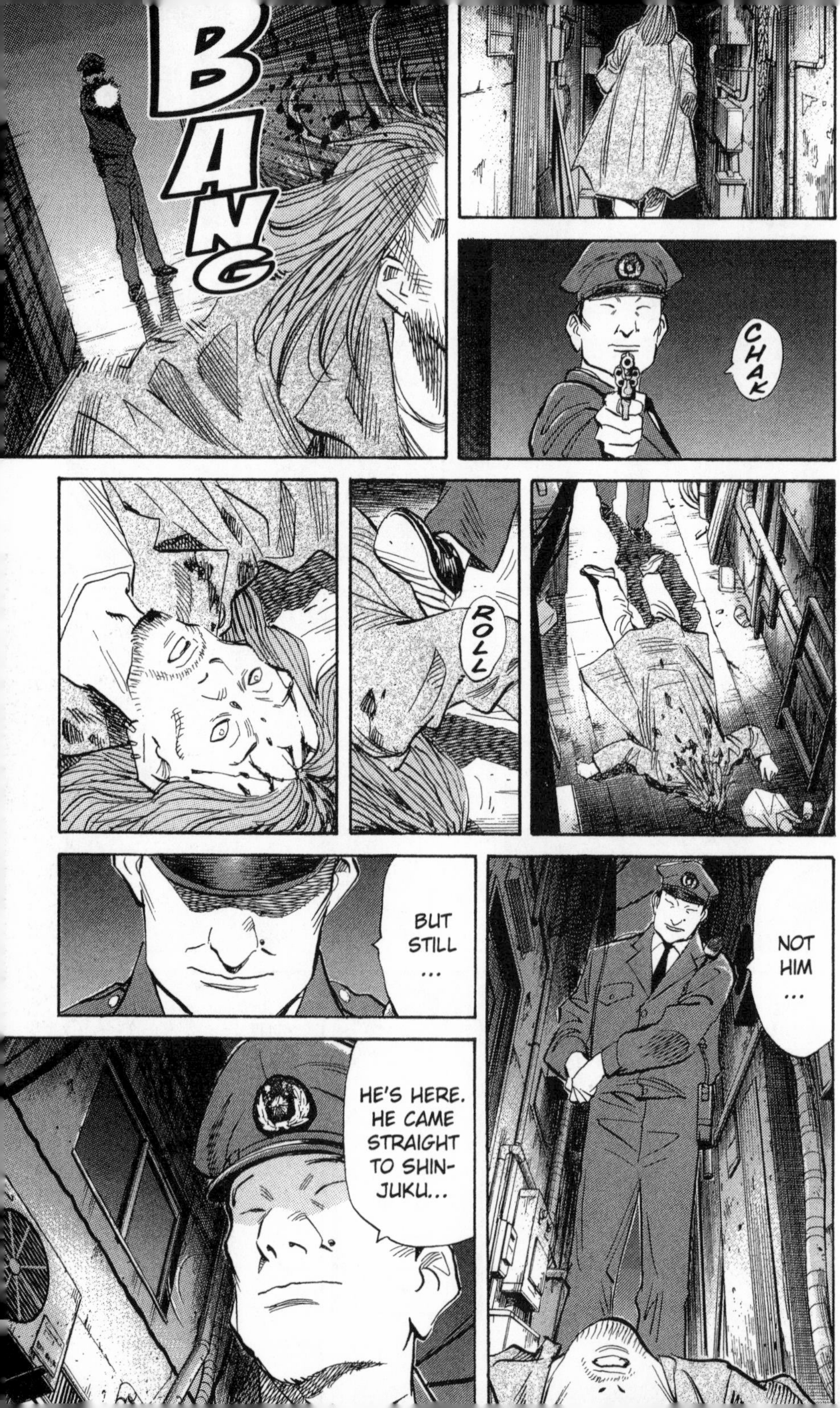
CHAK
BANG
ROLL
NOT HIM...
BUT STILL...
HE'S HERE. HE CAME STRAIGHT TO SHIN-JUKU...

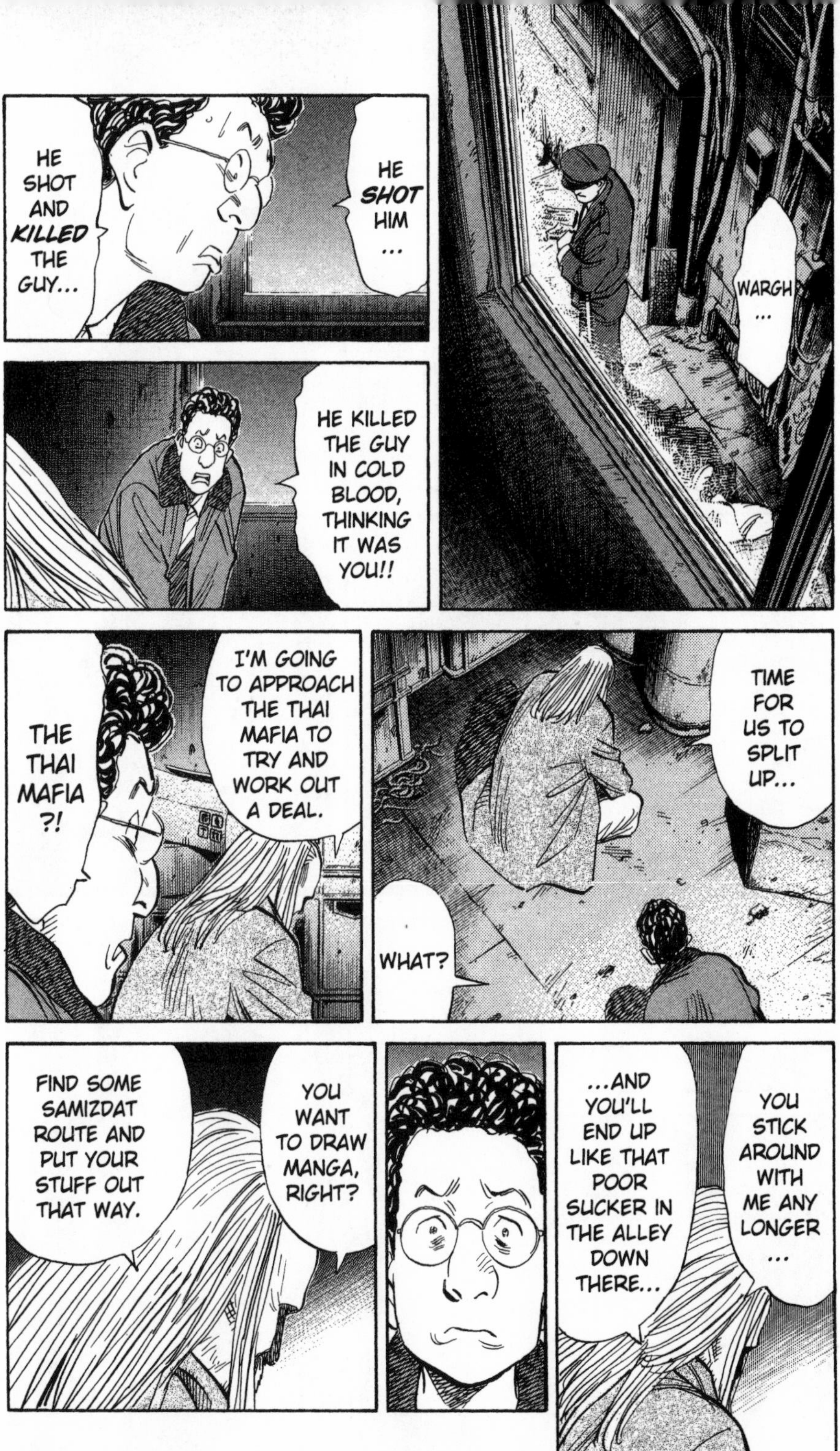
WARGH...
HE SHOT HIM...
HE SHOT AND KILLED THE GUY...
HE KILLED THE GUY IN COLD BLOOD, THINKING IT WAS YOU!!
TIME FOR US TO SPLIT UP...
WHAT?
I'M GOING TO APPROACH THE THAI MAFIA TO TRY AND WORK OUT A DEAL.
THE THAI MAFIA?!
YOU STICK AROUND WITH ME ANY LONGER...
...AND YOU'LL END UP LIKE THAT POOR SUCKER IN THE ALLEY DOWN THERE...
YOU WANT TO DRAW MANGA, RIGHT?
FIND SOME SAMIZDAT ROUTE AND PUT YOUR STUFF OUT THAT WAY.

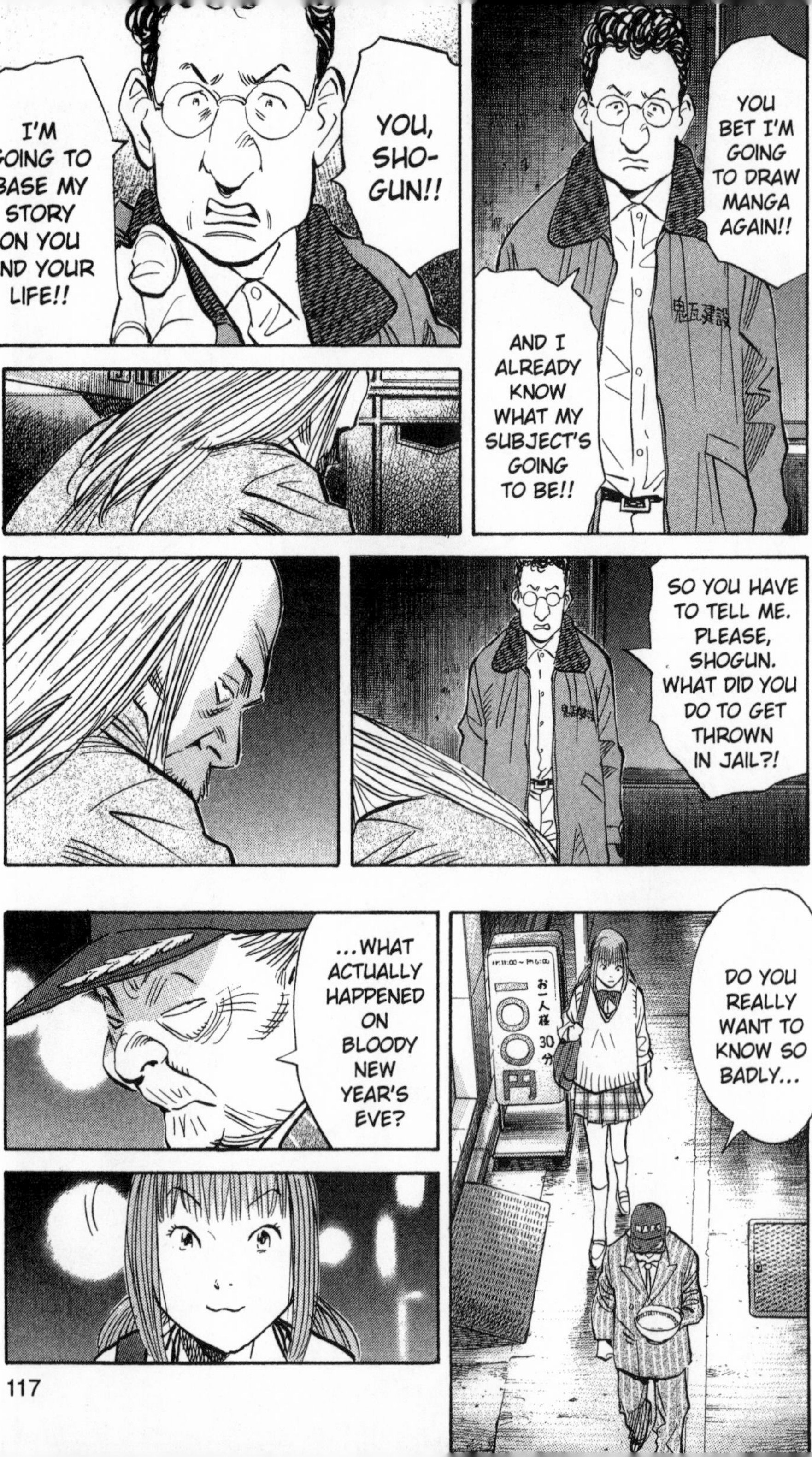
YOU BET I'M GOING TO DRAW MANGA AGAIN!!
AND I ALREADY KNOW WHAT MY SUBJECT'S GOING TO BE!!
YOU, SHO-GUN!!
I'M GOING TO BASE MY STORY ON YOU AND YOUR LIFE!!
SO YOU HAVE TO TELL ME. PLEASE, SHOGUN. WHAT DID YOU DO TO GET THROWN IN JAIL?!
DO YOU REALLY WANT TO KNOW SO BADLY...
...WHAT ACTUALLY HAPPENED ON BLOODY NEW YEAR'S EVE?

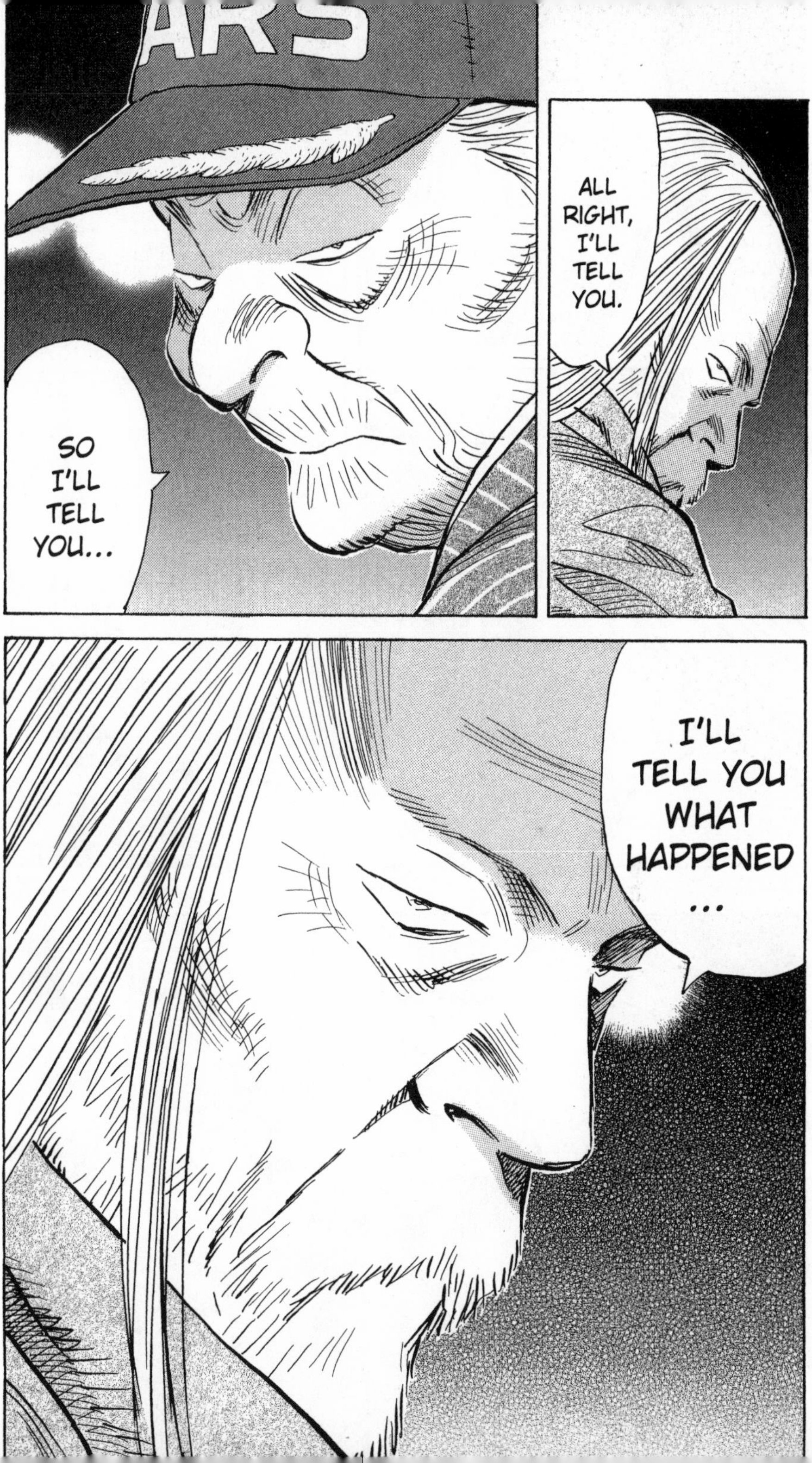
ALL RIGHT, I'LL TELL YOU.
SO I'LL TELL YOU...
I'LL TELL YOU WHAT HAPPENED ...

Chapter 7 The Truth

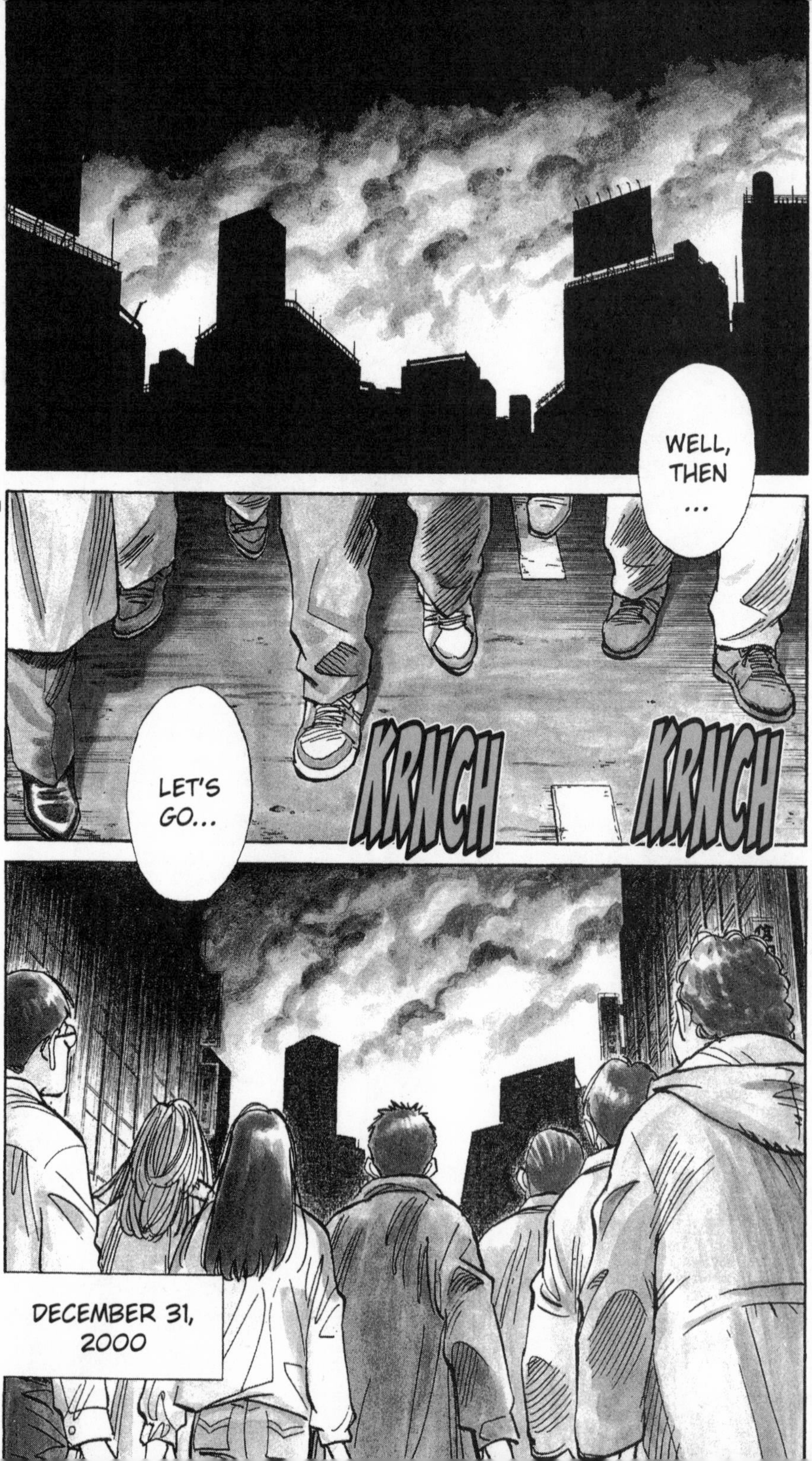

WELL, THEN ...
KRNCH
KRNCH
LET'S GO...
DECEMBER 31, 2000

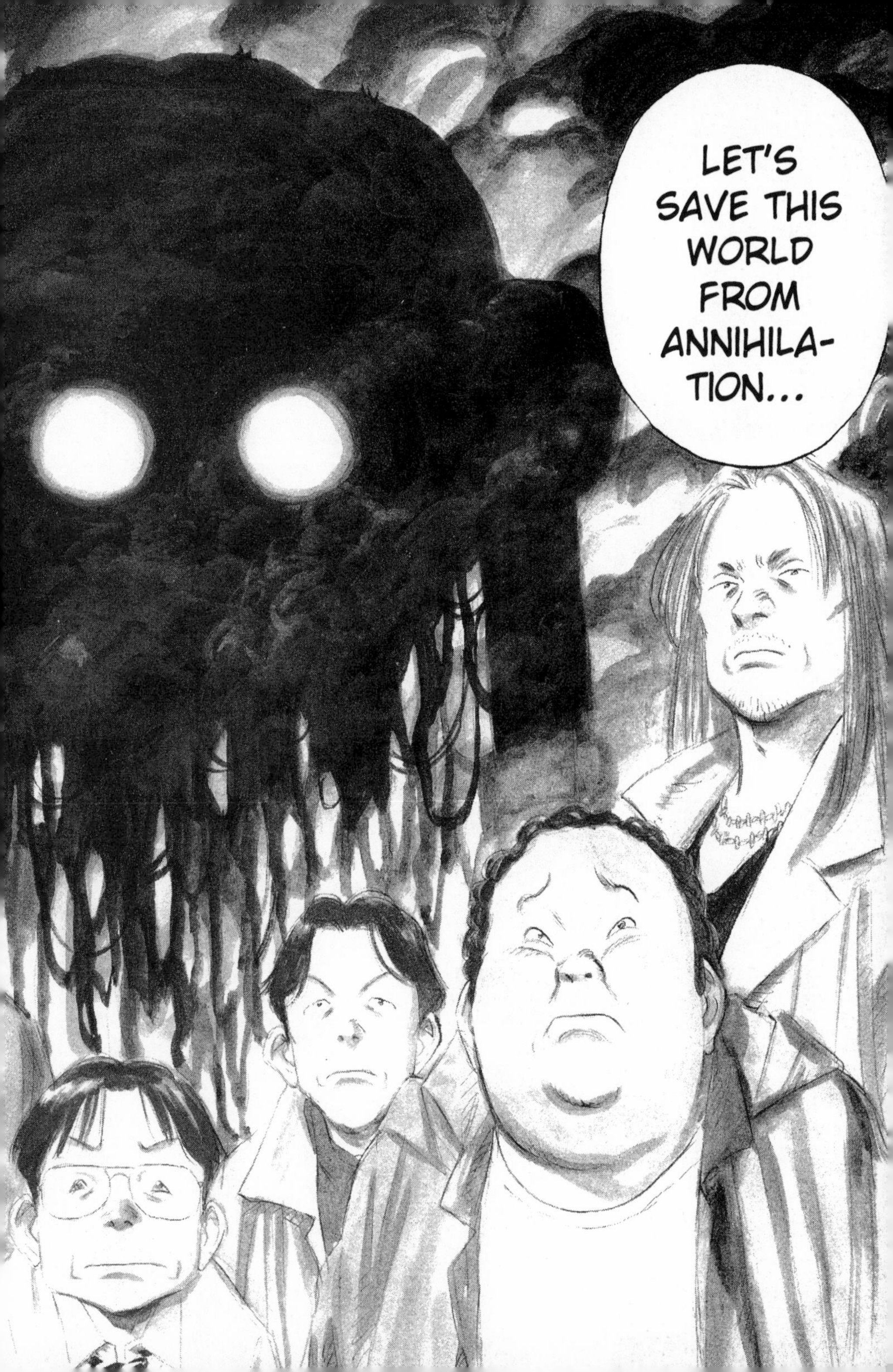
LET'S SAVE THIS WORLD FROM ANNIHILA- TION...

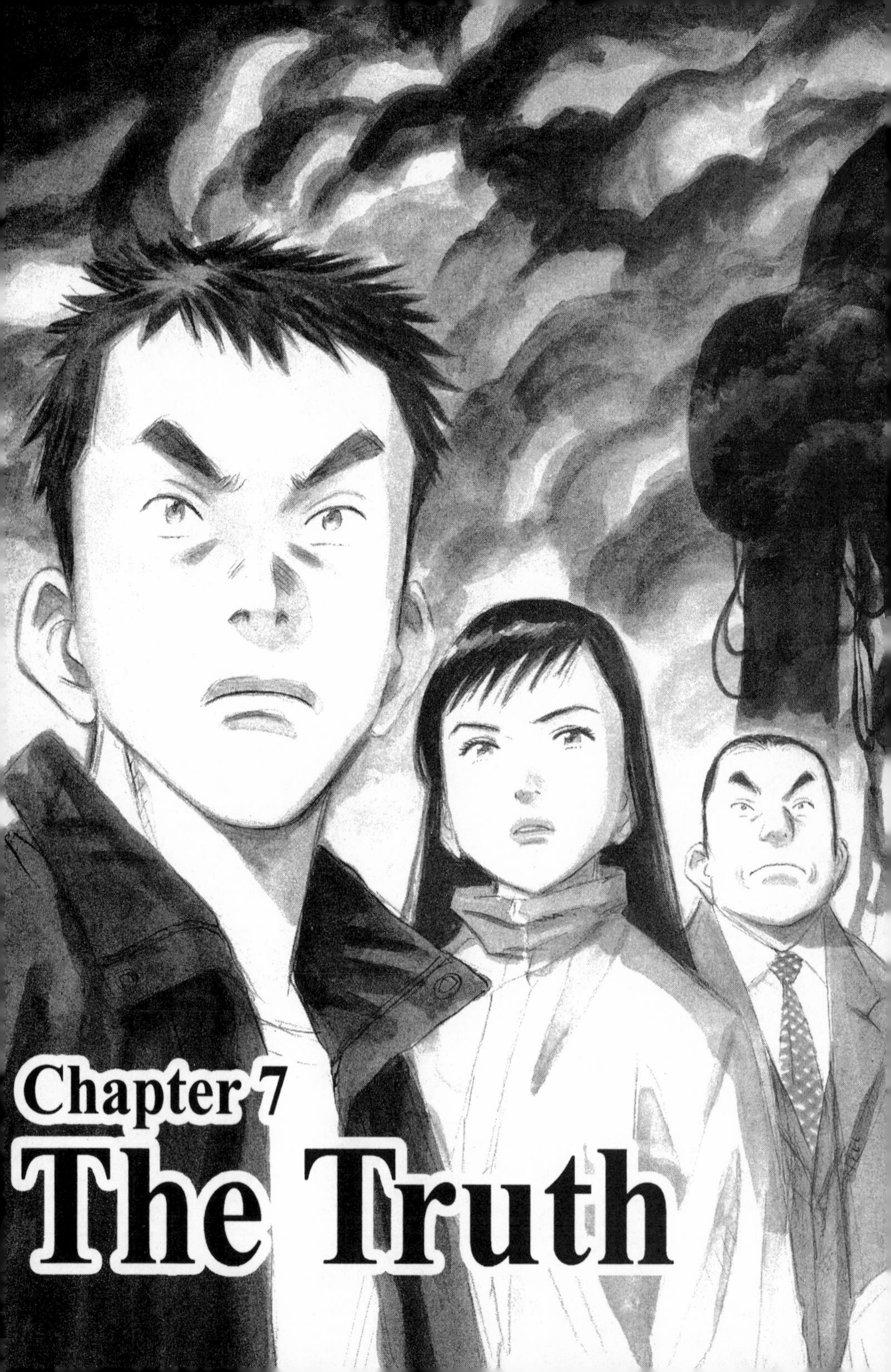
Chapter 7
The Truth

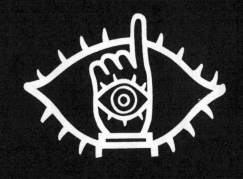

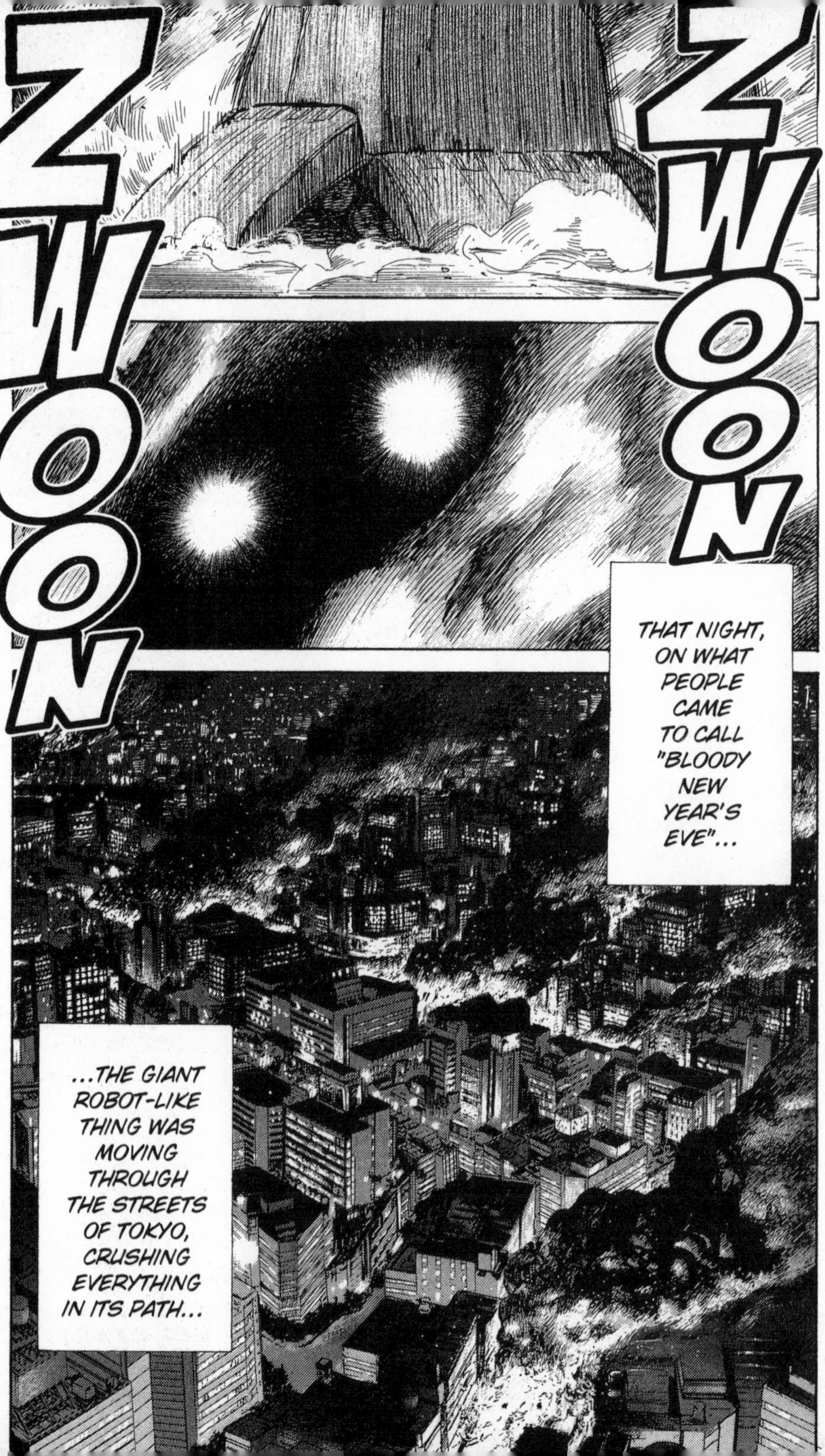
ZWOON
ZWOON
THAT NIGHT, ON WHAT PEOPLE CAME TO CALL "BLOODY NEW YEAR'S EVE"...
...THE GIANT ROBOT-LIKE THING WAS MOVING THROUGH THE STREETS OF TOKYO, CRUSHING EVERYTHING IN ITS PATH...

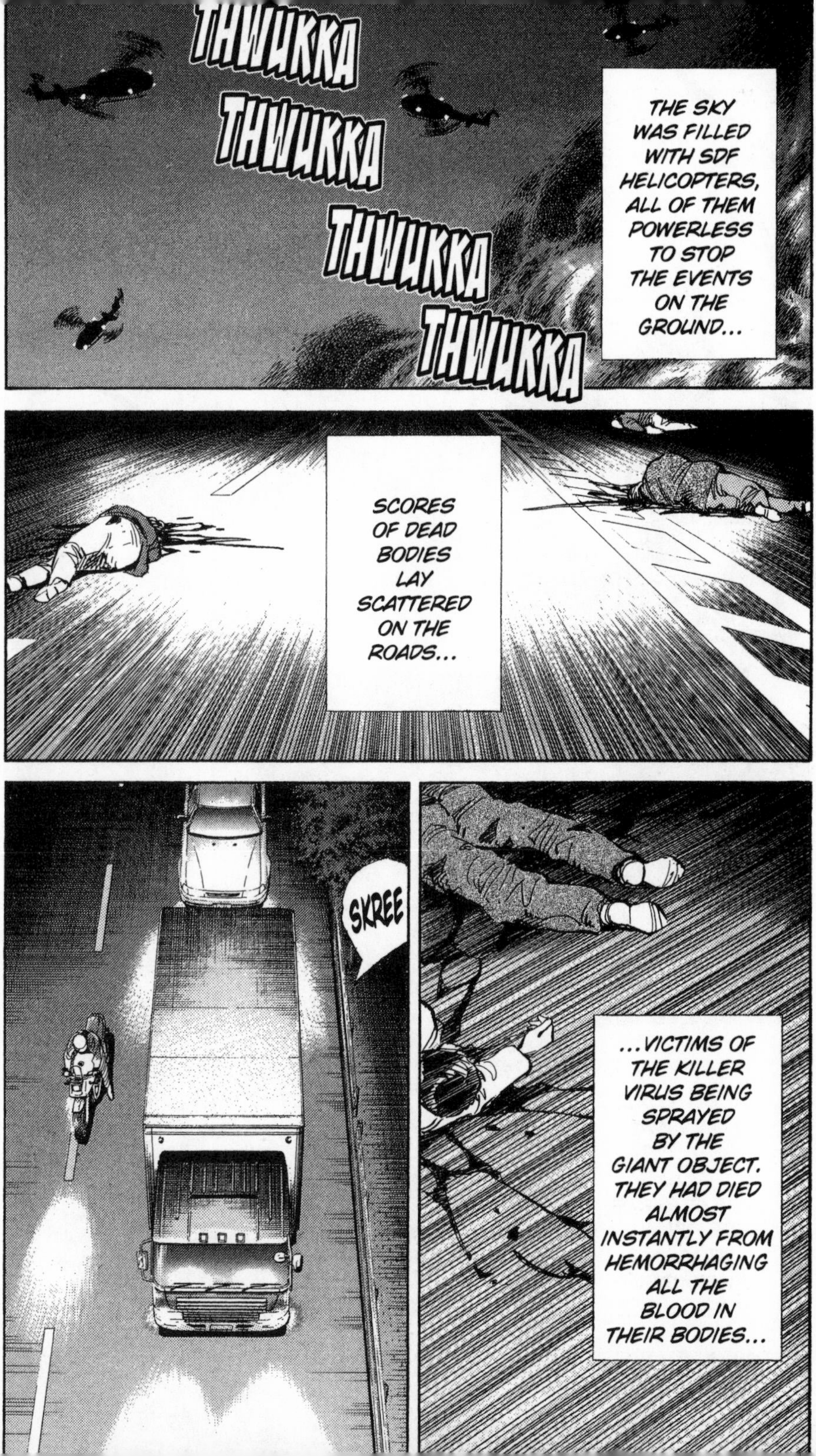
THWUKKA
THWUKKA
THWUKKA
THWUKKA
THE SKY WAS FILLED WITH SDF HELICOPTERS, ALL OF THEM POWERLESS TO STOP THE EVENTS ON THE GROUND...
SCORES OF DEAD BODIES LAY SCATTERED ON THE ROADS...
...VICTIMS OF THE KILLER VIRUS BEING SPRAYED BY THE GIANT OBJECT. THEY HAD DIED ALMOST INSTANTLY FROM HEMORRHAGING ALL THE BLOOD IN THEIR BODIES...
SKREE

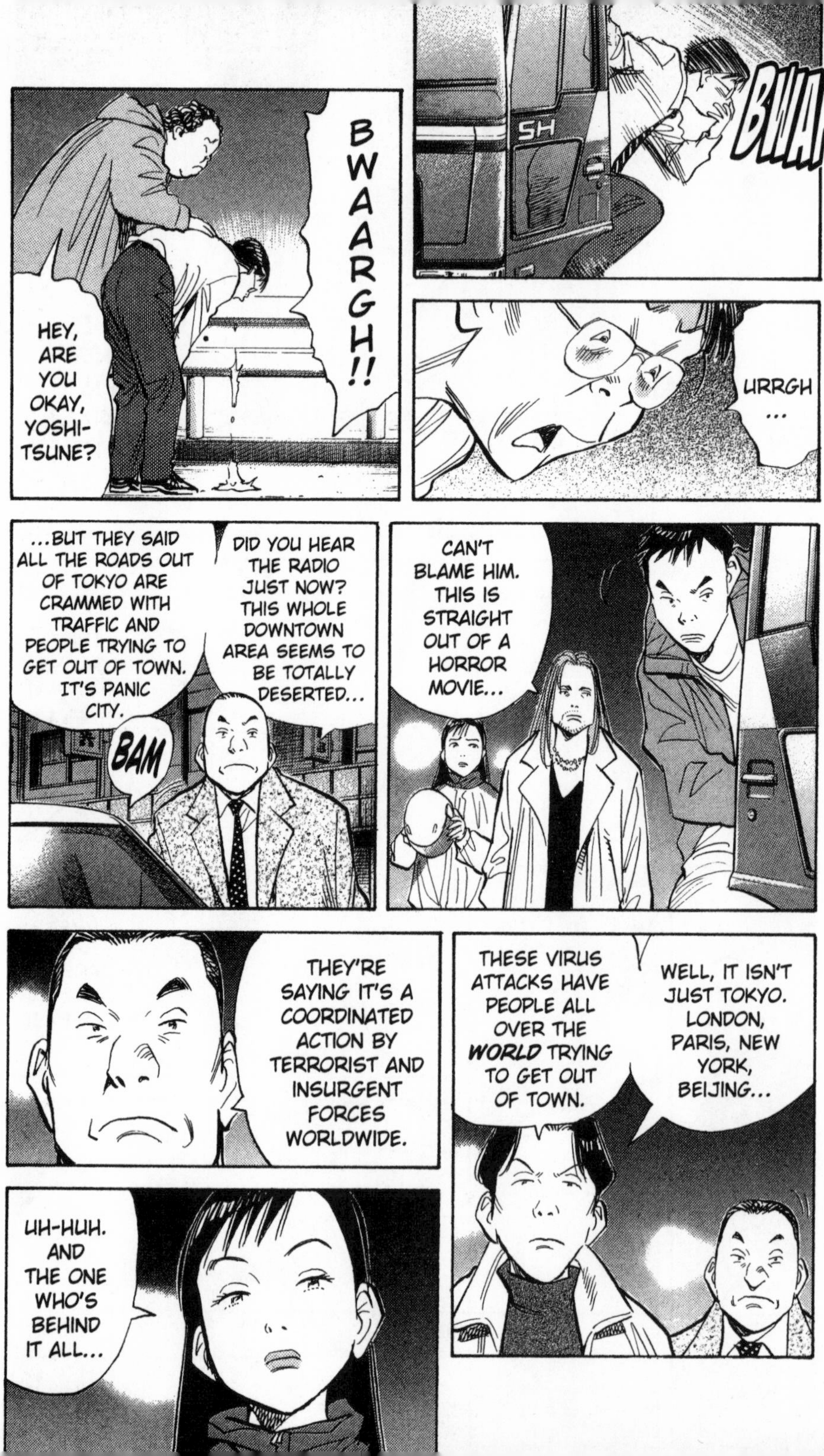
BWAP
URRGH...
BWAARGH!!
HEY, ARE YOU OKAY, YOSHI-TSUNE?
CAN'T BLAME HIM. THIS IS STRAIGHT OUT OF A HORROR MOVIE...
DID YOU HEAR THE RADIO JUST NOW? THIS WHOLE DOWNTOWN AREA SEEMS TO BE TOTALLY DESERTED...
...BUT THEY SAID ALL THE ROADS OUT OF TOKYO ARE CRAMMED WITH TRAFFIC AND PEOPLE TRYING TO GET OUT OF TOWN. IT'S PANIC CITY.
BAM
WELL, IT ISN'T JUST TOKYO. LONDON, PARIS, NEW YORK, BEIJING...
THESE VIRUS ATTACKS HAVE PEOPLE ALL OVER THE WORLD TRYING TO GET OUT OF TOWN.
THEY'RE SAYING IT'S A COORDINATED ACTION BY TERRORIST AND INSURGENT FORCES WORLDWIDE.
UH-HUH. AND THE ONE WHO'S BEHIND IT ALL...

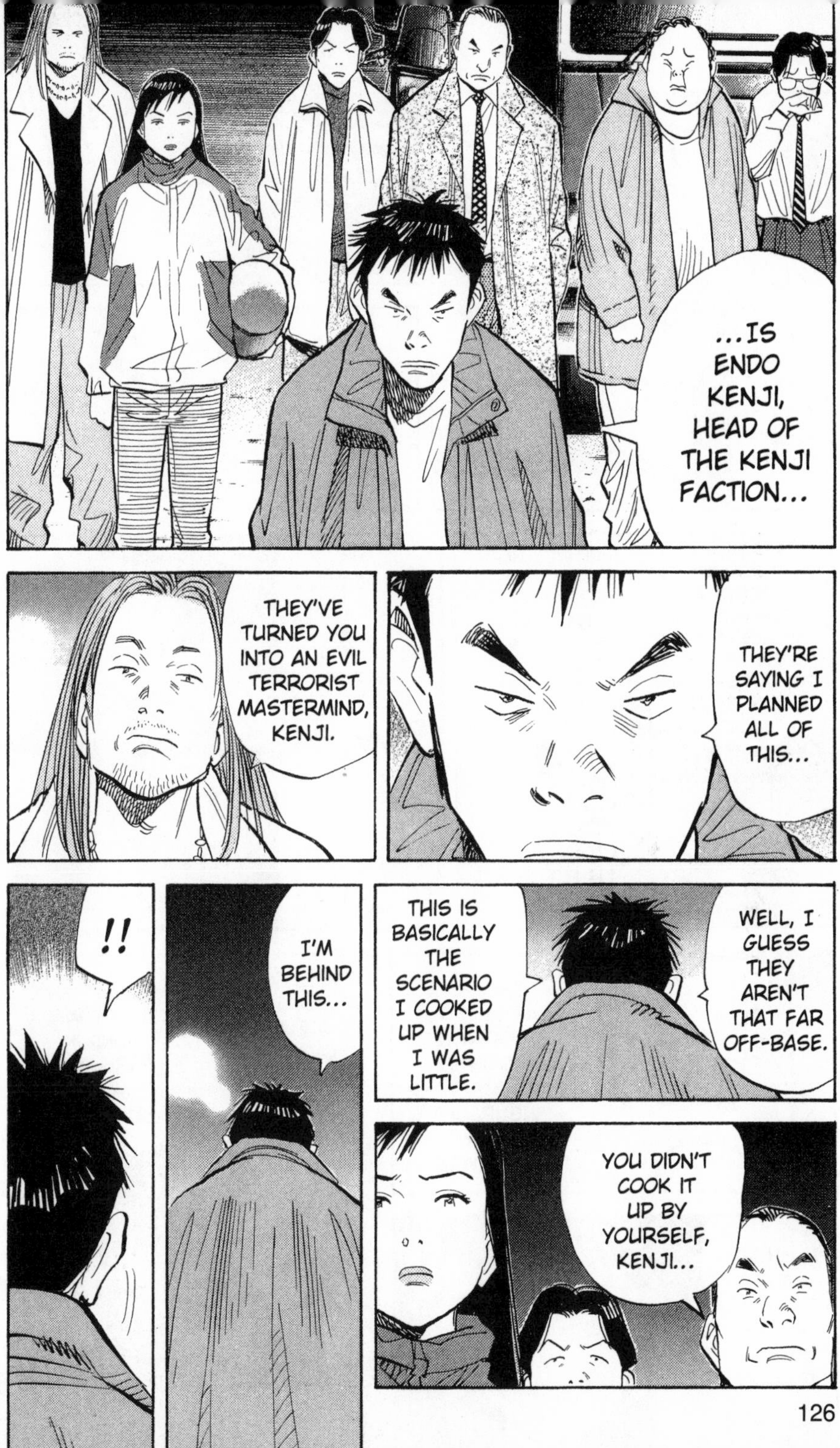
...IS ENDO KENJI, HEAD OF THE KENJI FACTION...
THEY'RE SAYING I PLANNED ALL OF THIS...
THEY'VE TURNED YOU INTO AN EVIL TERRORIST MASTERMIND, KENJI.
WELL, I GUESS THEY AREN'T THAT FAR OFF-BASE.
THIS IS BASICALLY THE SCENARIO I COOKED UP WHEN I WAS LITTLE.
YOU DIDN'T COOK IT UP BY YOURSELF, KENJI...
I'M BEHIND THIS...
!!

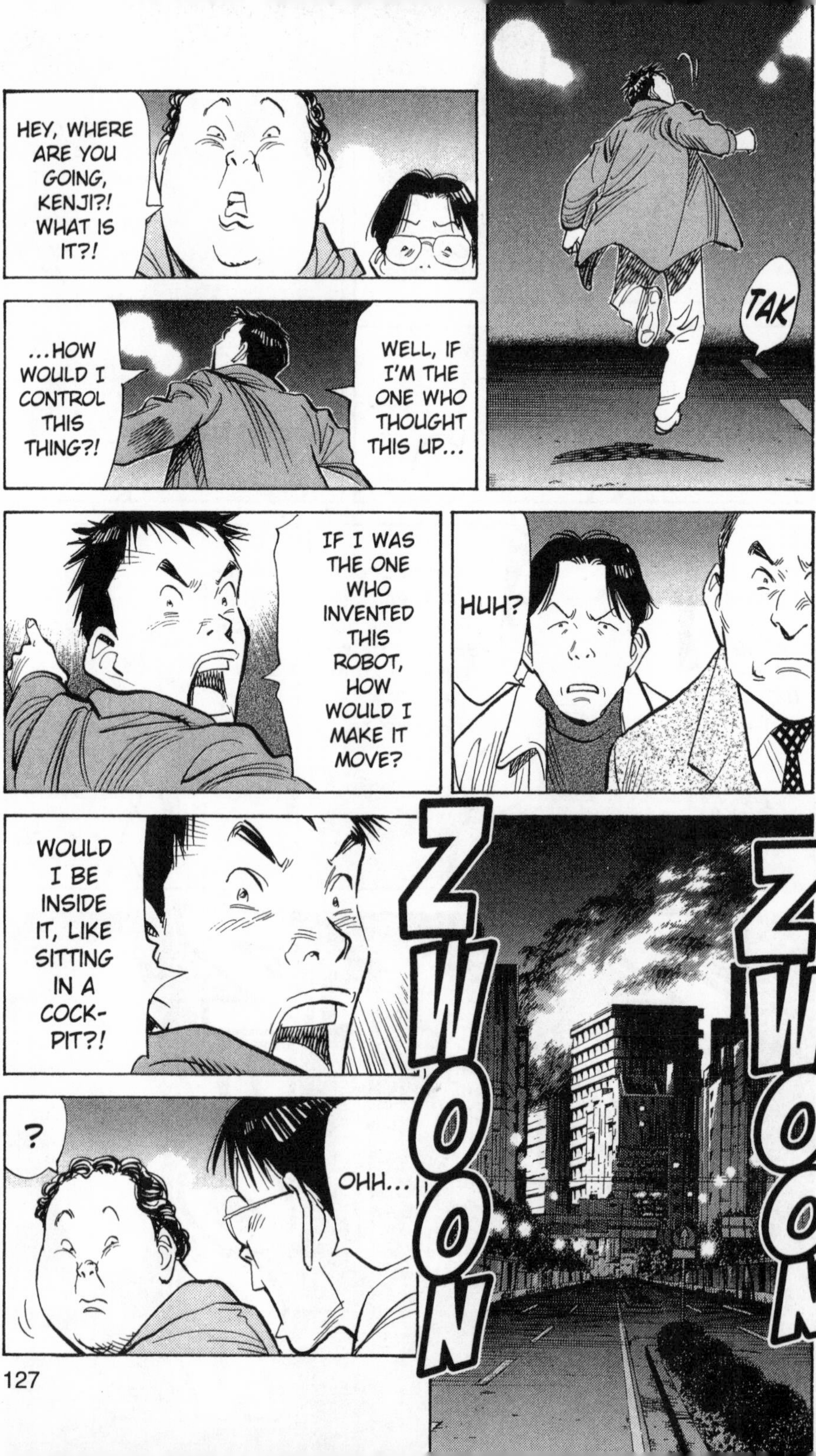
TAK
HEY, WHERE ARE YOU GOING, KENJI?! WHAT IS IT?!
WELL, IF I'M THE ONE WHO THOUGHT THIS UP...
...HOW WOULD I CONTROL THIS THING?!
HUH?
IF I WAS THE ONE WHO INVENTED THIS ROBOT, HOW WOULD I MAKE IT MOVE?
ZWOON
ZWOON
WOULD I BE INSIDE IT, LIKE SITTING IN A COCK-PIT?!
OHH...
?

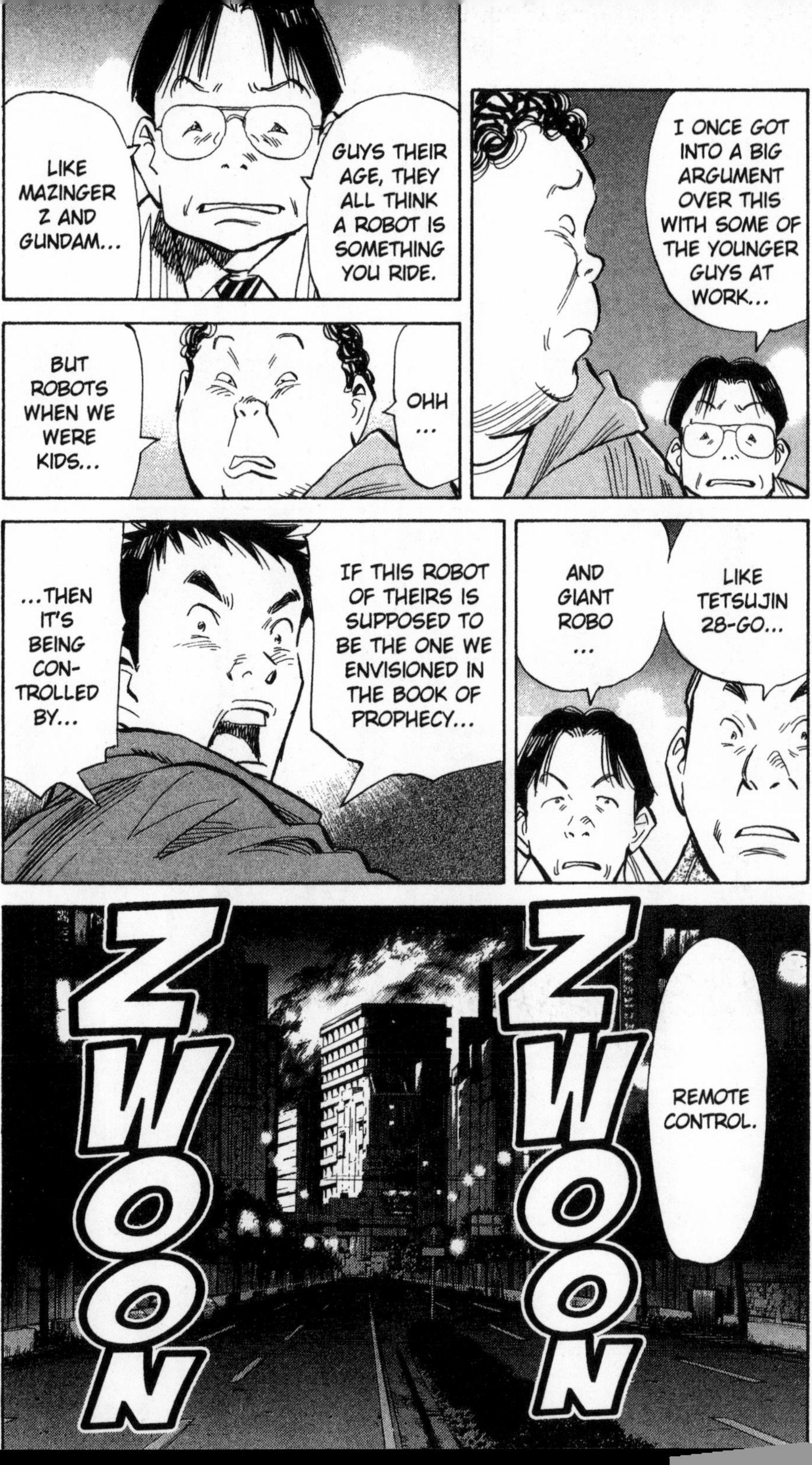
I ONCE GOT INTO A BIG ARGUMENT OVER THIS WITH SOME OF THE YOUNGER GUYS AT WORK...
GUYS THEIR AGE, THEY ALL THINK A ROBOT IS SOMETHING YOU RIDE.
LIKE MAZINGER Z AND GUNDAM...
OHH ...
BUT ROBOTS WHEN WE WERE KIDS...
LIKE TETSUJIN 28-GO...
AND GIANT ROBO ...
IF THIS ROBOT OF THEIRS IS SUPPOSED TO BE THE ONE WE ENVISIONED IN THE BOOK OF PROPHECY...
...THEN IT'S BEING CON-TROLLED BY...
REMOTE CONTROL.
ZWOON
ZWOON

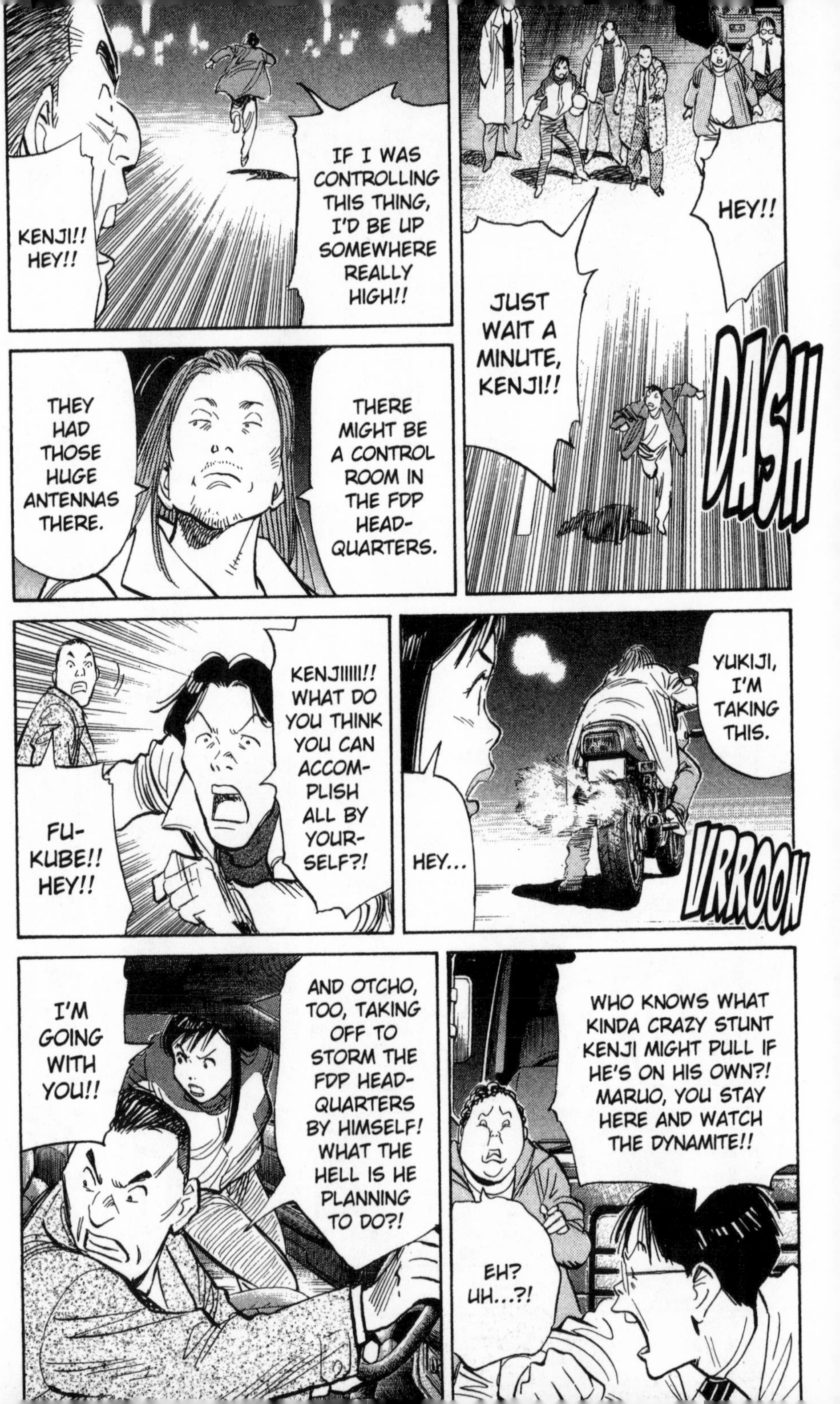
HEY!!
JUST WAIT A MINUTE, KENJI!!
DASH
IF I WAS CONTROLLING THIS THING, I'D BE UP SOMEWHERE REALLY HIGH!!
KENJI!! HEY!!
THERE MIGHT BE A CONTROL ROOM IN THE FDP HEAD-QUARTERS.
THEY HAD THOSE HUGE ANTENNAS THERE.
YUKIJI, I'M TAKING THIS.
VRROOM
HEY...
KENJIIIII!! WHAT DO YOU THINK YOU CAN ACCOM-PLISH ALL BY YOUR-SELF?!
FU-KUBE!! HEY!!
WHO KNOWS WHAT KINDA CRAZY STUNT KENJI MIGHT PULL IF HE'S ON HIS OWN?! MARUO, YOU STAY HERE AND WATCH THE DYNAMITE!!
EH? UH...?!
AND OTCHO, TOO, TAKING OFF TO STORM THE FDP HEAD-QUARTERS BY HIMSELF! WHAT THE HELL IS HE PLANNING TO DO?!
I'M GOING WITH YOU!!

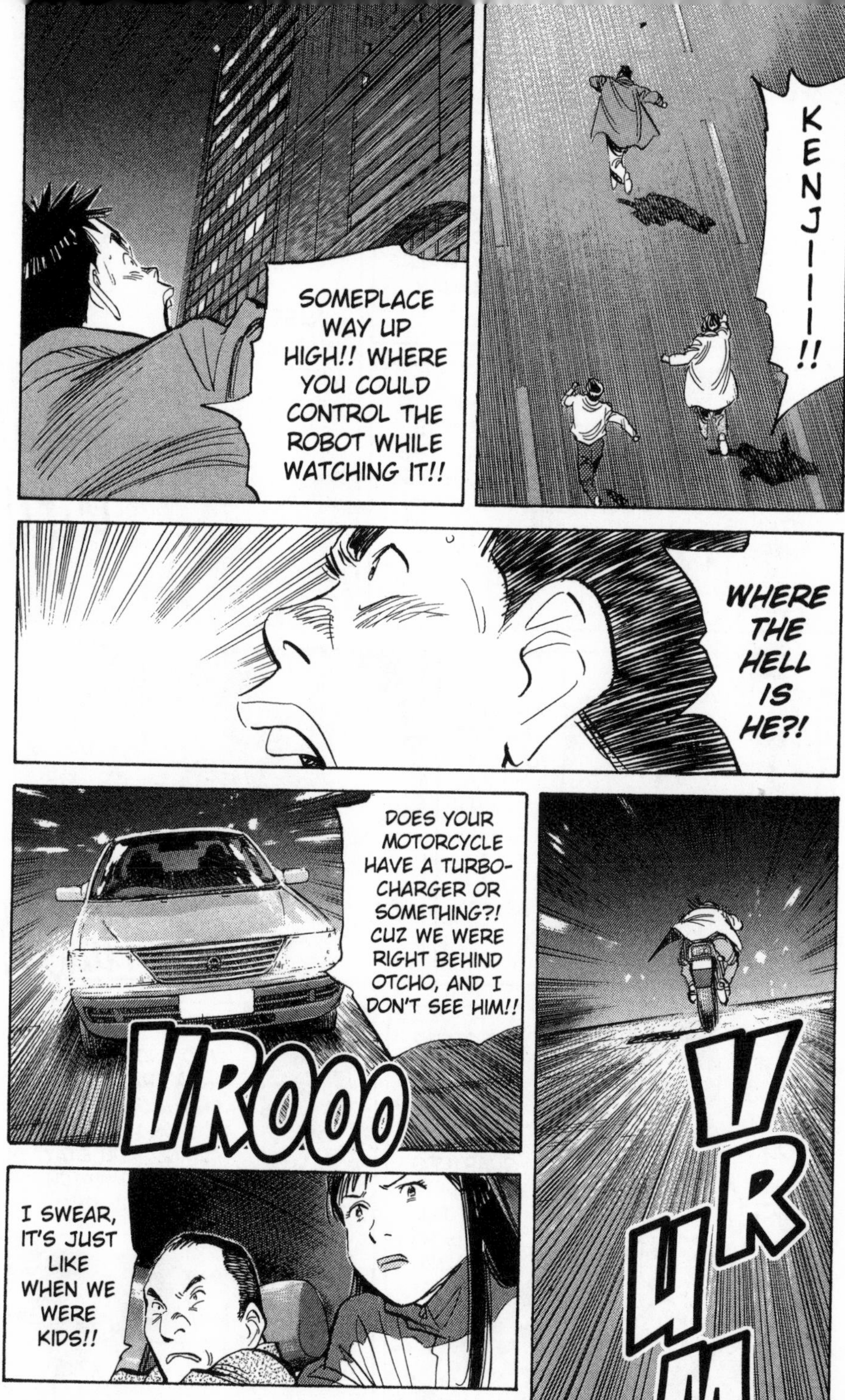
KENJIIIII!!
SOMEPLACE WAY UP HIGH!! WHERE YOU COULD CONTROL THE ROBOT WHILE WATCHING IT!!
WHERE THE HELL IS HE?!
VRUMM
DOES YOUR MOTORCYCLE HAVE A TURBO-CHARGER OR SOMETHING?! CUZ WE WERE RIGHT BEHIND OTCHO, AND I DON'T SEE HIM!!
VROOO
I SWEAR, IT'S JUST LIKE WHEN WE WERE KIDS!!

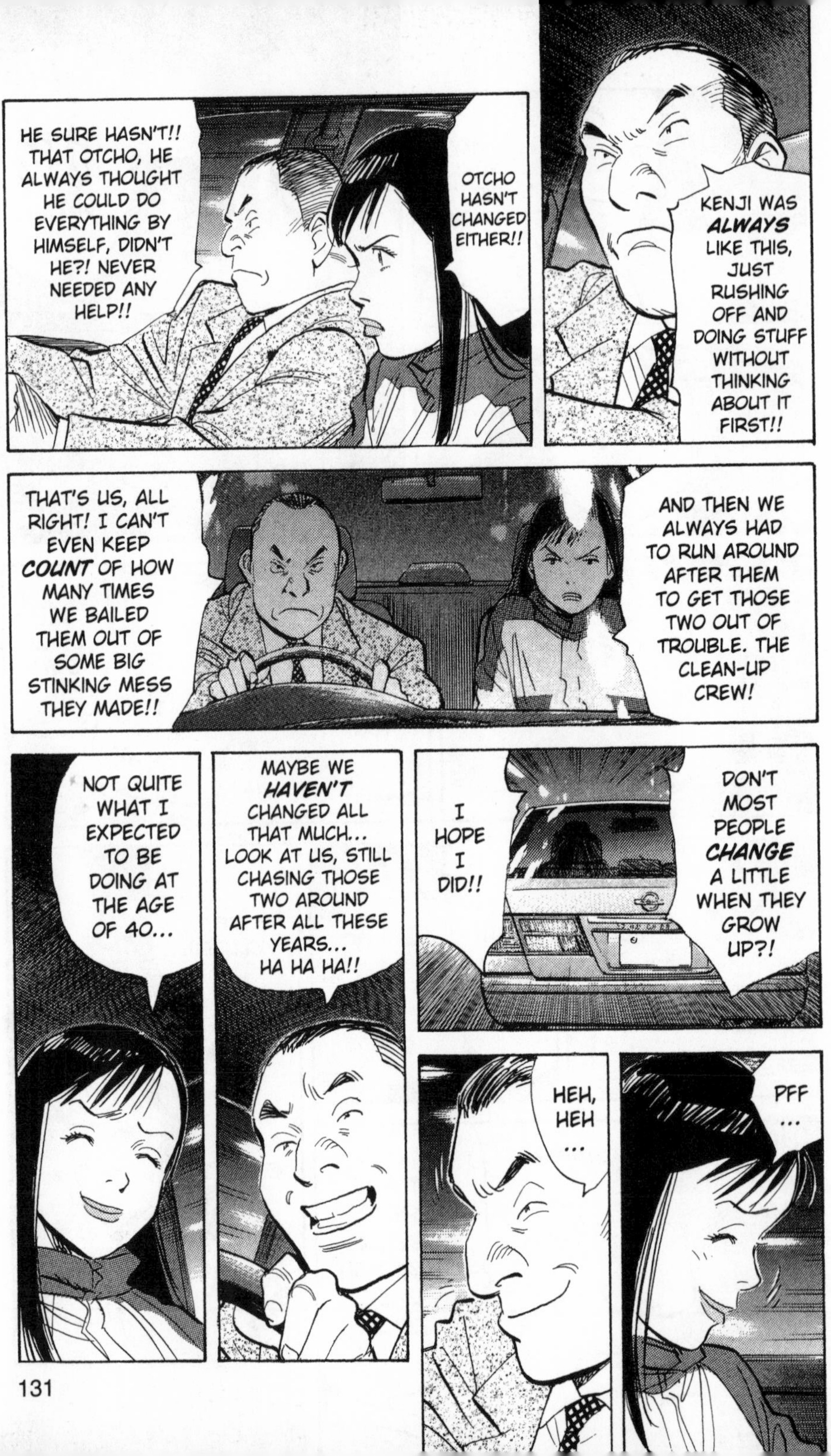
KENJI WAS ALWAYS LIKE THIS, JUST RUSHING OFF AND DOING STUFF WITHOUT THINKING ABOUT IT FIRST!!
OTCHO HASN'T CHANGED EITHER!!
HE SURE HASN'T!! THAT OTCHO, HE ALWAYS THOUGHT HE COULD DO EVERYTHING BY HIMSELF, DIDN'T HE?! NEVER NEEDED ANY HELP!!
AND THEN WE ALWAYS HAD TO RUN AROUND AFTER THEM TO GET THOSE TWO OUT OF TROUBLE. THE CLEAN-UP CREW!
THAT'S US, ALL RIGHT! I CAN'T EVEN KEEP COUNT OF HOW MANY TIMES WE BAILED THEM OUT OF SOME BIG STINKING MESS THEY MADE!!
DON'T MOST PEOPLE CHANGE A LITTLE WHEN THEY GROW UP?!
I HOPE I DID!!
PFF ...
HEH, HEH ...
MAYBE WE HAVEN'T CHANGED ALL THAT MUCH... LOOK AT US, STILL CHASING THOSE TWO AROUND AFTER ALL THESE YEARS... HA HA HA!!
NOT QUITE WHAT I EXPECTED TO BE DOING AT THE AGE OF 40...

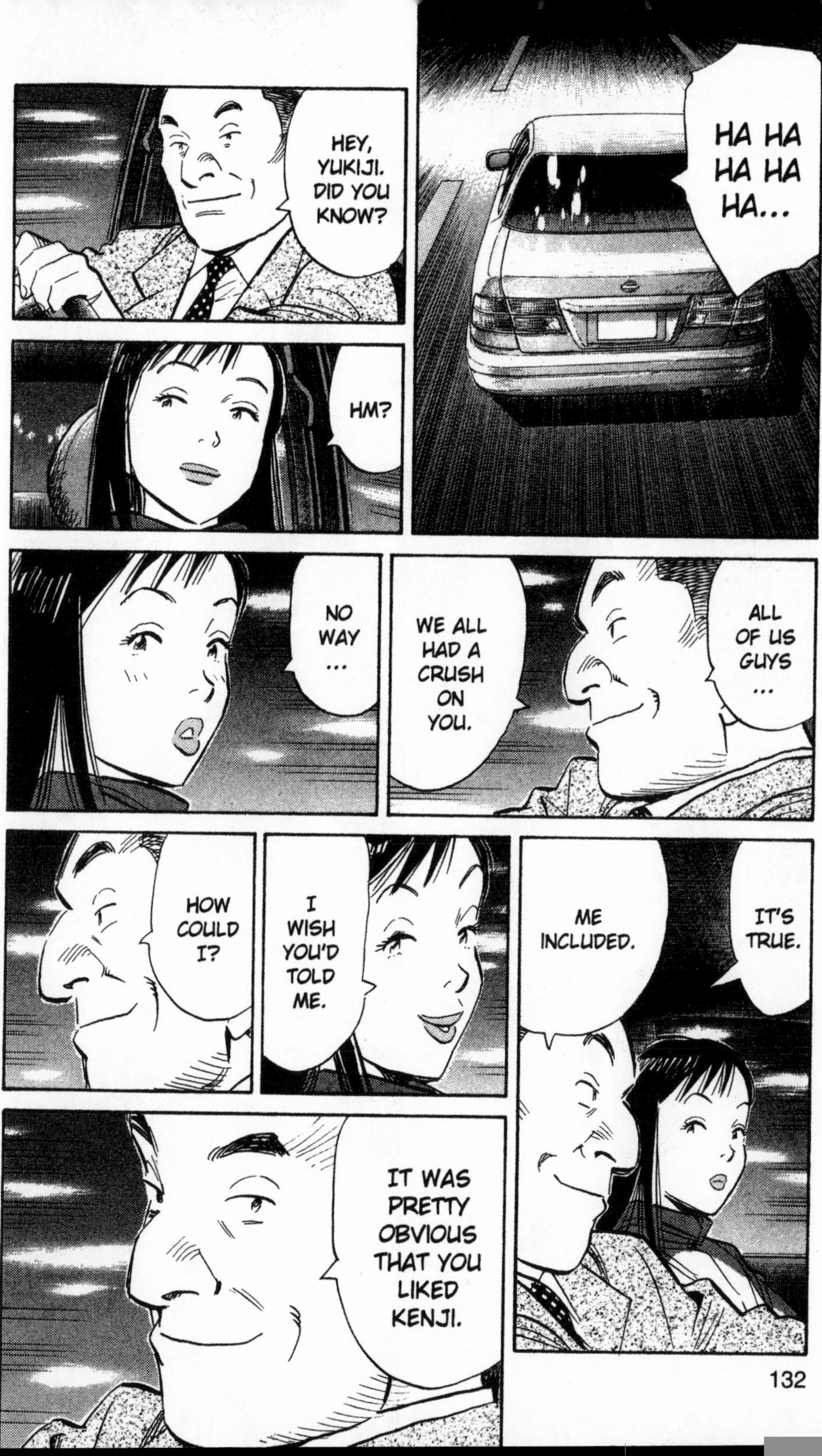
HA HA HA HA HA...
HEY, YUKIJI. DID YOU KNOW?
HM?
ALL OF US GUYS ...
WE ALL HAD A CRUSH ON YOU.
NO WAY ...
IT'S TRUE.
ME INCLUDED.
I WISH YOU'D TOLD ME.
HOW COULD I?
IT WAS PRETTY OBVIOUS THAT YOU LIKED KENJI.

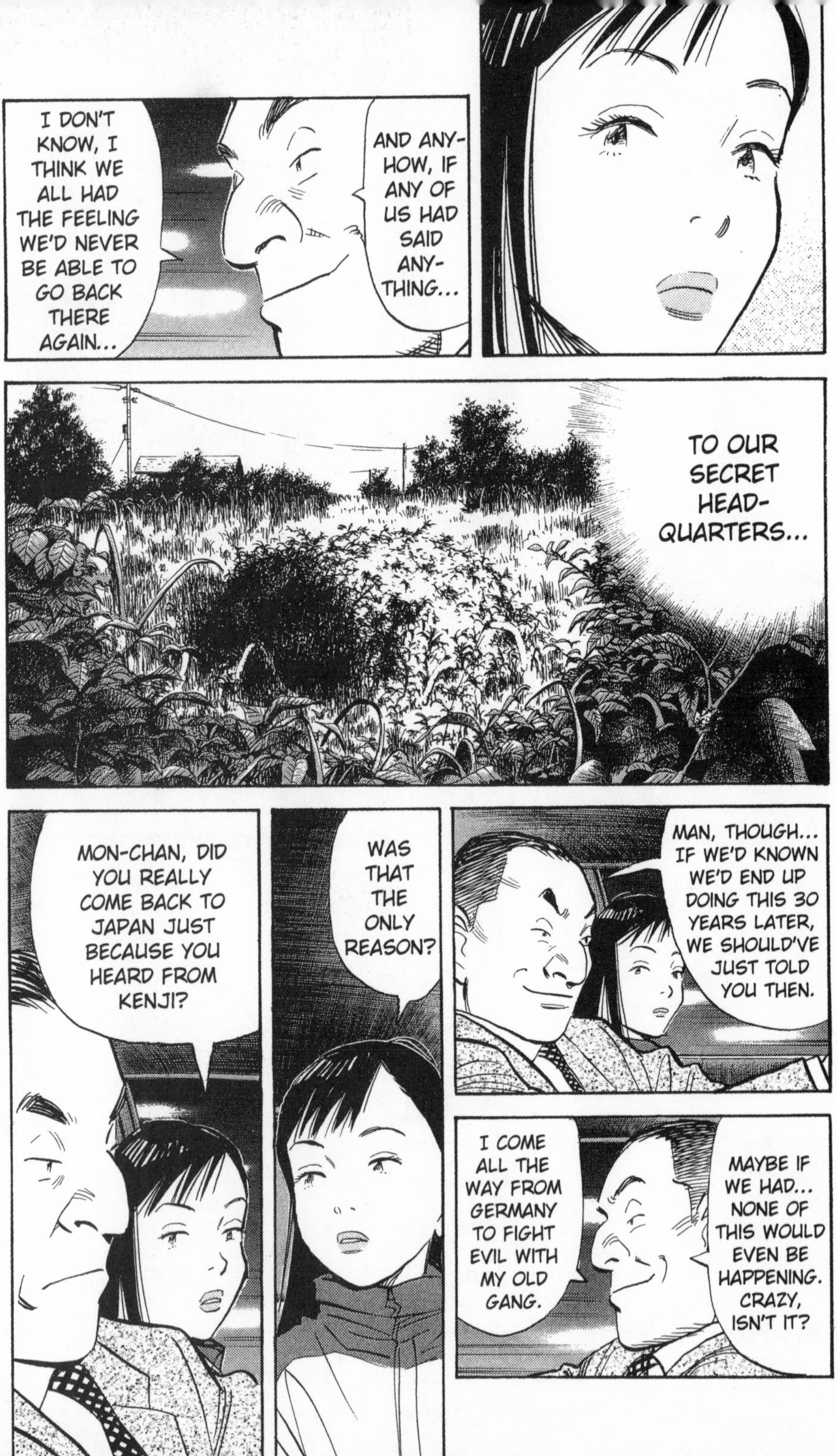
AND ANYHOW, IF ANY OF US HAD SAID ANYTHING...
I DON'T KNOW, I THINK WE ALL HAD THE FEELING WE'D NEVER BE ABLE TO GO BACK THERE AGAIN...
TO OUR SECRET HEADQUARTERS...
MAN, THOUGH... IF WE'D KNOWN WE'D END UP DOING THIS 30 YEARS LATER, WE SHOULD'VE JUST TOLD YOU THEN.
MAYBE IF WE HAD... NONE OF THIS WOULD EVEN BE HAPPENING. CRAZY, ISN'T IT?
I COME ALL THE WAY FROM GERMANY TO FIGHT EVIL WITH MY OLD GANG.
WAS THAT THE ONLY REASON?
MON-CHAN, DID YOU REALLY COME BACK TO JAPAN JUST BECAUSE YOU HEARD FROM KENJI?

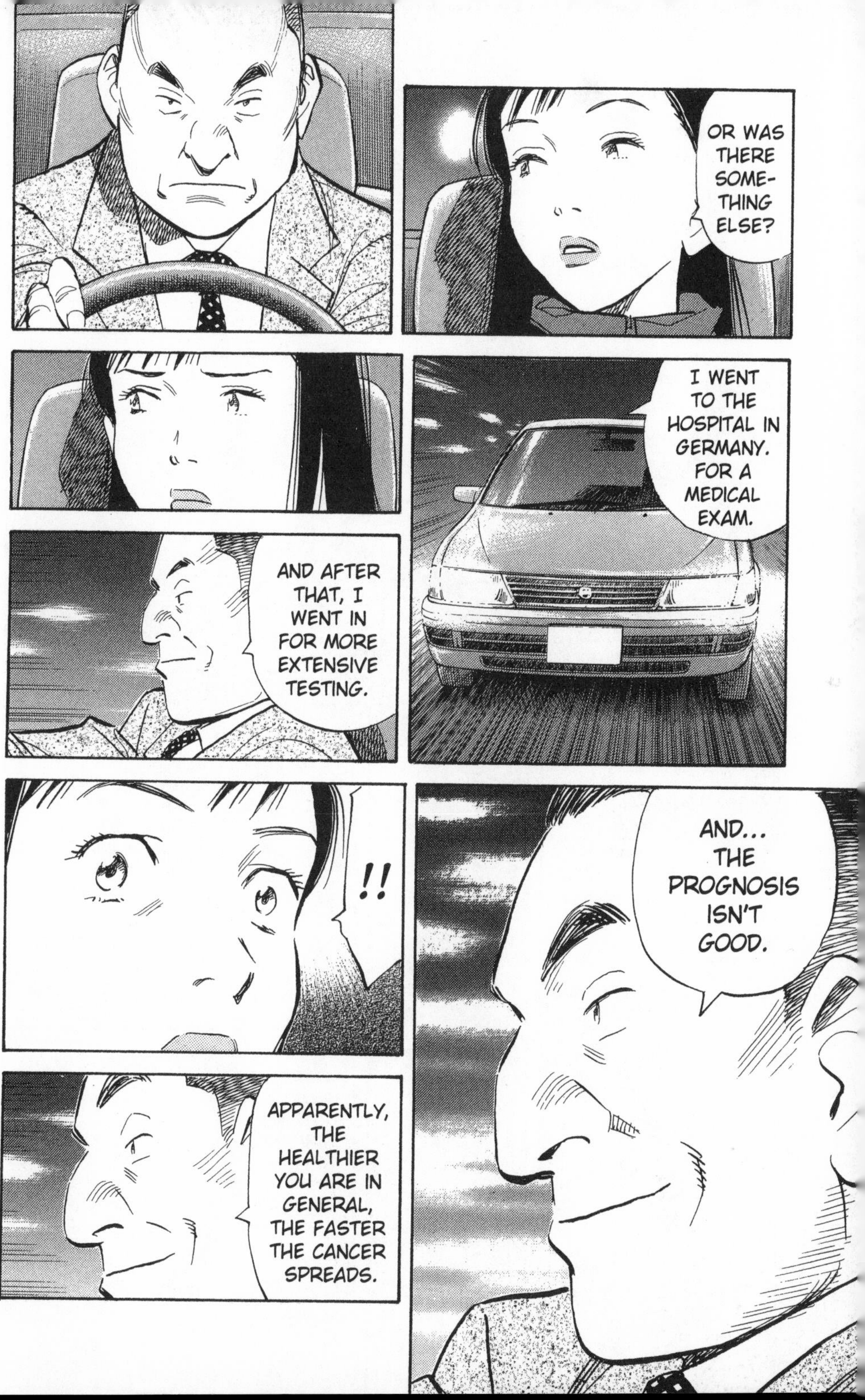
OR WAS THERE SOME-THING ELSE?
I WENT TO THE HOSPITAL IN GERMANY. FOR A MEDICAL EXAM.
AND AFTER THAT, I WENT IN FOR MORE EXTENSIVE TESTING.
AND... THE PROGNOSIS ISN'T GOOD.
!!
APPARENTLY, THE HEALTHIER YOU ARE IN GENERAL, THE FASTER THE CANCER SPREADS.

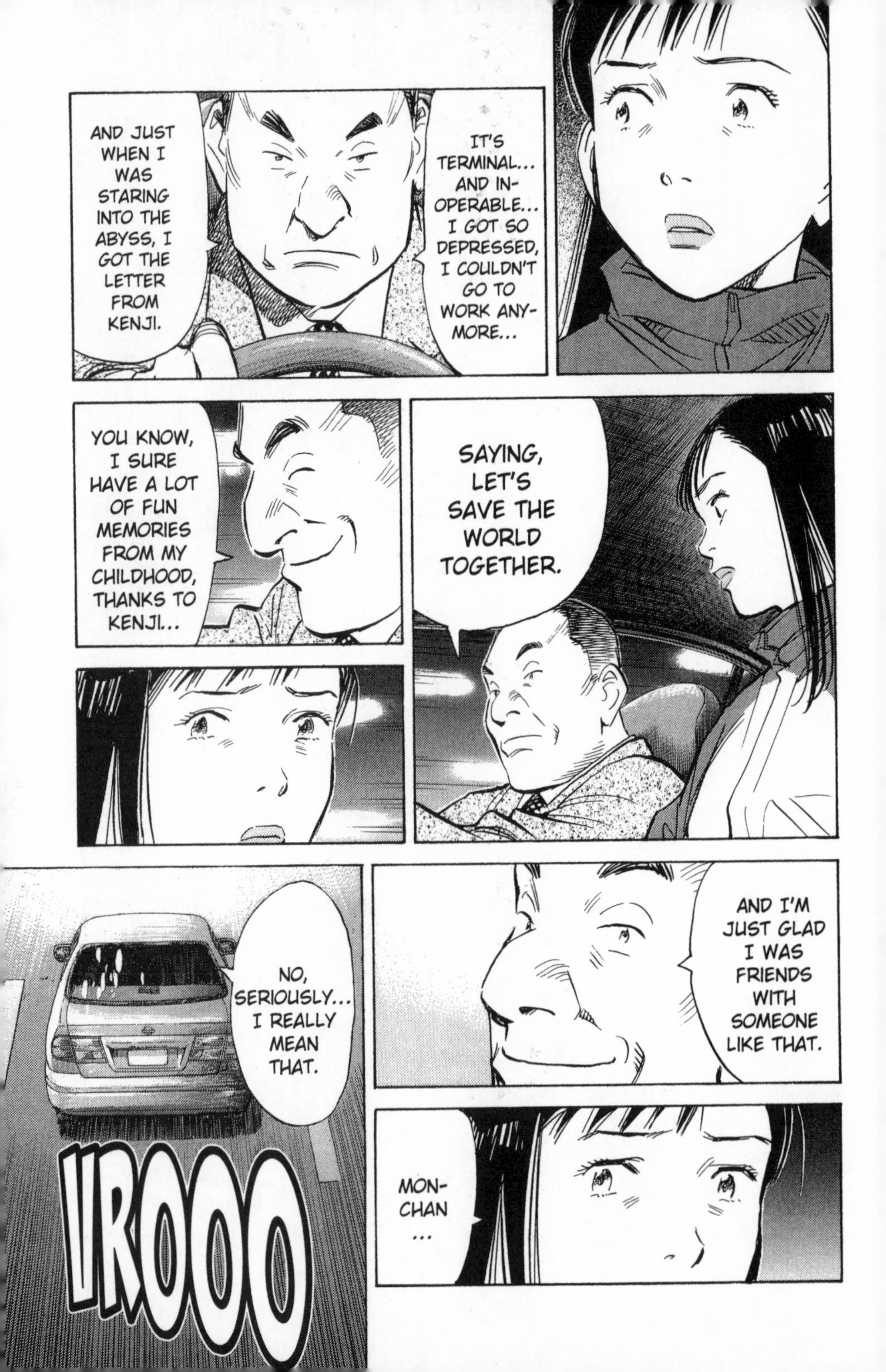
IT'S TERMINAL... AND IN-OPERABLE... I GOT SO DEPRESSED, I COULDN'T GO TO WORK ANY-MORE...
AND JUST WHEN I WAS STARING INTO THE ABYSS, I GOT THE LETTER FROM KENJI.
SAYING, LET'S SAVE THE WORLD TOGETHER.
YOU KNOW, I SURE HAVE A LOT OF FUN MEMORIES FROM MY CHILDHOOD, THANKS TO KENJI...
AND I'M JUST GLAD I WAS FRIENDS WITH SOMEONE LIKE THAT.
MON-CHAN ...
NO, SERIOUSLY... I REALLY MEAN THAT.
VROOO

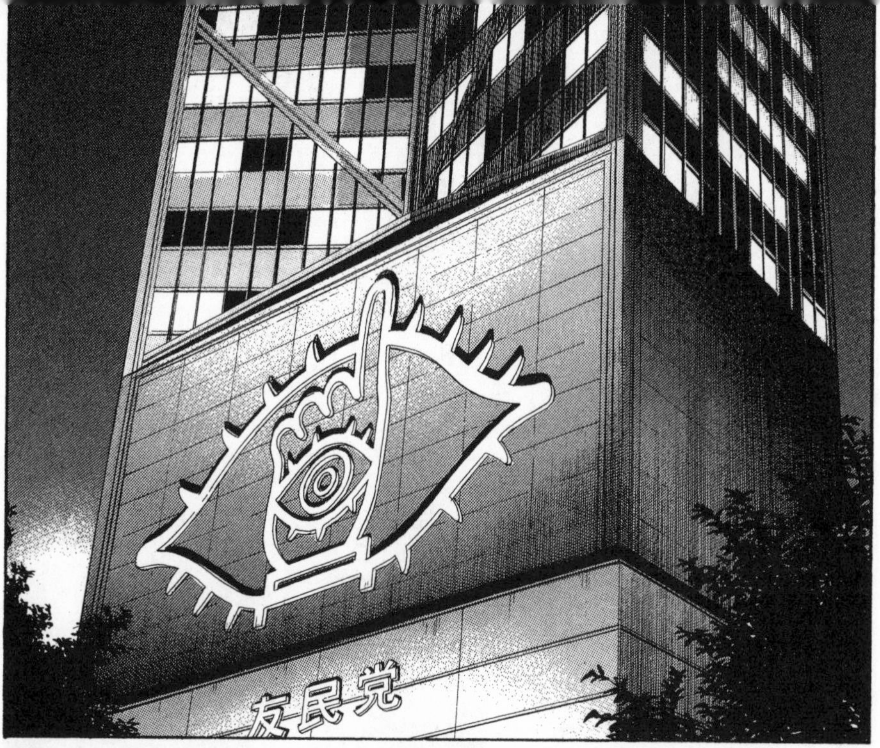
友民党

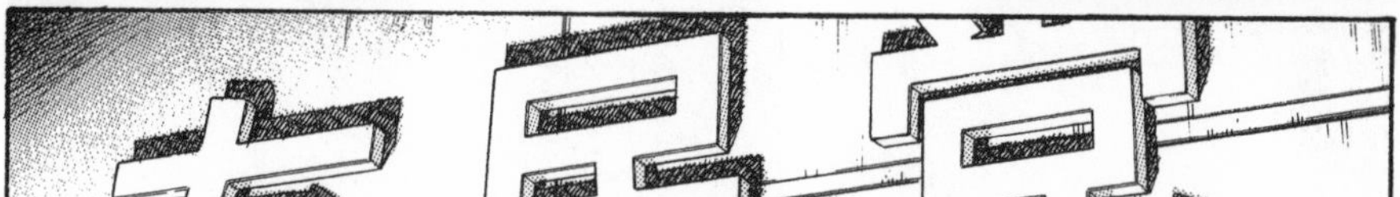
友民党

*Friendship and Democracy Party

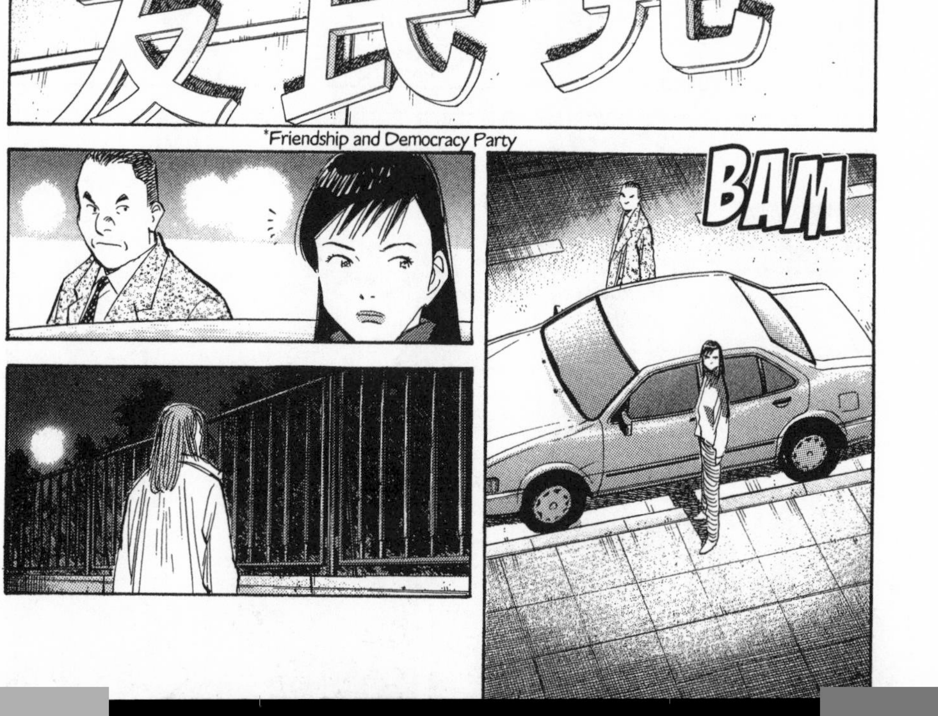
BAM

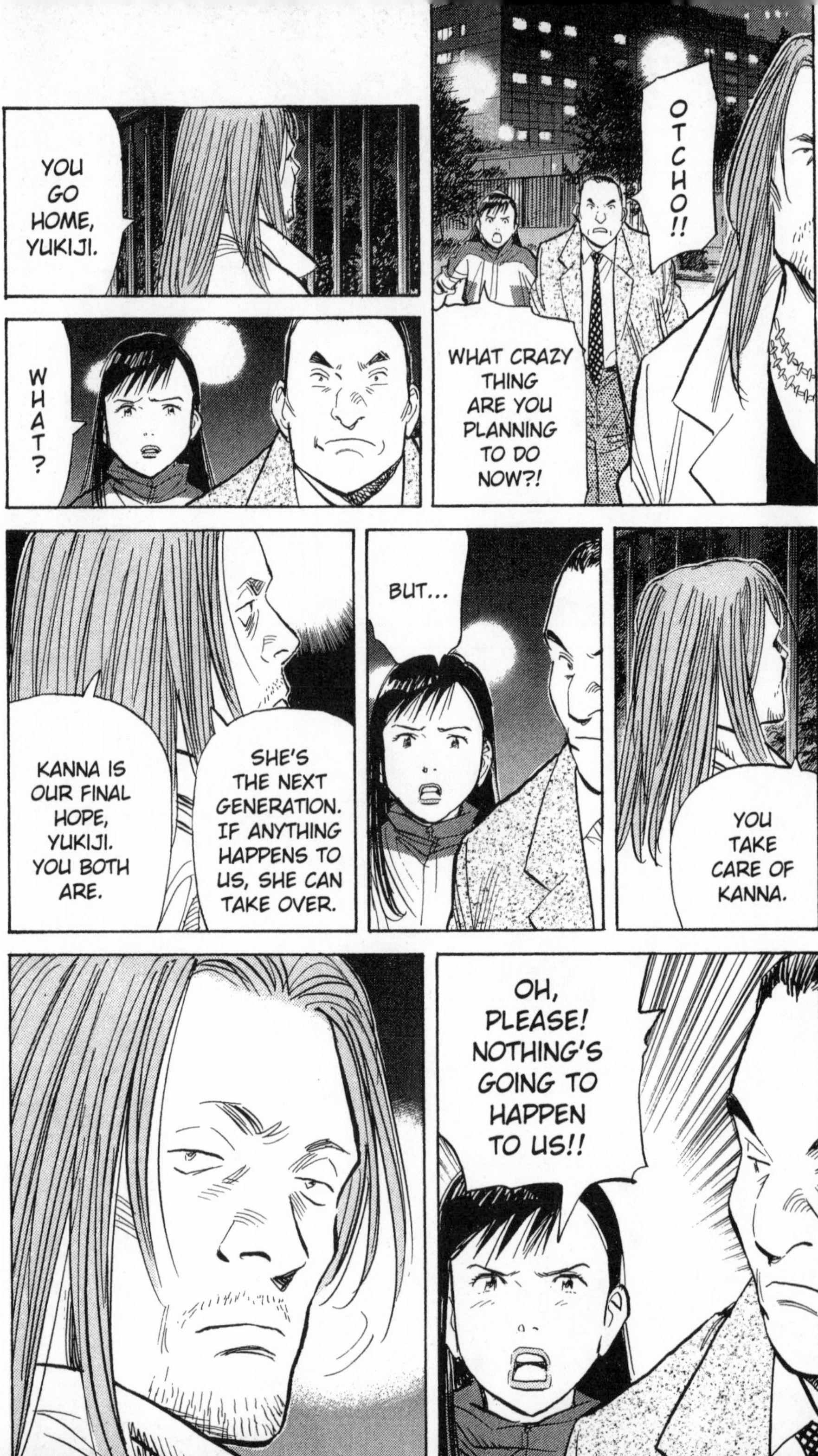
OTCHO!!
WHAT CRAZY THING ARE YOU PLANNING TO DO NOW?!
YOU GO HOME, YUKIJI.
WHAT?
YOU TAKE CARE OF KANNA.
BUT...
SHE'S THE NEXT GENERATION. IF ANYTHING HAPPENS TO US, SHE CAN TAKE OVER.
KANNA IS OUR FINAL HOPE, YUKIJI. YOU BOTH ARE.
OH, PLEASE! NOTHING'S GOING TO HAPPEN TO US!!

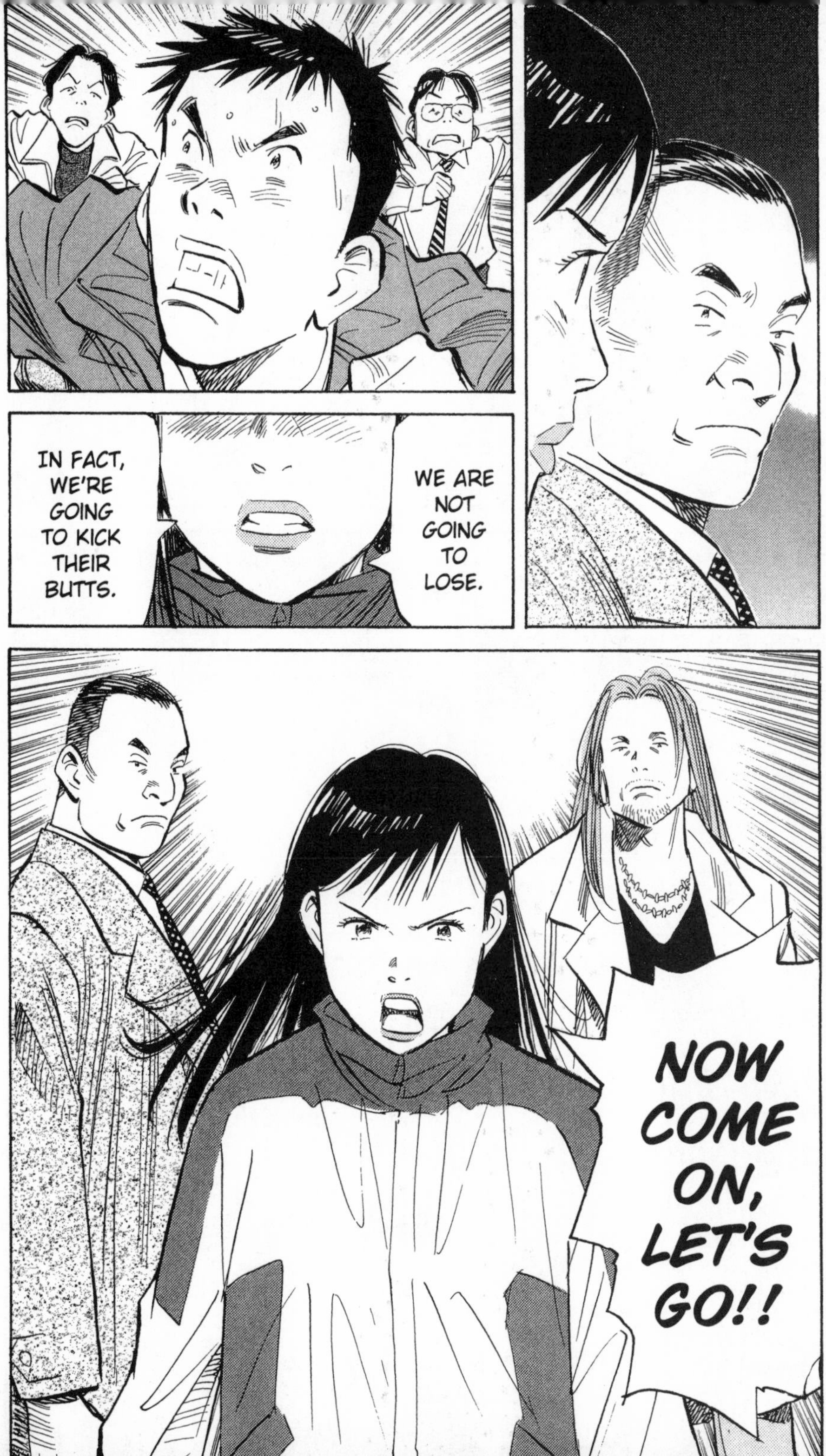
WE ARE NOT GOING TO LOSE.
IN FACT, WE'RE GOING TO KICK THEIR BUTTS.
NOW COME ON, LET'S GO!!

Chapter 8 Control Room

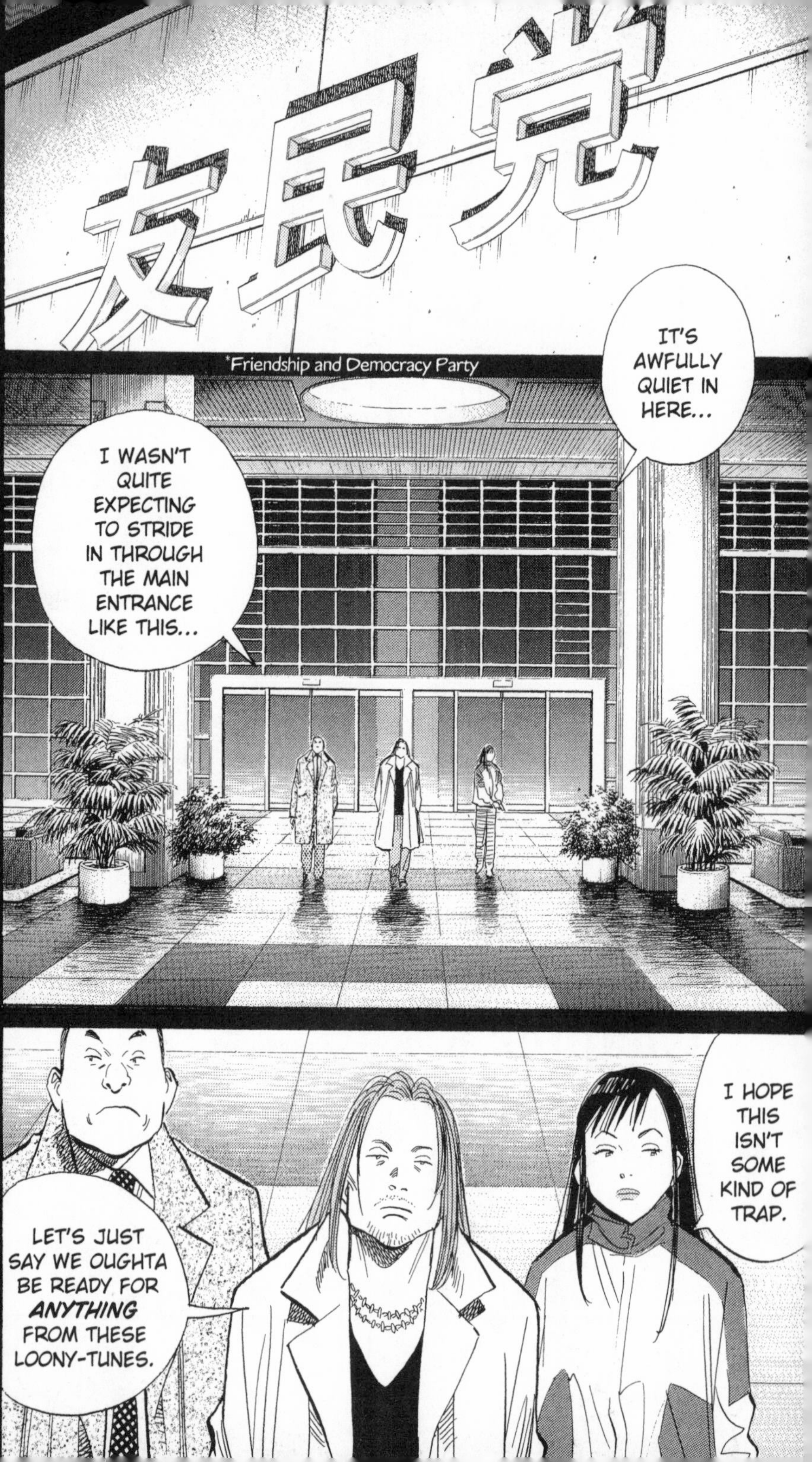
友民党
*Friendship and Democracy Party
IT'S AWFULLY QUIET IN HERE...
I WASN'T QUITE EXPECTING TO STRIDE IN THROUGH THE MAIN ENTRANCE LIKE THIS...
I HOPE THIS ISN'T SOME KIND OF TRAP.
LET'S JUST SAY WE OUGHTA BE READY FOR ***ANYTHING*** FROM THESE LOONY-TUNES.

Chapter 8
Control Room

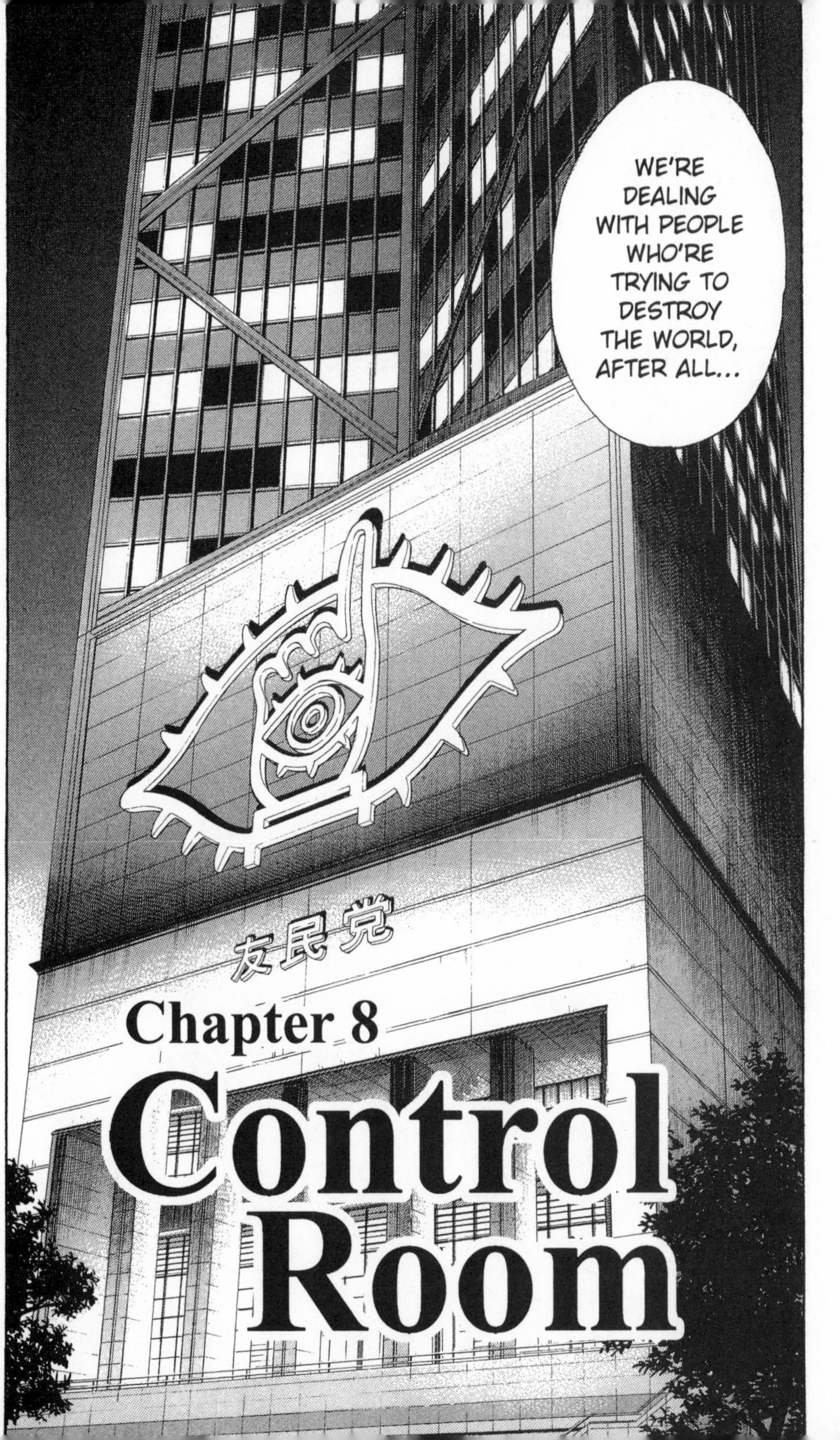
WE'RE DEALING WITH PEOPLE WHO'RE TRYING TO DESTROY THE WORLD, AFTER ALL...
友民党

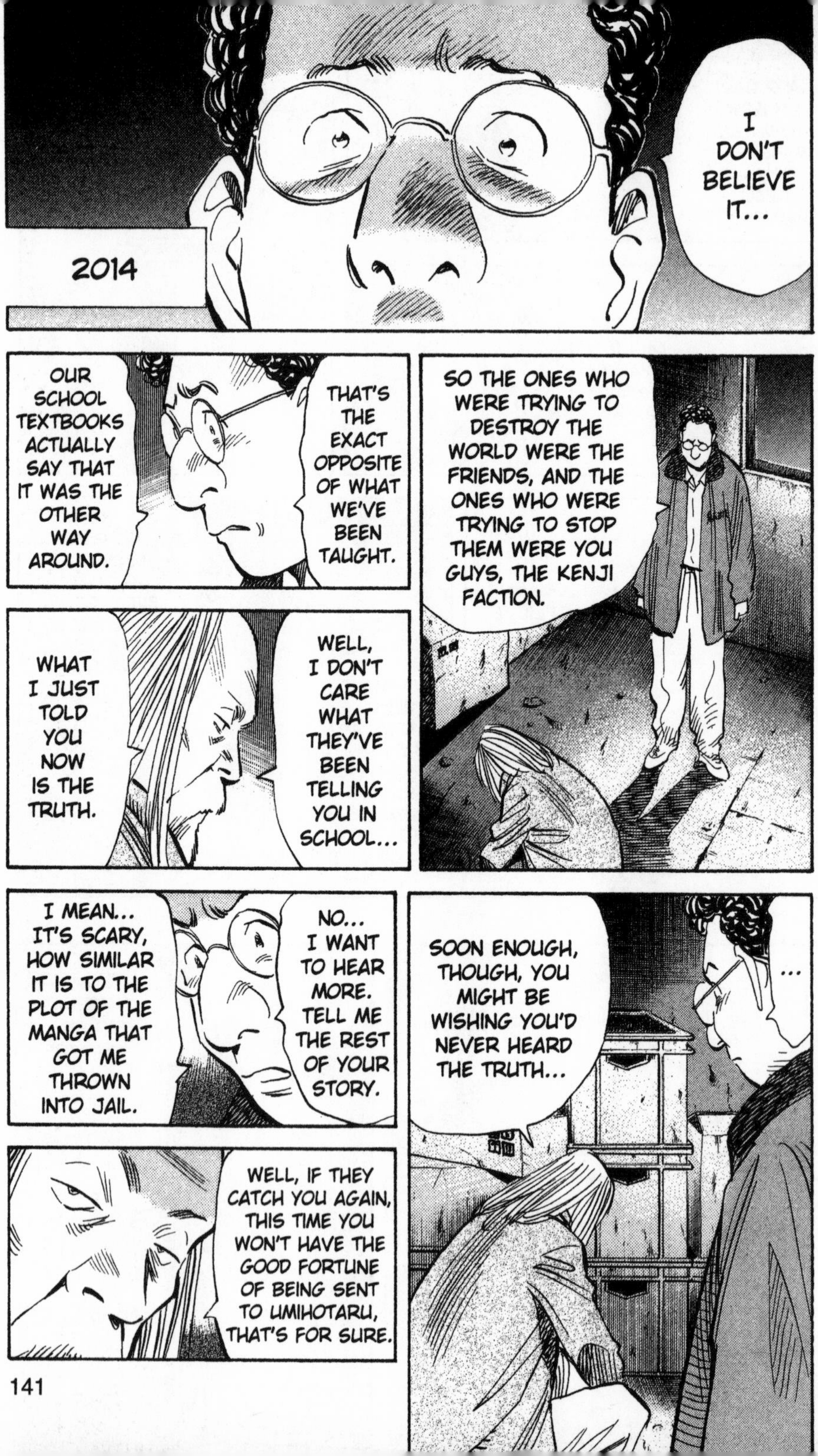
I DON'T BELIEVE IT...
2014
SO THE ONES WHO WERE TRYING TO DESTROY THE WORLD WERE THE FRIENDS, AND THE ONES WHO WERE TRYING TO STOP THEM WERE YOU GUYS, THE KENJI FACTION.
THAT'S THE EXACT OPPOSITE OF WHAT WE'VE BEEN TAUGHT.
OUR SCHOOL TEXTBOOKS ACTUALLY SAY THAT IT WAS THE OTHER WAY AROUND.
WELL, I DON'T CARE WHAT THEY'VE BEEN TELLING YOU IN SCHOOL...
WHAT I JUST TOLD YOU NOW IS THE TRUTH.
SOON ENOUGH, THOUGH, YOU MIGHT BE WISHING YOU'D NEVER HEARD THE TRUTH...
...
NO... I WANT TO HEAR MORE. TELL ME THE REST OF YOUR STORY.
I MEAN... IT'S SCARY, HOW SIMILAR IT IS TO THE PLOT OF THE MANGA THAT GOT ME THROWN INTO JAIL.
WELL, IF THEY CATCH YOU AGAIN, THIS TIME YOU WON'T HAVE THE GOOD FORTUNE OF BEING SENT TO UMIHOTARU, THAT'S FOR SURE.

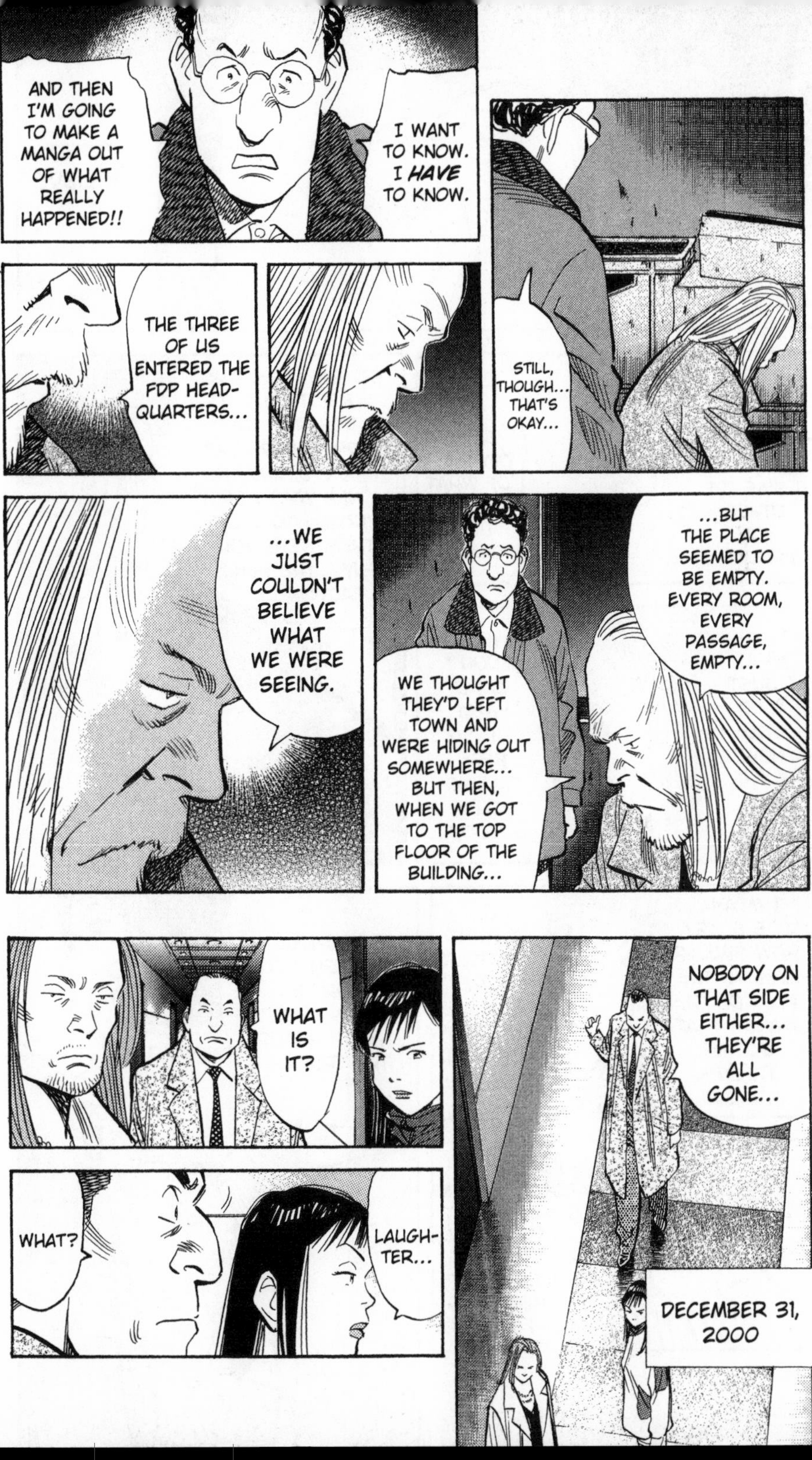
I WANT TO KNOW. I *HAVE* TO KNOW.
AND THEN I'M GOING TO MAKE A MANGA OUT OF WHAT REALLY HAPPENED!!
STILL, THOUGH... THAT'S OKAY...
THE THREE OF US ENTERED THE FDP HEAD-QUARTERS...
...BUT THE PLACE SEEMED TO BE EMPTY. EVERY ROOM, EVERY PASSAGE, EMPTY...
WE THOUGHT THEY'D LEFT TOWN AND WERE HIDING OUT SOMEWHERE... BUT THEN, WHEN WE GOT TO THE TOP FLOOR OF THE BUILDING...
...WE JUST COULDN'T BELIEVE WHAT WE WERE SEEING.
NOBODY ON THAT SIDE EITHER... THEY'RE ALL GONE...
DECEMBER 31, 2000
WHAT IS IT?
LAUGHTER...
WHAT?

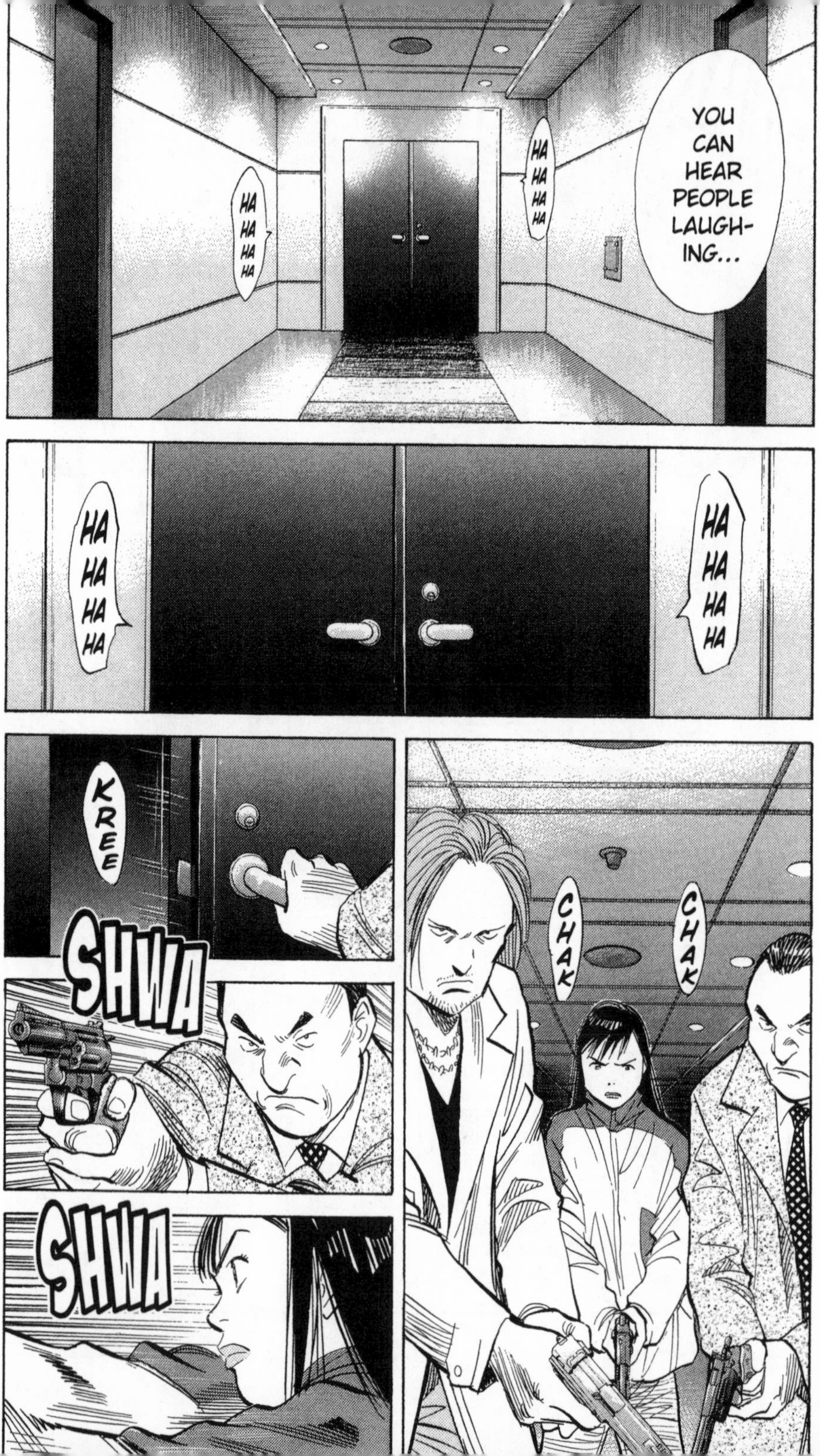
YOU CAN HEAR PEOPLE LAUGHING...
HA HA HA HA
HA HA HA HA
HA HA HA HA
HA HA HA HA
CHAK
CHAK
KREE
SHWA
SHWA

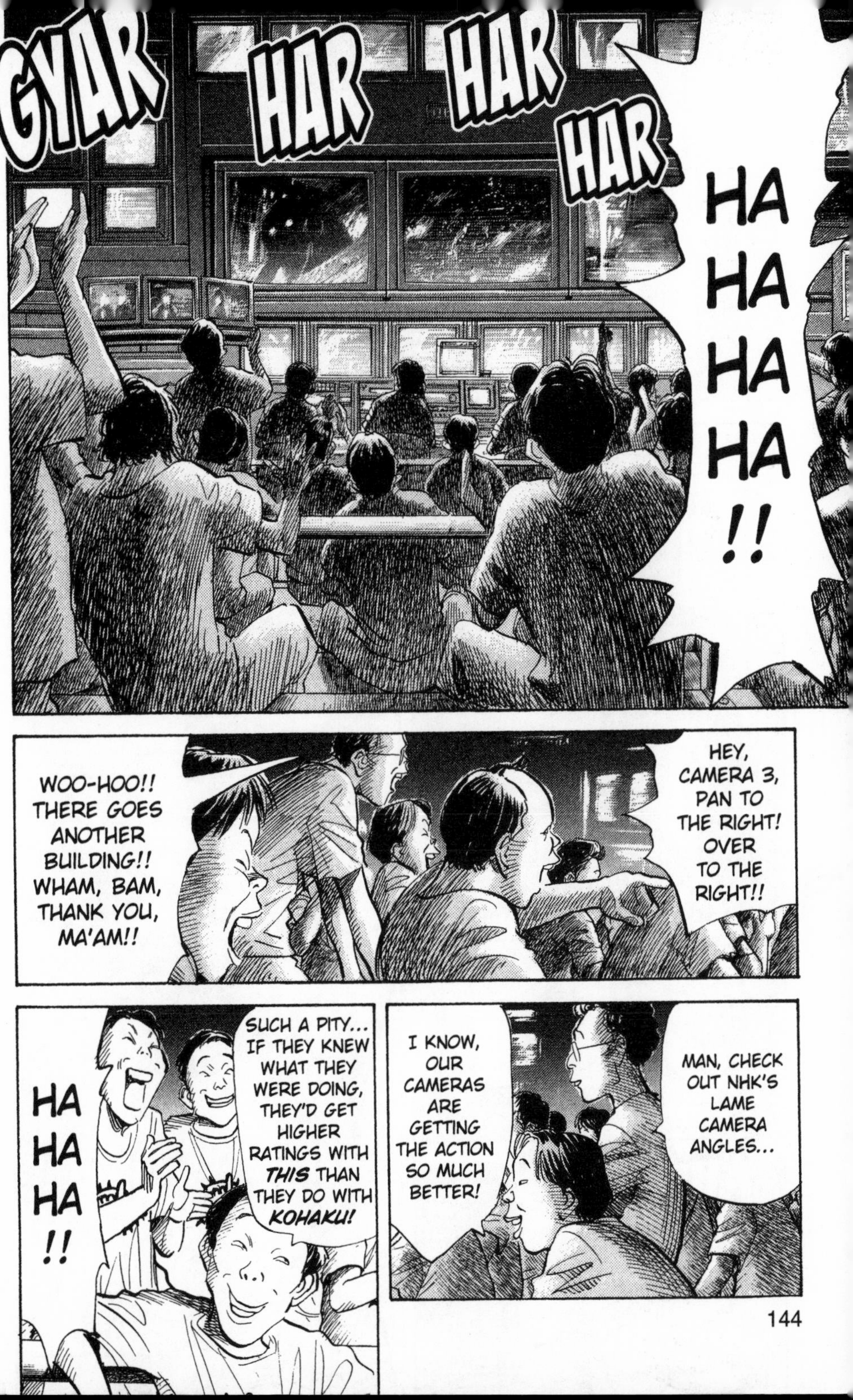
GYAR HAR HAR HAR
HA HA HA HA HA!!
HEY, CAMERA 3, PAN TO THE RIGHT! OVER TO THE RIGHT!!
WOO-HOO!! THERE GOES ANOTHER BUILDING!! WHAM, BAM, THANK YOU, MA'AM!!
MAN, CHECK OUT NHK'S LAME CAMERA ANGLES...
I KNOW, OUR CAMERAS ARE GETTING THE ACTION SO MUCH BETTER!
SUCH A PITY... IF THEY KNEW WHAT THEY WERE DOING, THEY'D GET HIGHER RATINGS WITH *THIS* THAN THEY DO WITH *KOHAKU!*
HA HA HA!!

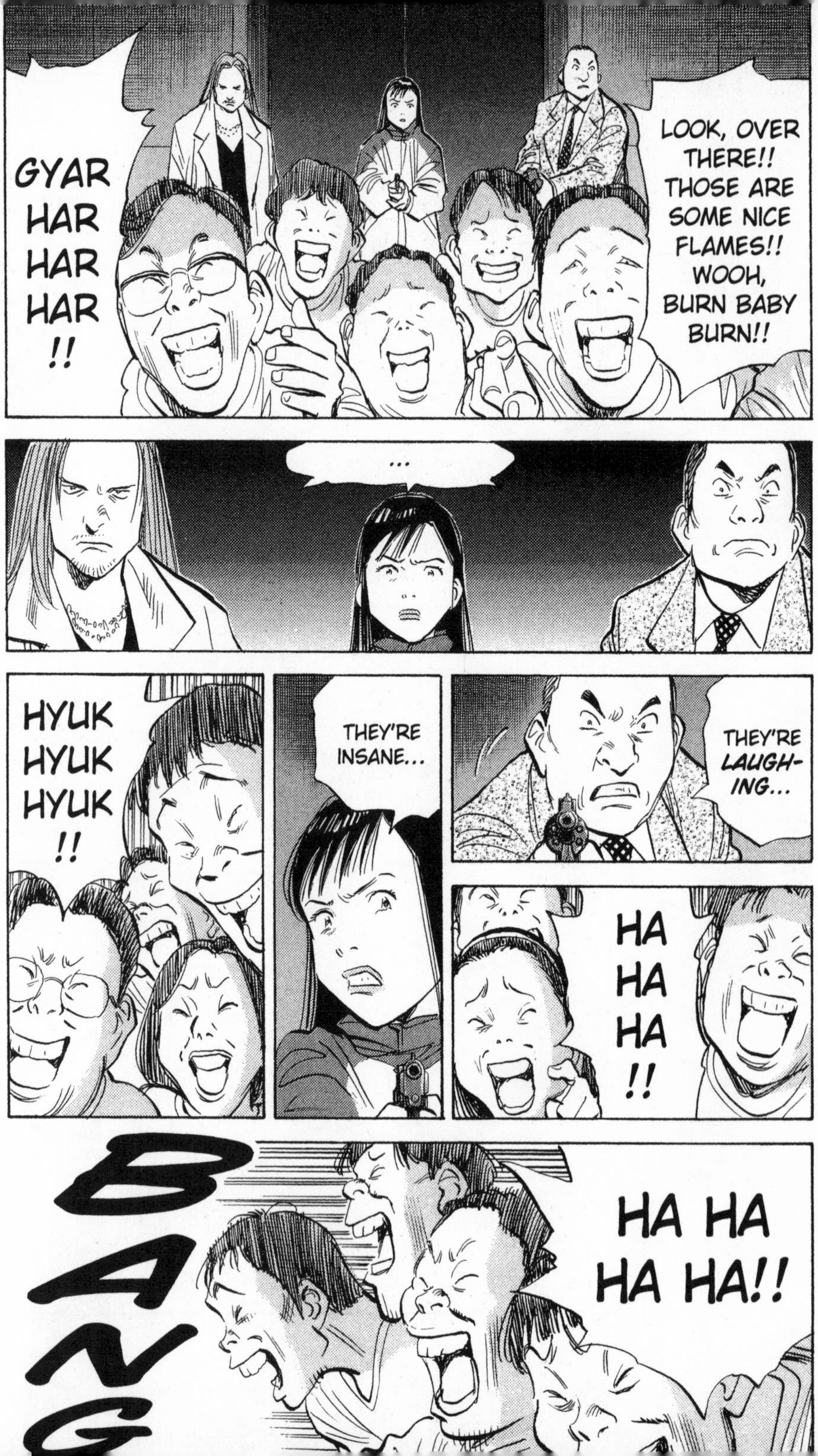
LOOK, OVER THERE!! THOSE ARE SOME NICE FLAMES!! WOOH, BURN BABY BURN!!
GYAR HAR HAR HAR!!
...
THEY'RE *LAUGHING*...
HA HA HA!!
THEY'RE INSANE...
HYUK HYUK HYUK!!
HA HA HA HA!!
BANG

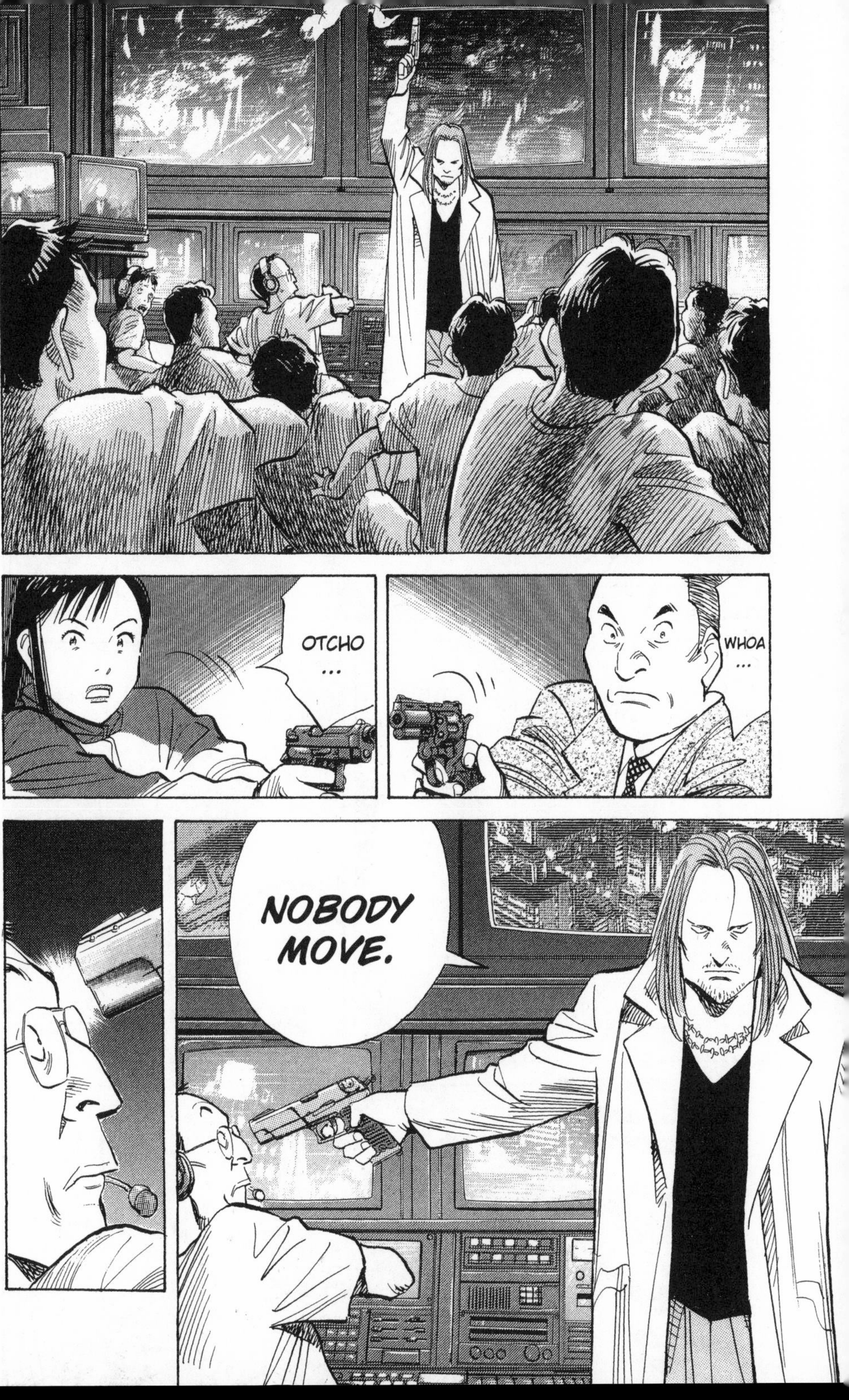
WHOA ...
OTCHO ...
NOBODY MOVE.

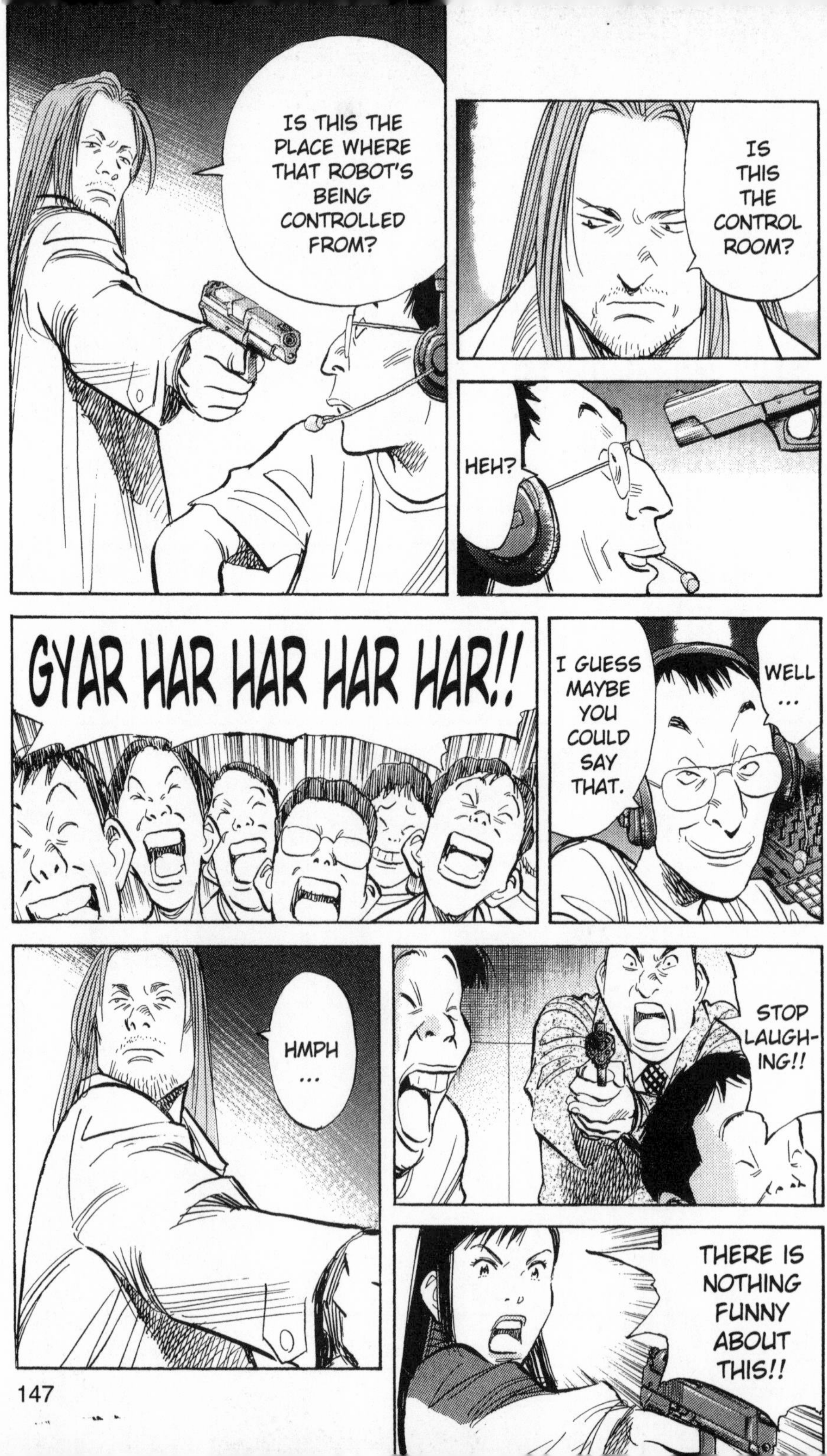
IS THIS THE CONTROL ROOM?
HEH?
IS THIS THE PLACE WHERE THAT ROBOT'S BEING CONTROLLED FROM?
WELL ...
I GUESS MAYBE YOU COULD SAY THAT.
GYAR HAR HAR HAR HAR!!
STOP LAUGH-ING!!
THERE IS NOTHING FUNNY ABOUT THIS!!
HMPH ...

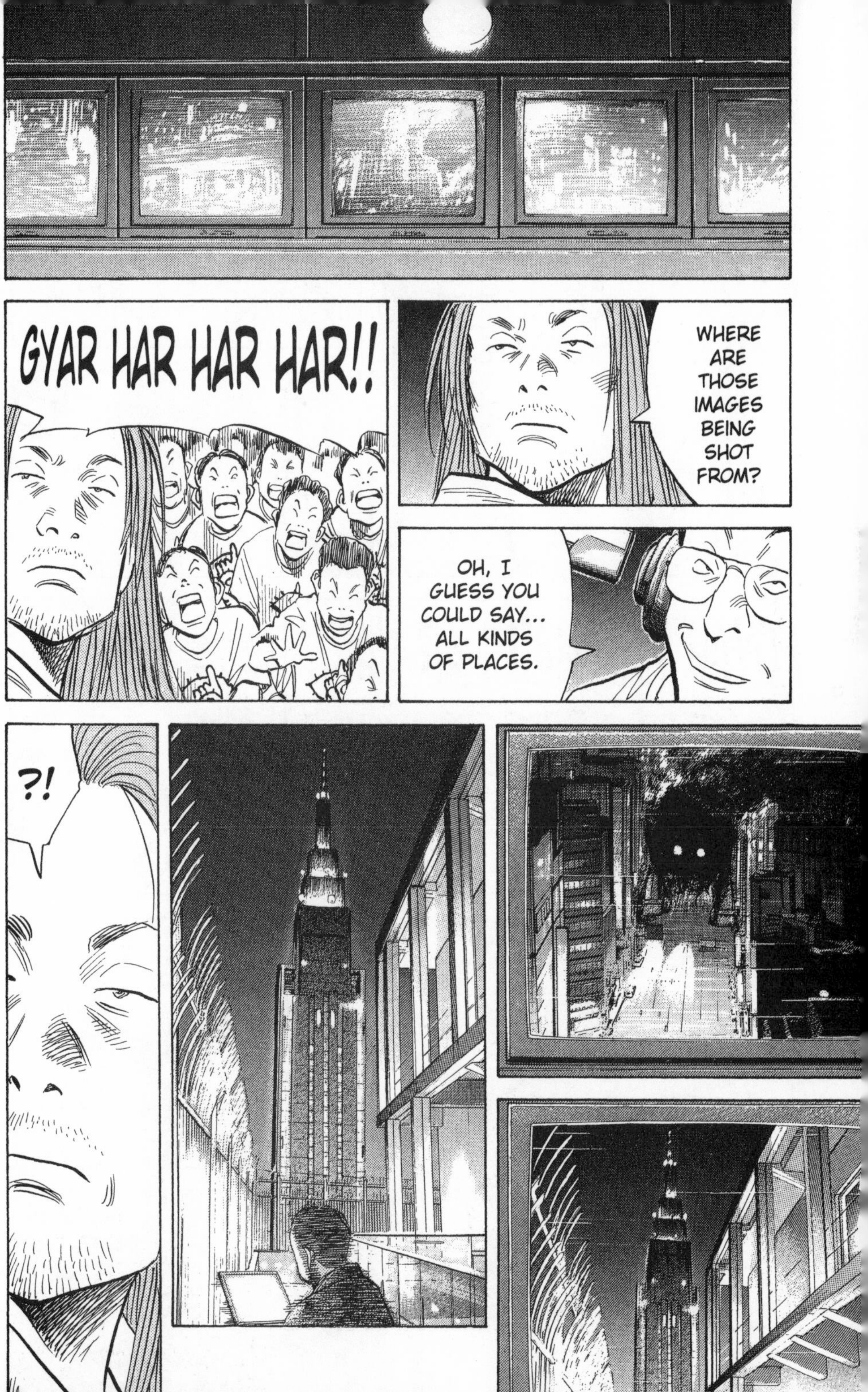
WHERE ARE THOSE IMAGES BEING SHOT FROM?
OH, I GUESS YOU COULD SAY... ALL KINDS OF PLACES.
GYAR HAR HAR HAR!!
?!

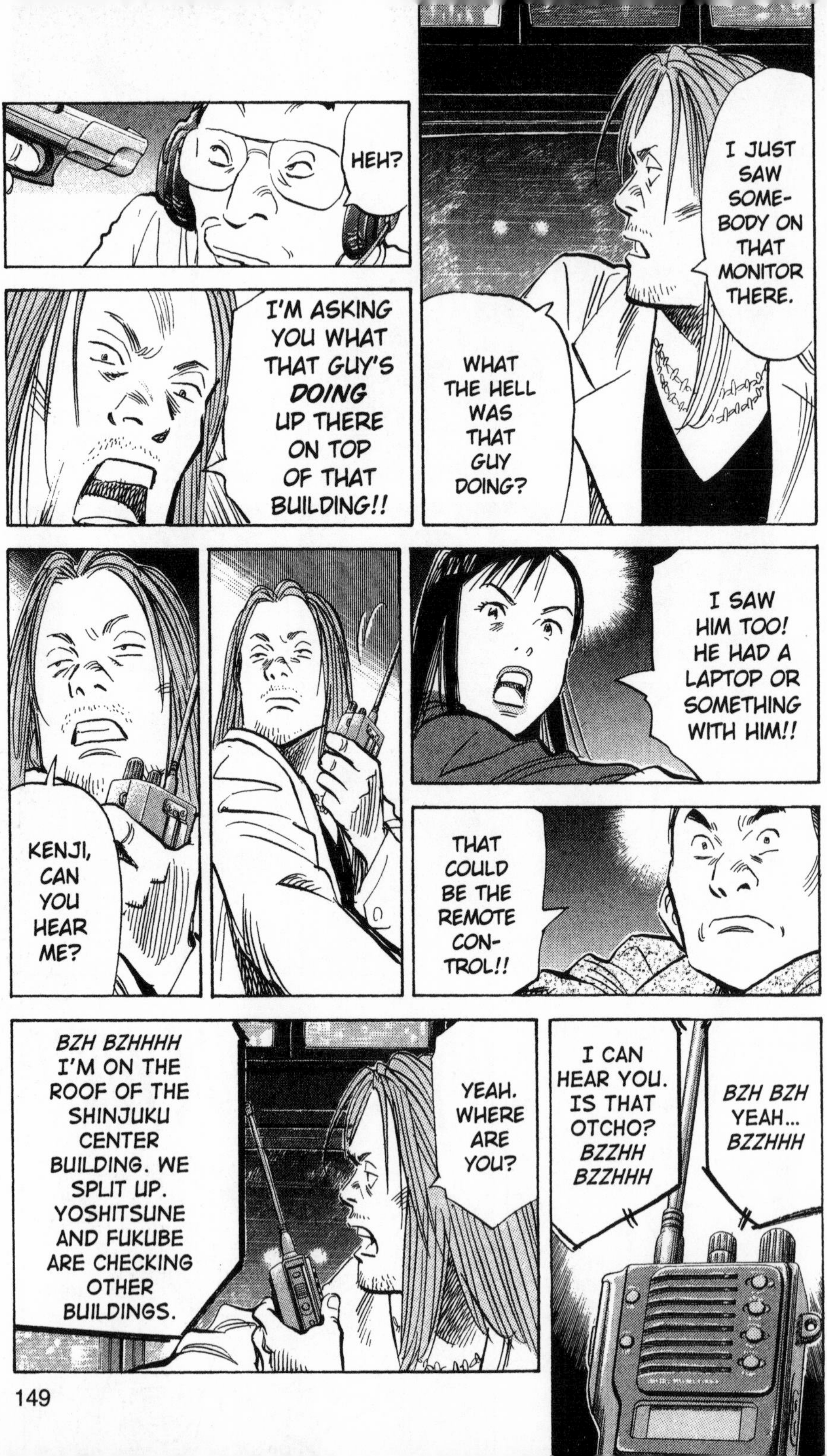
I JUST SAW SOMEBODY ON THAT MONITOR THERE.
WHAT THE HELL WAS THAT GUY DOING?
HEH?
I'M ASKING YOU WHAT THAT GUY'S *DOING* UP THERE ON TOP OF THAT BUILDING!!
I SAW HIM TOO! HE HAD A LAPTOP OR SOMETHING WITH HIM!!
THAT COULD BE THE REMOTE CON-TROL!!
KENJI, CAN YOU HEAR ME?
BZH BZH YEAH... *BZZHHH*
I CAN HEAR YOU. IS THAT OTCHO? *BZZHH BZZHHH*
YEAH. WHERE ARE YOU?
BZH BZHHHH I'M ON THE ROOF OF THE SHINJUKU CENTER BUILDING. WE SPLIT UP. YOSHITSUNE AND FUKUBE ARE CHECKING OTHER BUILDINGS.

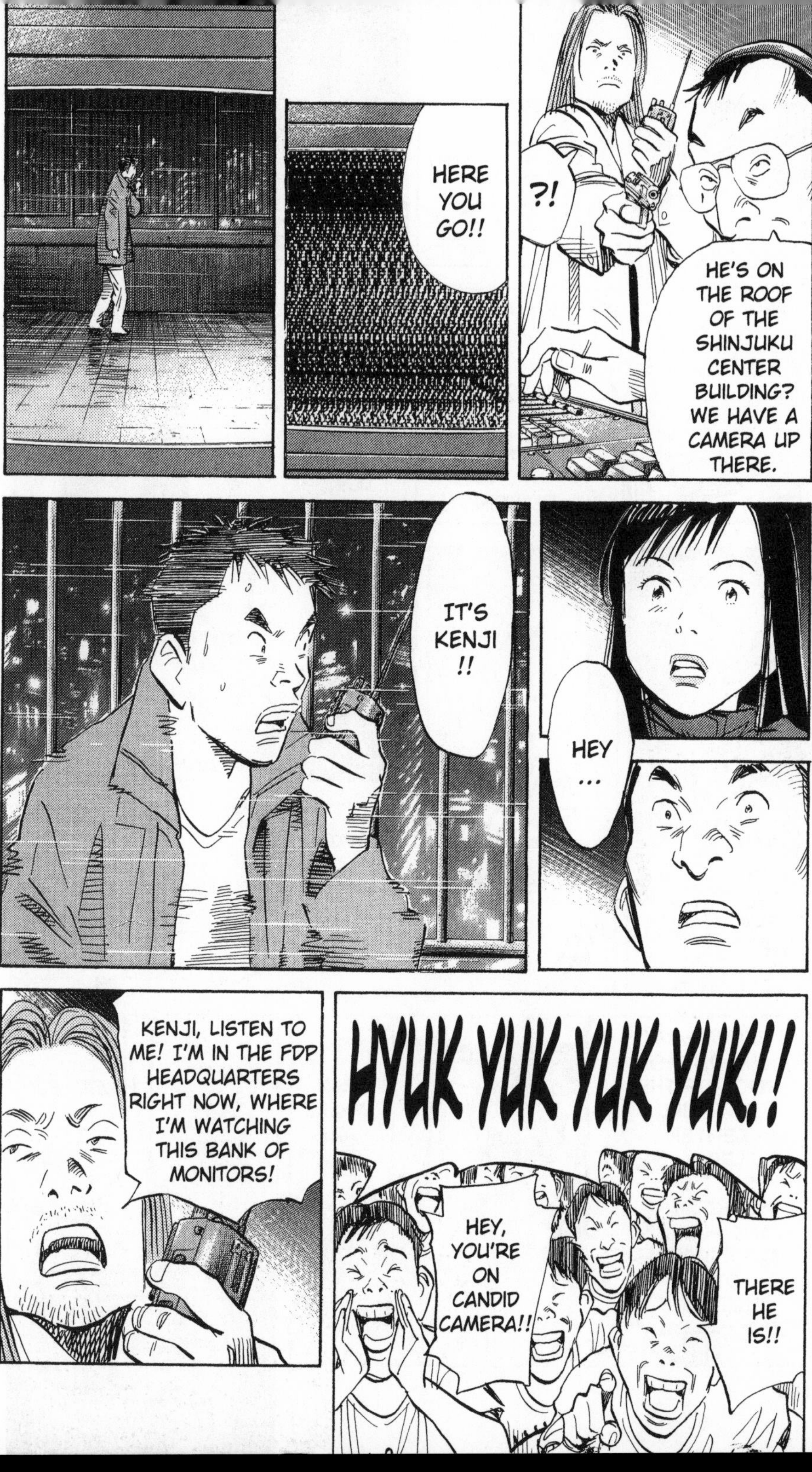
?!
HE'S ON THE ROOF OF THE SHINJUKU CENTER BUILDING? WE HAVE A CAMERA UP THERE.
HERE YOU GO!!
HEY ...
IT'S KENJI !!
HYUK YUK YUK YUK!!
HEY, YOU'RE ON CANDID CAMERA!!
THERE HE IS!!
KENJI, LISTEN TO ME! I'M IN THE FDP HEADQUARTERS RIGHT NOW, WHERE I'M WATCHING THIS BANK OF MONITORS!

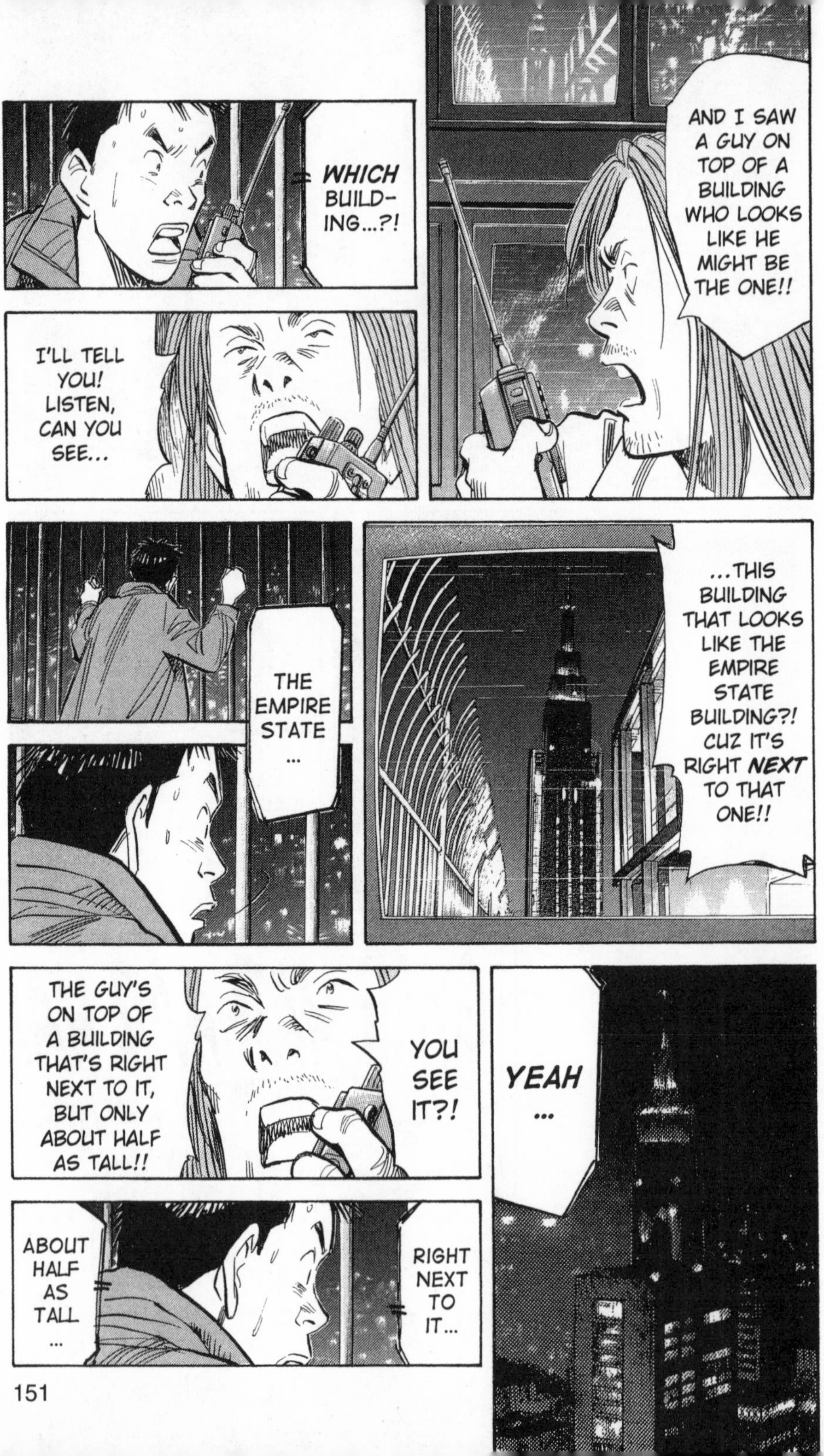
AND I SAW A GUY ON TOP OF A BUILDING WHO LOOKS LIKE HE MIGHT BE THE ONE!!
WHICH BUILDING...?!
I'LL TELL YOU! LISTEN, CAN YOU SEE...
...THIS BUILDING THAT LOOKS LIKE THE EMPIRE STATE BUILDING?! CUZ IT'S RIGHT NEXT TO THAT ONE!!
THE EMPIRE STATE ...
YEAH ...
THE GUY'S ON TOP OF A BUILDING THAT'S RIGHT NEXT TO IT, BUT ONLY ABOUT HALF AS TALL!!
YOU SEE IT?!
RIGHT NEXT TO IT...
ABOUT HALF AS TALL ...

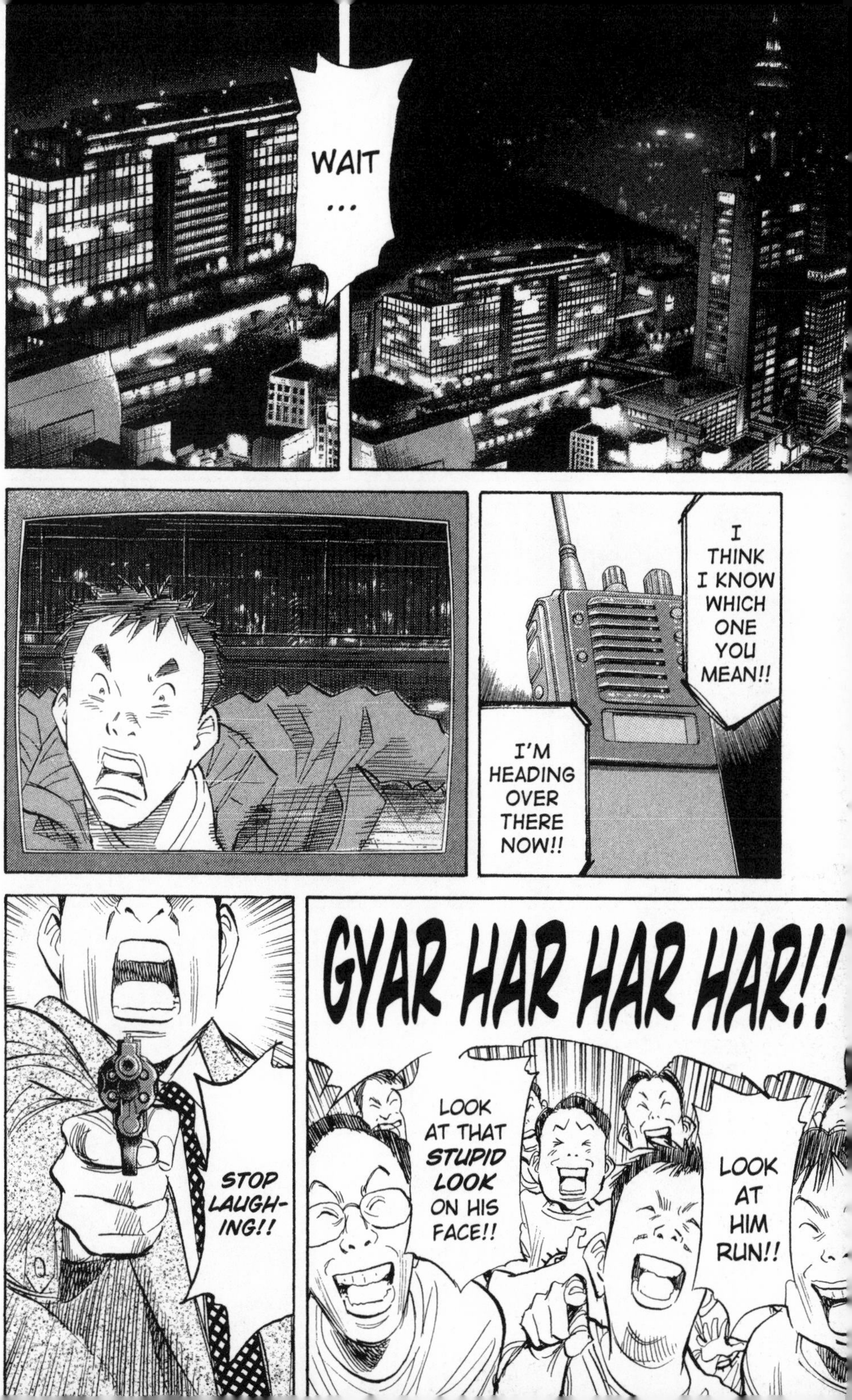
WAIT ...
I THINK I KNOW WHICH ONE YOU MEAN!!
I'M HEADING OVER THERE NOW!!
GYAR HAR HAR HAR!!
LOOK AT HIM RUN!!
LOOK AT THAT *STUPID LOOK* ON HIS FACE!!
STOP LAUGHING!!

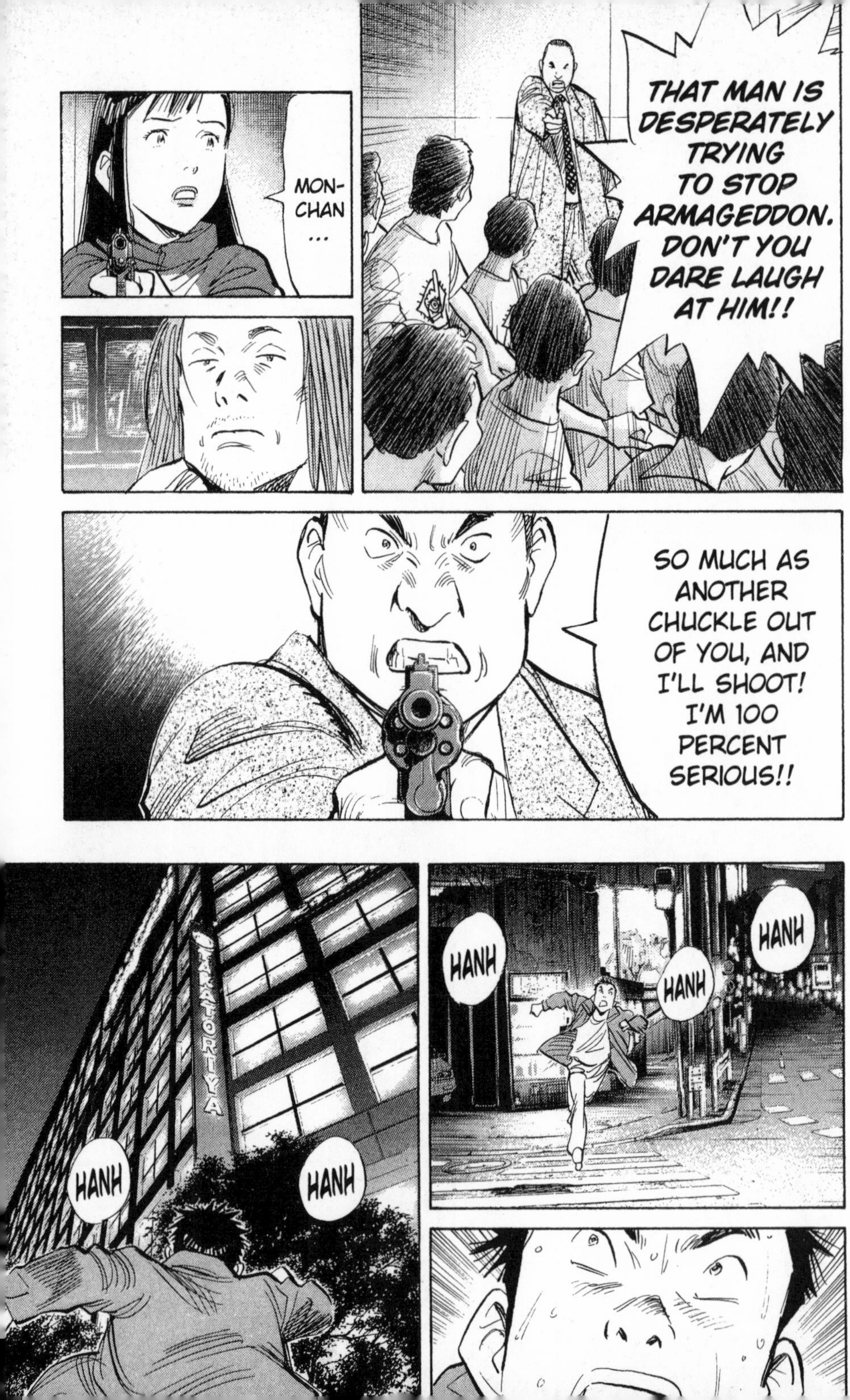
THAT MAN IS DESPERATELY TRYING TO STOP ARMAGEDDON. DON'T YOU DARE LAUGH AT HIM!!
MON-CHAN ...
SO MUCH AS ANOTHER CHUCKLE OUT OF YOU, AND I'LL SHOOT! I'M 100 PERCENT SERIOUS!!
HANH
HANH
HANH
TAKATORIYA
HANH
HANH

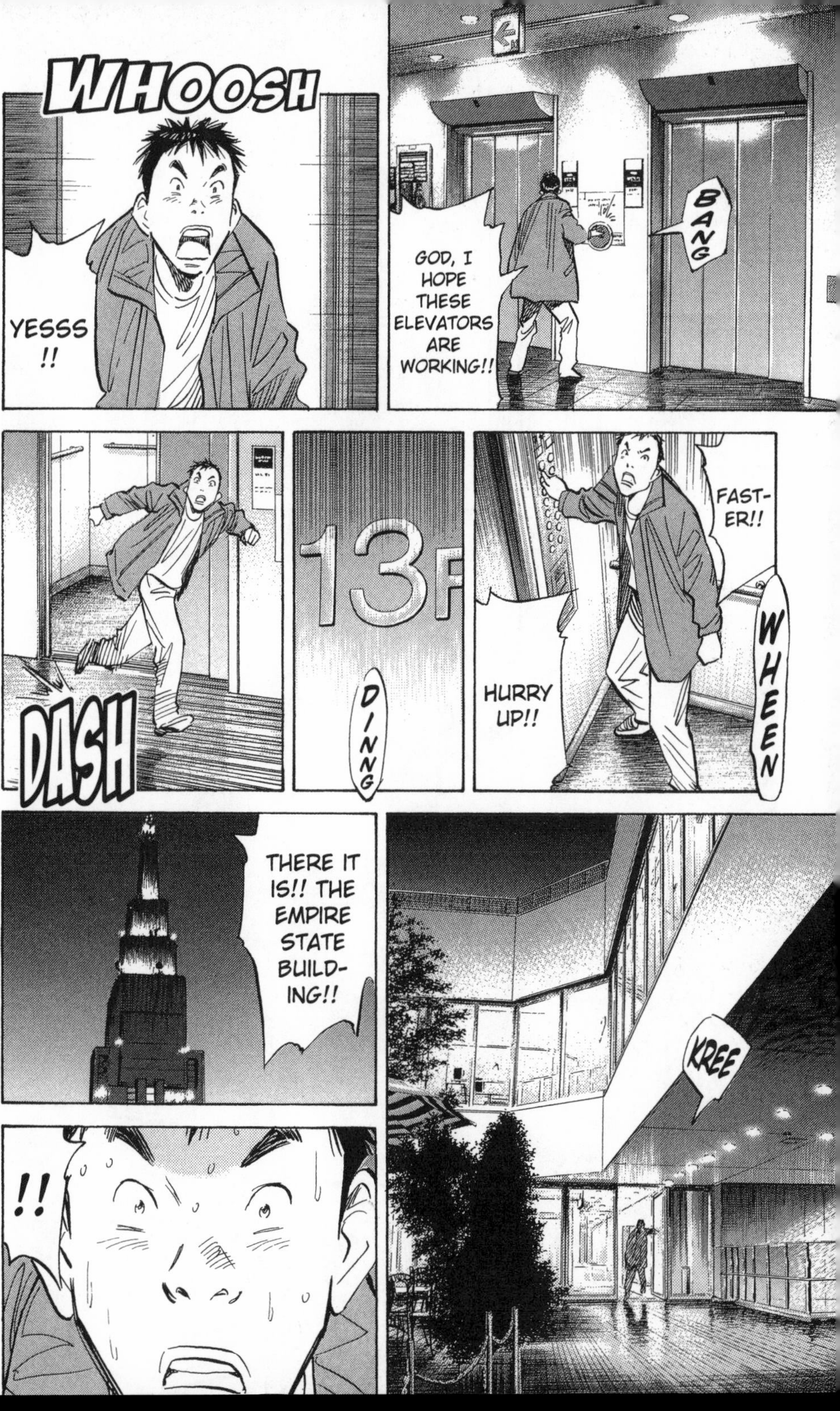
BANG
GOD, I HOPE THESE ELEVATORS ARE WORKING!!
WHOOSH
YESSS!!
FASTER!!
WHEEN
HURRY UP!!
13F
DINNG
DASH
KREE
THERE IT IS!! THE EMPIRE STATE BUILDING!!
!!

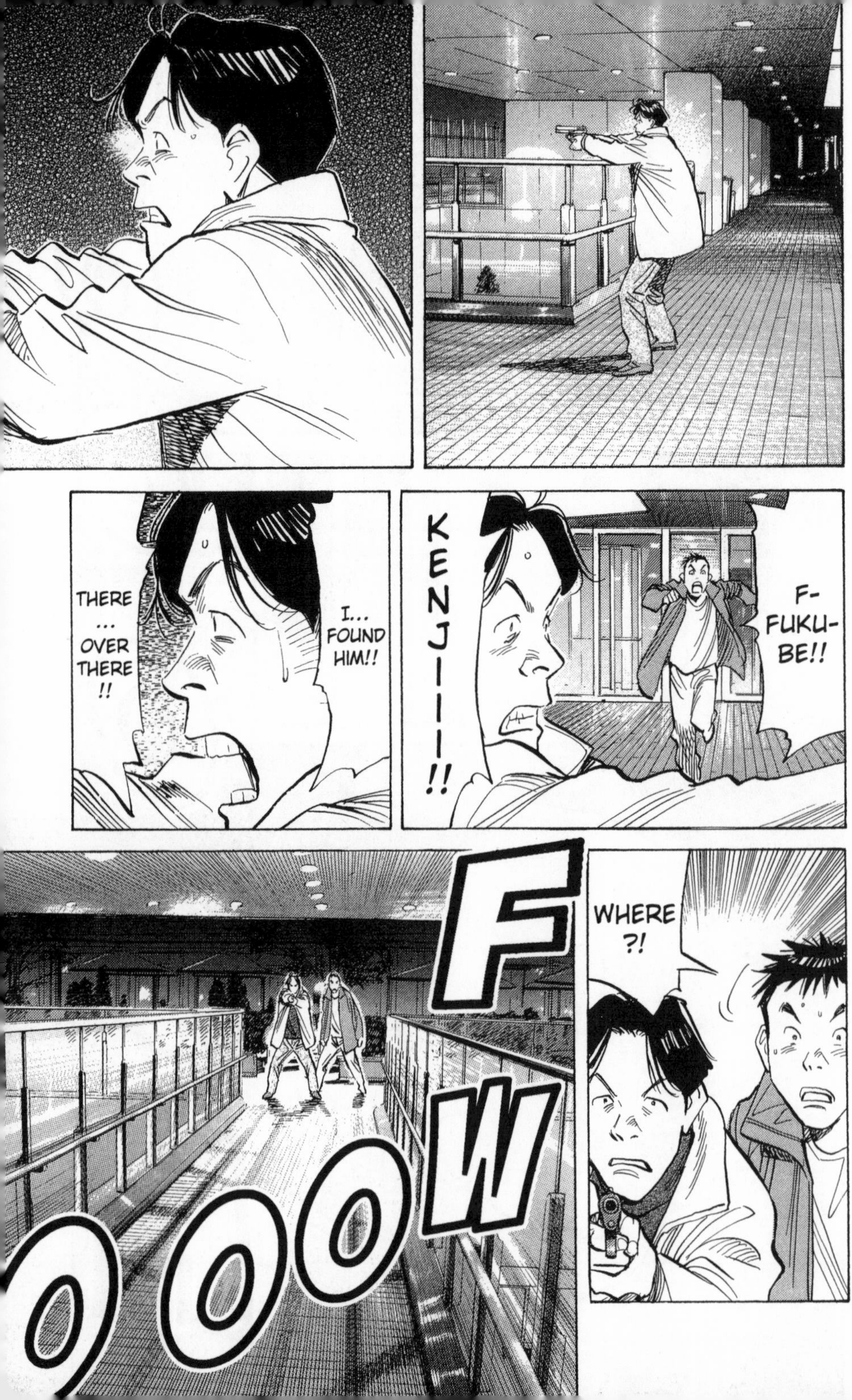
F-FUKUBE!!
KENJIIIII!!
I... FOUND HIM!!
THERE... OVER THERE!!
WHERE?!
FWOOO

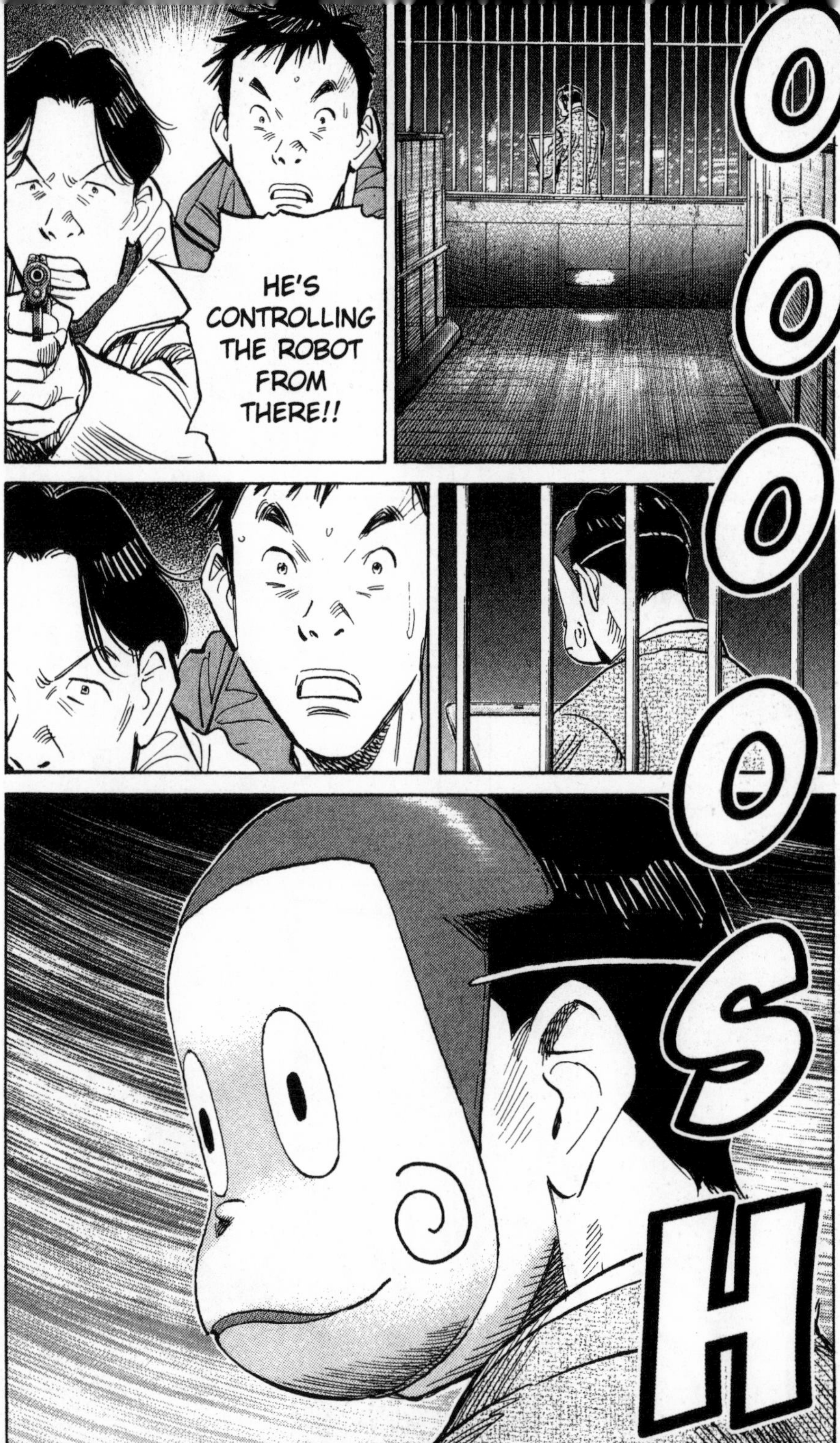
HE'S CONTROLLING THE ROBOT FROM THERE!!
OOOOOOSH

20世紀少年
Twentieth Century Boys

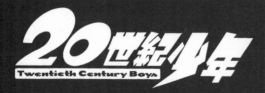

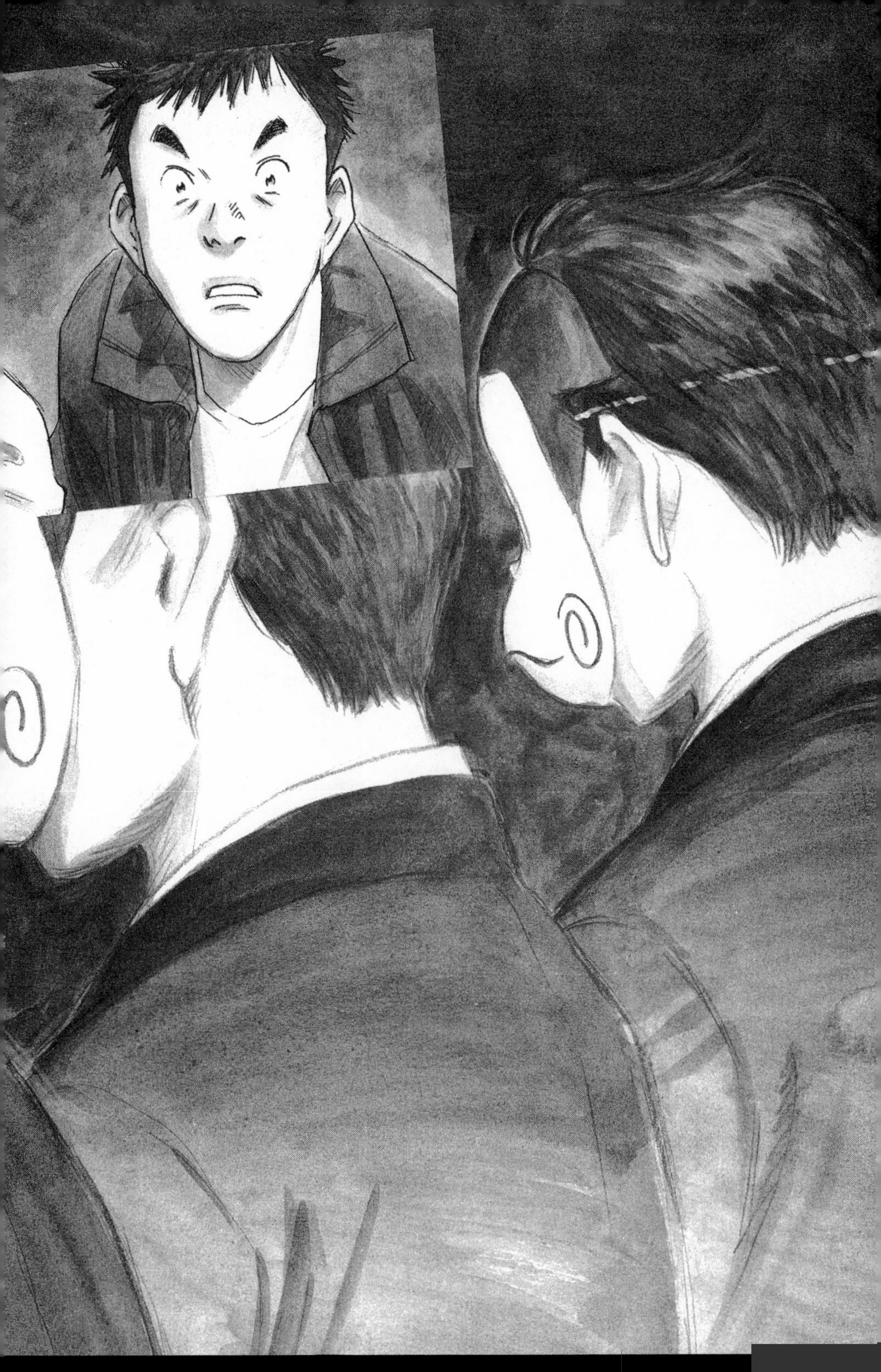

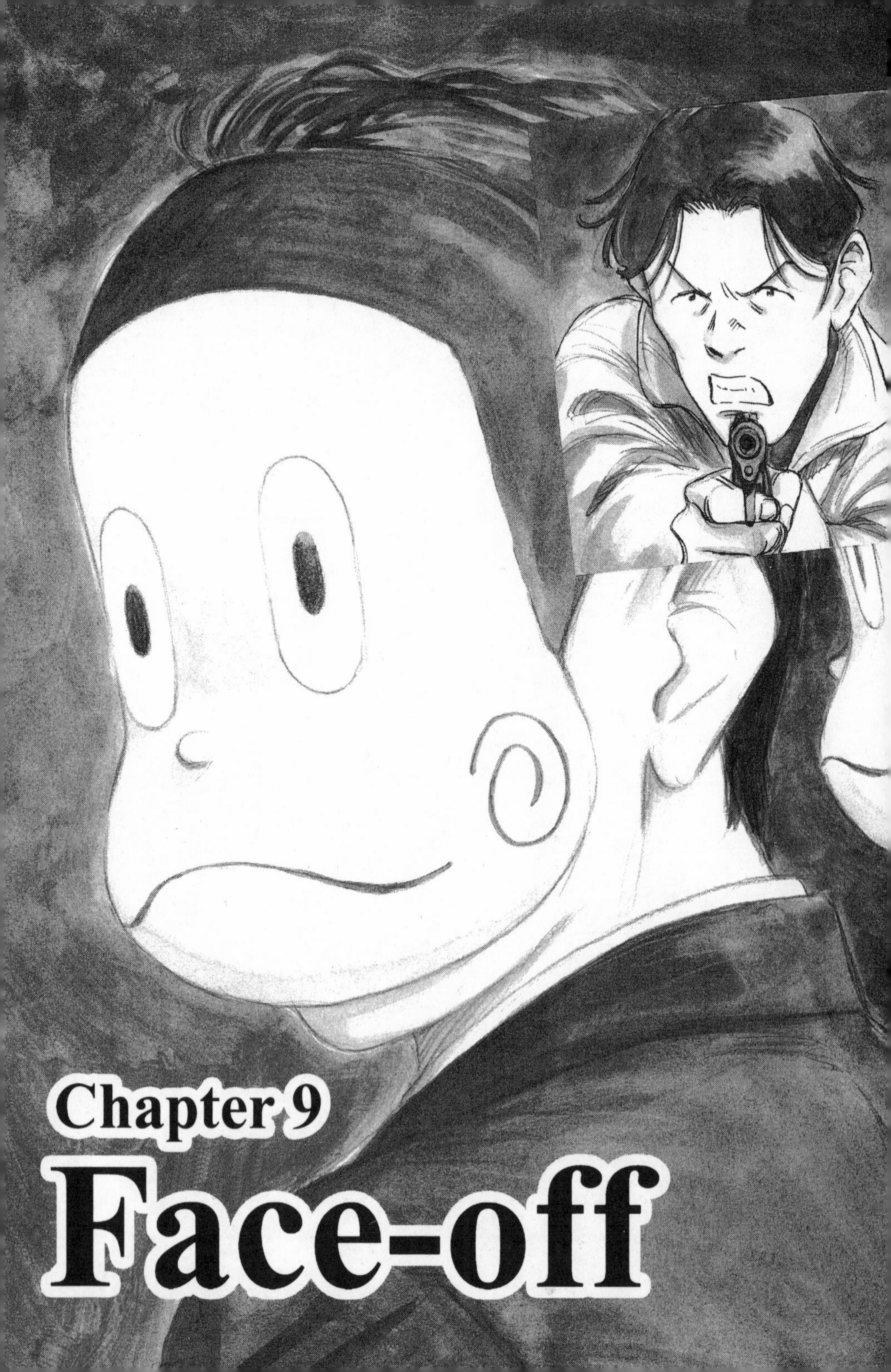
Chapter 9
Face-off

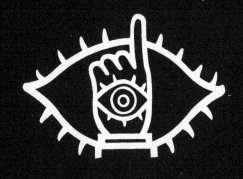

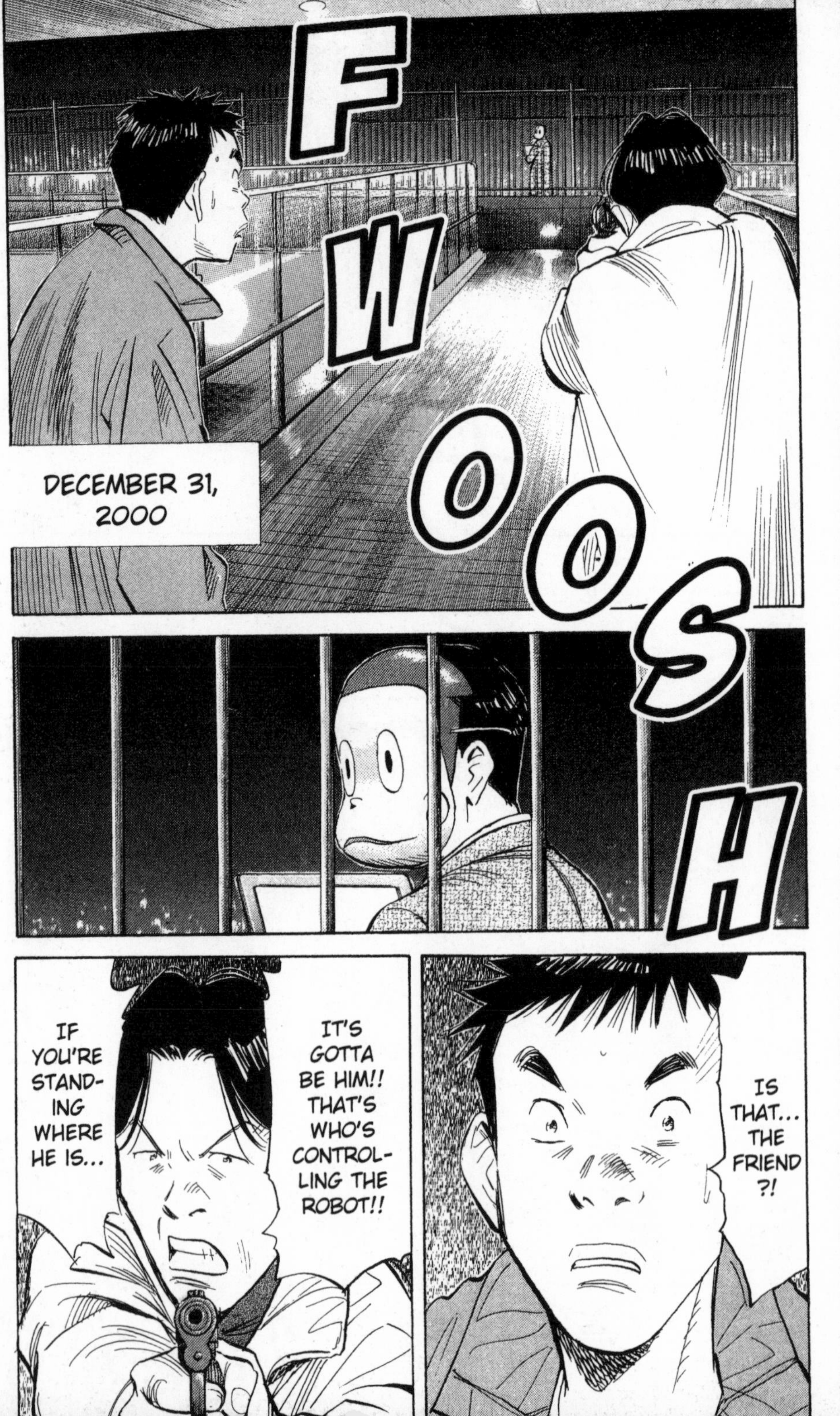
FWOOSH
DECEMBER 31, 2000
IS THAT... THE FRIEND?!
IT'S GOTTA BE HIM!! THAT'S WHO'S CONTROLLING THE ROBOT!!
IF YOU'RE STANDING WHERE HE IS...

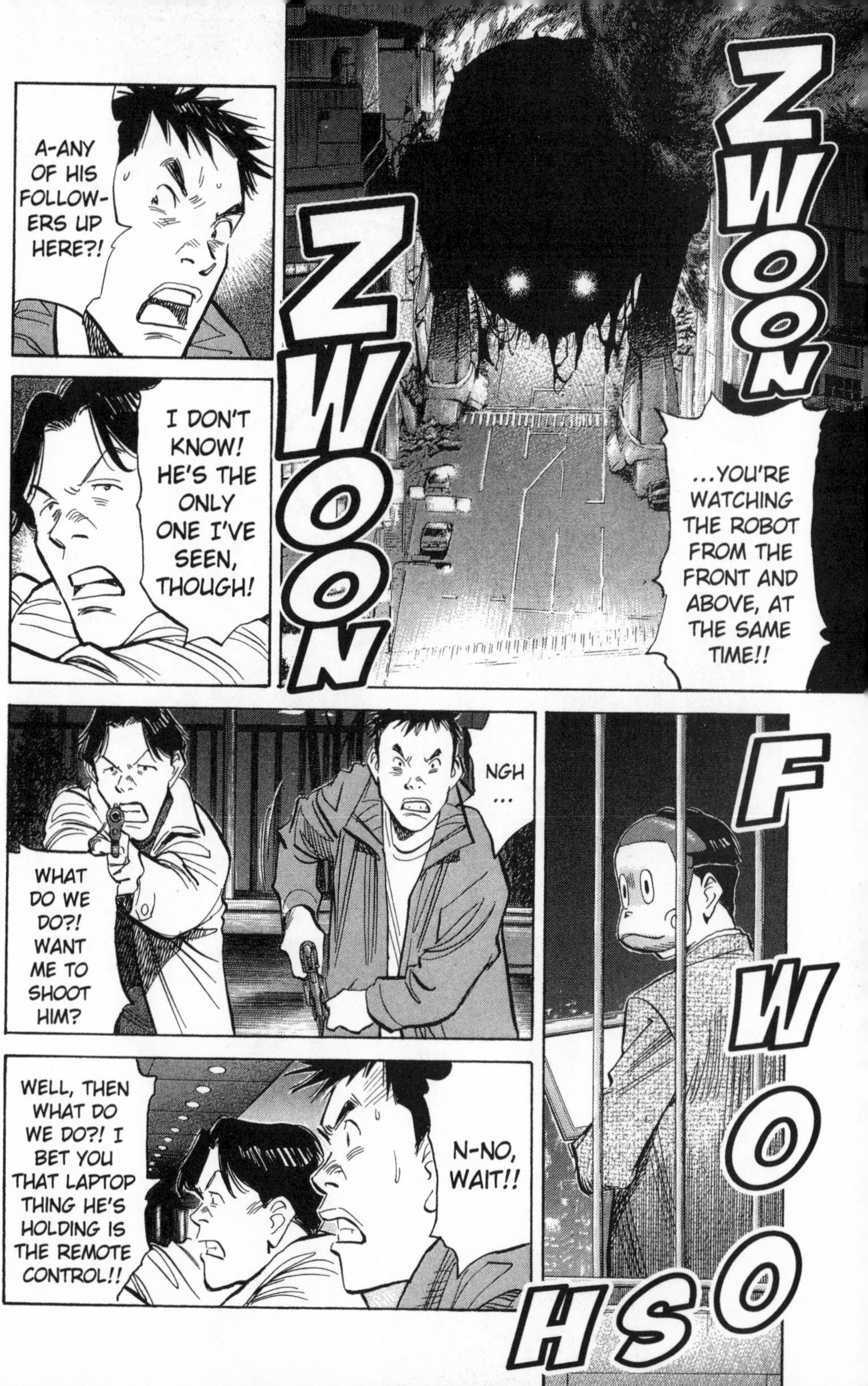
ZWOON
...YOU'RE WATCHING THE ROBOT FROM THE FRONT AND ABOVE, AT THE SAME TIME!!
ZWOON
A-ANY OF HIS FOLLOWERS UP HERE?!
I DON'T KNOW! HE'S THE ONLY ONE I'VE SEEN, THOUGH!
FWOOOSH
NGH ...
WHAT DO WE DO?! WANT ME TO SHOOT HIM?
N-NO, WAIT!!
WELL, THEN WHAT DO WE DO?! I BET YOU THAT LAPTOP THING HE'S HOLDING IS THE REMOTE CONTROL!!

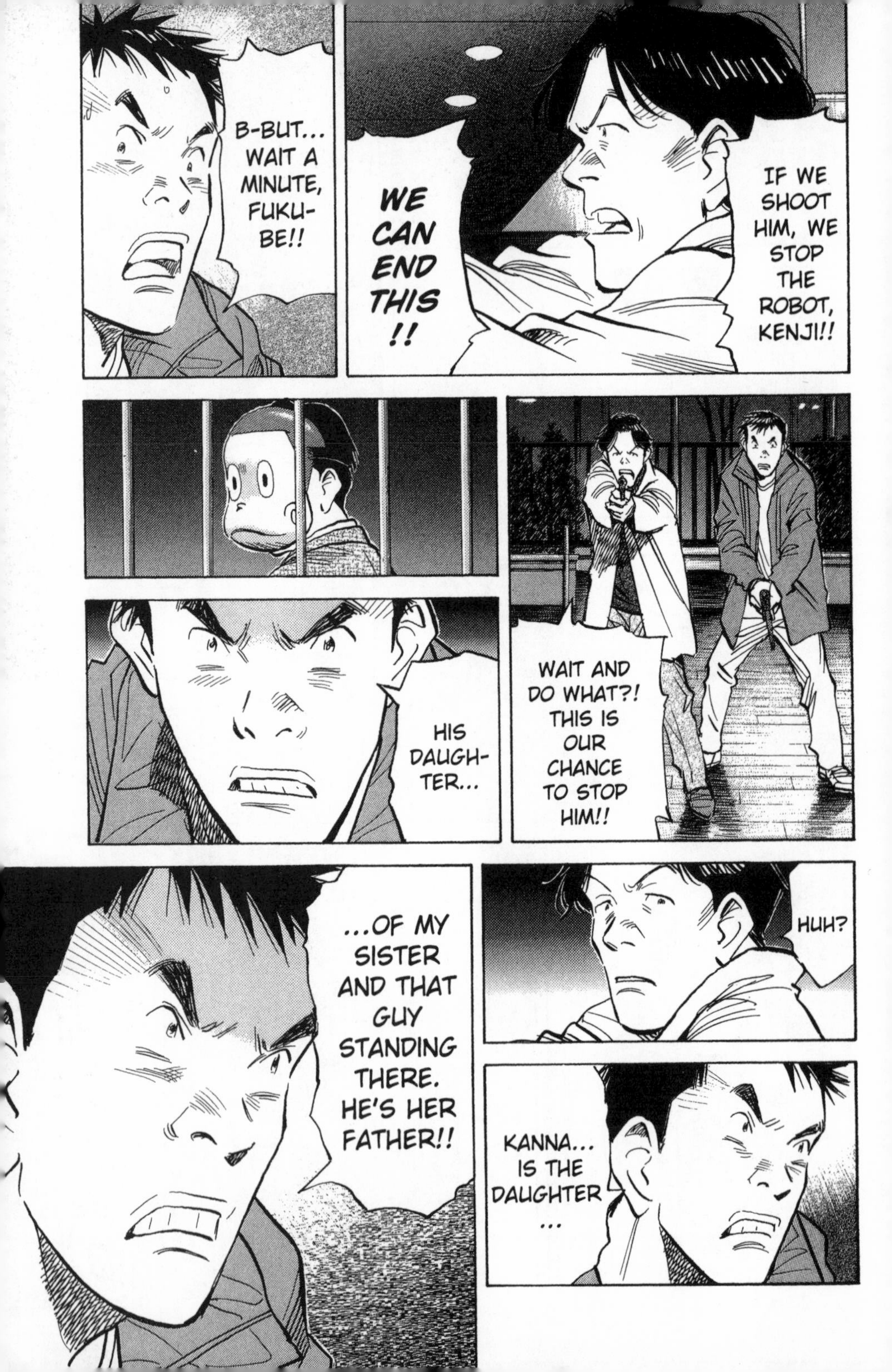
IF WE SHOOT HIM, WE STOP THE ROBOT, KENJI!!
WE CAN END THIS!!
B-BUT... WAIT A MINUTE, FUKU-BE!!
WAIT AND DO WHAT?! THIS IS OUR CHANCE TO STOP HIM!!
HIS DAUGH-TER...
HUH?
KANNA... IS THE DAUGHTER ...
...OF MY SISTER AND THAT GUY STANDING THERE. HE'S HER FATHER!!

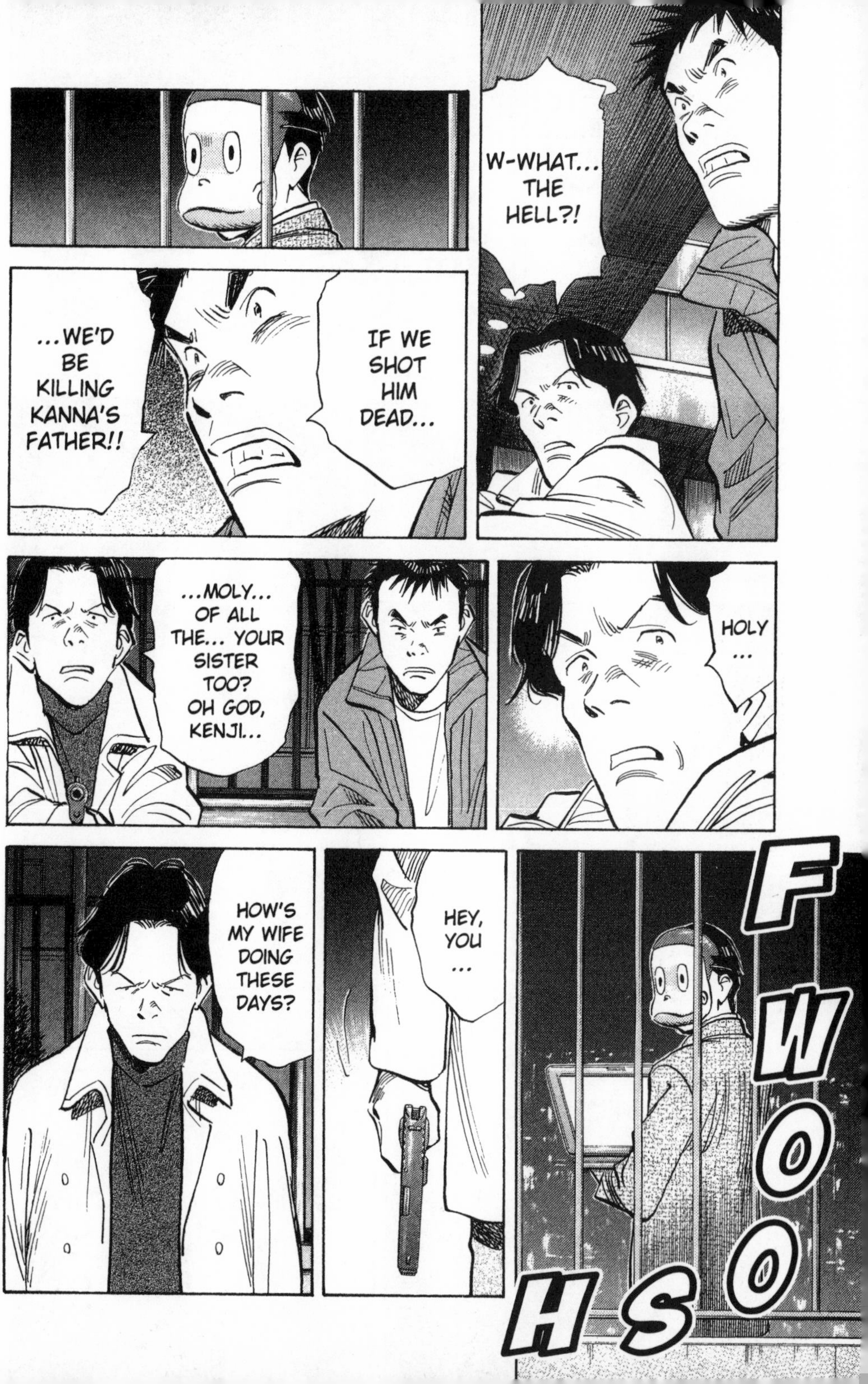
W-WHAT... THE HELL?!
IF WE SHOT HIM DEAD...
...WE'D BE KILLING KANNA'S FATHER!!
HOLY ...
...MOLY... OF ALL THE... YOUR SISTER TOO? OH GOD, KENJI...
FWOOSH
HEY, YOU ...
HOW'S MY WIFE DOING THESE DAYS?

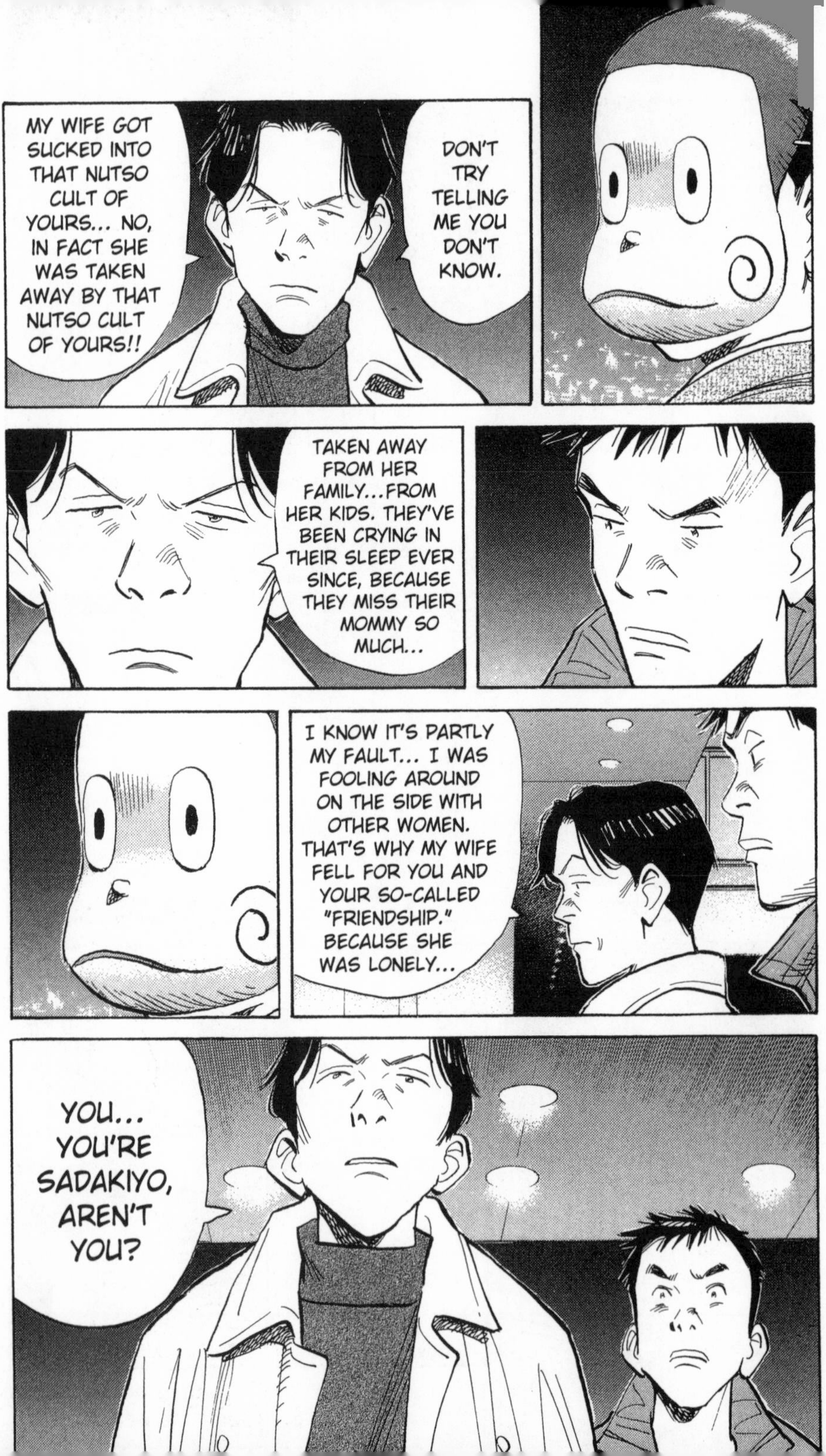
DON'T TRY TELLING ME YOU DON'T KNOW.
MY WIFE GOT SUCKED INTO THAT NUTSO CULT OF YOURS... NO, IN FACT SHE WAS TAKEN AWAY BY THAT NUTSO CULT OF YOURS!!
TAKEN AWAY FROM HER FAMILY...FROM HER KIDS. THEY'VE BEEN CRYING IN THEIR SLEEP EVER SINCE, BECAUSE THEY MISS THEIR MOMMY SO MUCH...
I KNOW IT'S PARTLY MY FAULT... I WAS FOOLING AROUND ON THE SIDE WITH OTHER WOMEN. THAT'S WHY MY WIFE FELL FOR YOU AND YOUR SO-CALLED "FRIENDSHIP." BECAUSE SHE WAS LONELY...
YOU... YOU'RE SADAKIYO, AREN'T YOU?

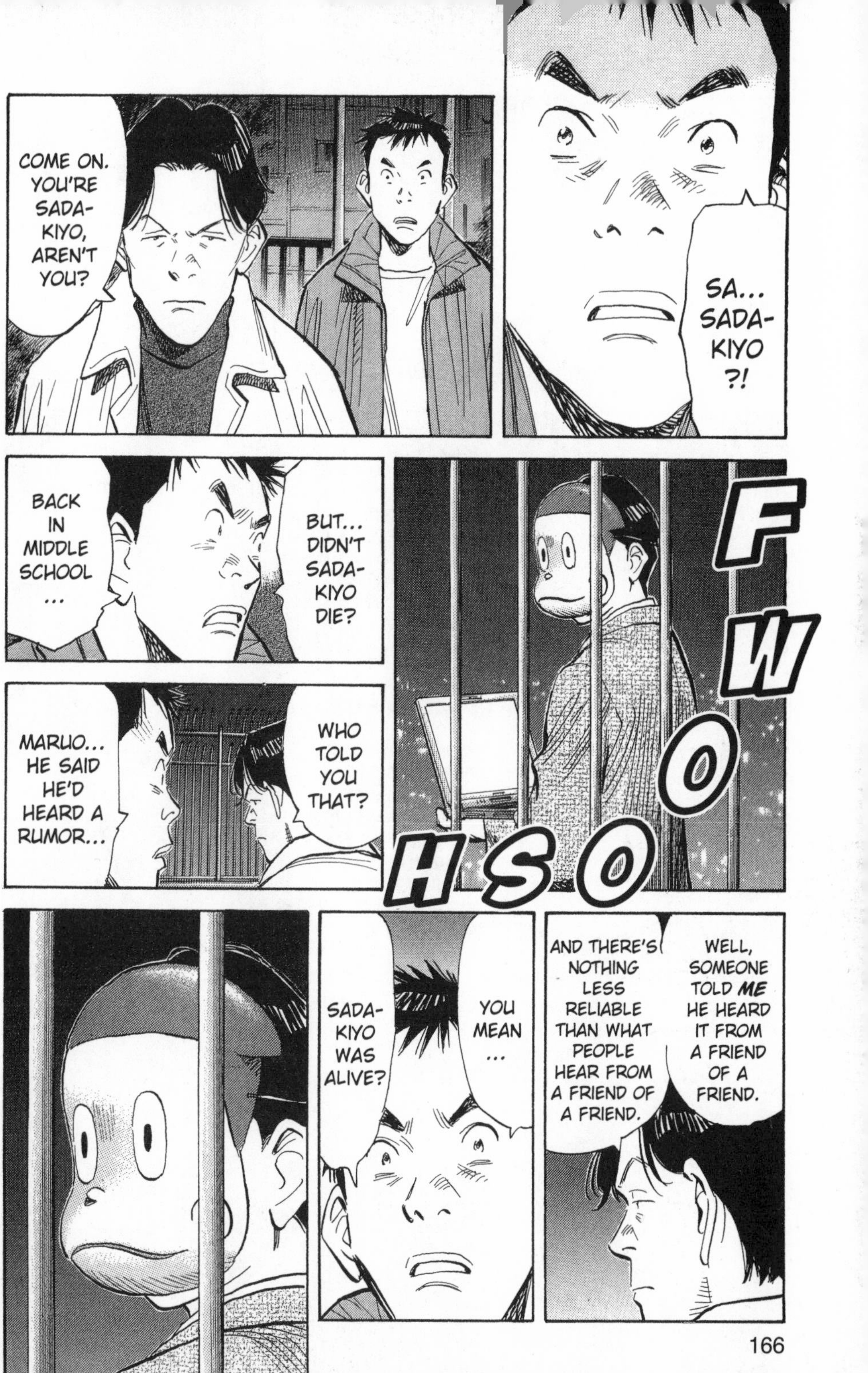
SA... SADAKIYO ?!
COME ON. YOU'RE SADAKIYO, AREN'T YOU?
FWOOSH
BUT... DIDN'T SADAKIYO DIE?
BACK IN MIDDLE SCHOOL...
WHO TOLD YOU THAT?
MARUO... HE SAID HE'D HEARD A RUMOR...
WELL, SOMEONE TOLD *ME* HE HEARD IT FROM A FRIEND OF A FRIEND.
AND THERE'S NOTHING LESS RELIABLE THAN WHAT PEOPLE HEAR FROM A FRIEND OF A FRIEND.
YOU MEAN...
SADAKIYO WAS ALIVE?

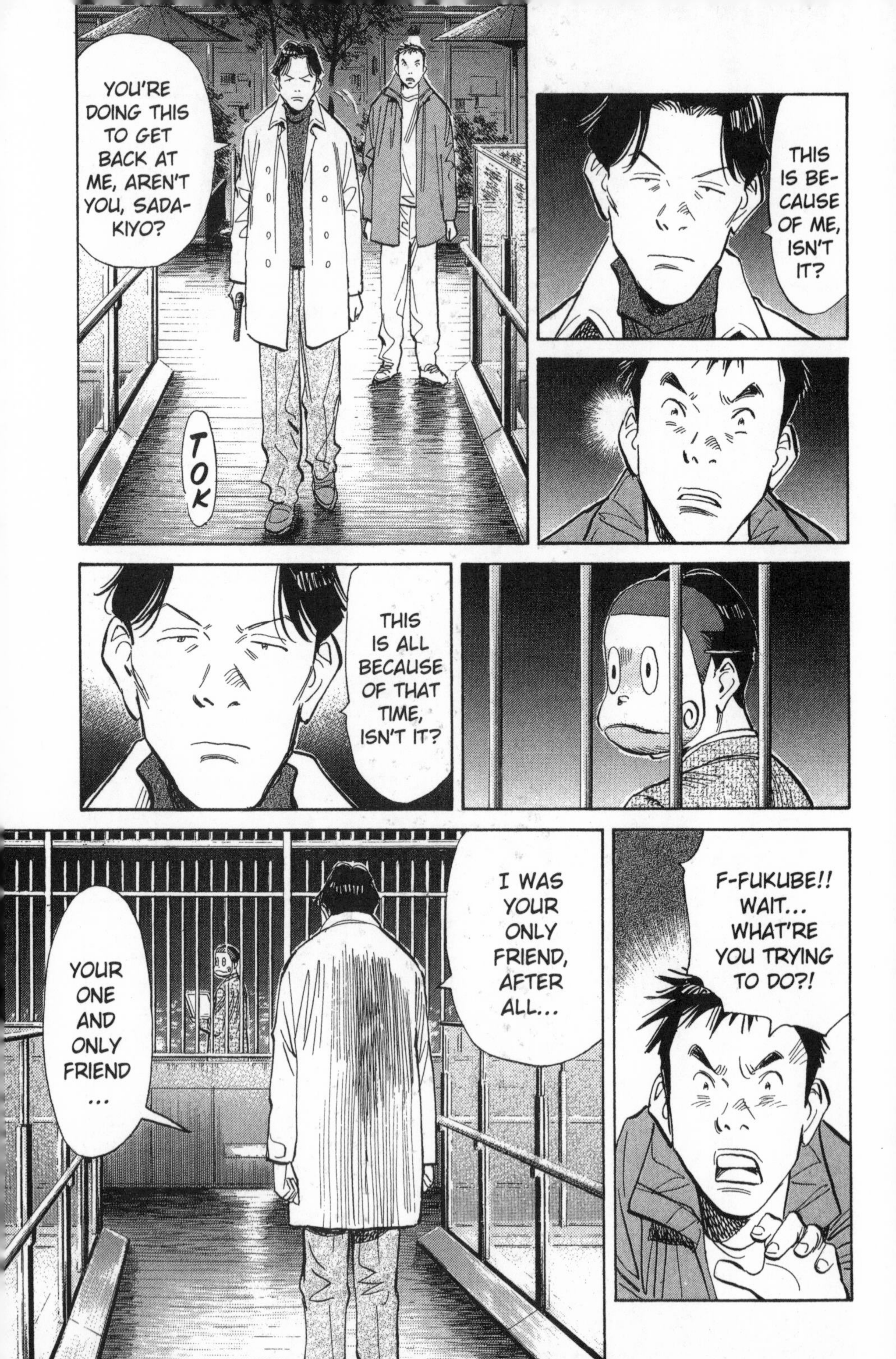
THIS IS BE-CAUSE OF ME, ISN'T IT?
YOU'RE DOING THIS TO GET BACK AT ME, AREN'T YOU, SADA-KIYO?
TOK
THIS IS ALL BECAUSE OF THAT TIME, ISN'T IT?
F-FUKUBE!! WAIT... WHAT'RE YOU TRYING TO DO?!
I WAS YOUR ONLY FRIEND, AFTER ALL...
YOUR ONE AND ONLY FRIEND...

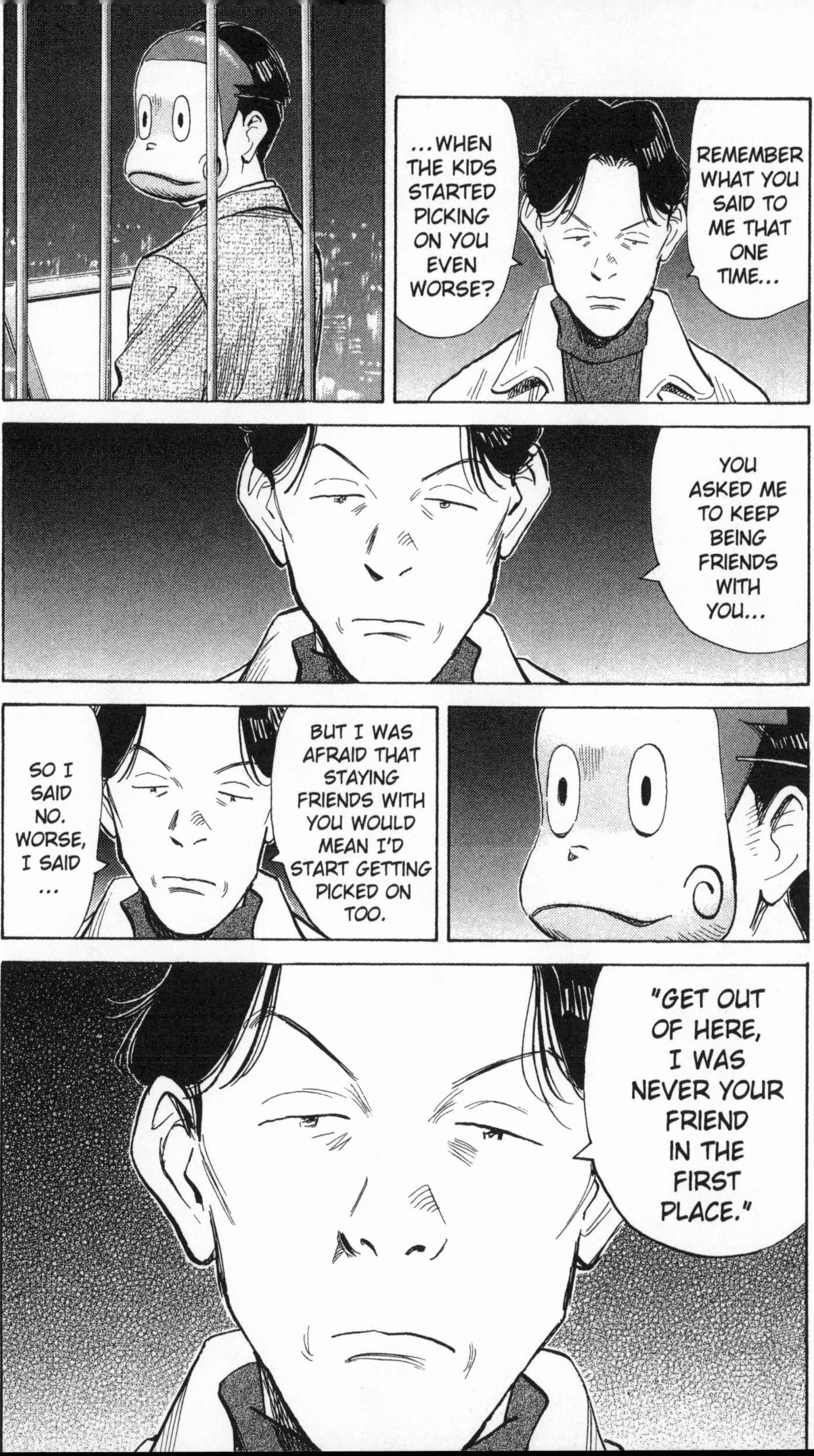
REMEMBER WHAT YOU SAID TO ME THAT ONE TIME...
...WHEN THE KIDS STARTED PICKING ON YOU EVEN WORSE?
YOU ASKED ME TO KEEP BEING FRIENDS WITH YOU...
BUT I WAS AFRAID THAT STAYING FRIENDS WITH YOU WOULD MEAN I'D START GETTING PICKED ON TOO.
SO I SAID NO. WORSE, I SAID ...
"GET OUT OF HERE, I WAS NEVER YOUR FRIEND IN THE FIRST PLACE."

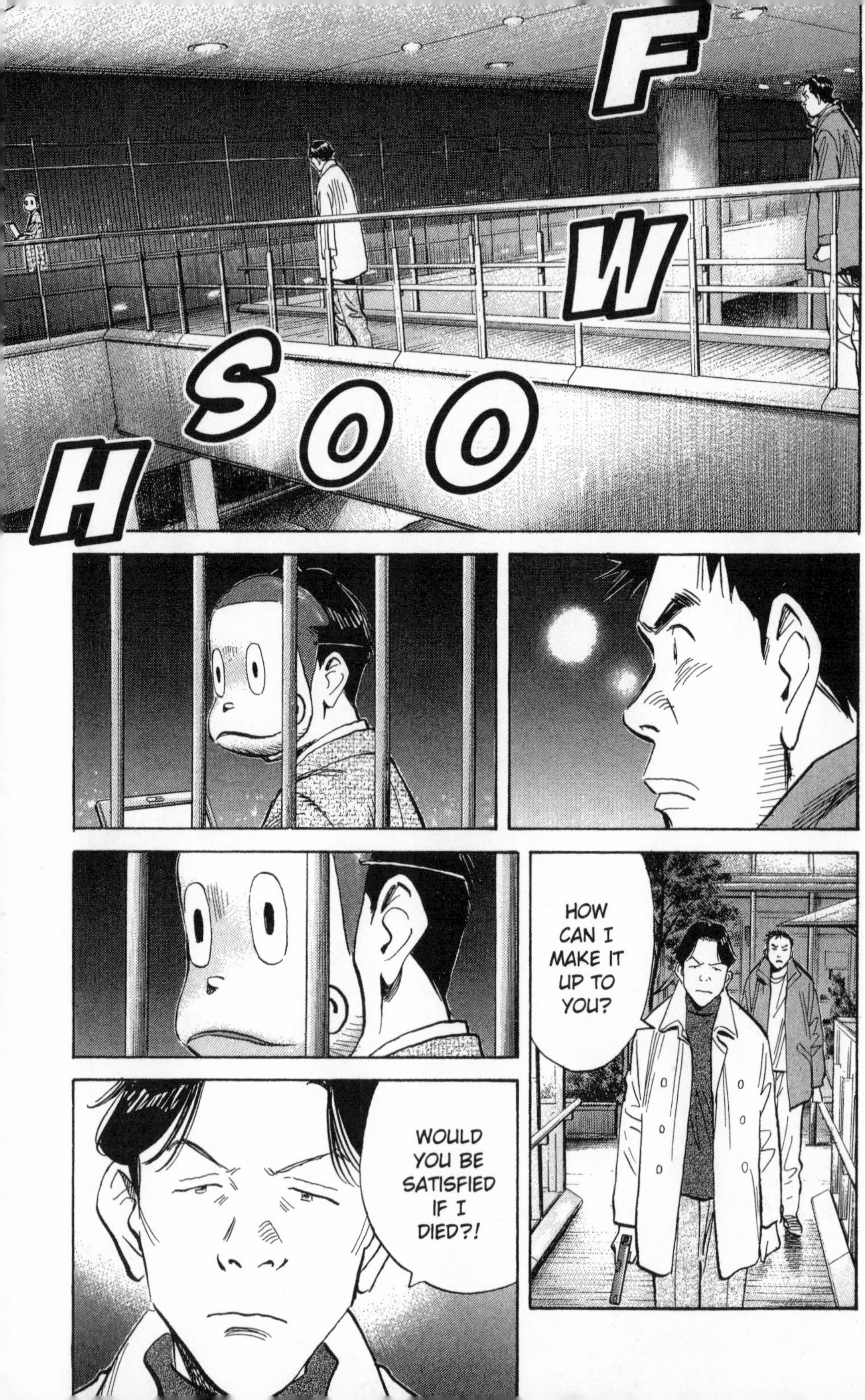
FWOOSH
HOW CAN I MAKE IT UP TO YOU?
WOULD YOU BE SATISFIED IF I DIED?!

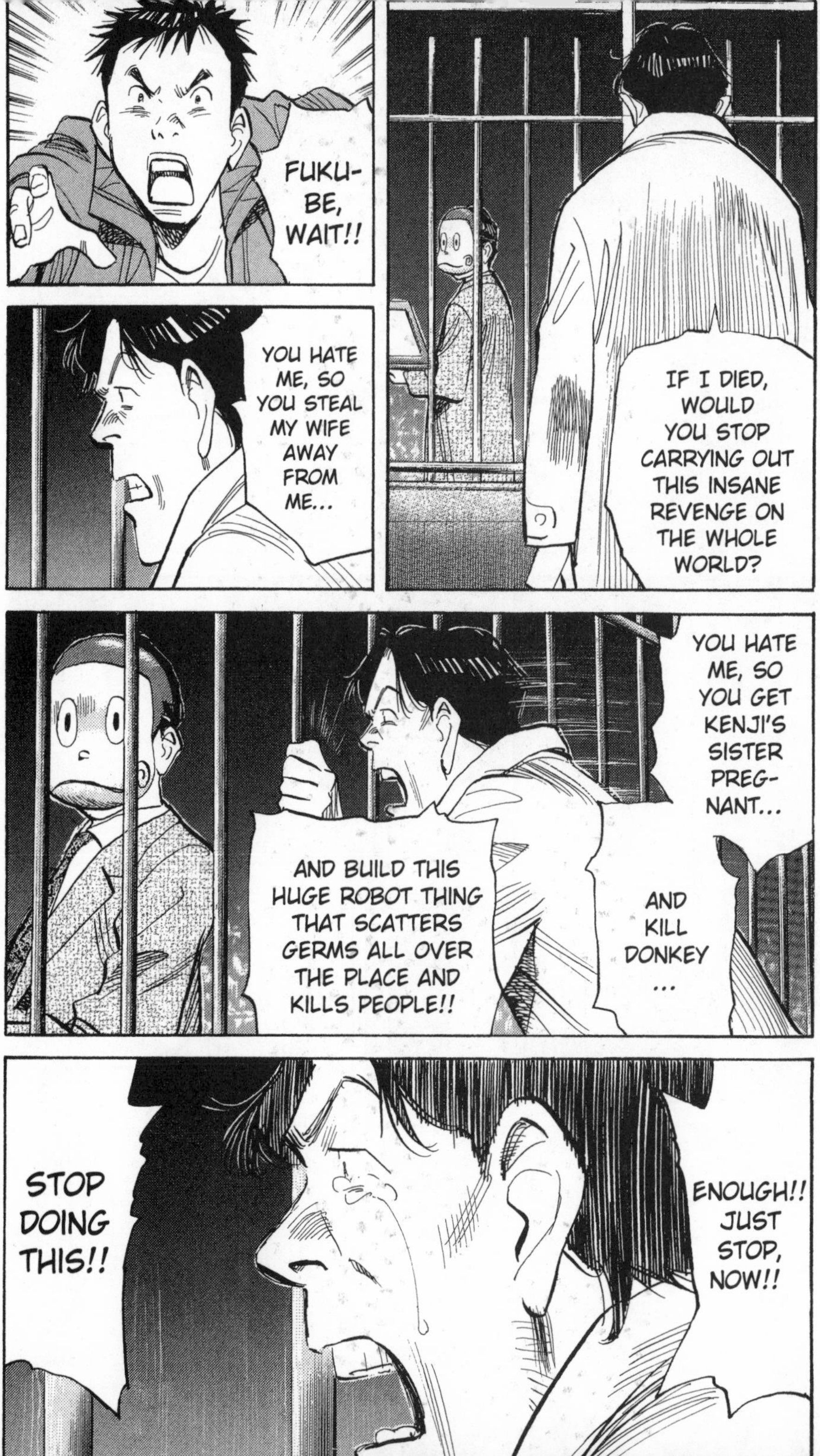
IF I DIED, WOULD YOU STOP CARRYING OUT THIS INSANE REVENGE ON THE WHOLE WORLD?
FUKU-BE, WAIT!!
YOU HATE ME, SO YOU STEAL MY WIFE AWAY FROM ME...
YOU HATE ME, SO YOU GET KENJI'S SISTER PREG-NANT...
AND KILL DONKEY ...
AND BUILD THIS HUGE ROBOT THING THAT SCATTERS GERMS ALL OVER THE PLACE AND KILLS PEOPLE!!
ENOUGH!! JUST STOP, NOW!!
STOP DOING THIS!!

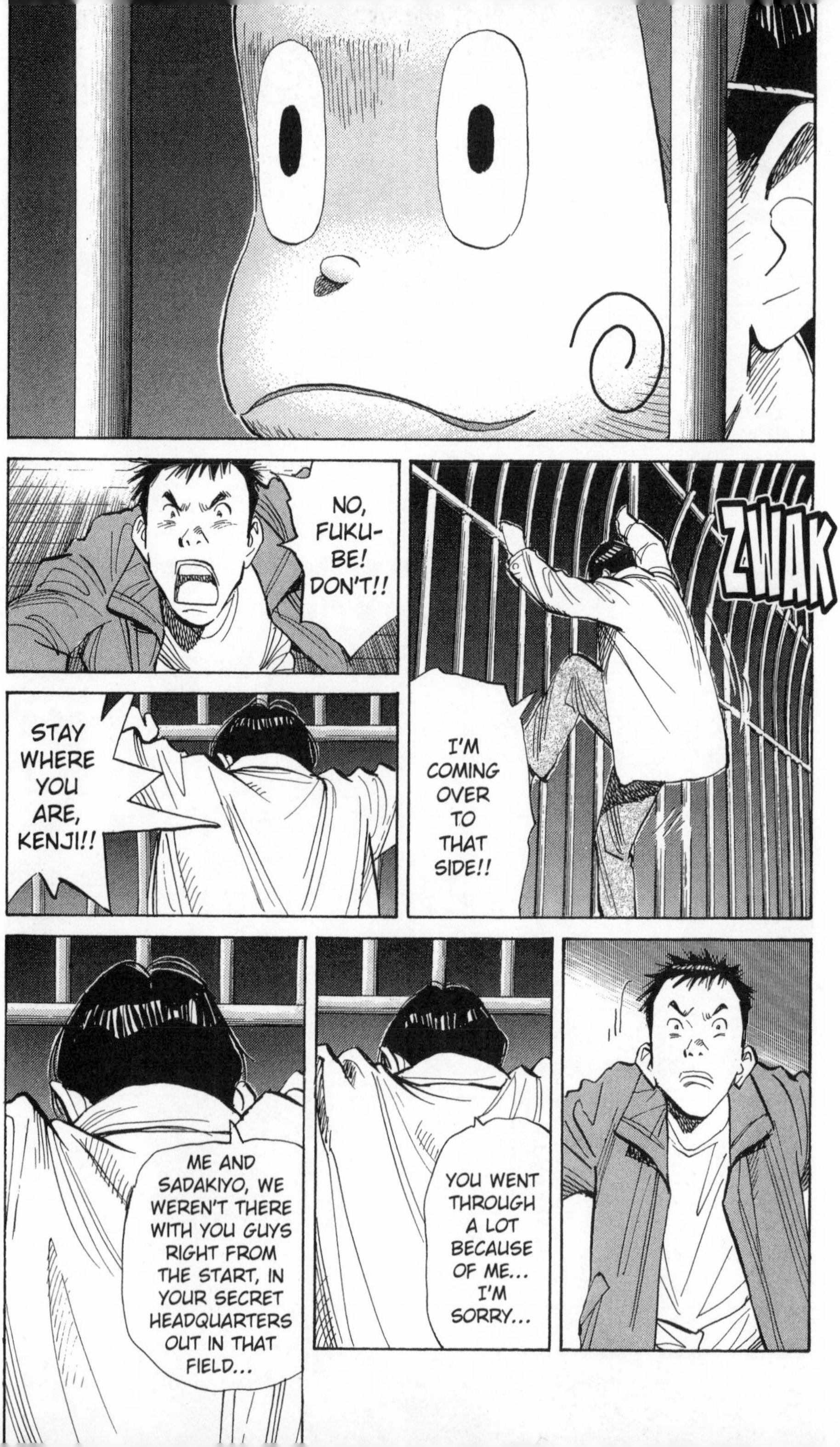
ZWAK
I'M COMING OVER TO THAT SIDE!!
NO, FUKUBE! DON'T!!
STAY WHERE YOU ARE, KENJI!!
YOU WENT THROUGH A LOT BECAUSE OF ME... I'M SORRY...
ME AND SADAKIYO, WE WEREN'T THERE WITH YOU GUYS RIGHT FROM THE START, IN YOUR SECRET HEADQUARTERS OUT IN THAT FIELD...

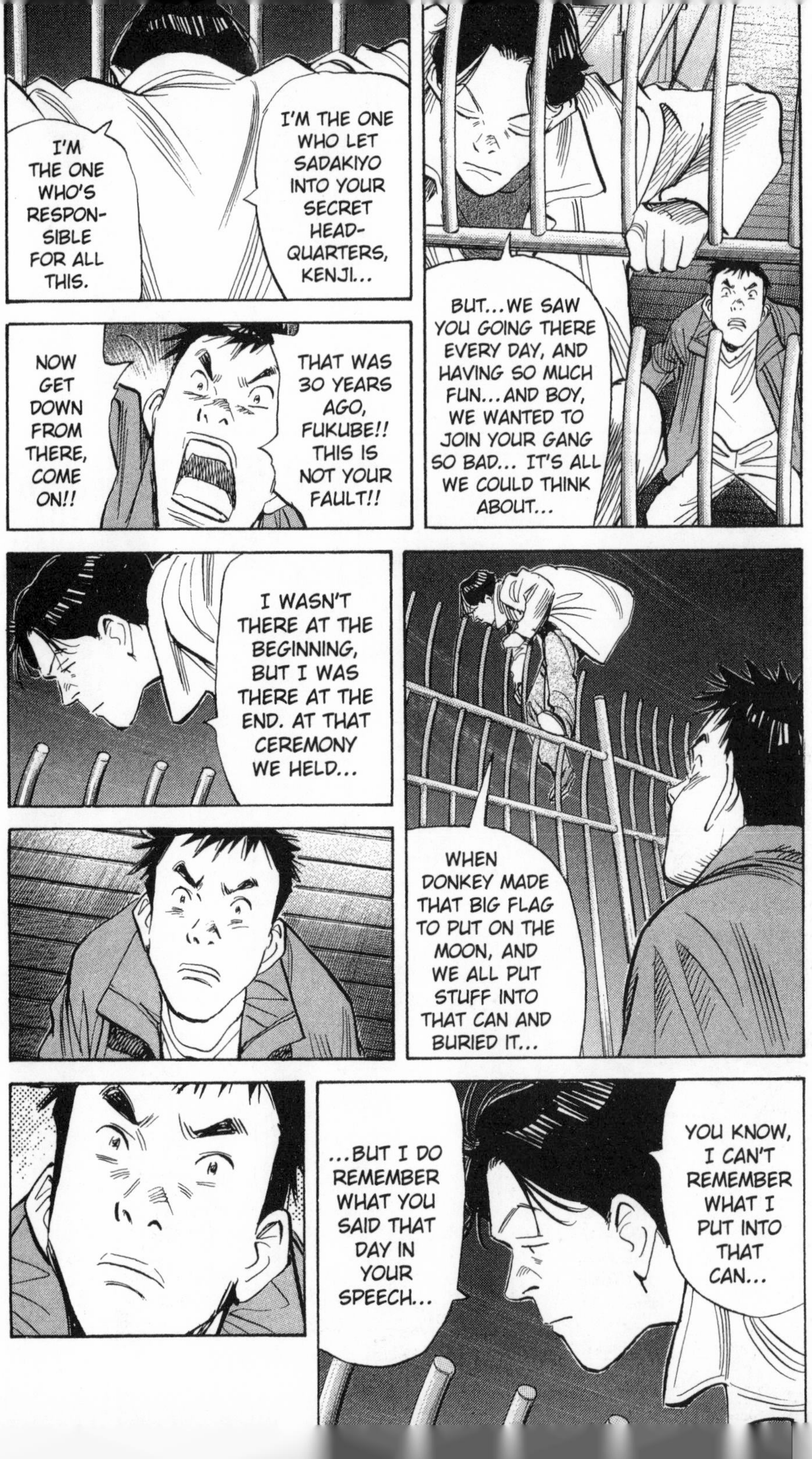
BUT...WE SAW YOU GOING THERE EVERY DAY, AND HAVING SO MUCH FUN...AND BOY, WE WANTED TO JOIN YOUR GANG SO BAD... IT'S ALL WE COULD THINK ABOUT...
I'M THE ONE WHO LET SADAKIYO INTO YOUR SECRET HEAD-QUARTERS, KENJI...
I'M THE ONE WHO'S RESPON-SIBLE FOR ALL THIS.
THAT WAS 30 YEARS AGO, FUKUBE!! THIS IS NOT YOUR FAULT!!
NOW GET DOWN FROM THERE, COME ON!!
WHEN DONKEY MADE THAT BIG FLAG TO PUT ON THE MOON, AND WE ALL PUT STUFF INTO THAT CAN AND BURIED IT...
I WASN'T THERE AT THE BEGINNING, BUT I WAS THERE AT THE END. AT THAT CEREMONY WE HELD...
YOU KNOW, I CAN'T REMEMBER WHAT I PUT INTO THAT CAN...
...BUT I DO REMEMBER WHAT YOU SAID THAT DAY IN YOUR SPEECH...

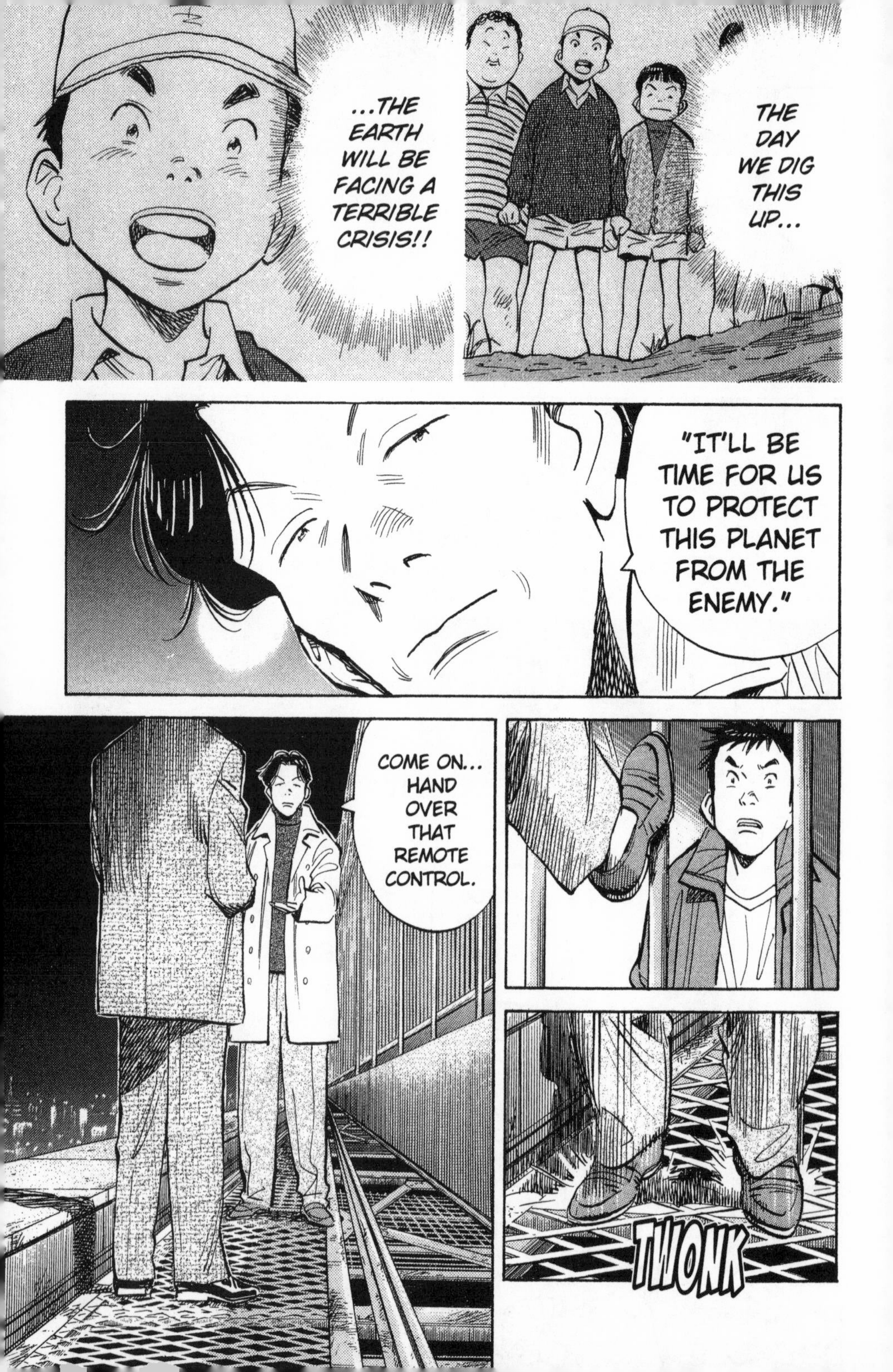
THE DAY WE DIG THIS UP...
...THE EARTH WILL BE FACING A TERRIBLE CRISIS!!
"IT'LL BE TIME FOR US TO PROTECT THIS PLANET FROM THE ENEMY."
TWONK
COME ON... HAND OVER THAT REMOTE CONTROL.

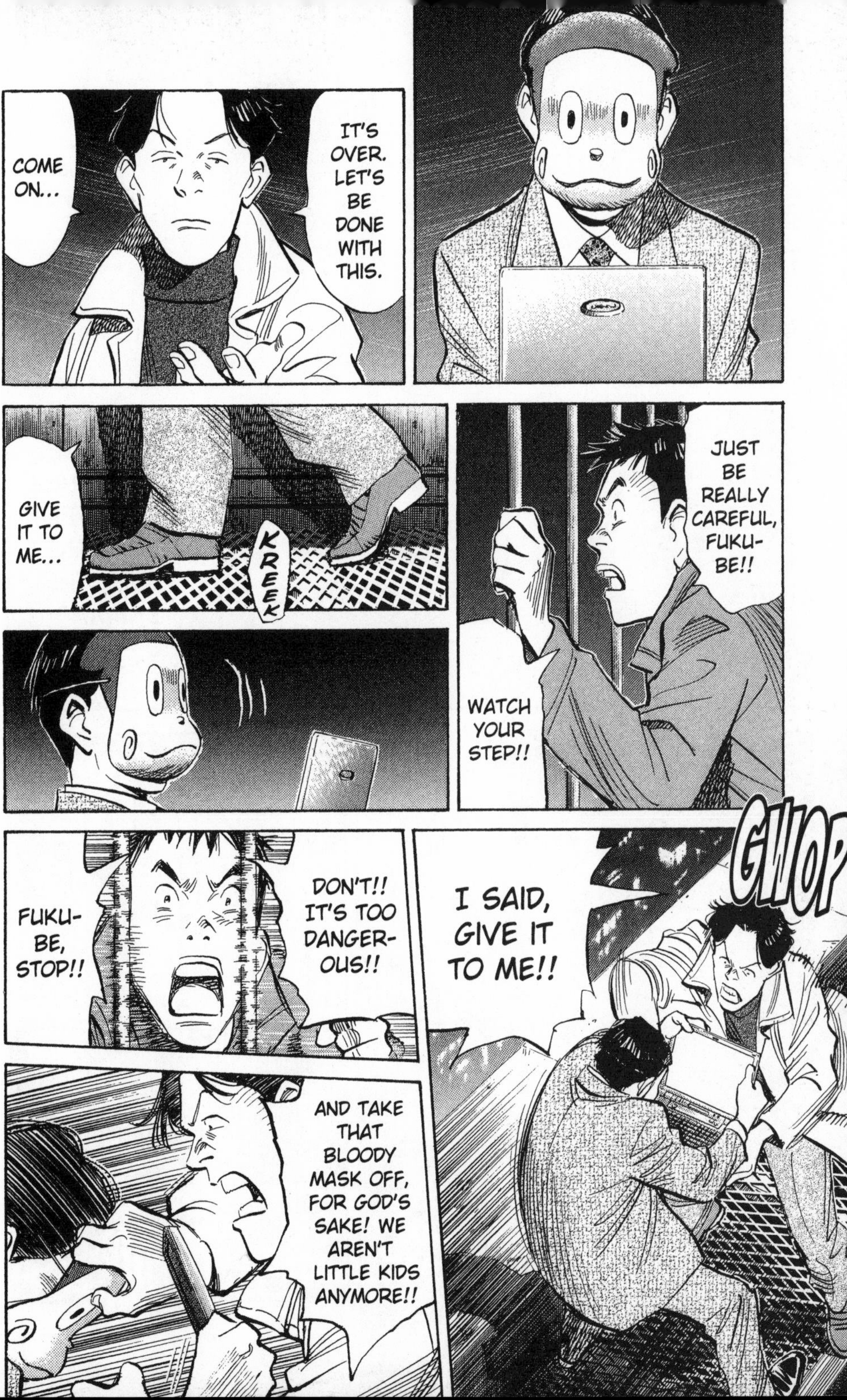
IT'S OVER. LET'S BE DONE WITH THIS.
COME ON...
JUST BE REALLY CAREFUL, FUKU-BE!!
WATCH YOUR STEP!!
GIVE IT TO ME...
KREEK
GWOP
I SAID, GIVE IT TO ME!!
DON'T!! IT'S TOO DANGER-OUS!!
FUKU-BE, STOP!!
AND TAKE THAT BLOODY MASK OFF, FOR GOD'S SAKE! WE AREN'T LITTLE KIDS ANYMORE!!

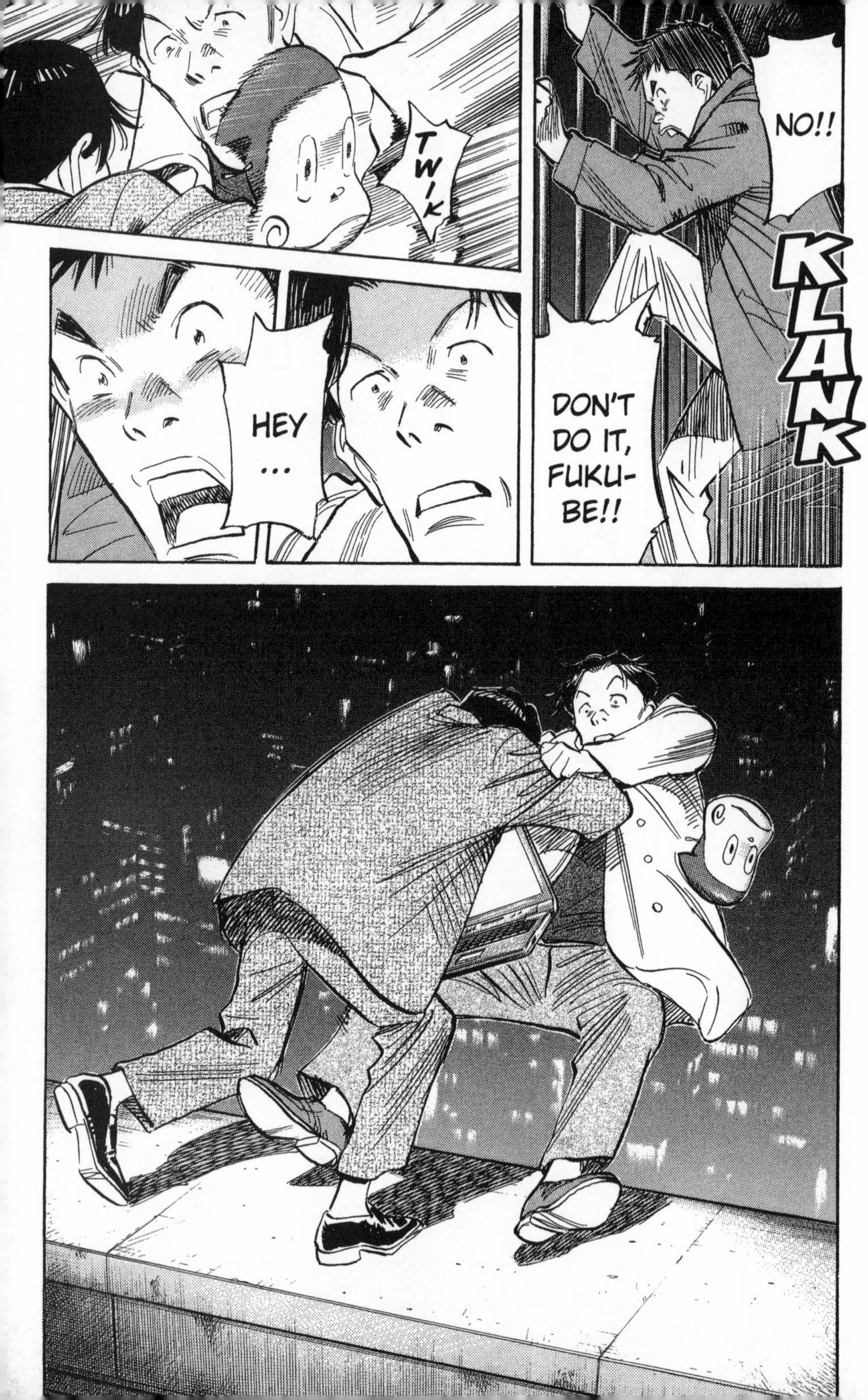
NO!!
KLANK
DON'T DO IT, FUKU-BE!!
TWIK
HEY ...

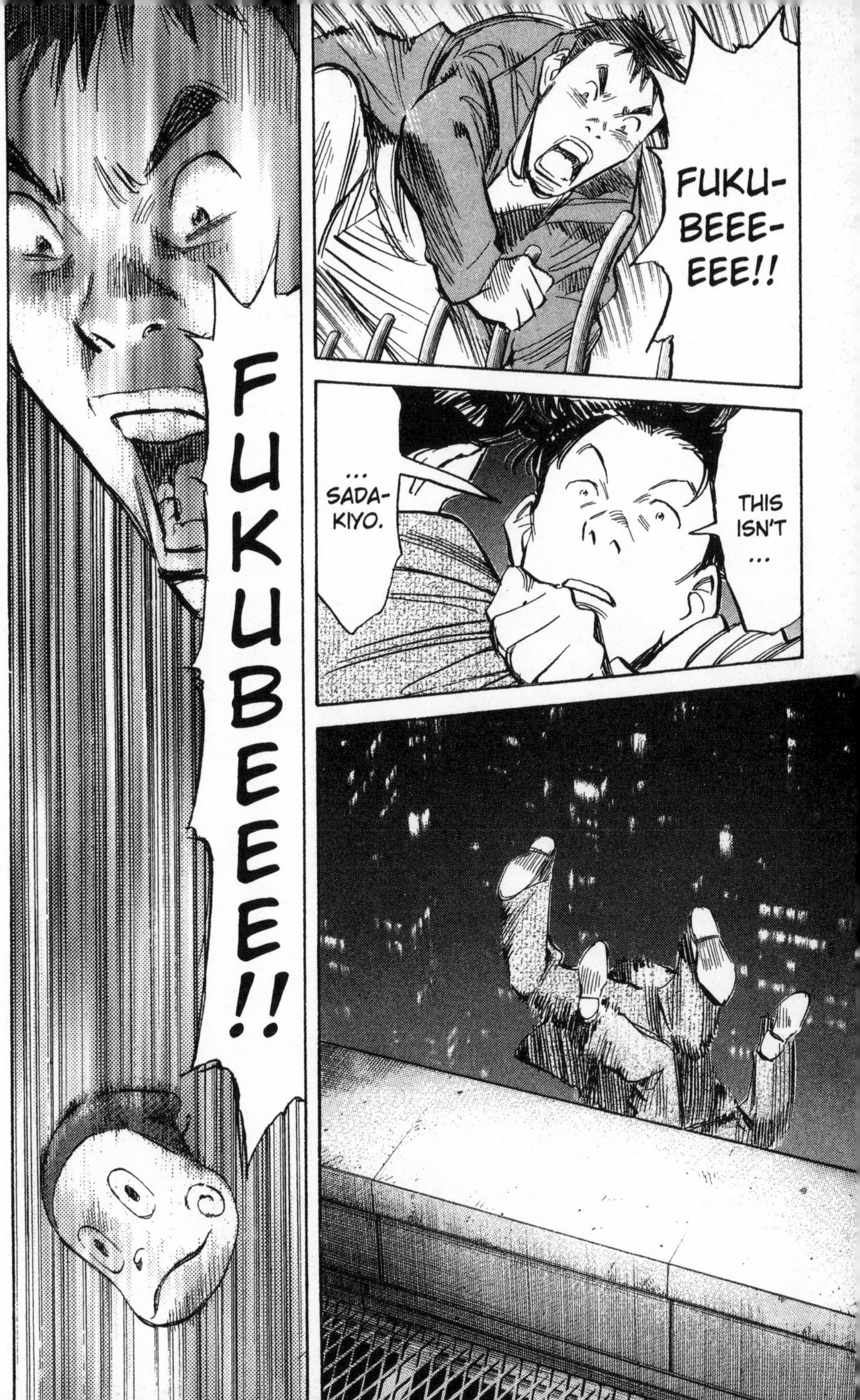
FUKU-
BEEE-
EEE!!
THIS ISN'T ...
... SADA-KIYO.
FUKUBEEE!!

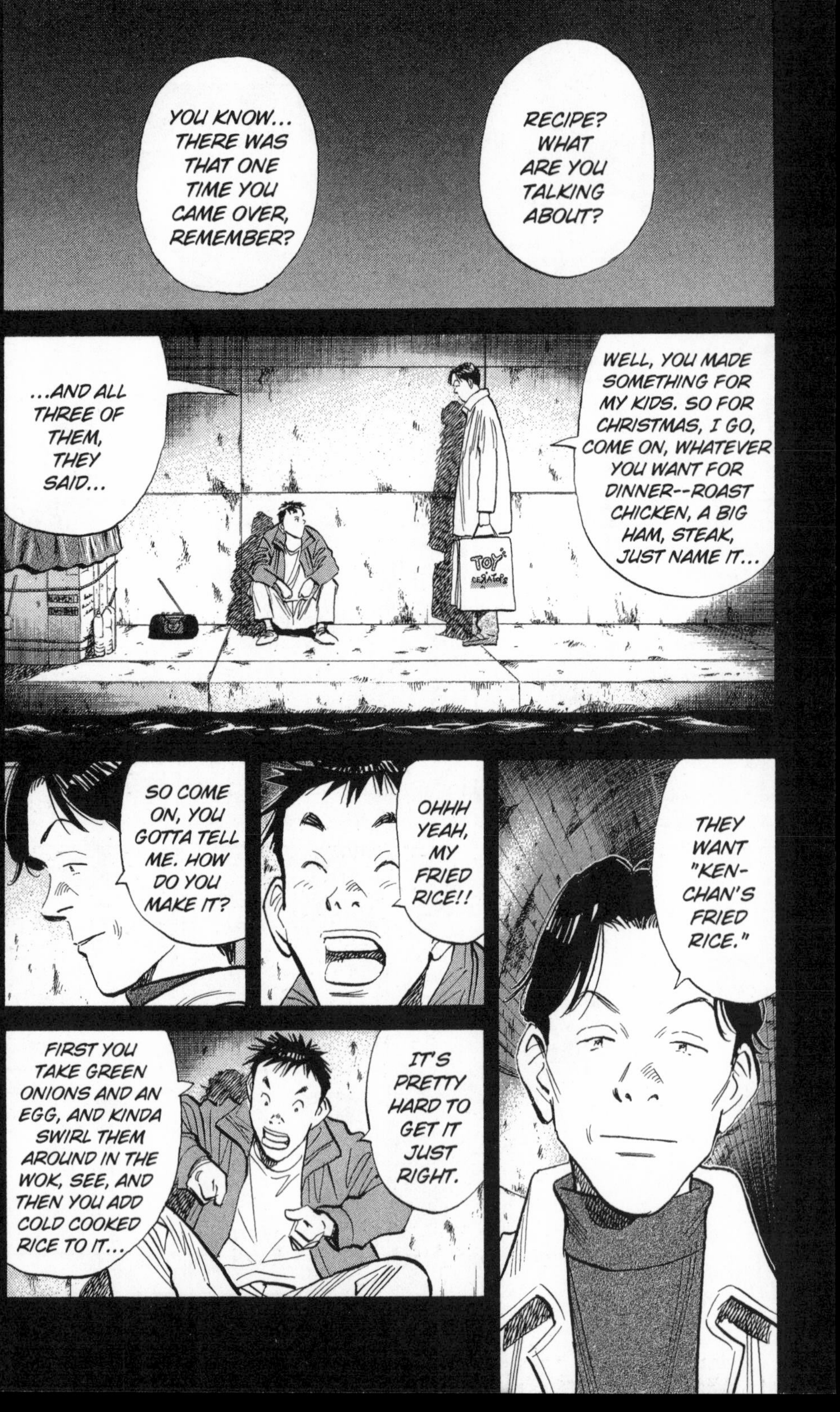
RECIPE? WHAT ARE YOU TALKING ABOUT?
YOU KNOW... THERE WAS THAT ONE TIME YOU CAME OVER, REMEMBER?
WELL, YOU MADE SOMETHING FOR MY KIDS. SO FOR CHRISTMAS, I GO, COME ON, WHATEVER YOU WANT FOR DINNER--ROAST CHICKEN, A BIG HAM, STEAK, JUST NAME IT...
...AND ALL THREE OF THEM, THEY SAID...
THEY WANT "KEN-CHAN'S FRIED RICE."
OHHH YEAH, MY FRIED RICE!!
SO COME ON, YOU GOTTA TELL ME. HOW DO YOU MAKE IT?
IT'S PRETTY HARD TO GET IT JUST RIGHT.
FIRST YOU TAKE GREEN ONIONS AND AN EGG, AND KINDA SWIRL THEM AROUND IN THE WOK, SEE, AND THEN YOU ADD COLD COOKED RICE TO IT...

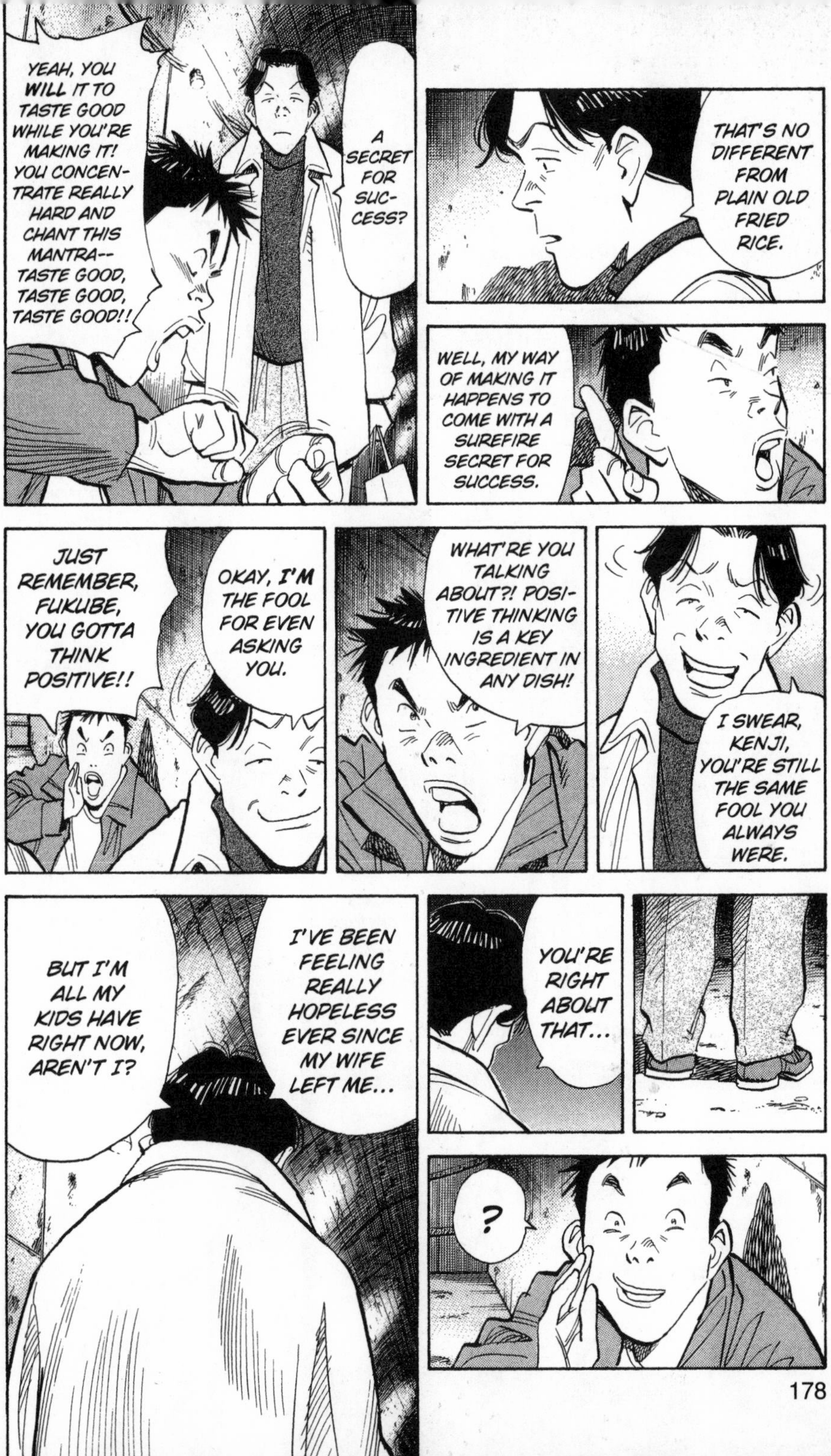
THAT'S NO DIFFERENT FROM PLAIN OLD FRIED RICE.
WELL, MY WAY OF MAKING IT HAPPENS TO COME WITH A SUREFIRE SECRET FOR SUCCESS.
A SECRET FOR SUC-CESS?
YEAH, YOU **WILL** IT TO TASTE GOOD WHILE YOU'RE MAKING IT! YOU CONCEN-TRATE REALLY HARD AND CHANT THIS MANTRA-- TASTE GOOD, TASTE GOOD, TASTE GOOD!!
I SWEAR, KENJI, YOU'RE STILL THE SAME FOOL YOU ALWAYS WERE.
WHAT'RE YOU TALKING ABOUT?! POSI-TIVE THINKING IS A KEY INGREDIENT IN ANY DISH!
OKAY, **I'M** THE FOOL FOR EVEN ASKING YOU.
JUST REMEMBER, FUKUBE, YOU GOTTA THINK POSITIVE!!
YOU'RE RIGHT ABOUT THAT...
?
I'VE BEEN FEELING REALLY HOPELESS EVER SINCE MY WIFE LEFT ME...
BUT I'M ALL MY KIDS HAVE RIGHT NOW, AREN'T I?

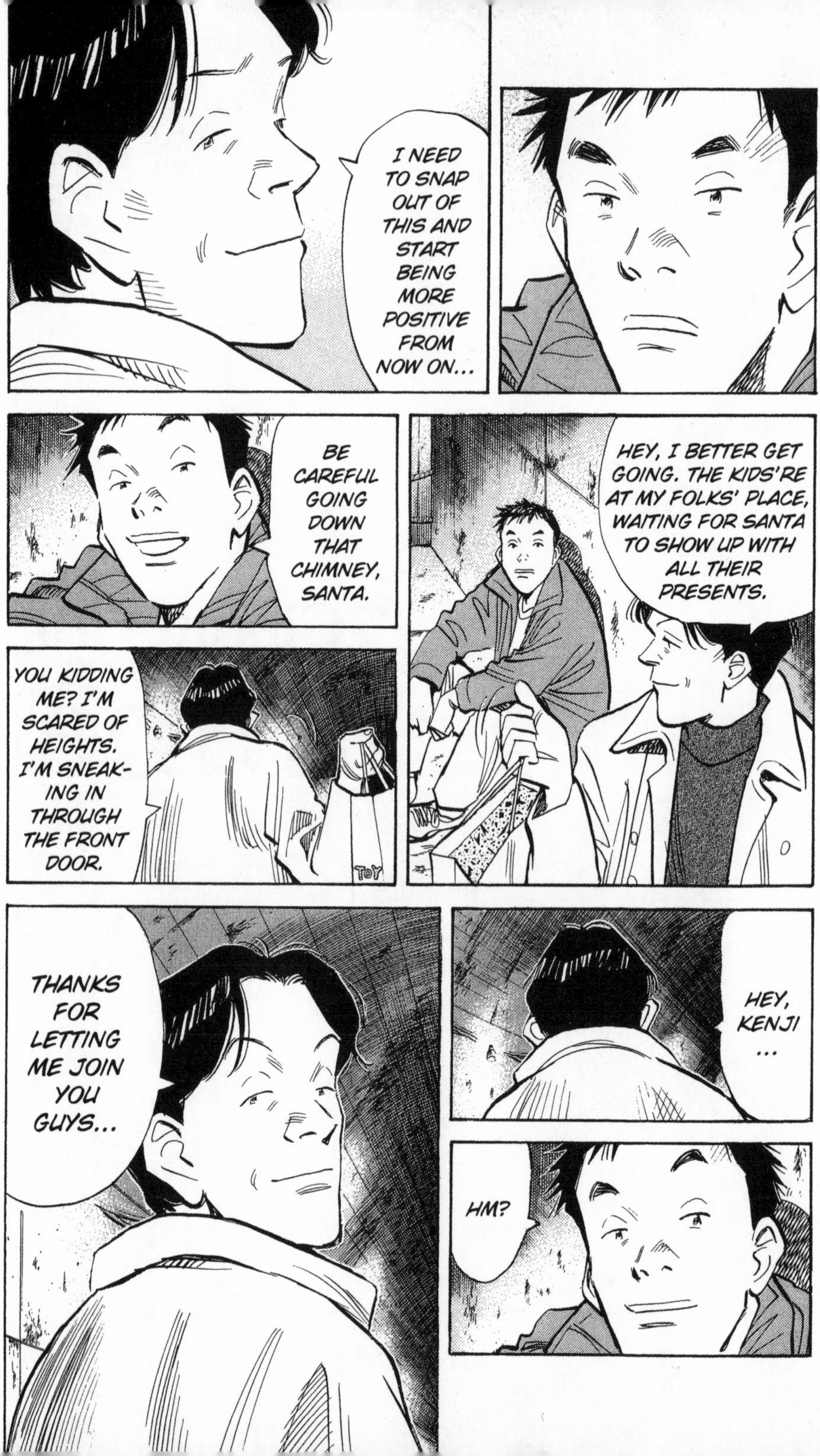

I NEED TO SNAP OUT OF THIS AND START BEING MORE POSITIVE FROM NOW ON...
HEY, I BETTER GET GOING. THE KIDS'RE AT MY FOLKS' PLACE, WAITING FOR SANTA TO SHOW UP WITH ALL THEIR PRESENTS.
BE CAREFUL GOING DOWN THAT CHIMNEY, SANTA.
YOU KIDDING ME? I'M SCARED OF HEIGHTS. I'M SNEAK-ING IN THROUGH THE FRONT DOOR.
TOY
HEY, KENJI...
HM?
THANKS FOR LETTING ME JOIN YOU GUYS...

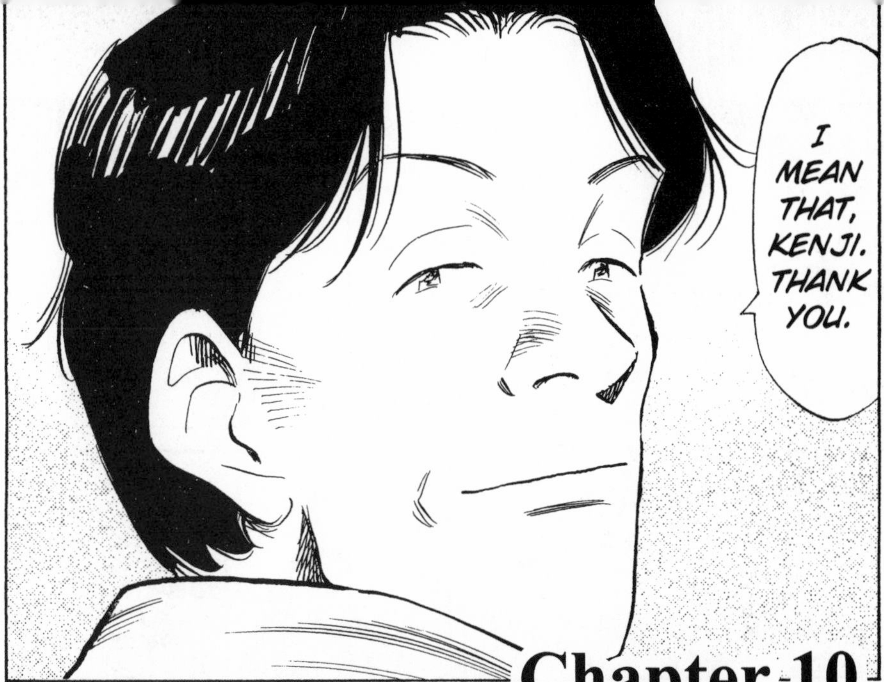
I MEAN THAT, KENJI. THANK YOU.

Chapter 10
Fukube

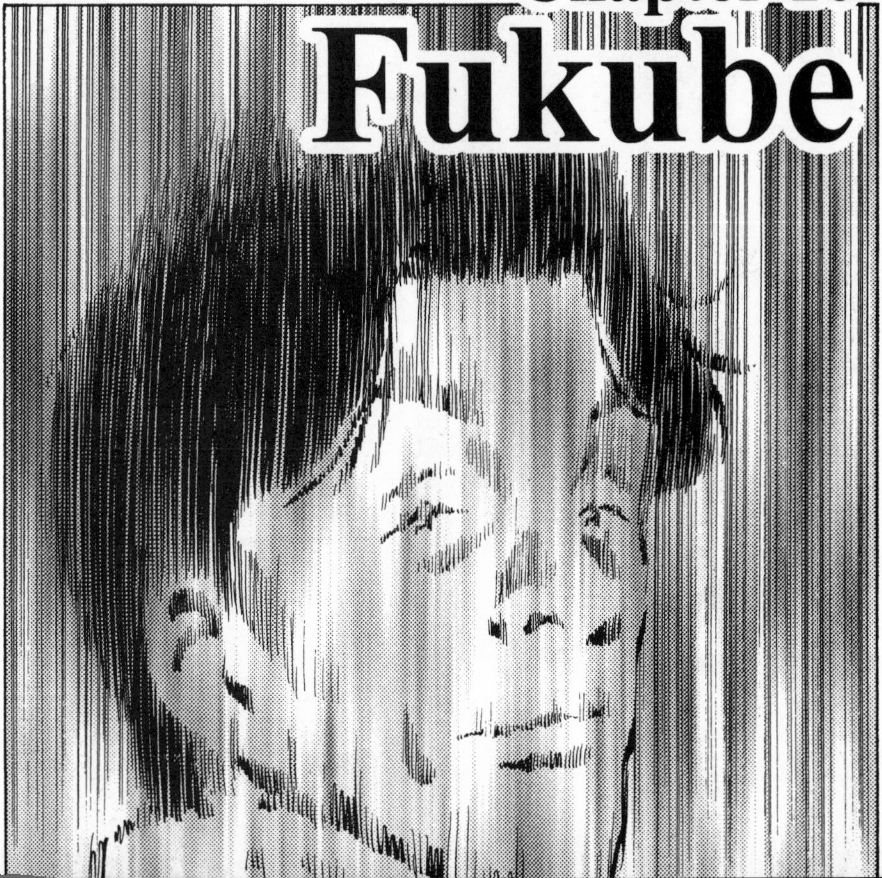

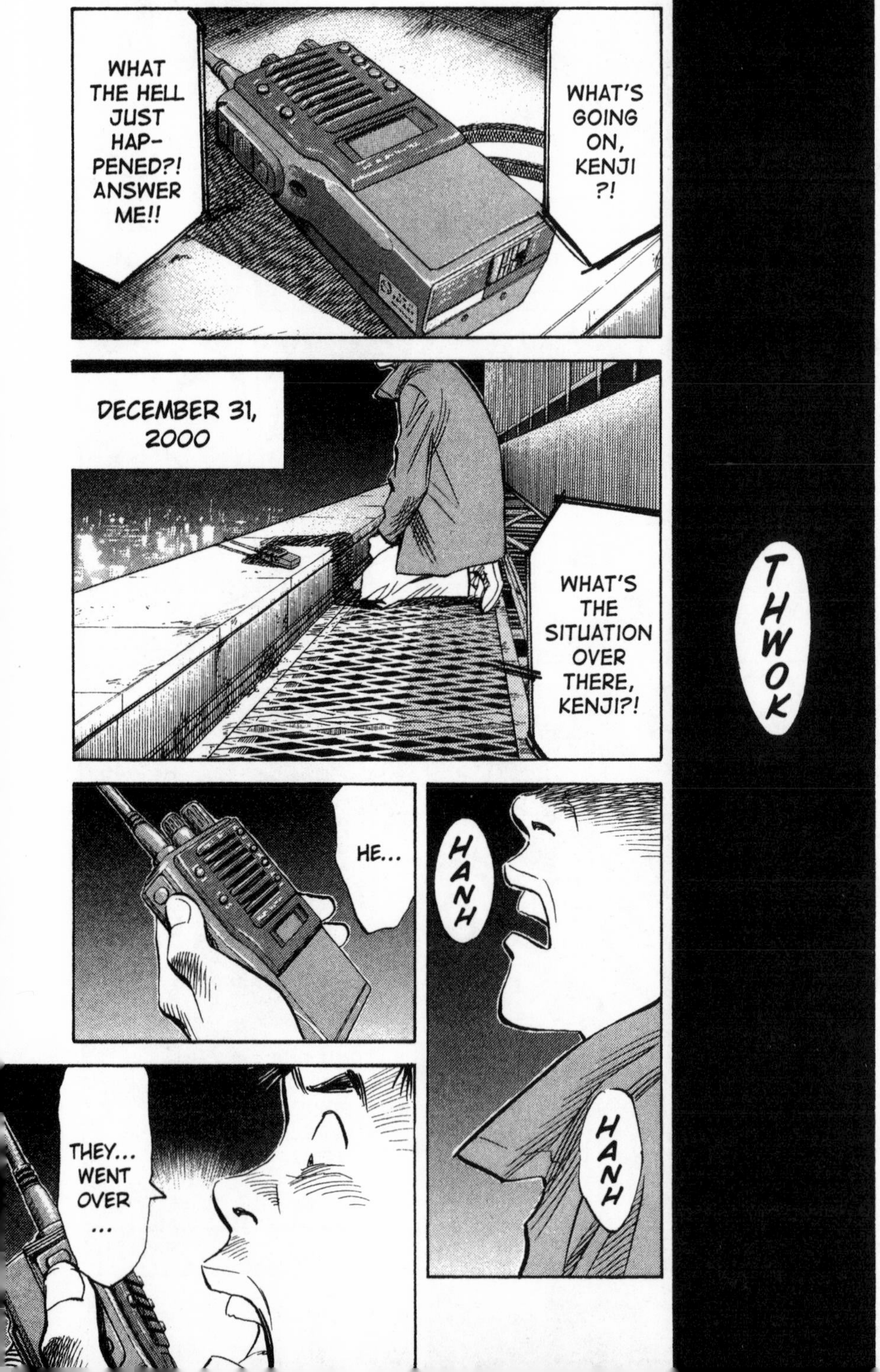
THWOK
WHAT'S GOING ON, KENJI?!
WHAT THE HELL JUST HAP-PENED?! ANSWER ME!!
DECEMBER 31, 2000
WHAT'S THE SITUATION OVER THERE, KENJI?!
HANH
HANH
HE...
THEY... WENT OVER ...

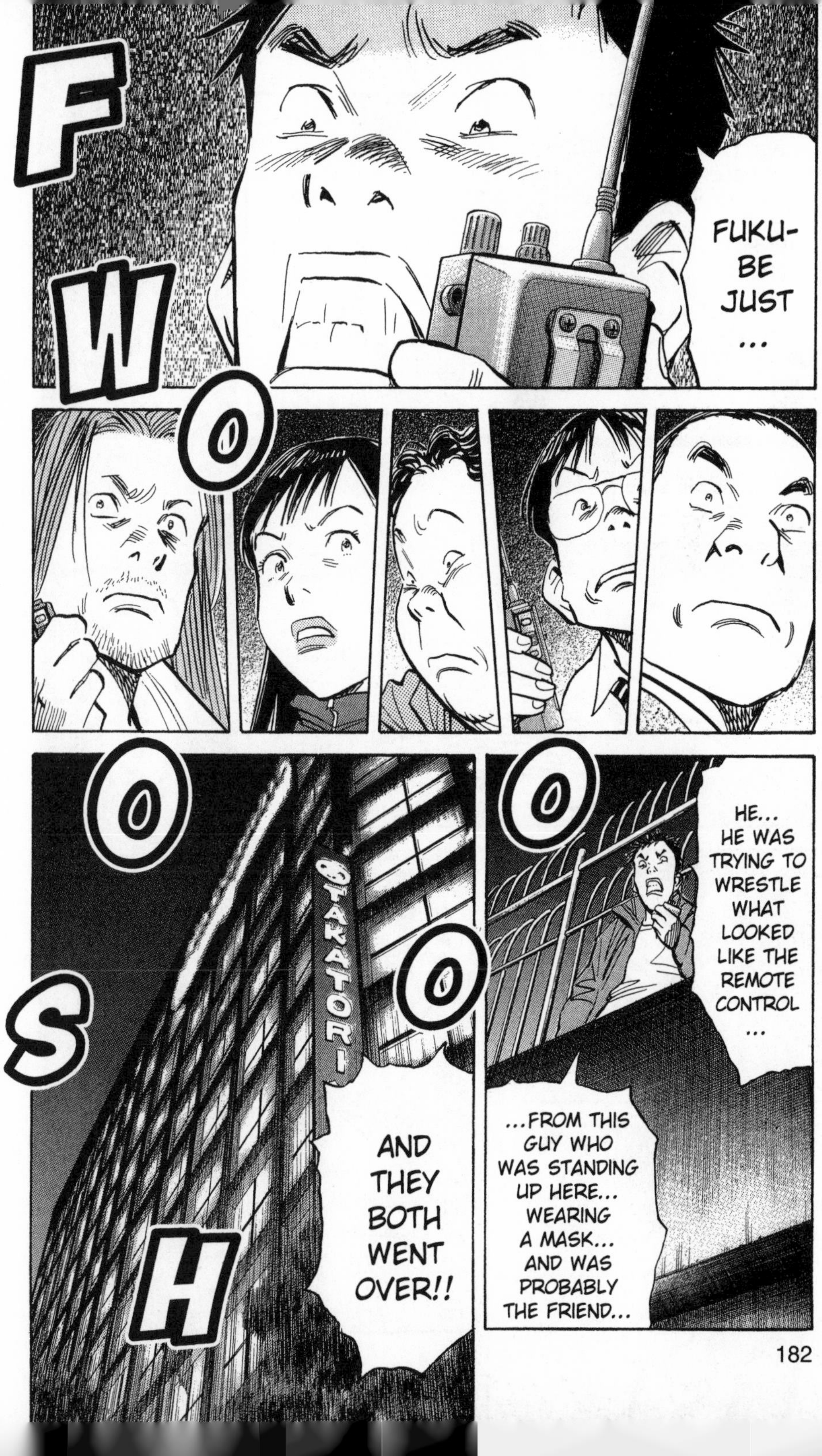
FUKU-BE JUST...
FWOOOOSH
HE... HE WAS TRYING TO WRESTLE WHAT LOOKED LIKE THE REMOTE CONTROL...
...FROM THIS GUY WHO WAS STANDING UP HERE... WEARING A MASK... AND WAS PROBABLY THE FRIEND...
TAKATORI
AND THEY BOTH WENT OVER!!

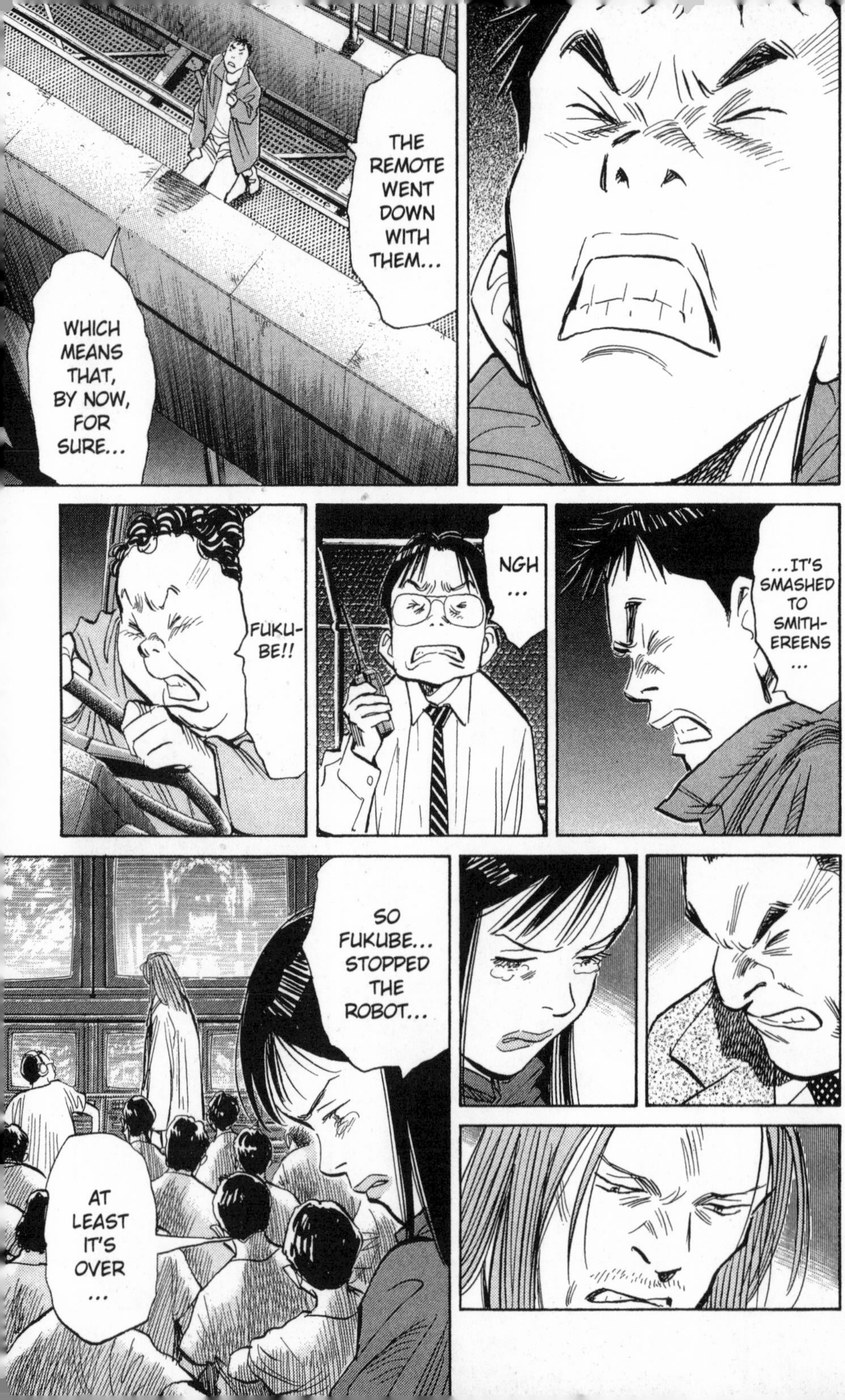
THE REMOTE WENT DOWN WITH THEM...
WHICH MEANS THAT, BY NOW, FOR SURE...
...IT'S SMASHED TO SMITH-EREENS...
NGH...
FUKU-BE!!
SO FUKUBE... STOPPED THE ROBOT...
AT LEAST IT'S OVER...

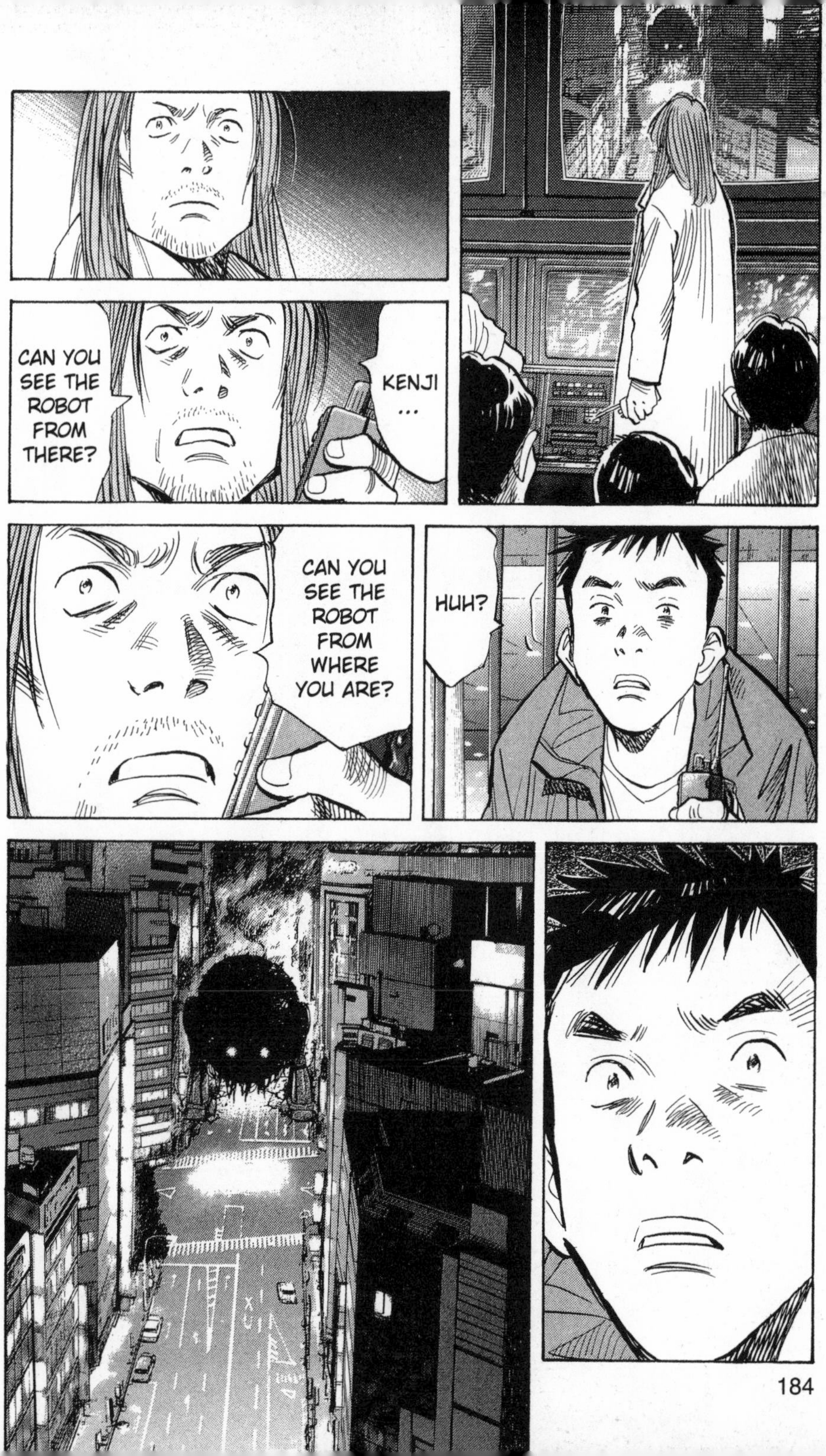
KENJI ...
CAN YOU SEE THE ROBOT FROM THERE?
HUH?
CAN YOU SEE THE ROBOT FROM WHERE YOU ARE?

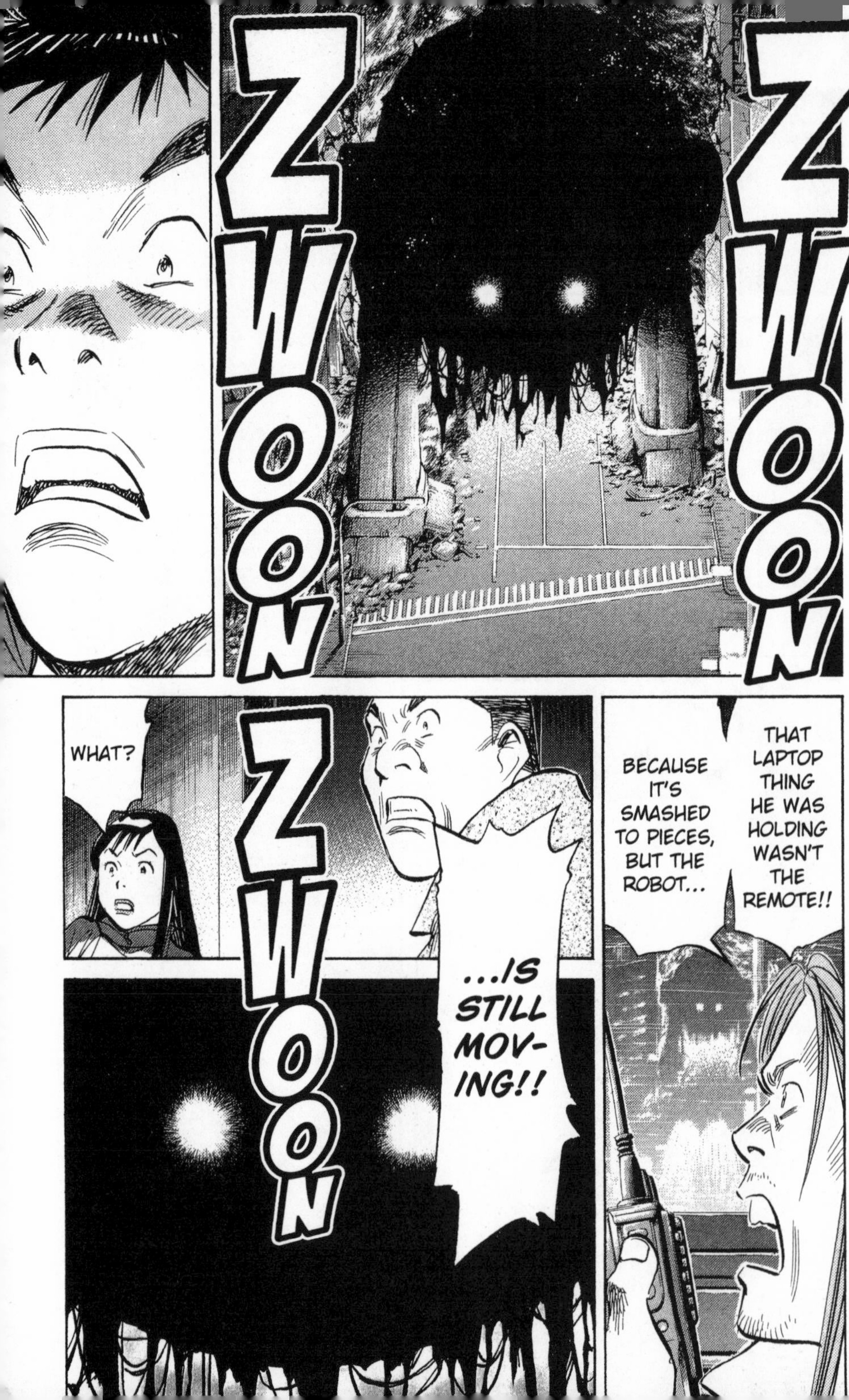
ZWOOON
ZWOOON
THAT LAPTOP THING HE WAS HOLDING WASN'T THE REMOTE!!
BECAUSE IT'S SMASHED TO PIECES, BUT THE ROBOT...
...IS STILL MOV-ING!!
WHAT?
ZWOOON

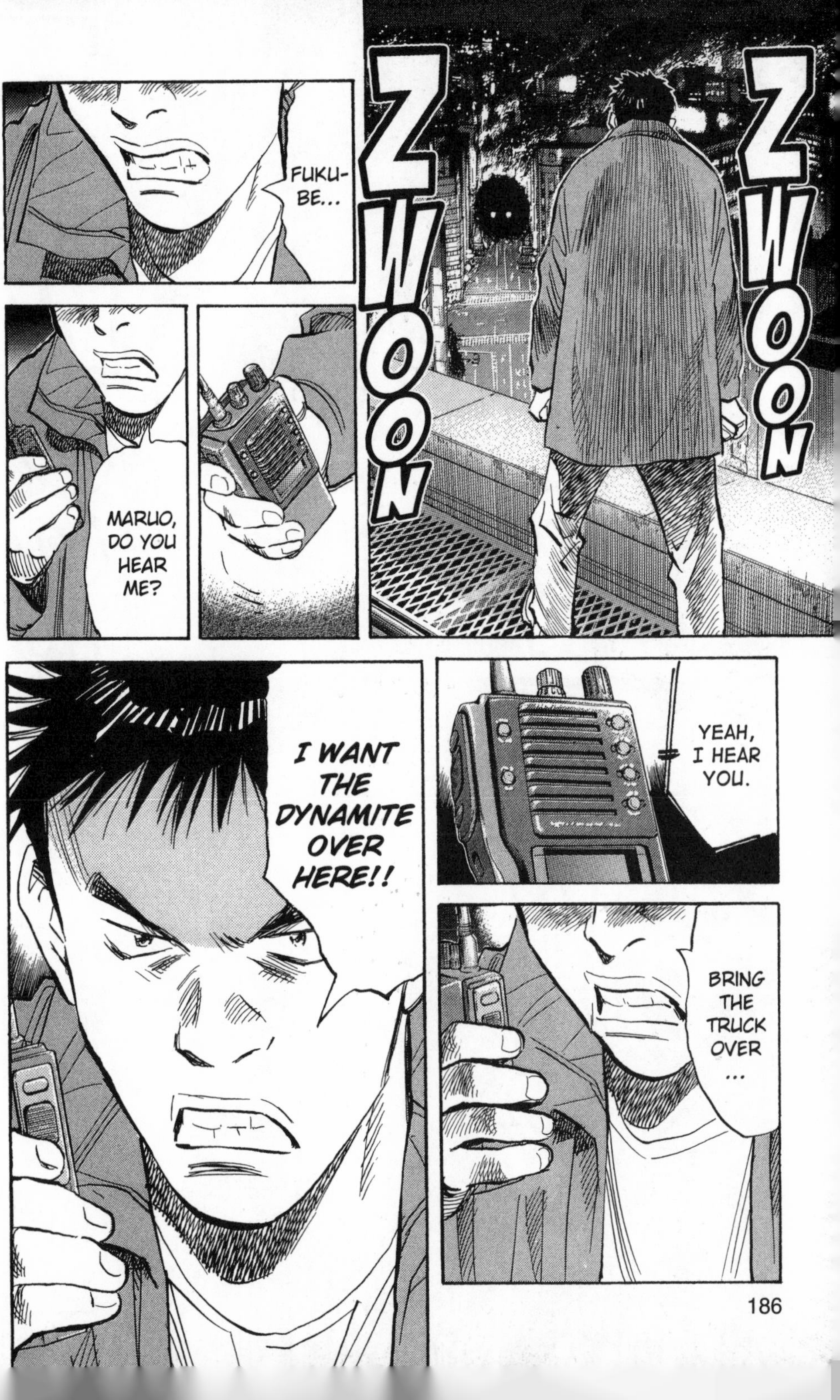
ZWOON
ZWOON
FUKU-BE...
MARUO, DO YOU HEAR ME?
YEAH, I HEAR YOU.
BRING THE TRUCK OVER ...
I WANT THE DYNAMITE OVER HERE!!

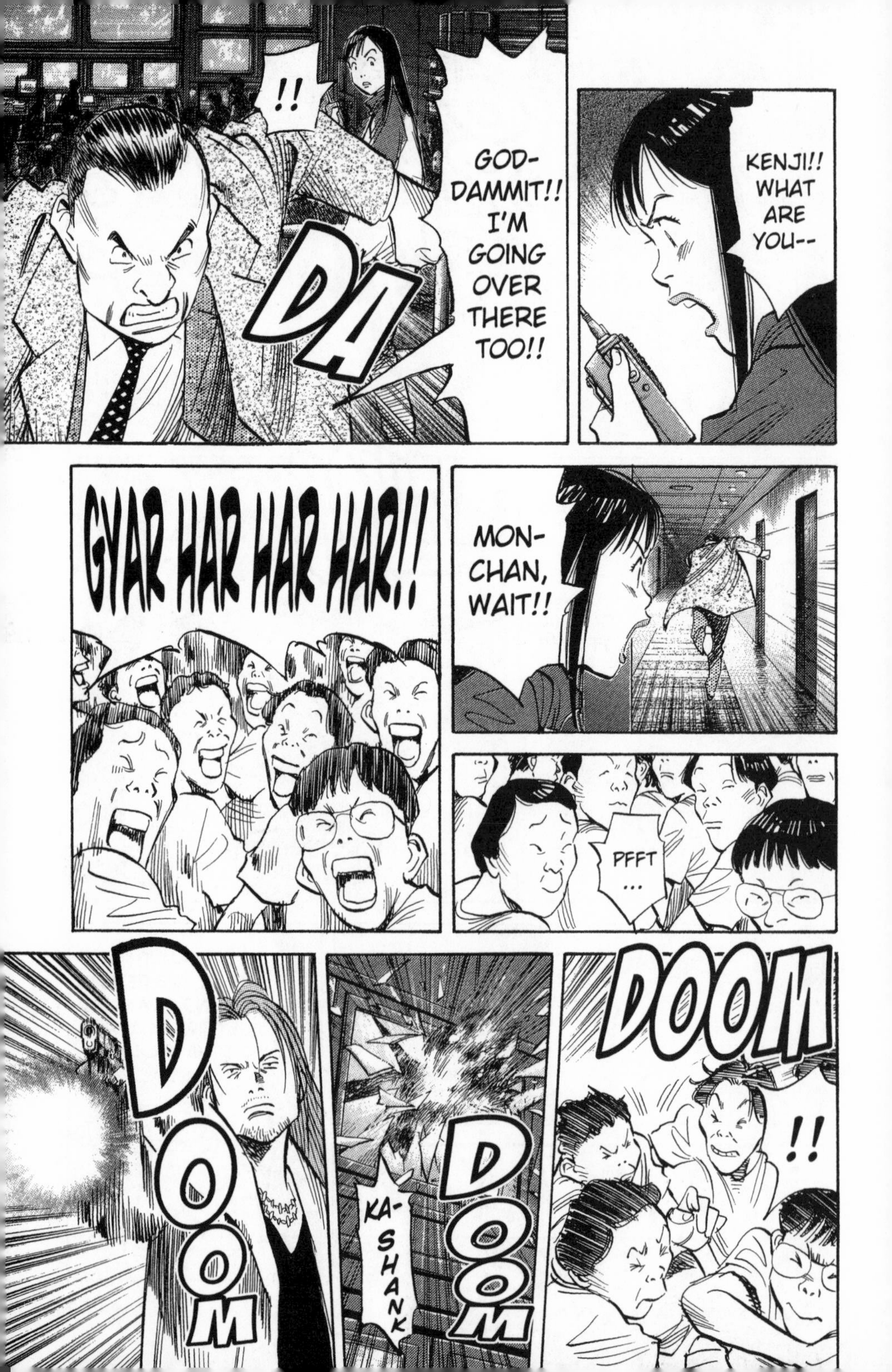
KENJI!! WHAT ARE YOU--
GOD-DAMMIT!! I'M GOING OVER THERE TOO!!
!!
DA
MON-CHAN, WAIT!!
PFFT ...
GYAR HAR HAR HAR!!
DOOM
!!
DOOOM
KA-SHANK
DOOOM

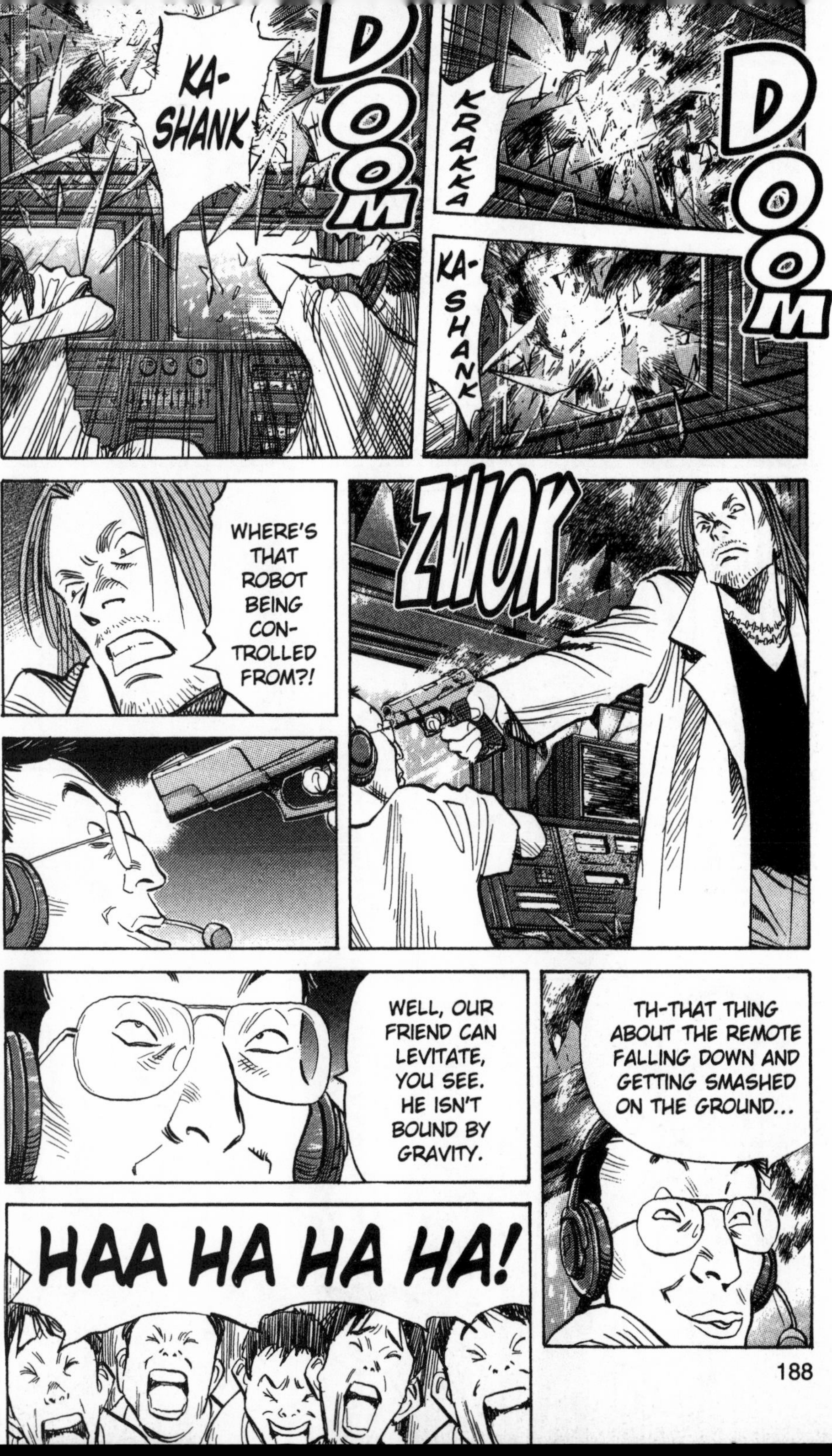
DOOM
KRAKKA
KA-SHANK
DOOM
KA-SHANK
ZWOK
WHERE'S THAT ROBOT BEING CON-TROLLED FROM?!
TH-THAT THING ABOUT THE REMOTE FALLING DOWN AND GETTING SMASHED ON THE GROUND...
WELL, OUR FRIEND CAN LEVITATE, YOU SEE. HE ISN'T BOUND BY GRAVITY.
HAA HA HA HA HA!

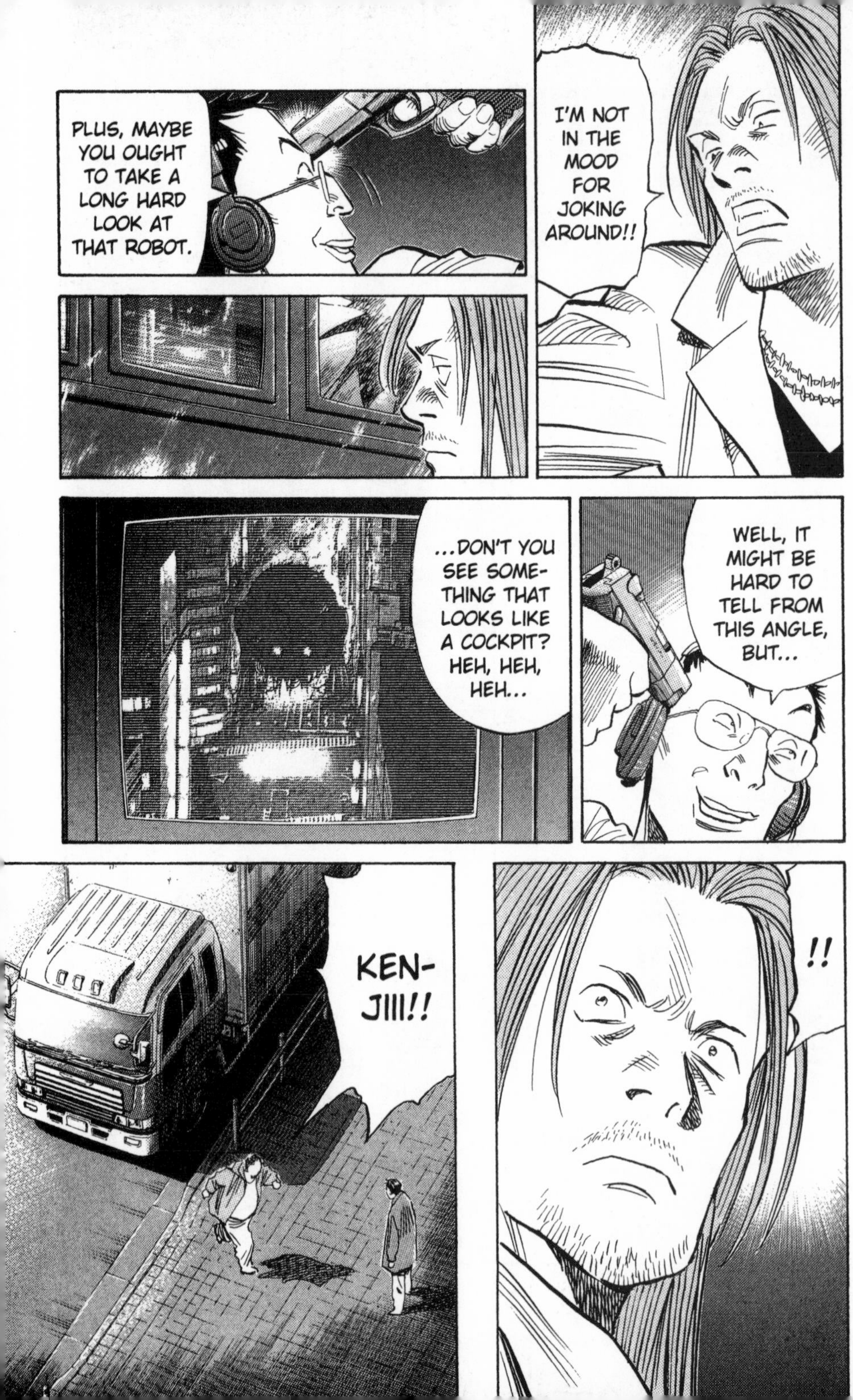
I'M NOT IN THE MOOD FOR JOKING AROUND!!
PLUS, MAYBE YOU OUGHT TO TAKE A LONG HARD LOOK AT THAT ROBOT.
WELL, IT MIGHT BE HARD TO TELL FROM THIS ANGLE, BUT...
...DON'T YOU SEE SOME-THING THAT LOOKS LIKE A COCKPIT? HEH, HEH, HEH...
!!
KEN-JIII!!

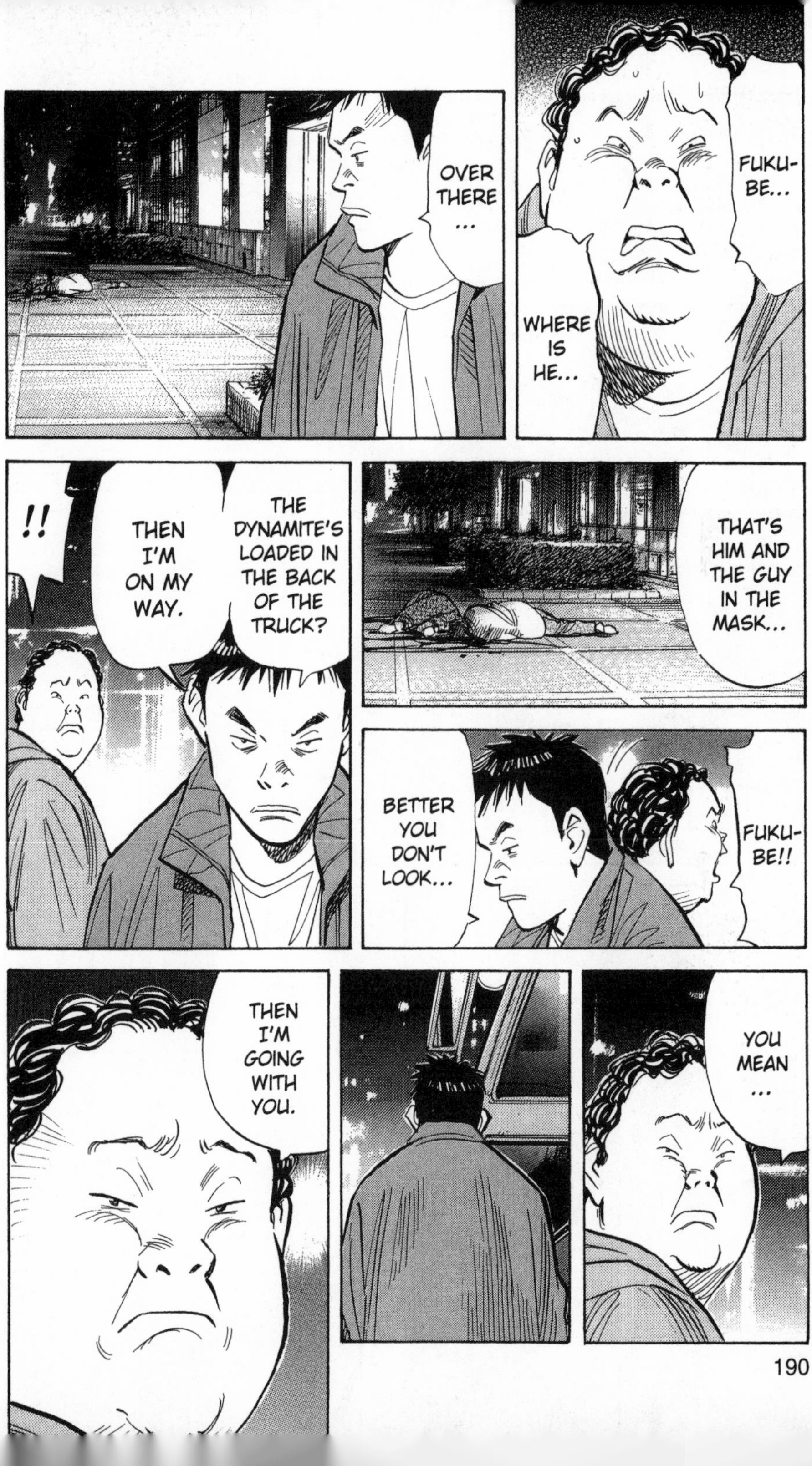
FUKU-BE...
WHERE IS HE...
OVER THERE ...
THAT'S HIM AND THE GUY IN THE MASK...
FUKU-BE!!
BETTER YOU DON'T LOOK...
THE DYNAMITE'S LOADED IN THE BACK OF THE TRUCK?
THEN I'M ON MY WAY.
!!
YOU MEAN ...
THEN I'M GOING WITH YOU.

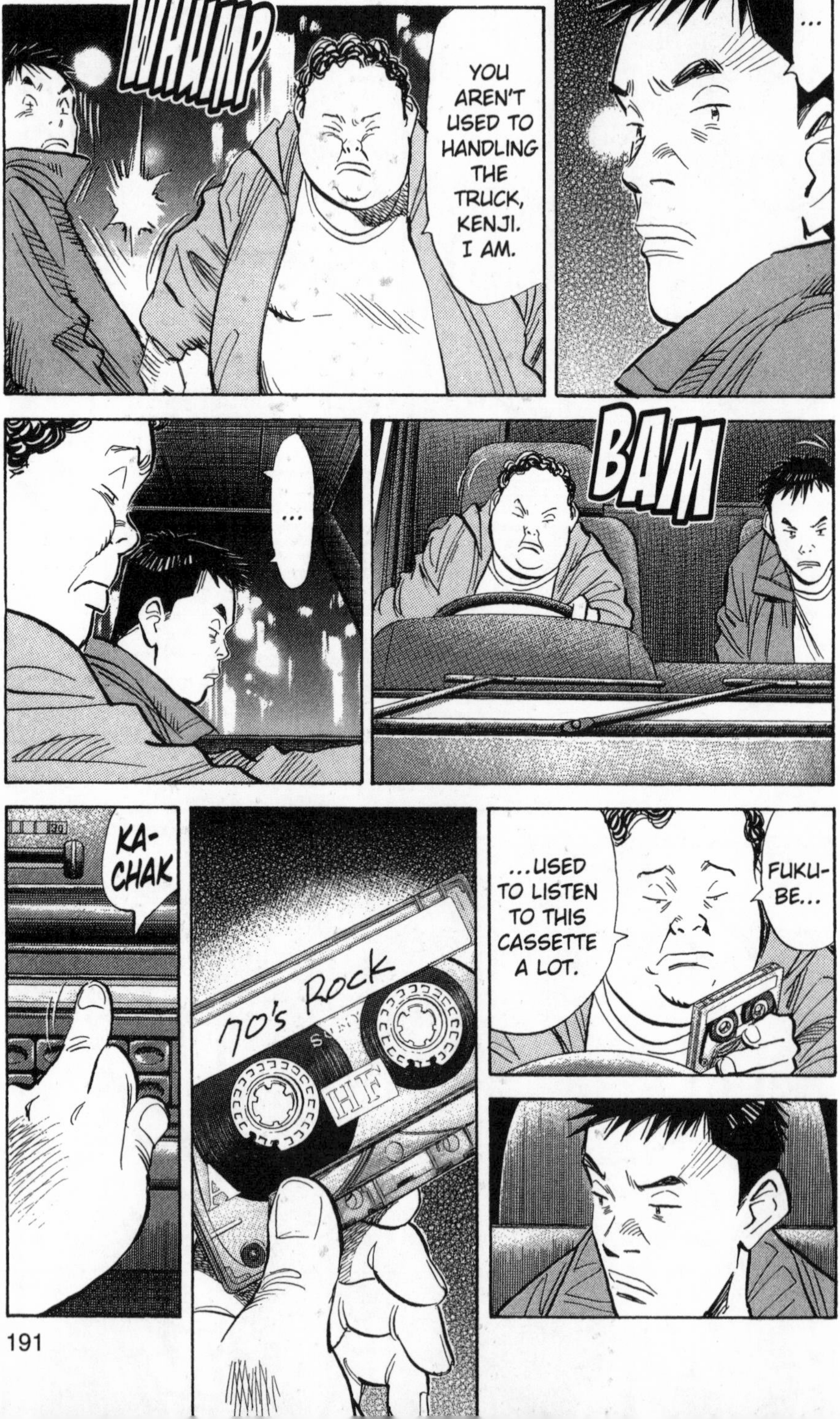
...
YOU AREN'T USED TO HANDLING THE TRUCK, KENJI. I AM.
WHUMP
BAM
...
FUKU-BE...
...USED TO LISTEN TO THIS CASSETTE A LOT.
70's Rock
HF
KA-CHAK

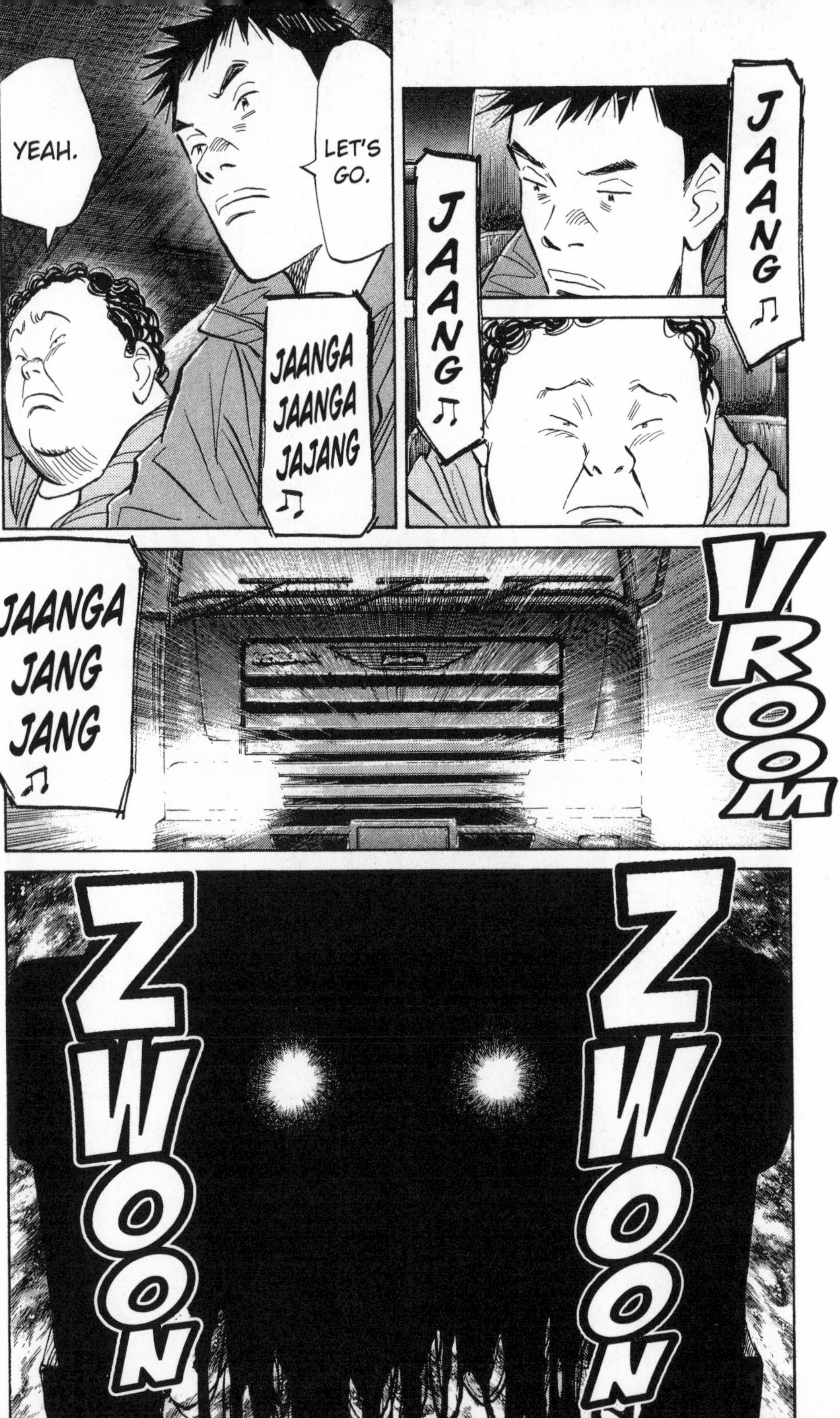
JAAANG ♫
JAAANG ♫
LET'S GO.
YEAH.
JAANGA JAANGA JAJANG ♫
VROOM
JAANGA JANG JANG ♫
ZWOOON
ZWOOON

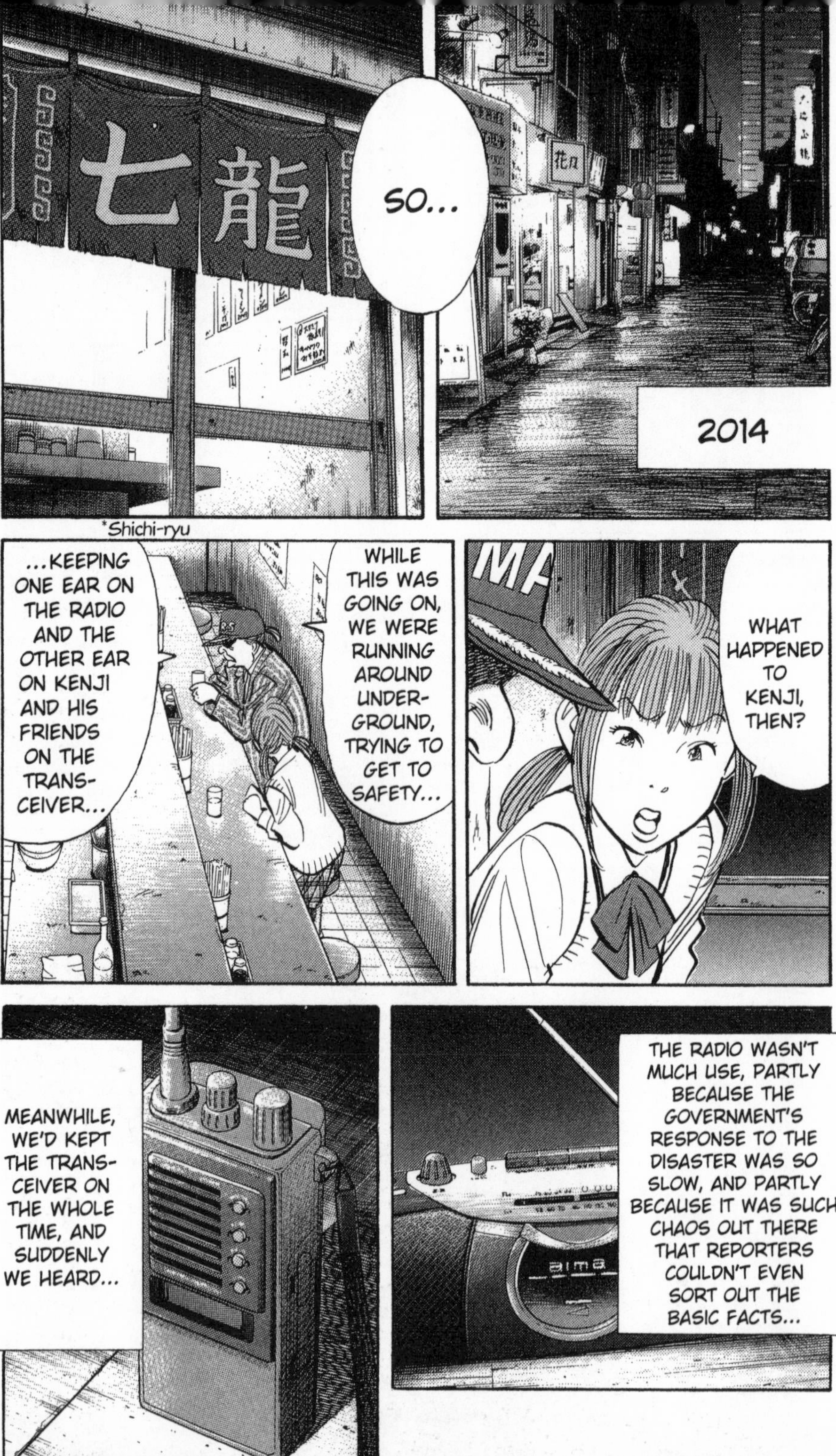
SO...
2014
七龍
*Shichi-ryu
WHAT HAPPENED TO KENJI, THEN?
WHILE THIS WAS GOING ON, WE WERE RUNNING AROUND UNDER-GROUND, TRYING TO GET TO SAFETY...
...KEEPING ONE EAR ON THE RADIO AND THE OTHER EAR ON KENJI AND HIS FRIENDS ON THE TRANS-CEIVER...
THE RADIO WASN'T MUCH USE, PARTLY BECAUSE THE GOVERNMENT'S RESPONSE TO THE DISASTER WAS SO SLOW, AND PARTLY BECAUSE IT WAS SUCH CHAOS OUT THERE THAT REPORTERS COULDN'T EVEN SORT OUT THE BASIC FACTS...
MEANWHILE, WE'D KEPT THE TRANS-CEIVER ON THE WHOLE TIME, AND SUDDENLY WE HEARD...

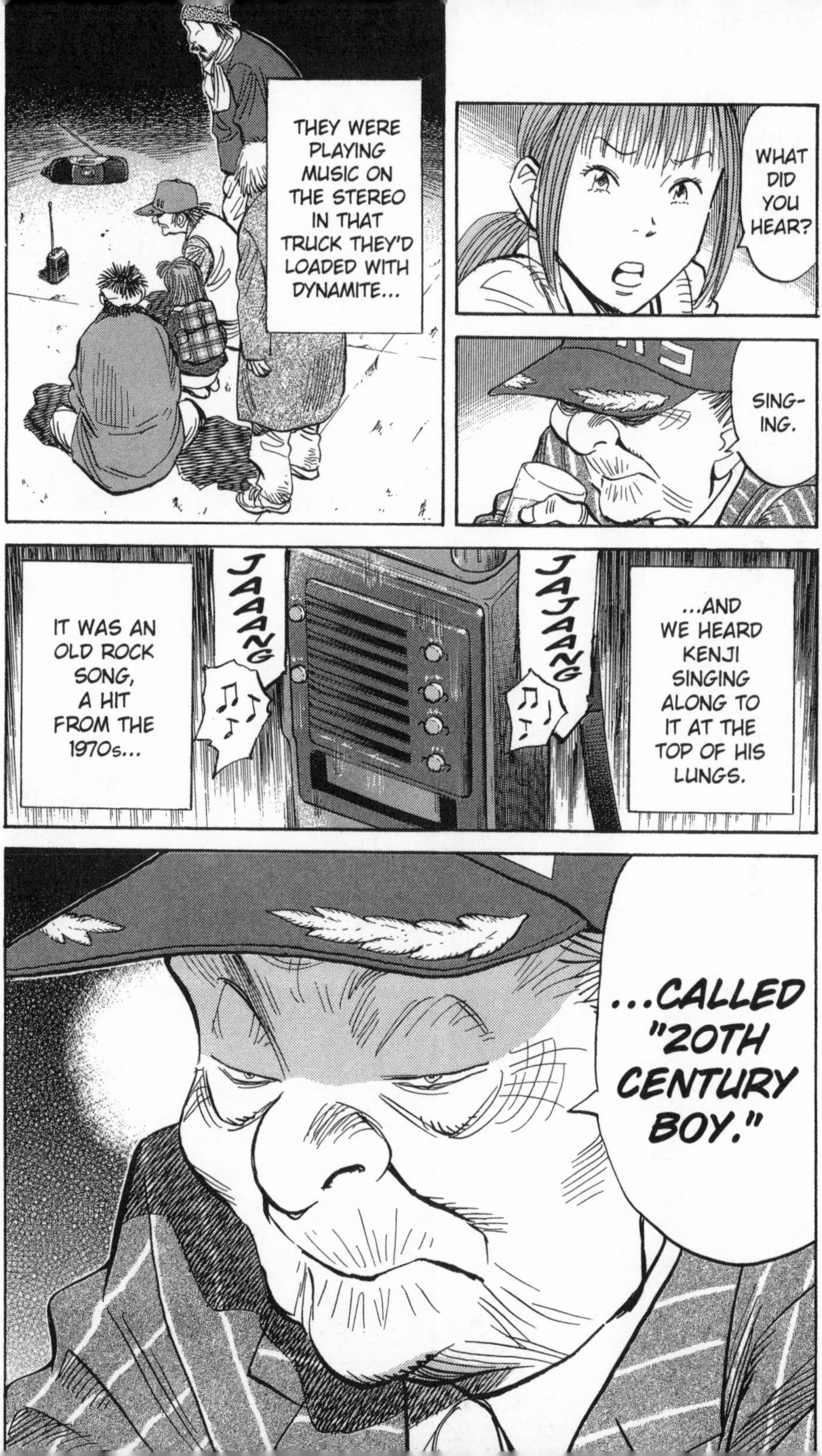
WHAT DID YOU HEAR?
SING-ING.
THEY WERE PLAYING MUSIC ON THE STEREO IN THAT TRUCK THEY'D LOADED WITH DYNAMITE...
...AND WE HEARD KENJI SINGING ALONG TO IT AT THE TOP OF HIS LUNGS.
JAJAANG
JAAAANG
IT WAS AN OLD ROCK SONG, A HIT FROM THE 1970s...
...CALLED "20TH CENTURY BOY."

Chapter 11 Charge

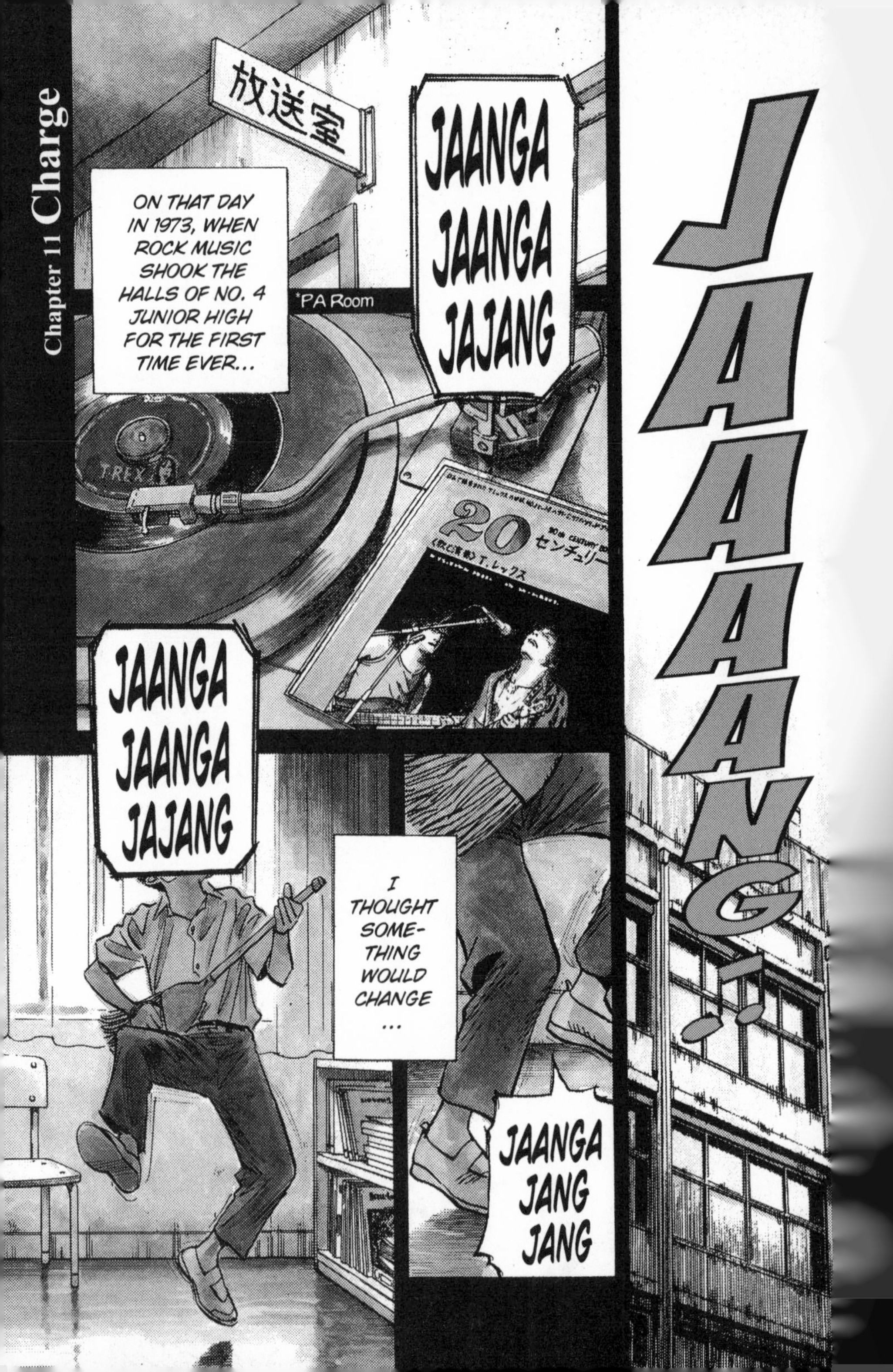
JAAAAANG
放送室
JAANGA JAANGA JAJANG
ON THAT DAY IN 1973, WHEN ROCK MUSIC SHOOK THE HALLS OF NO. 4 JUNIOR HIGH FOR THE FIRST TIME EVER...
*PA Room
20
センチュリー
T. レックス
I THOUGHT SOME-THING WOULD CHANGE ...
JAANGA JANG JANG
JAANGA JAANGA JAJANG

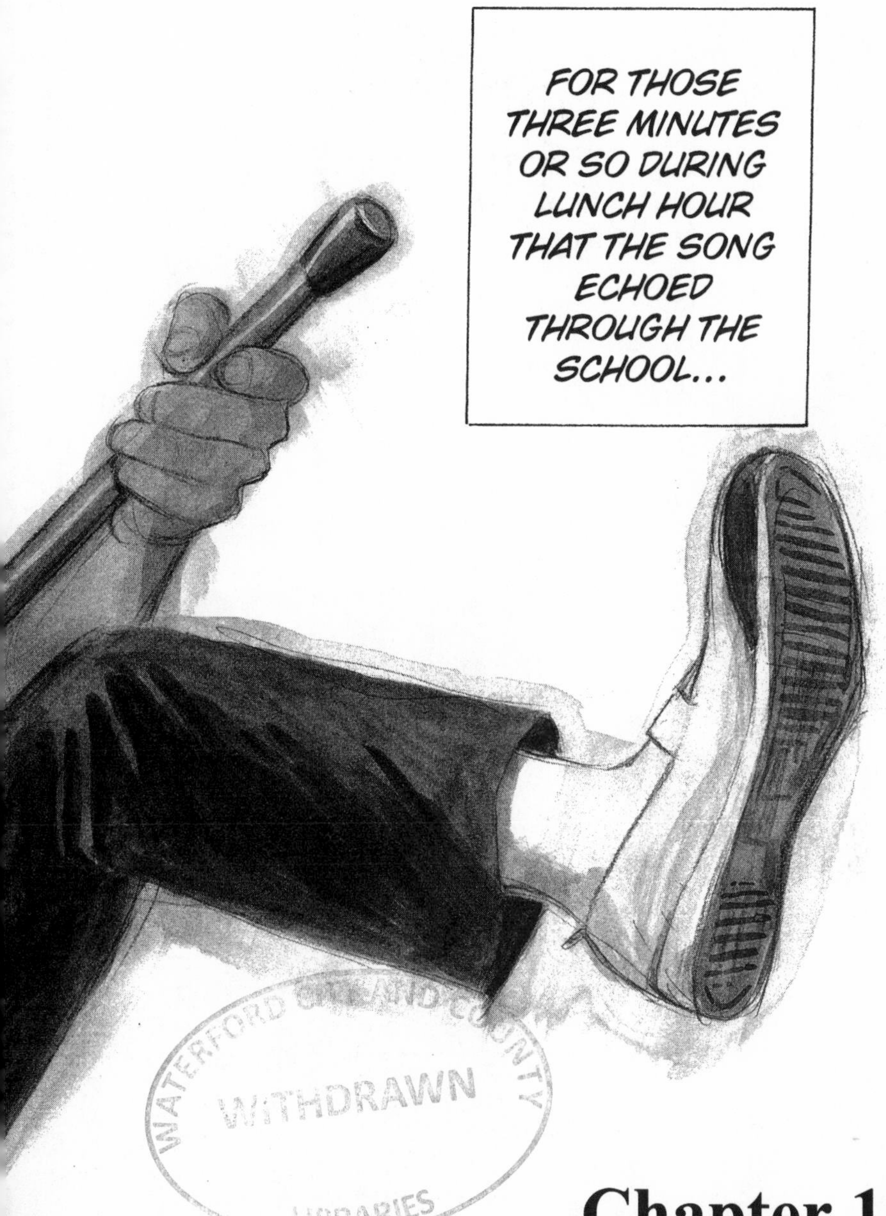
FOR THOSE THREE MINUTES OR SO DURING LUNCH HOUR THAT THE SONG ECHOED THROUGH THE SCHOOL...

Chapter 11
Charge

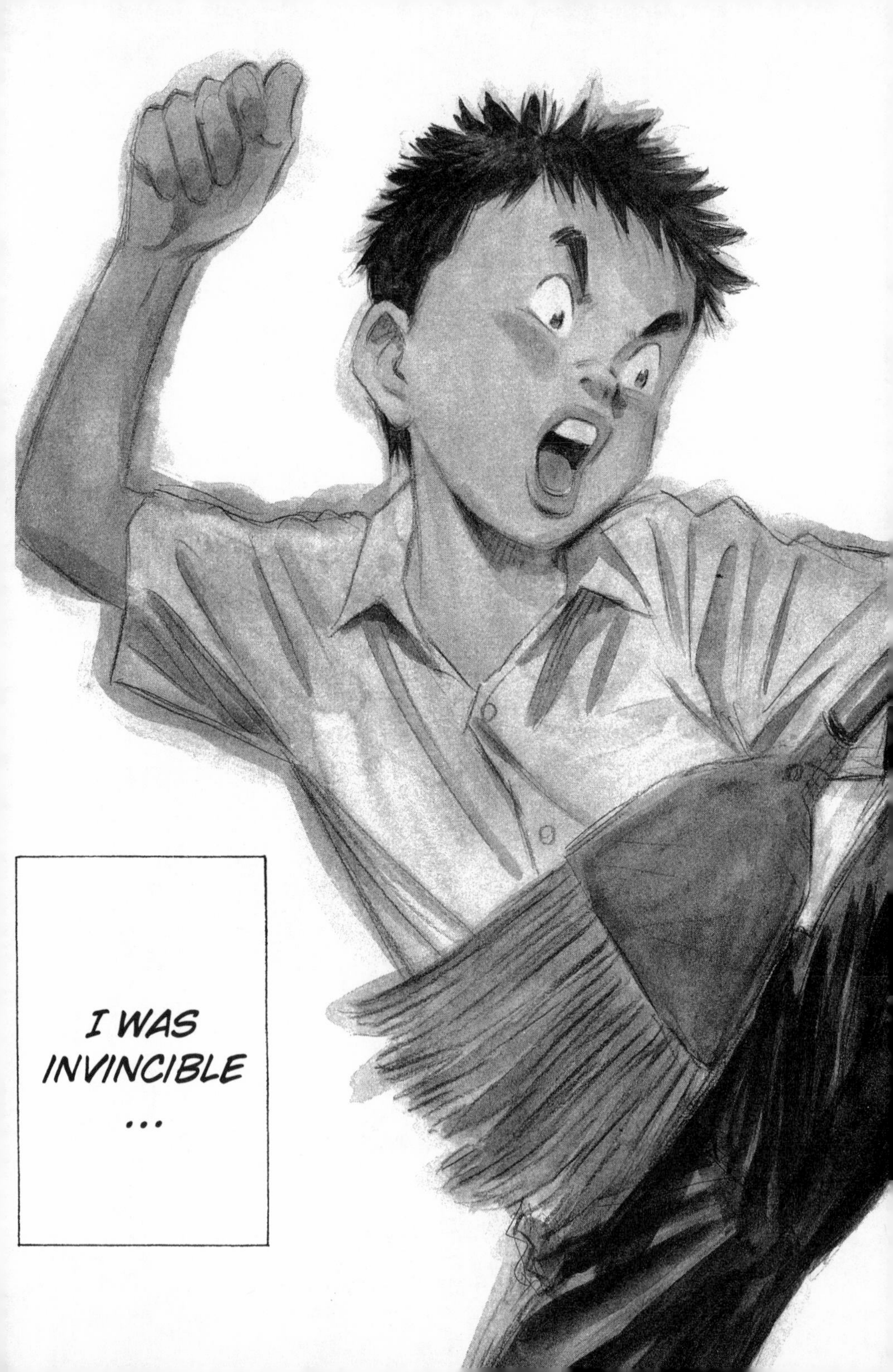
I WAS INVINCIBLE ...

20世紀少年
Twentieth Century Boys

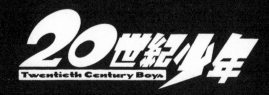

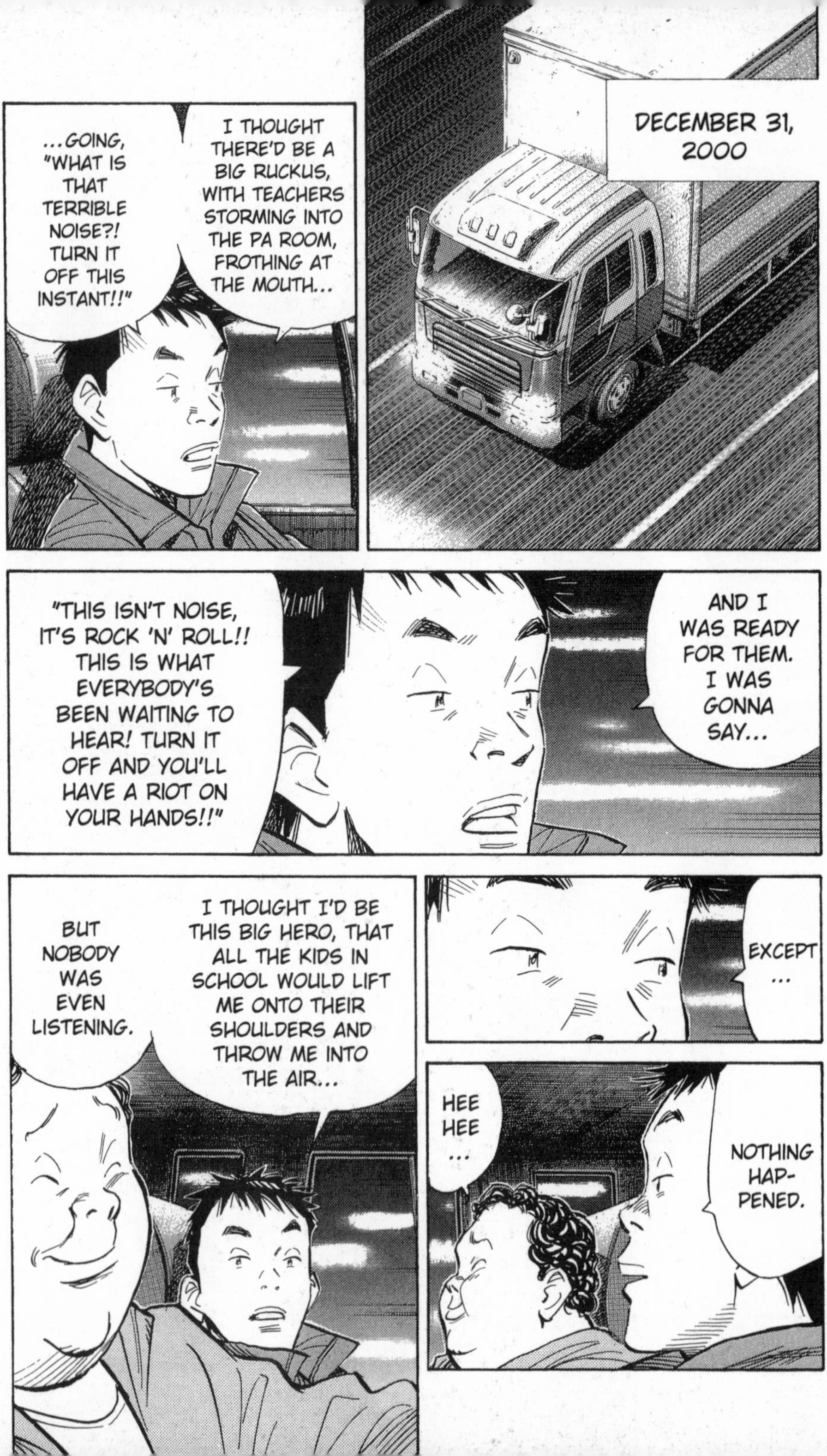
DECEMBER 31, 2000
I THOUGHT THERE'D BE A BIG RUCKUS, WITH TEACHERS STORMING INTO THE PA ROOM, FROTHING AT THE MOUTH...
...GOING, "WHAT IS THAT TERRIBLE NOISE?! TURN IT OFF THIS INSTANT!!"
AND I WAS READY FOR THEM. I WAS GONNA SAY...
"THIS ISN'T NOISE, IT'S ROCK 'N' ROLL!! THIS IS WHAT EVERYBODY'S BEEN WAITING TO HEAR! TURN IT OFF AND YOU'LL HAVE A RIOT ON YOUR HANDS!!"
EXCEPT...
NOTHING HAP-PENED.
HEE HEE...
I THOUGHT I'D BE THIS BIG HERO, THAT ALL THE KIDS IN SCHOOL WOULD LIFT ME ONTO THEIR SHOULDERS AND THROW ME INTO THE AIR...
BUT NOBODY WAS EVEN LISTENING.

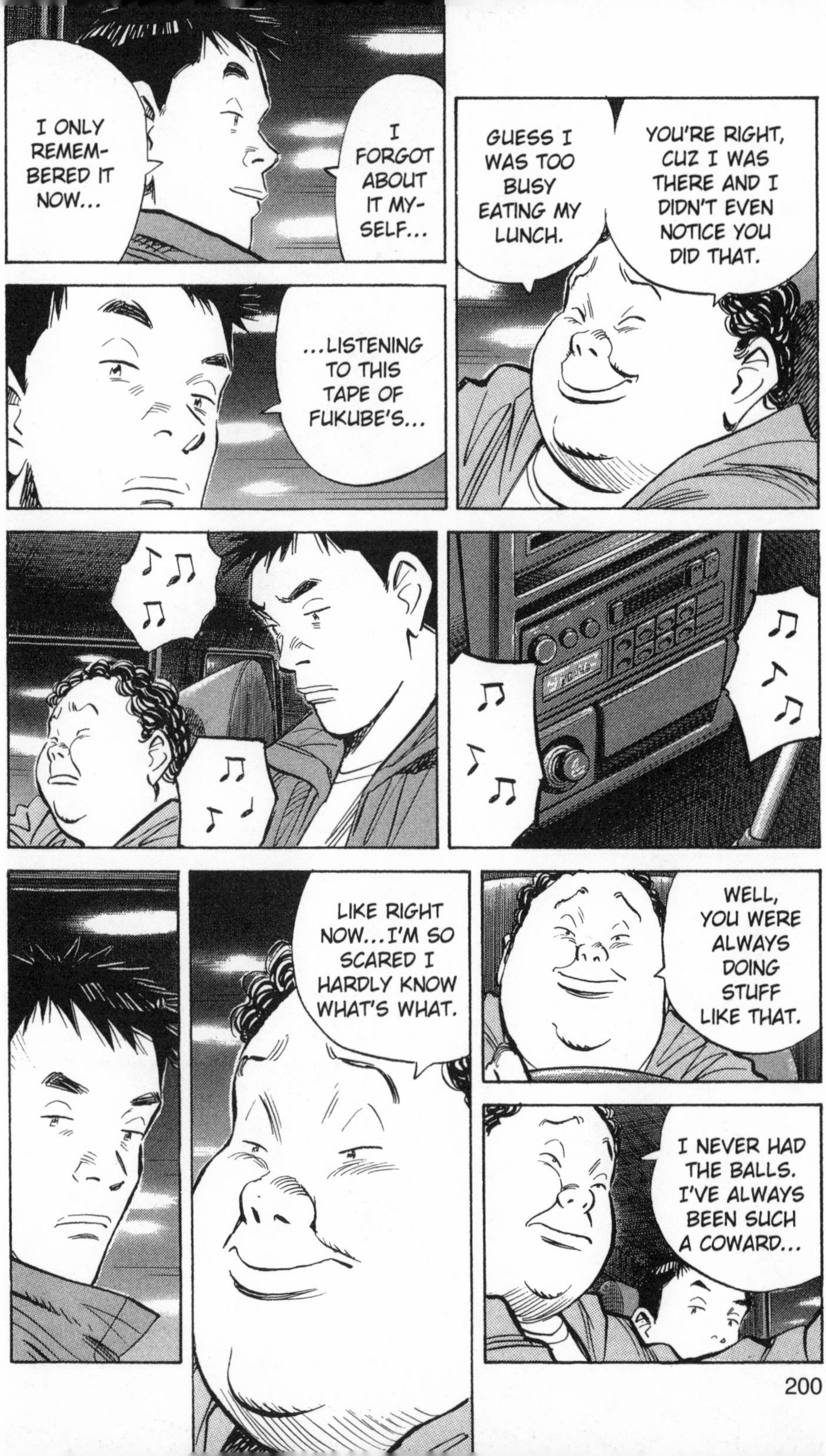
YOU'RE RIGHT, CUZ I WAS THERE AND I DIDN'T EVEN NOTICE YOU DID THAT.
GUESS I WAS TOO BUSY EATING MY LUNCH.
I FORGOT ABOUT IT MY-SELF...
I ONLY REMEM-BERED IT NOW...
...LISTENING TO THIS TAPE OF FUKUBE'S...
WELL, YOU WERE ALWAYS DOING STUFF LIKE THAT.
I NEVER HAD THE BALLS. I'VE ALWAYS BEEN SUCH A COWARD...
LIKE RIGHT NOW...I'M SO SCARED I HARDLY KNOW WHAT'S WHAT.

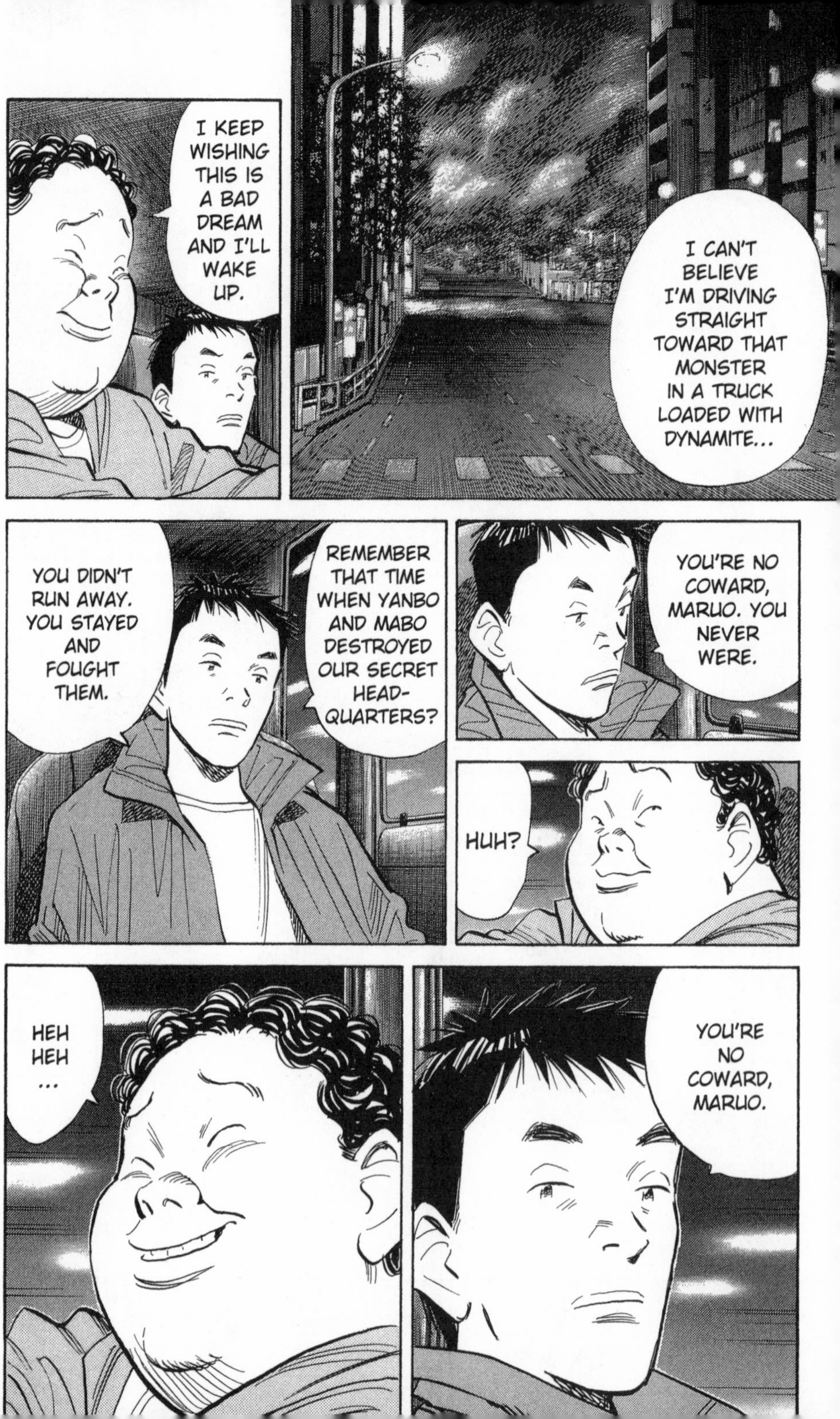
I CAN'T BELIEVE I'M DRIVING STRAIGHT TOWARD THAT MONSTER IN A TRUCK LOADED WITH DYNAMITE...
I KEEP WISHING THIS IS A BAD DREAM AND I'LL WAKE UP.
YOU'RE NO COWARD, MARUO. YOU NEVER WERE.
HUH?
REMEMBER THAT TIME WHEN YANBO AND MABO DESTROYED OUR SECRET HEAD-QUARTERS?
YOU DIDN'T RUN AWAY. YOU STAYED AND FOUGHT THEM.
YOU'RE NO COWARD, MARUO.
HEH HEH ...

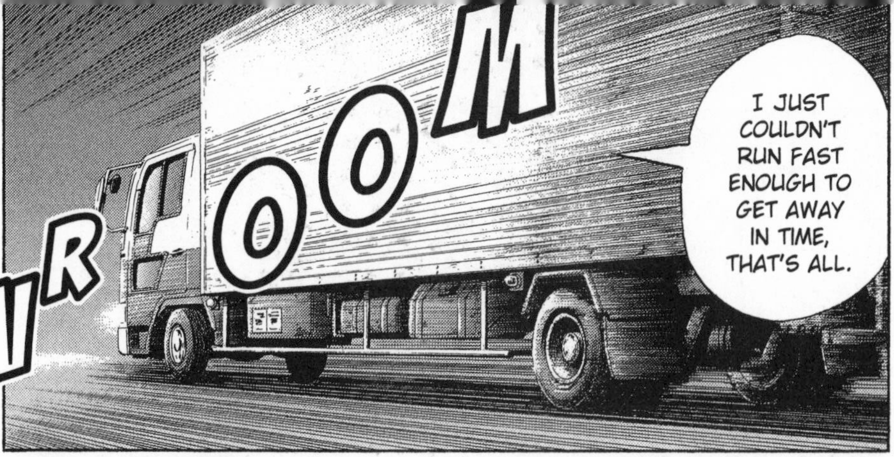
VROOOM
I JUST COULDN'T RUN FAST ENOUGH TO GET AWAY IN TIME, THAT'S ALL.

*National Crisis Control Committee

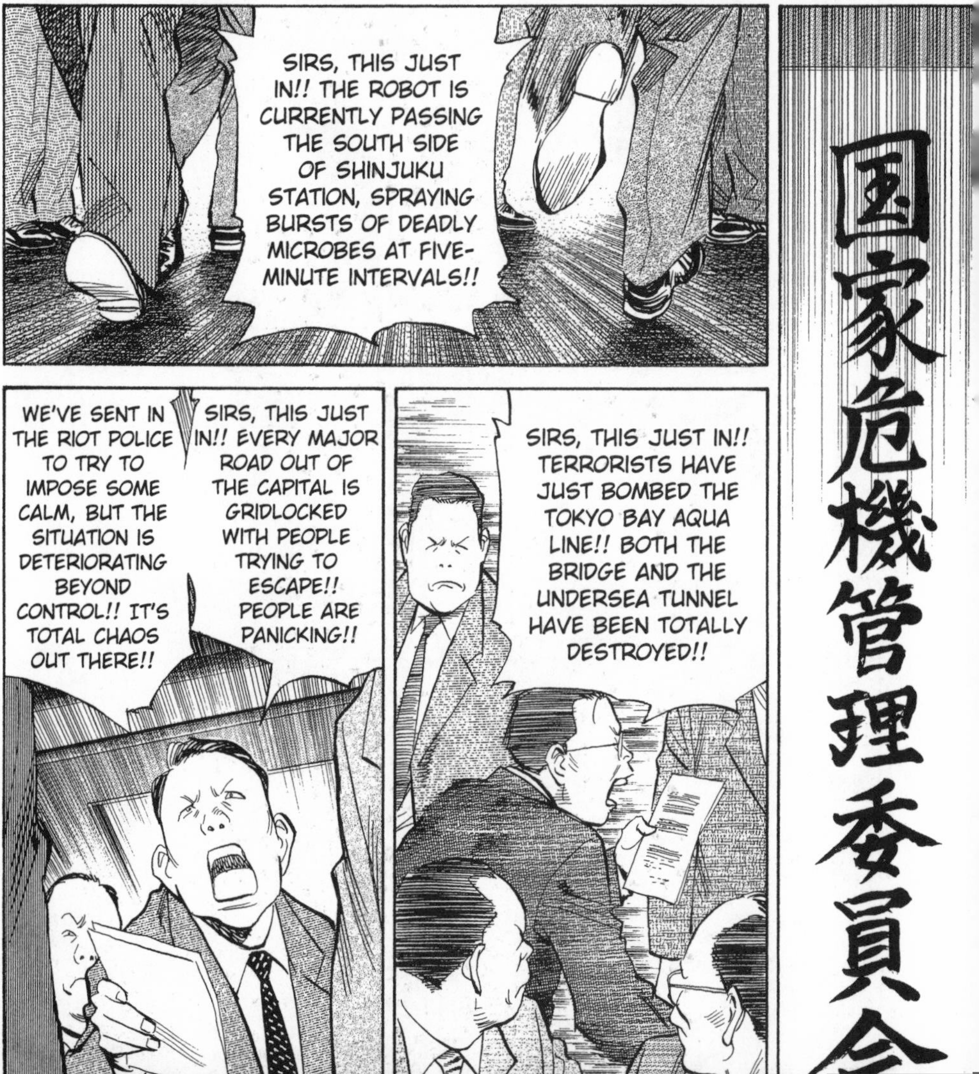
国家危機管理委員会
SIRS, THIS JUST IN!! THE ROBOT IS CURRENTLY PASSING THE SOUTH SIDE OF SHINJUKU STATION, SPRAYING BURSTS OF DEADLY MICROBES AT FIVE-MINUTE INTERVALS!!
SIRS, THIS JUST IN!! TERRORISTS HAVE JUST BOMBED THE TOKYO BAY AQUA LINE!! BOTH THE BRIDGE AND THE UNDERSEA TUNNEL HAVE BEEN TOTALLY DESTROYED!!
SIRS, THIS JUST IN!! EVERY MAJOR ROAD OUT OF THE CAPITAL IS GRIDLOCKED WITH PEOPLE TRYING TO ESCAPE!! PEOPLE ARE PANICKING!!
WE'VE SENT IN THE RIOT POLICE TO TRY TO IMPOSE SOME CALM, BUT THE SITUATION IS DETERIORATING BEYOND CONTROL!! IT'S TOTAL CHAOS OUT THERE!!

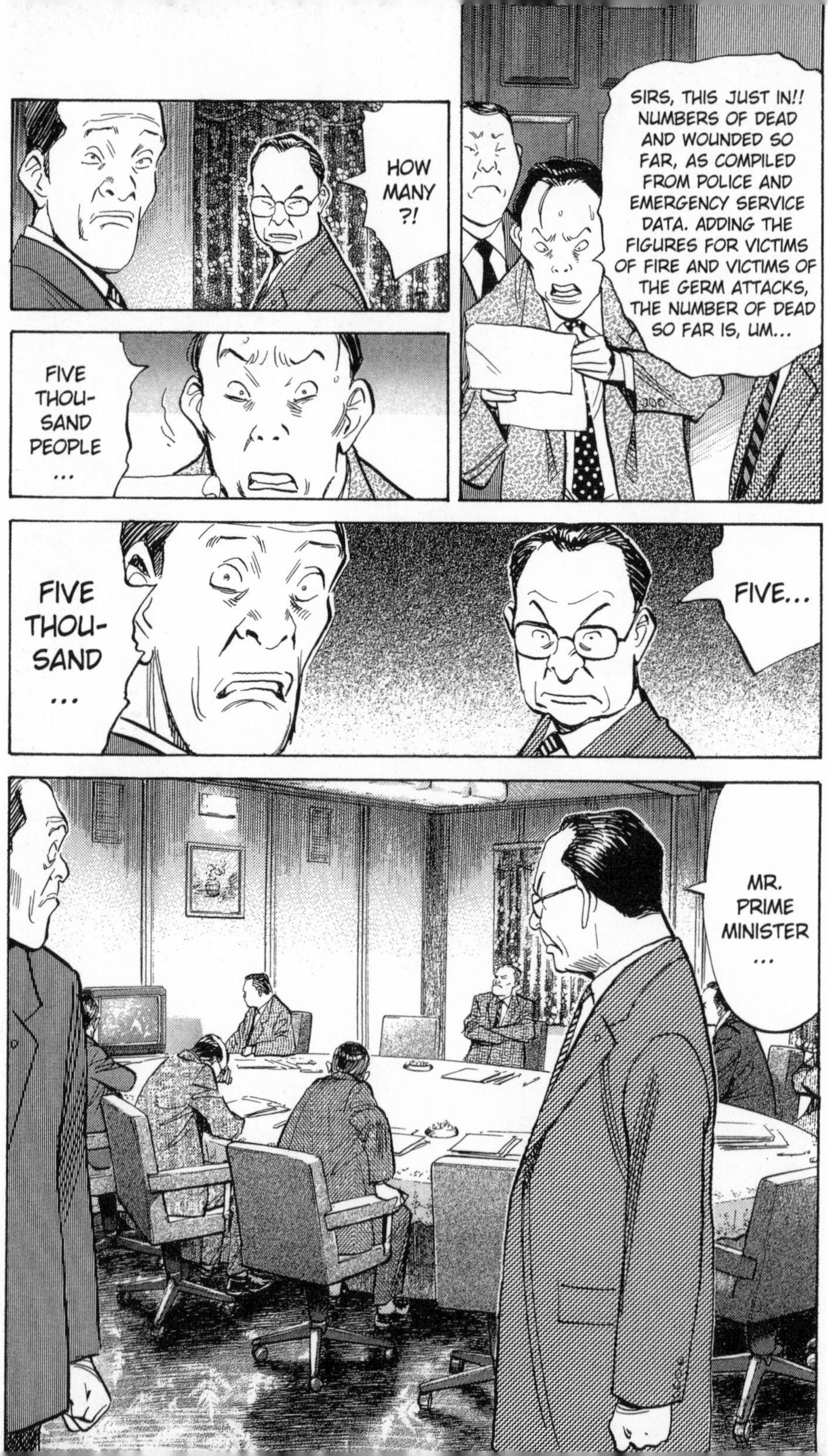
SIRS, THIS JUST IN!! NUMBERS OF DEAD AND WOUNDED SO FAR, AS COMPILED FROM POLICE AND EMERGENCY SERVICE DATA. ADDING THE FIGURES FOR VICTIMS OF FIRE AND VICTIMS OF THE GERM ATTACKS, THE NUMBER OF DEAD SO FAR IS, UM...
HOW MANY?!
FIVE THOUSAND PEOPLE...
FIVE...
FIVE THOUSAND...
MR. PRIME MINISTER...

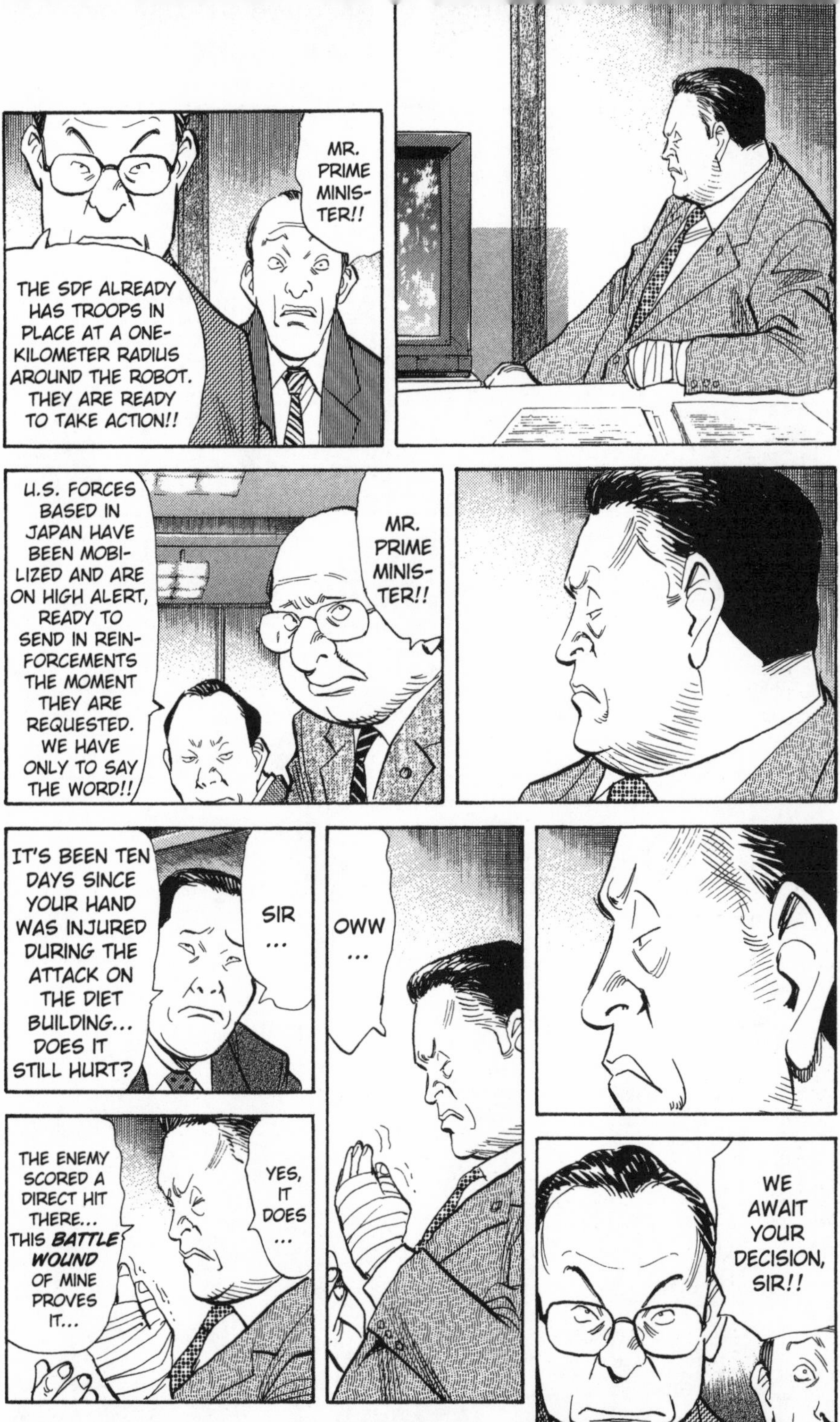

MR. PRIME MINISTER!!
THE SDF ALREADY HAS TROOPS IN PLACE AT A ONE-KILOMETER RADIUS AROUND THE ROBOT. THEY ARE READY TO TAKE ACTION!!
MR. PRIME MINISTER!!
U.S. FORCES BASED IN JAPAN HAVE BEEN MOBILIZED AND ARE ON HIGH ALERT, READY TO SEND IN REINFORCEMENTS THE MOMENT THEY ARE REQUESTED. WE HAVE ONLY TO SAY THE WORD!!
WE AWAIT YOUR DECISION, SIR!!
OWW ...
SIR ...
IT'S BEEN TEN DAYS SINCE YOUR HAND WAS INJURED DURING THE ATTACK ON THE DIET BUILDING... DOES IT STILL HURT?
YES, IT DOES ...
THE ENEMY SCORED A DIRECT HIT THERE... THIS ***BATTLE WOUND*** OF MINE PROVES IT...

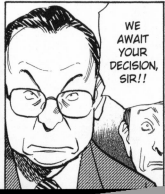

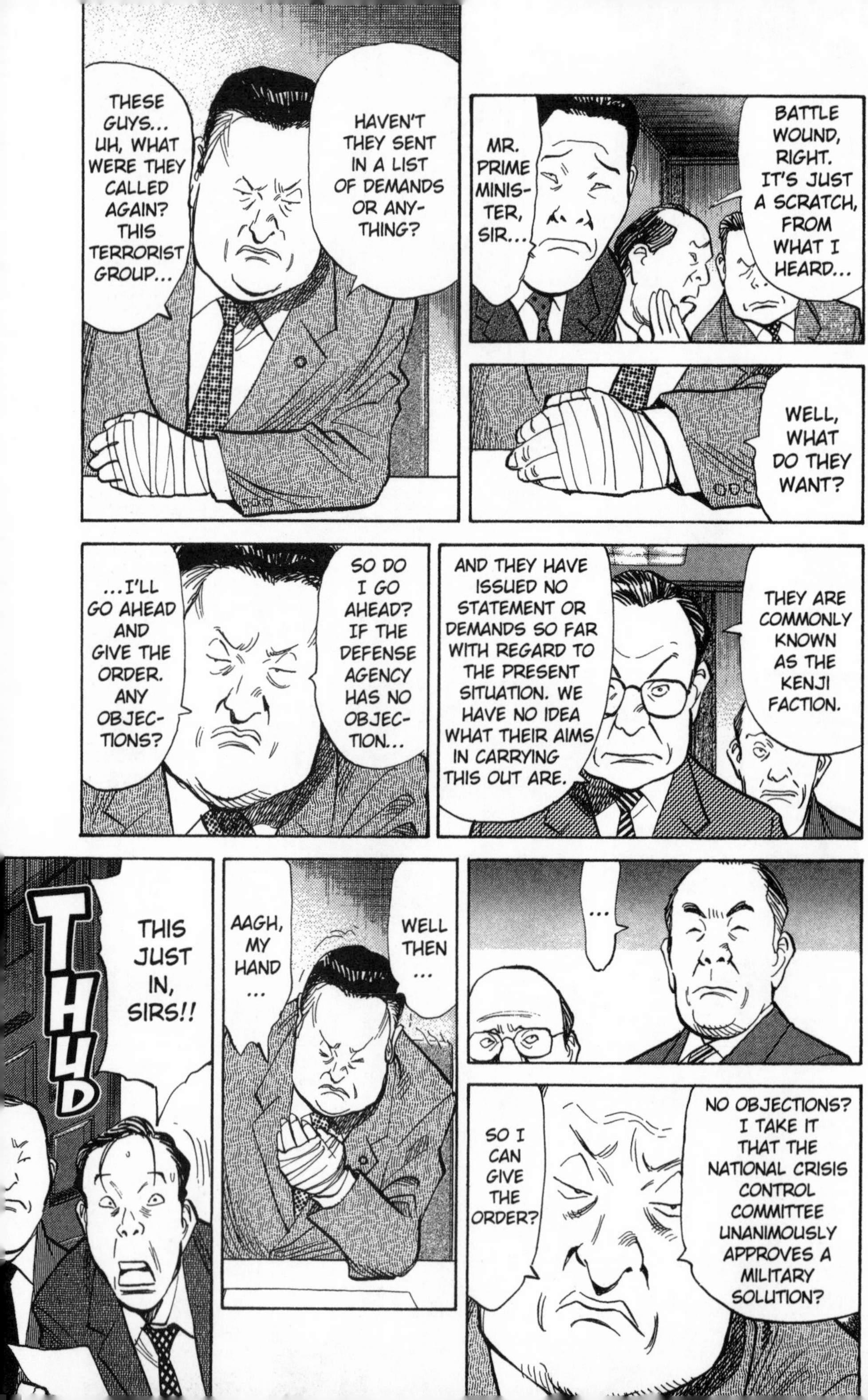
BATTLE WOUND, RIGHT. IT'S JUST A SCRATCH, FROM WHAT I HEARD...
MR. PRIME MINISTER, SIR...
WELL, WHAT DO THEY WANT?
HAVEN'T THEY SENT IN A LIST OF DEMANDS OR ANYTHING?
THESE GUYS... UH, WHAT WERE THEY CALLED AGAIN? THIS TERRORIST GROUP...
THEY ARE COMMONLY KNOWN AS THE KENJI FACTION.
AND THEY HAVE ISSUED NO STATEMENT OR DEMANDS SO FAR WITH REGARD TO THE PRESENT SITUATION. WE HAVE NO IDEA WHAT THEIR AIMS IN CARRYING THIS OUT ARE.
SO DO I GO AHEAD? IF THE DEFENSE AGENCY HAS NO OBJECTION...
...I'LL GO AHEAD AND GIVE THE ORDER. ANY OBJECTIONS?
...
NO OBJECTIONS? I TAKE IT THAT THE NATIONAL CRISIS CONTROL COMMITTEE UNANIMOUSLY APPROVES A MILITARY SOLUTION?
SO I CAN GIVE THE ORDER?
WELL THEN...
AAGH, MY HAND...
THIS JUST IN, SIRS!!
THUD

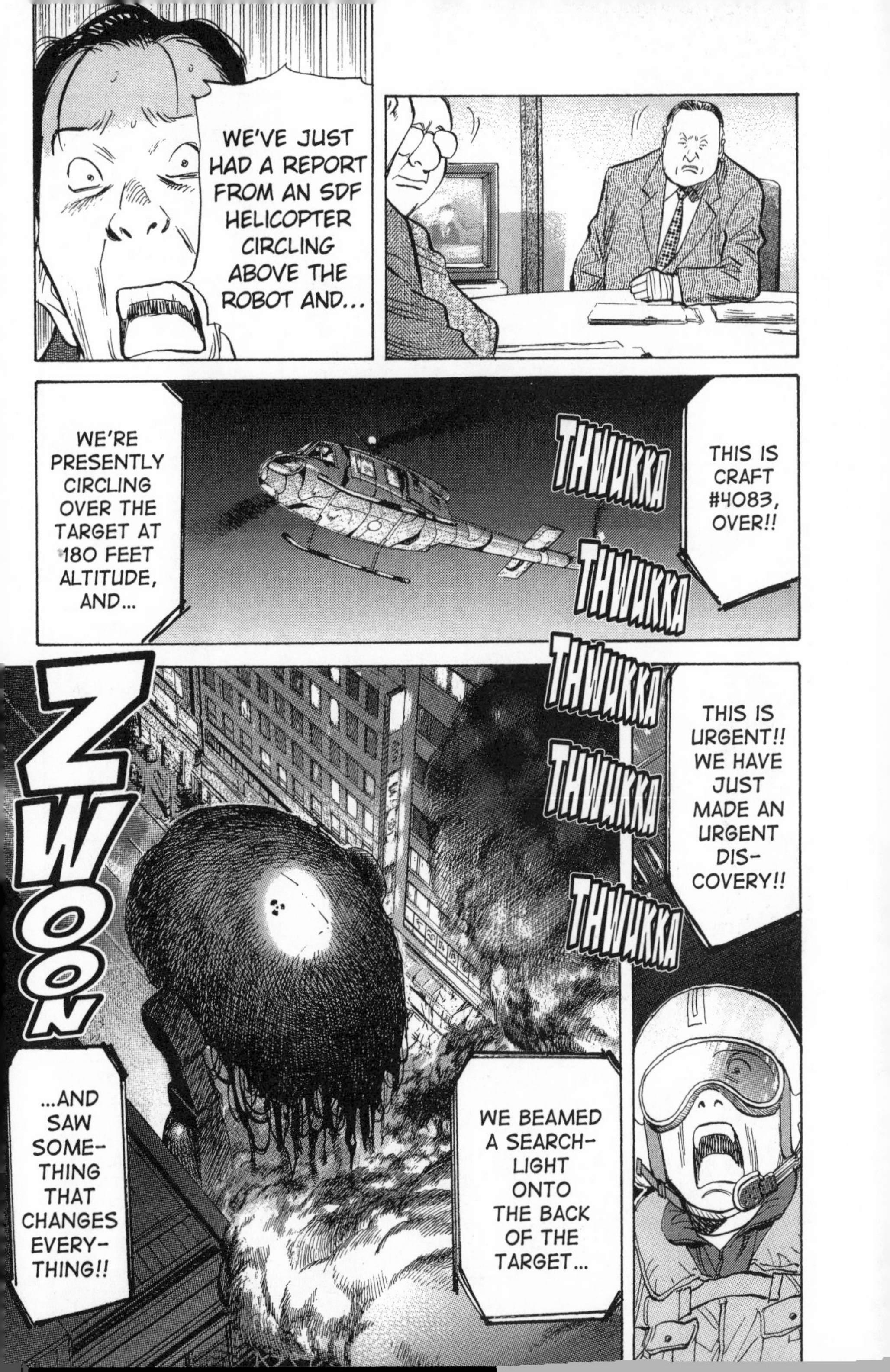
WE'VE JUST HAD A REPORT FROM AN SDF HELICOPTER CIRCLING ABOVE THE ROBOT AND...
THIS IS CRAFT #4083, OVER!!
THWUKKA
THWUKKA
WE'RE PRESENTLY CIRCLING OVER THE TARGET AT 180 FEET ALTITUDE, AND...
THWUKKA
THWUKKA
THWUKKA
THIS IS URGENT!! WE HAVE JUST MADE AN URGENT DIS-COVERY!!
WE BEAMED A SEARCH-LIGHT ONTO THE BACK OF THE TARGET...
...AND SAW SOME-THING THAT CHANGES EVERY-THING!!
ZWOOON

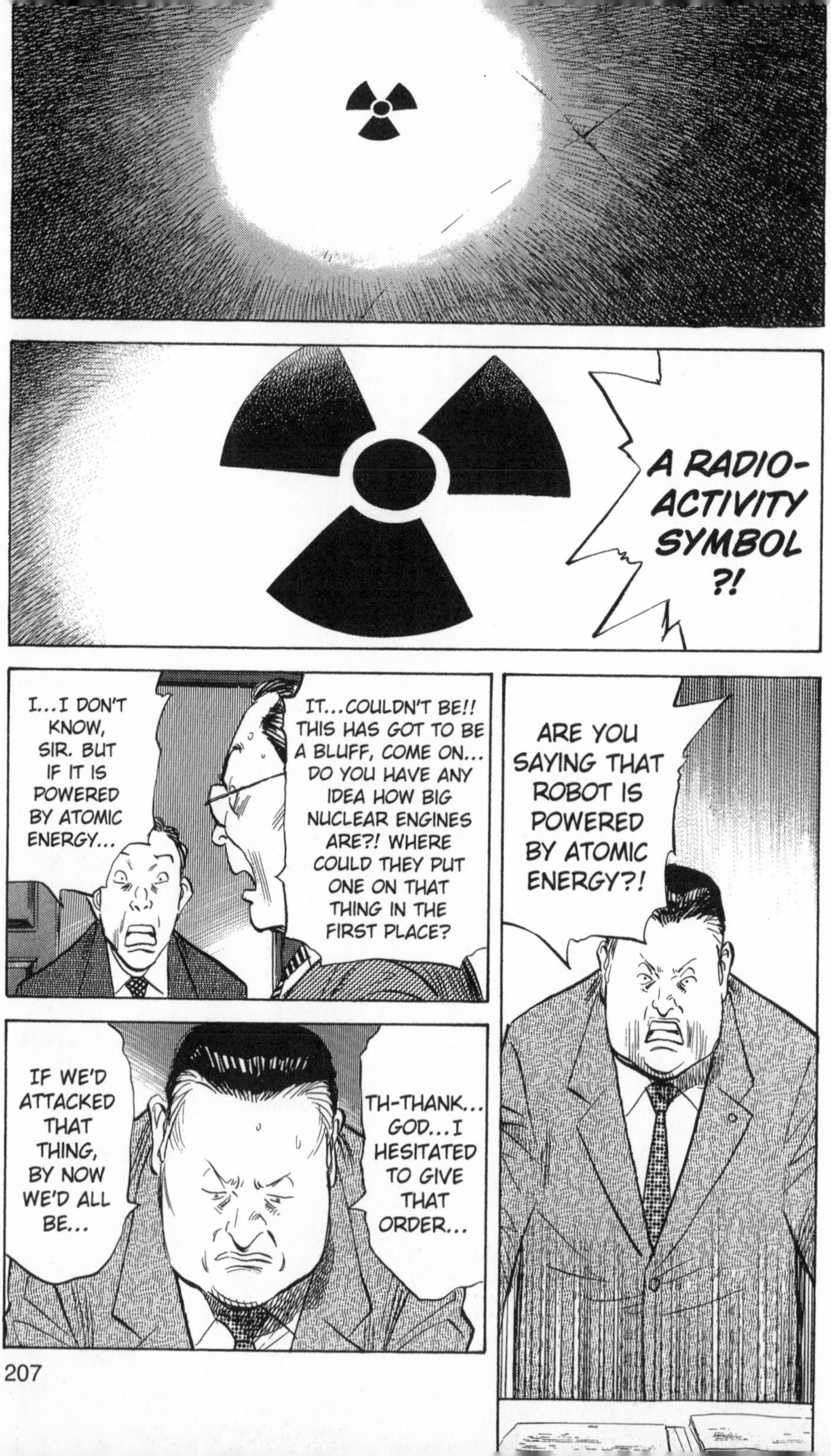
A RADIO-ACTIVITY SYMBOL ?!
ARE YOU SAYING THAT ROBOT IS POWERED BY ATOMIC ENERGY?!
IT...COULDN'T BE!! THIS HAS GOT TO BE A BLUFF, COME ON... DO YOU HAVE ANY IDEA HOW BIG NUCLEAR ENGINES ARE?! WHERE COULD THEY PUT ONE ON THAT THING IN THE FIRST PLACE?
I...I DON'T KNOW, SIR. BUT IF IT IS POWERED BY ATOMIC ENERGY...
TH-THANK... GOD...I HESITATED TO GIVE THAT ORDER...
IF WE'D ATTACKED THAT THING, BY NOW WE'D ALL BE...

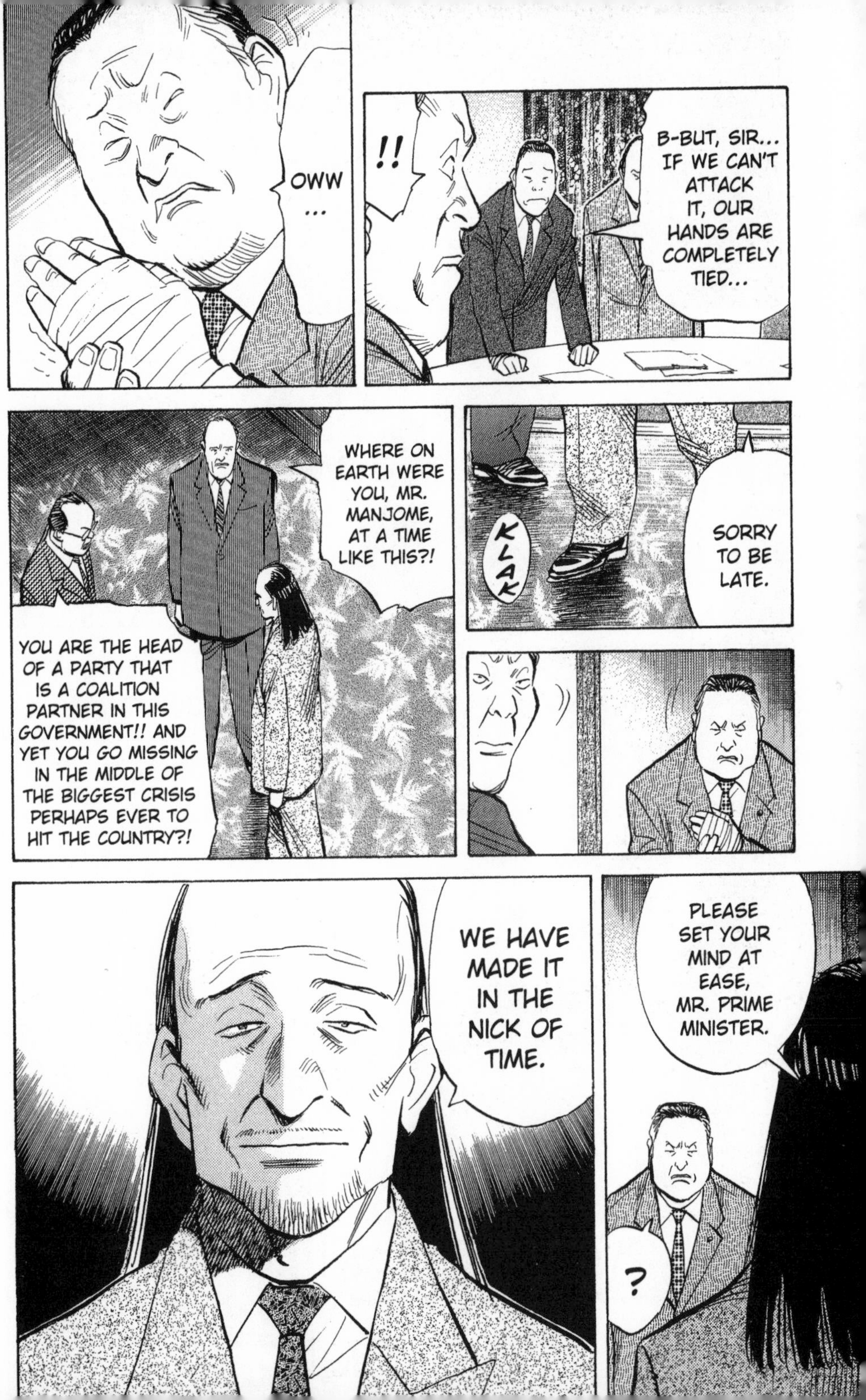

B-BUT, SIR... IF WE CAN'T ATTACK IT, OUR HANDS ARE COMPLETELY TIED...
!!
OWW ...
SORRY TO BE LATE.
KLAK
WHERE ON EARTH WERE YOU, MR. MANJOME, AT A TIME LIKE THIS?!
YOU ARE THE HEAD OF A PARTY THAT IS A COALITION PARTNER IN THIS GOVERNMENT!! AND YET YOU GO MISSING IN THE MIDDLE OF THE BIGGEST CRISIS PERHAPS EVER TO HIT THE COUNTRY?!
PLEASE SET YOUR MIND AT EASE, MR. PRIME MINISTER.
?
WE HAVE MADE IT IN THE NICK OF TIME.

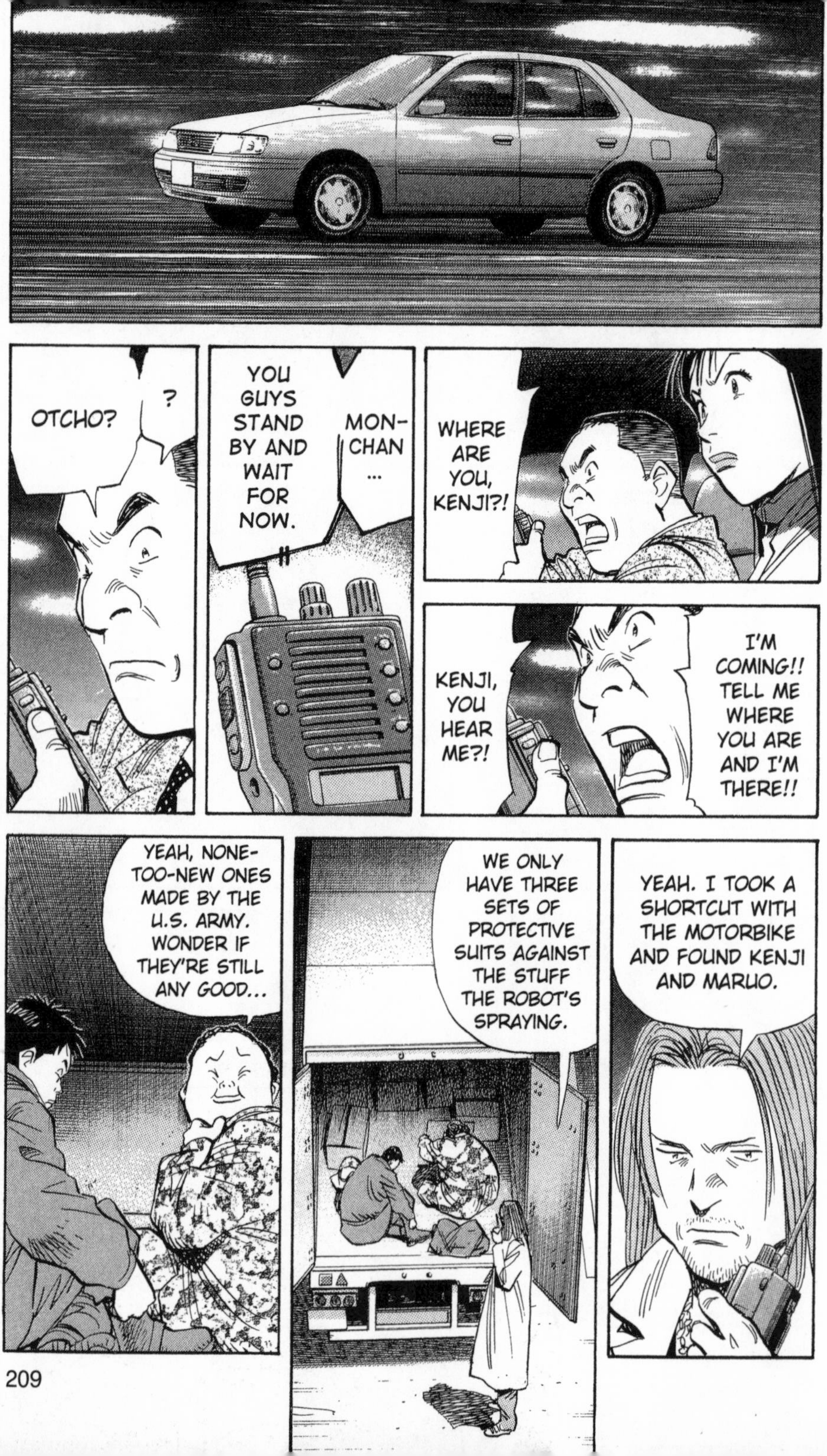
WHERE ARE YOU, KENJI?!
I'M COMING!! TELL ME WHERE YOU ARE AND I'M THERE!!
KENJI, YOU HEAR ME?!
MON-CHAN ...
YOU GUYS STAND BY AND WAIT FOR NOW.
?
OTCHO?
YEAH. I TOOK A SHORTCUT WITH THE MOTORBIKE AND FOUND KENJI AND MARUO.
WE ONLY HAVE THREE SETS OF PROTECTIVE SUITS AGAINST THE STUFF THE ROBOT'S SPRAYING.
YEAH, NONE-TOO-NEW ONES MADE BY THE U.S. ARMY. WONDER IF THEY'RE STILL ANY GOOD...

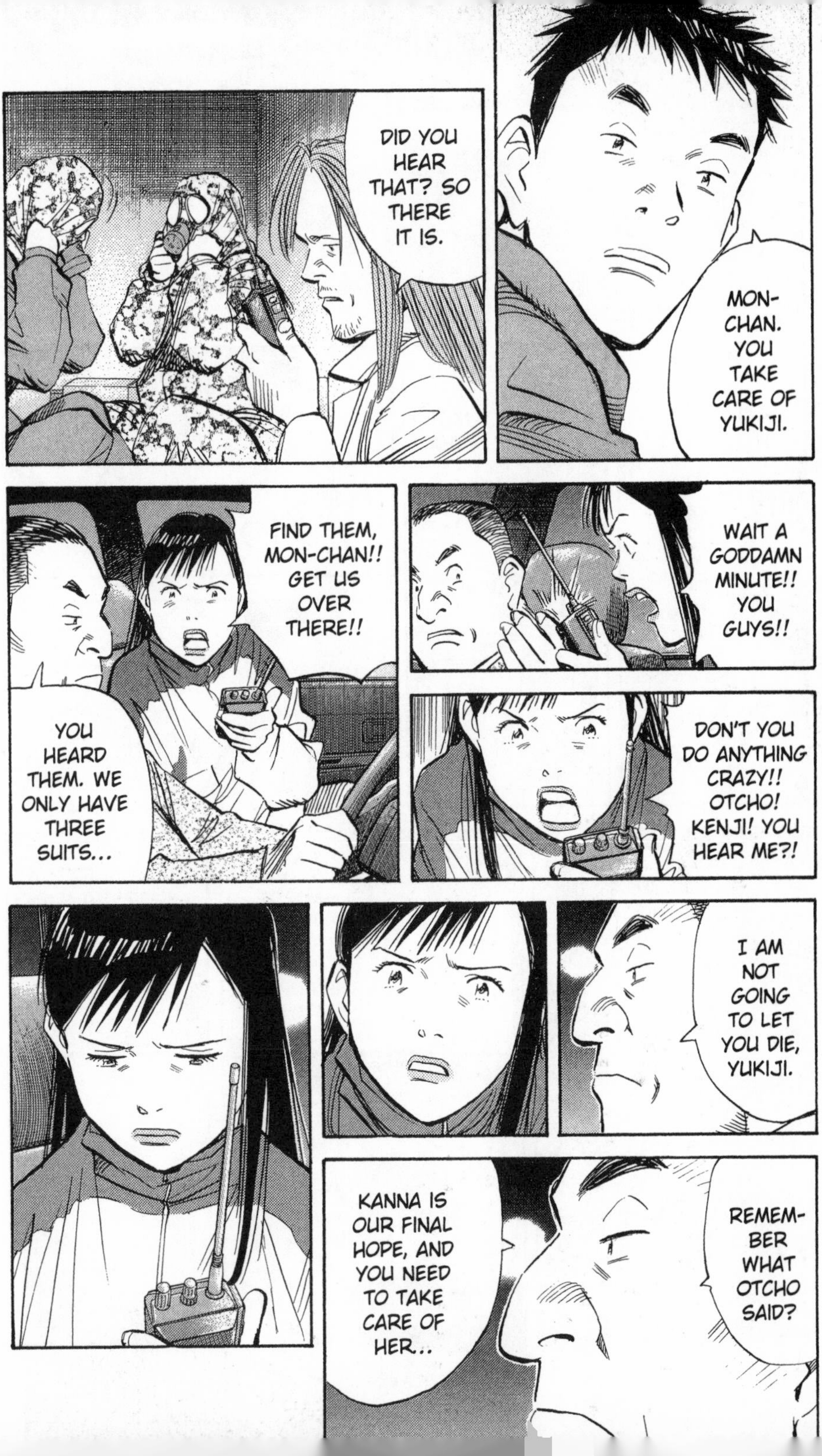
MON-CHAN. YOU TAKE CARE OF YUKIJI.
DID YOU HEAR THAT? SO THERE IT IS.
WAIT A GODDAMN MINUTE!! YOU GUYS!!
DON'T YOU DO ANYTHING CRAZY!! OTCHO! KENJI! YOU HEAR ME?!
FIND THEM, MON-CHAN!! GET US OVER THERE!!
YOU HEARD THEM. WE ONLY HAVE THREE SUITS...
I AM NOT GOING TO LET YOU DIE, YUKIJI.
REMEMBER WHAT OTCHO SAID?
KANNA IS OUR FINAL HOPE, AND YOU NEED TO TAKE CARE OF HER...

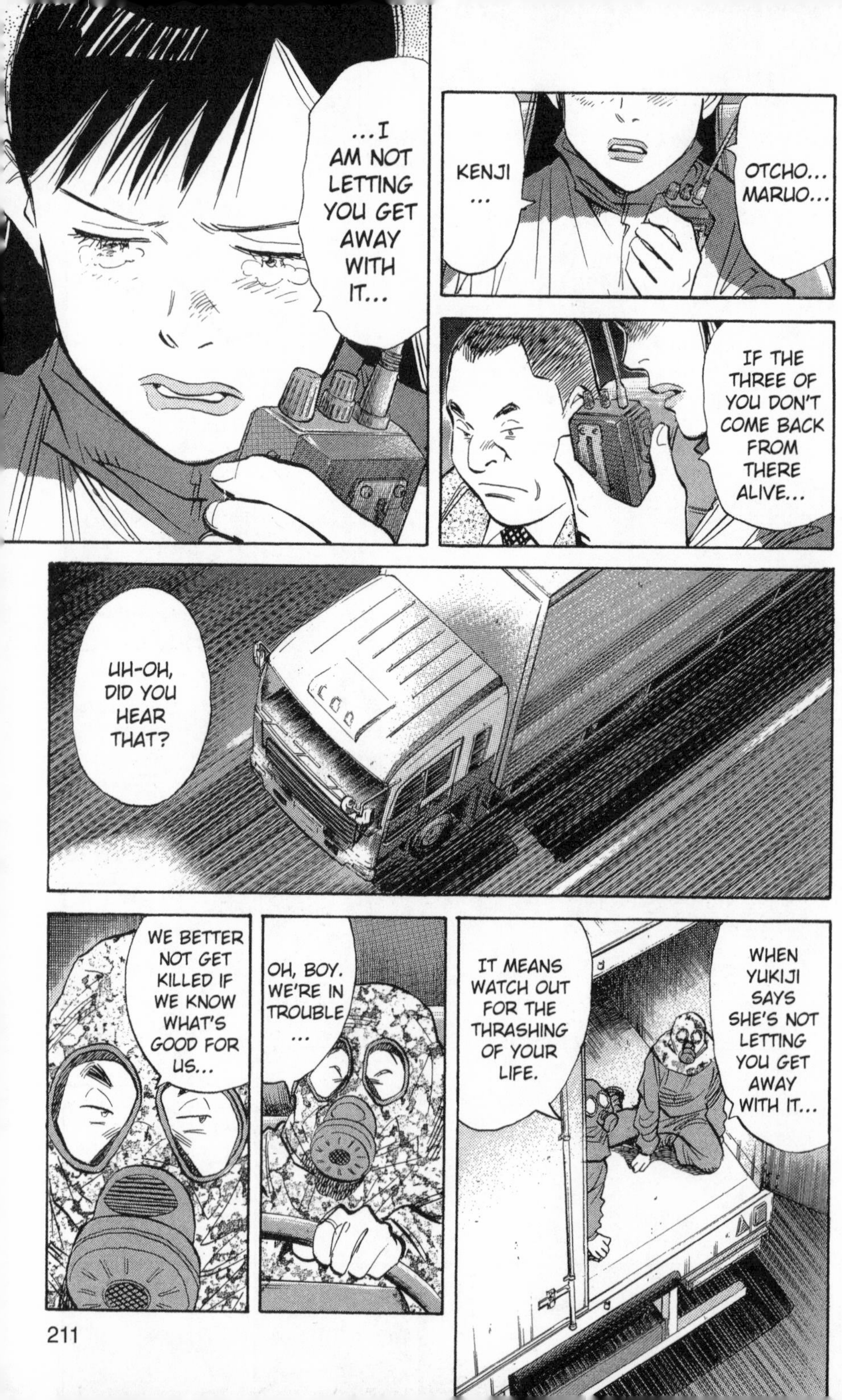
OTCHO... MARUO...
KENJI ...
IF THE THREE OF YOU DON'T COME BACK FROM THERE ALIVE...
...I AM NOT LETTING YOU GET AWAY WITH IT...
UH-OH, DID YOU HEAR THAT?
WHEN YUKIJI SAYS SHE'S NOT LETTING YOU GET AWAY WITH IT...
IT MEANS WATCH OUT FOR THE THRASHING OF YOUR LIFE.
OH, BOY. WE'RE IN TROUBLE ...
WE BETTER NOT GET KILLED IF WE KNOW WHAT'S GOOD FOR US...

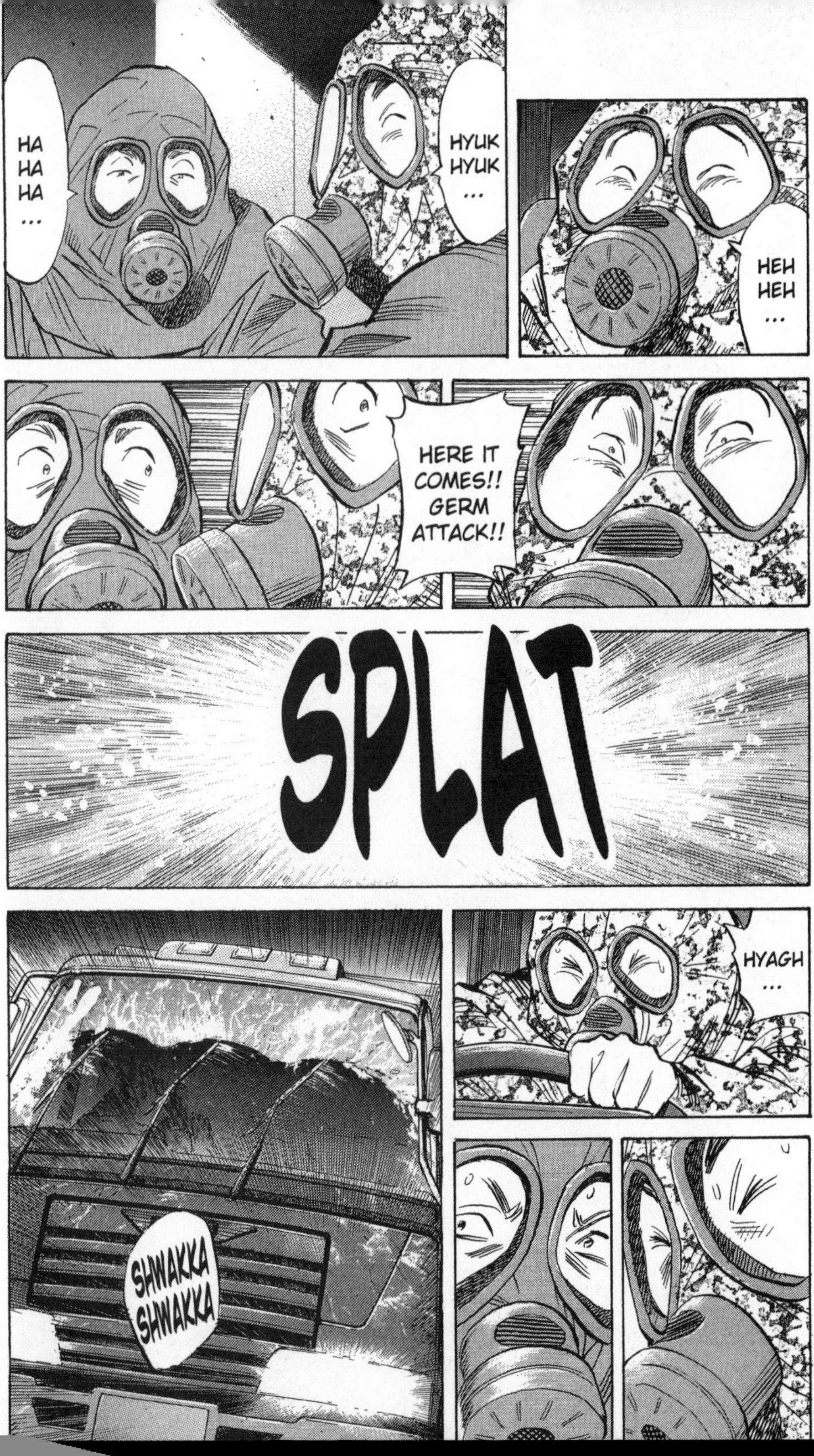
HEH HEH ...
HYUK HYUK ...
HA HA HA ...
HERE IT COMES!! GERM ATTACK!!
SPLAT
HYAGH ...
SHWAKKA SHWAKKA

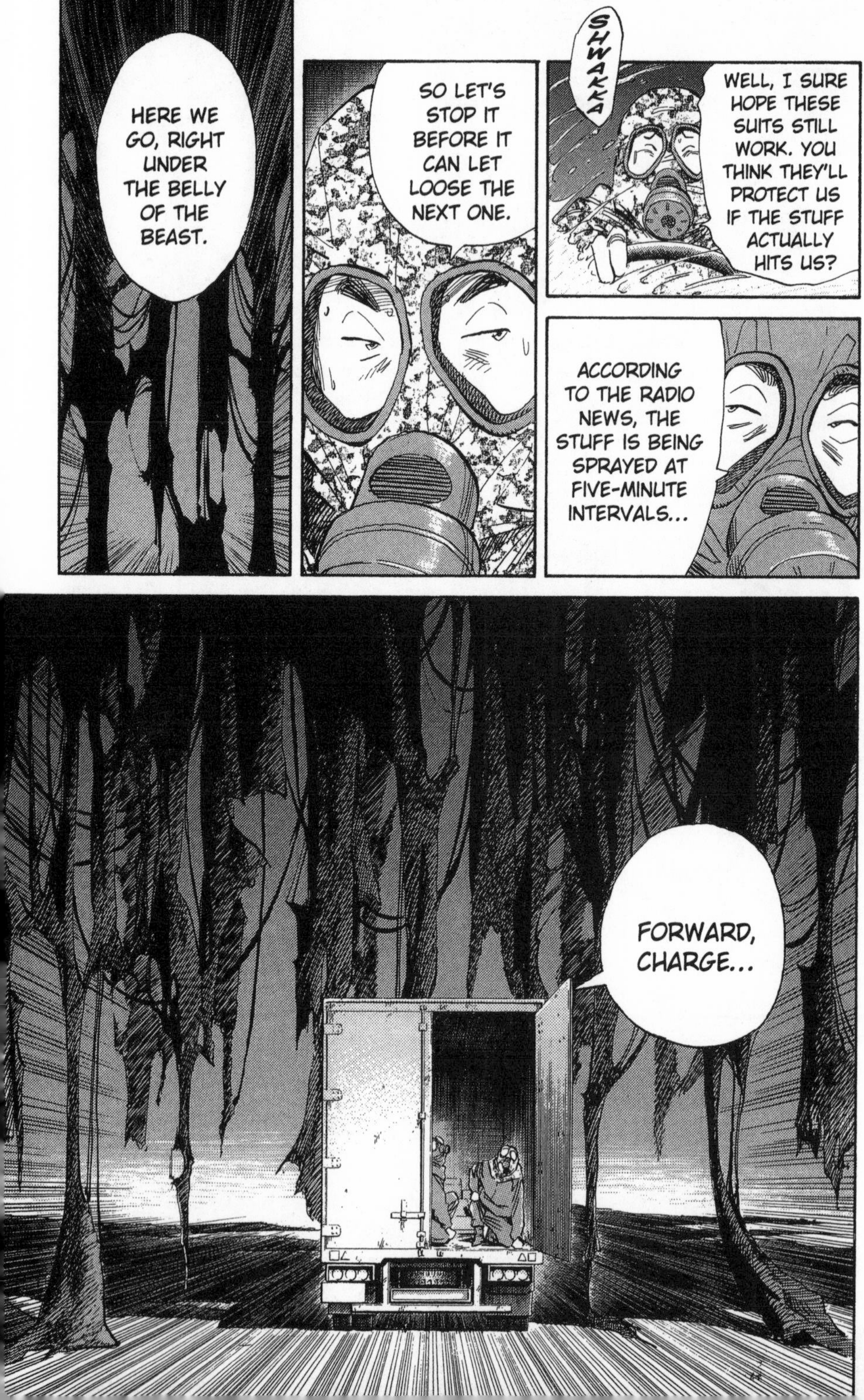
SHWAKKA
WELL, I SURE HOPE THESE SUITS STILL WORK. YOU THINK THEY'LL PROTECT US IF THE STUFF ACTUALLY HITS US?
ACCORDING TO THE RADIO NEWS, THE STUFF IS BEING SPRAYED AT FIVE-MINUTE INTERVALS...
SO LET'S STOP IT BEFORE IT CAN LET LOOSE THE NEXT ONE.
HERE WE GO, RIGHT UNDER THE BELLY OF THE BEAST.
FORWARD, CHARGE...

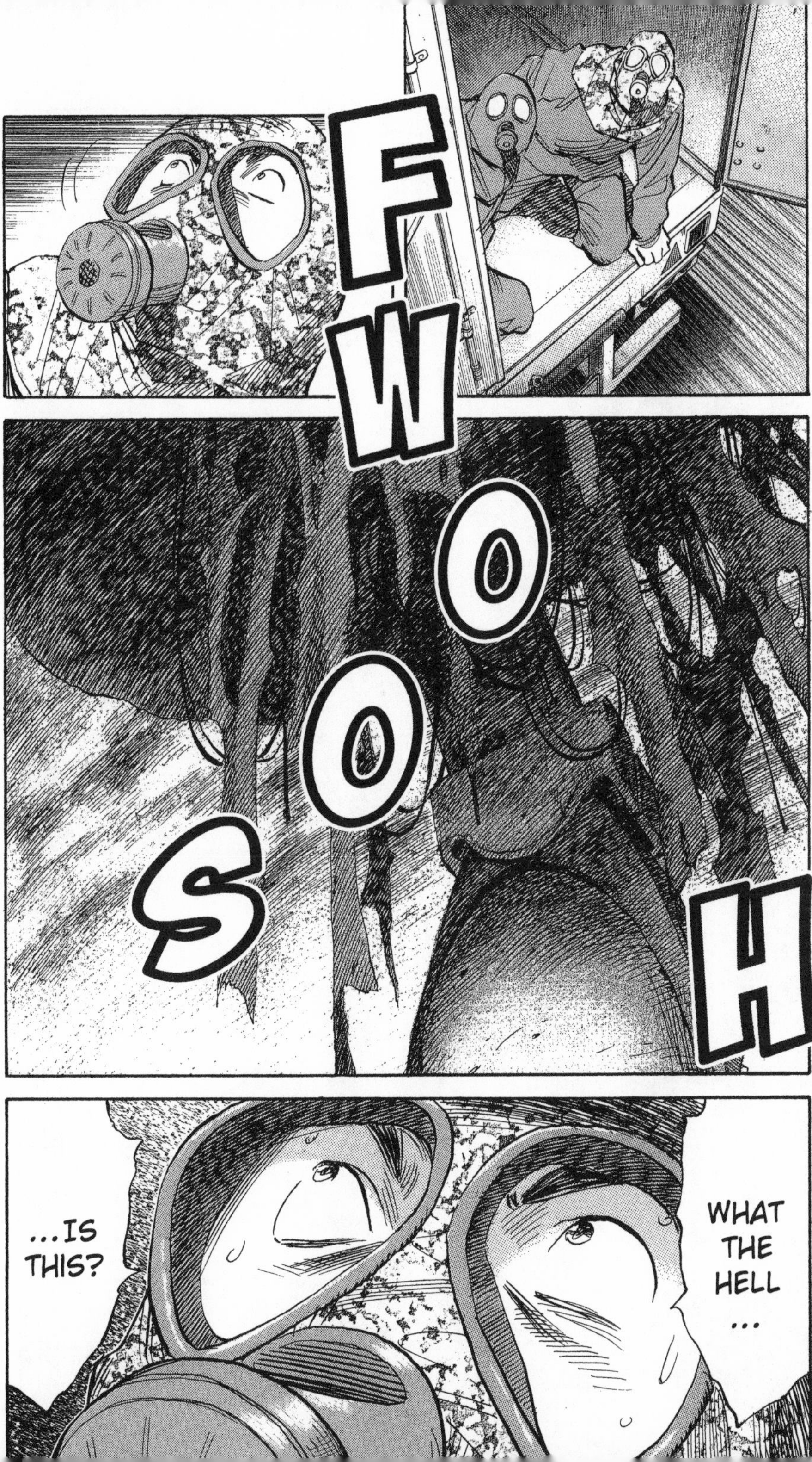
FWOOSH
WHAT THE HELL ...
...IS THIS?

TO BE CONTINUED

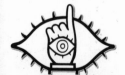

NOTES FROM THE TRANSLATOR

This series follows the Japanese naming convention, with a character's family name followed by their given name. Honorifics such as -*san* and -*kun* are also preserved.

Page 27: A *dagashiya* is a local neighborhood candy store crammed with sweets, toys, vinegared squid and other items. They often include a raffle board where one can win prizes.

Page 80: *Onmyoji*, literally "yin yang masters," were practitioners of divination who advised the emperor on all kinds of issues in the Heian period.

Page 80: Heian-kyo, literally "tranquil capital," is what the imperial capital was called during the Heian period (794-1185). Today it is known as Kyoto.

Page 85: *Kohaku*, short for *Kohaku Uta Gassen*, is a yearly televised singing competition that airs on New Year's Eve in Japan. Broadcasted on NHK, *Kohaku* features musical performances from popular singers and groups.

Page 128: In Japanese, Mon-chan says "Tetsujin 28-go," literally "Ironman No. 28," a series better known in the U.S. as *Gigantor*.

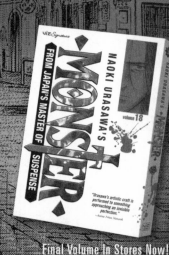

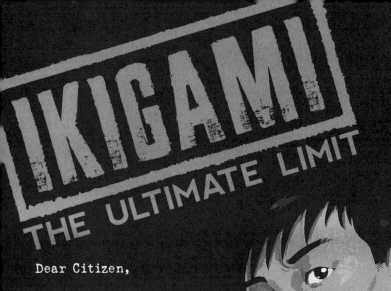
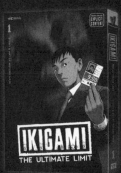

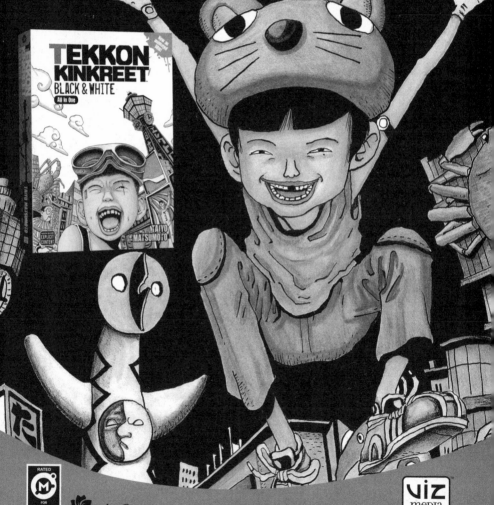

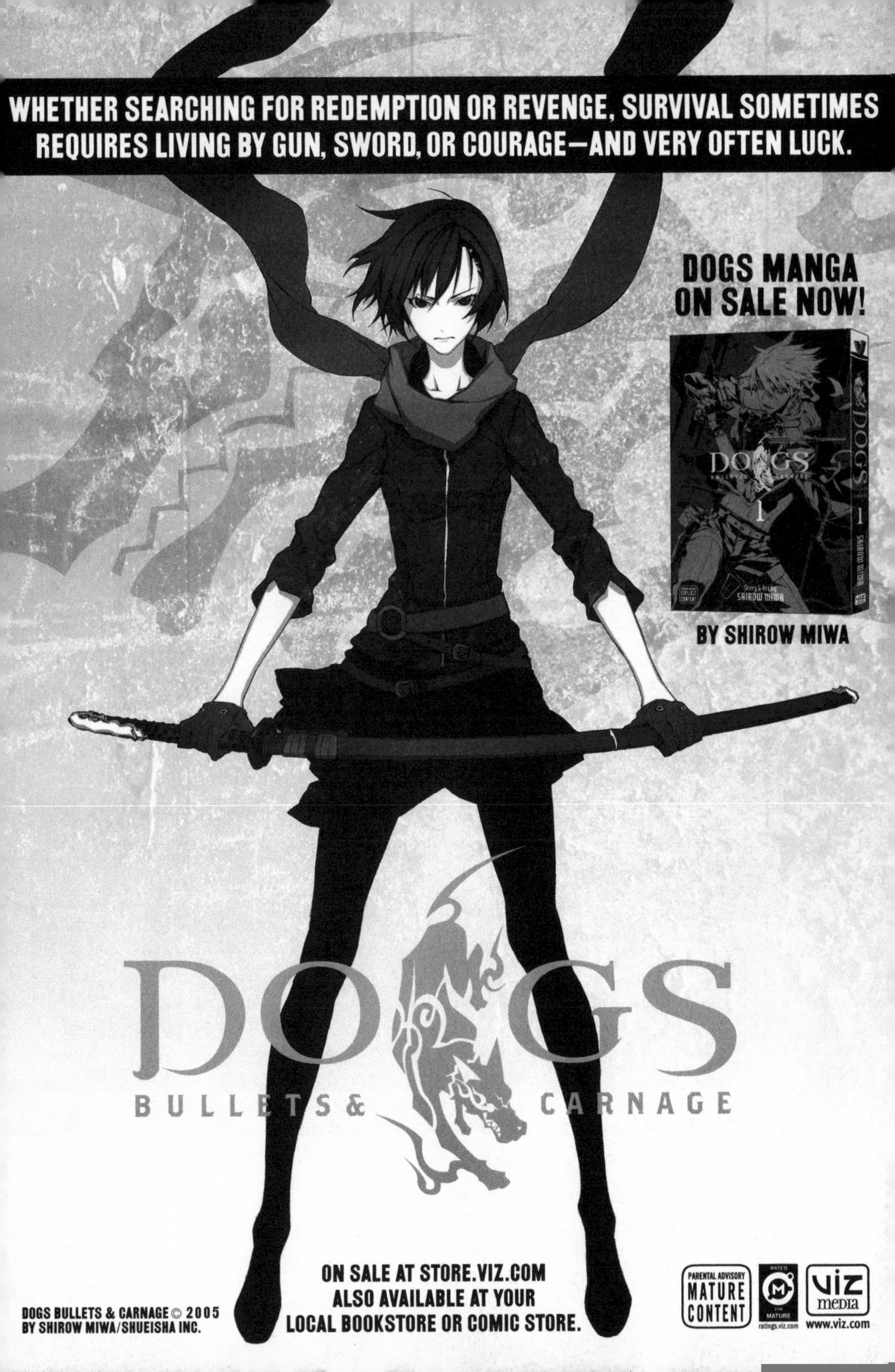
WHETHER SEARCHING FOR REDEMPTION OR REVENGE, SURVIVAL SOMETIMES REQUIRES LIVING BY GUN, SWORD, OR COURAGE—AND VERY OFTEN LUCK.
DOGS MANGA ON SALE NOW!
DOGS
1
Story & Art by SHIROW MIWA
BY SHIROW MIWA
DOGS
BULLETS & CARNAGE
ON SALE AT STORE.VIZ.COM
ALSO AVAILABLE AT YOUR LOCAL BOOKSTORE OR COMIC STORE.
DOGS BULLETS & CARNAGE © 2005 BY SHIROW MIWA/SHUEISHA INC.
PARENTAL ADVISORY MATURE CONTENT
RATED M FOR MATURE
ratings.viz.com
VIZ media
www.viz.com

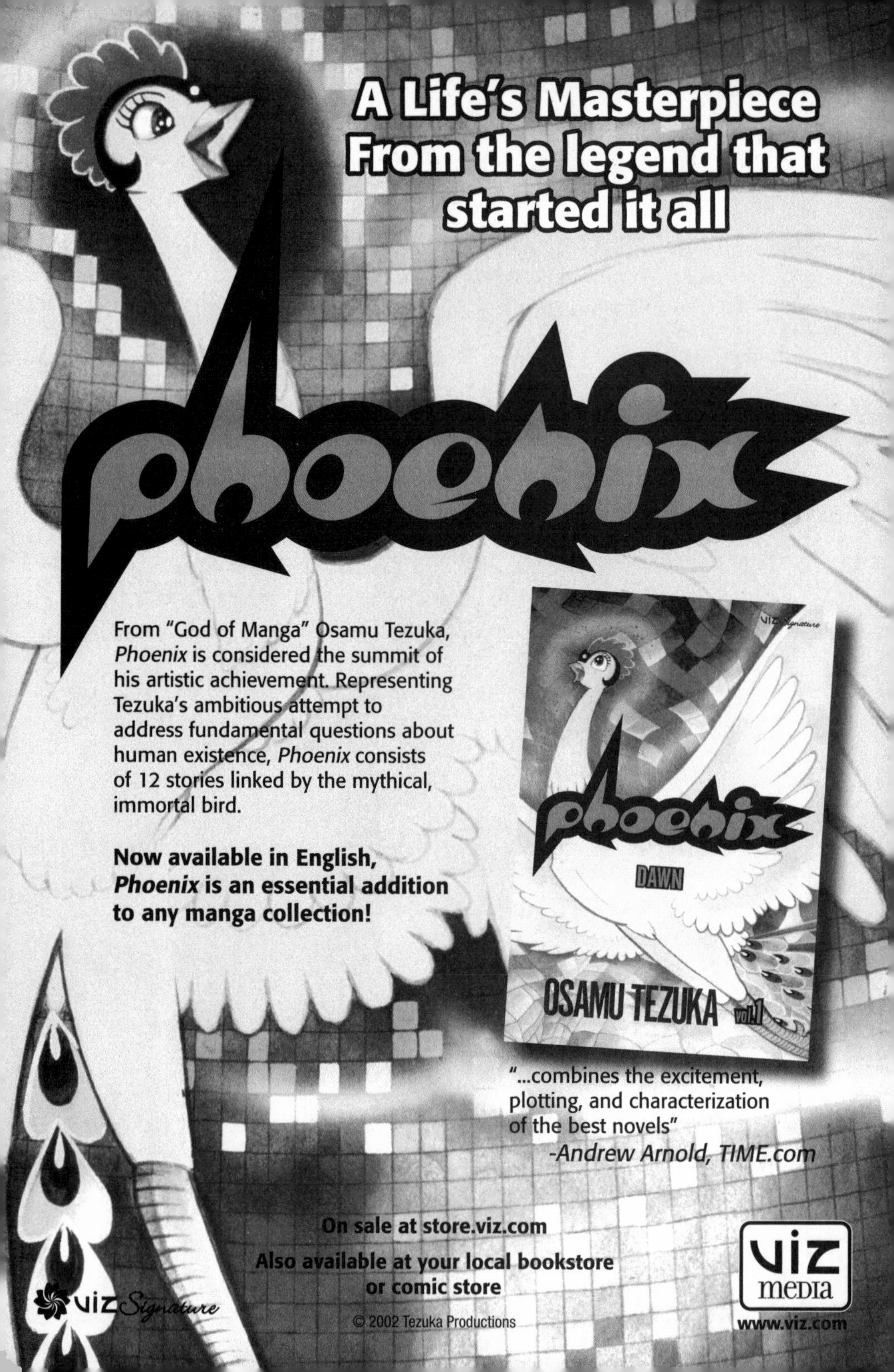
A Life's Masterpiece
From the legend that
started it all
Phoenix
From "God of Manga" Osamu Tezuka, Phoenix is considered the summit of his artistic achievement. Representing Tezuka's ambitious attempt to address fundamental questions about human existence, Phoenix consists of 12 stories linked by the mythical, immortal bird.
Now available in English, Phoenix is an essential addition to any manga collection!
VIZ Signature
Phoenix
DAWN
OSAMU TEZUKA vol.1
"...combines the excitement, plotting, and characterization of the best novels"
-Andrew Arnold, TIME.com
On sale at store.viz.com
Also available at your local bookstore or comic store
© 2002 Tezuka Productions
VIZ Signature
VIZ MEDIA
www.viz.com

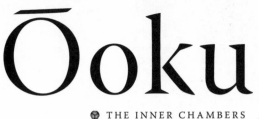
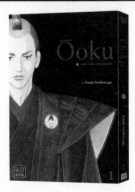

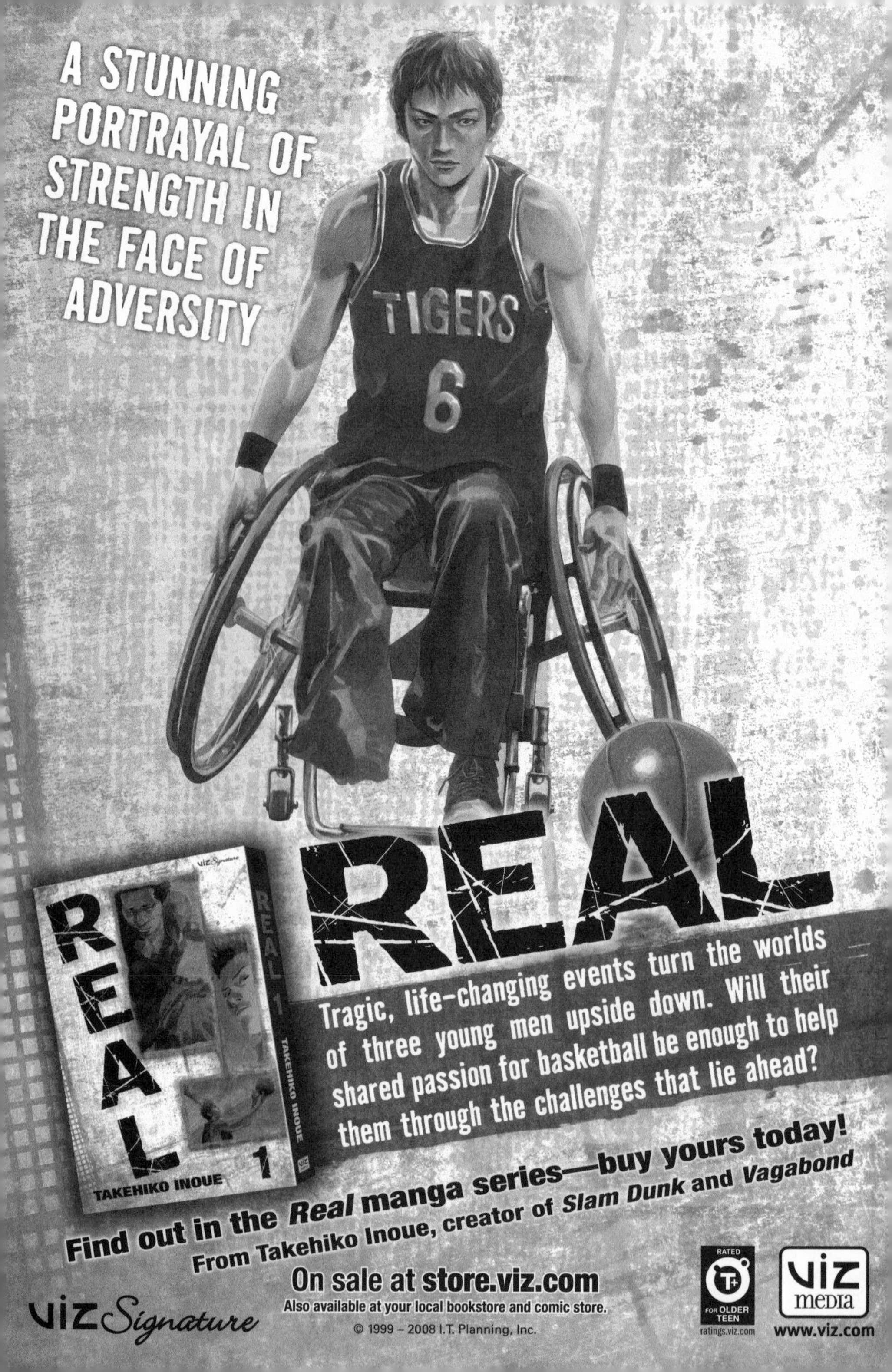
A STUNNING PORTRAYAL OF STRENGTH IN THE FACE OF ADVERSITY
TIGERS
6
REAL
viz Signature
REAL 1
TAKEHIKO INOUE
Tragic, life-changing events turn the worlds of three young men upside down. Will their shared passion for basketball be enough to help them through the challenges that lie ahead?
Find out in the Real manga series—buy yours today!
From Takehiko Inoue, creator of Slam Dunk and Vagabond
On sale at store.viz.com
Also available at your local bookstore and comic store.
viz Signature
© 1999 – 2008 I.T. Planning, Inc.
RATED T+ FOR OLDER TEEN
ratings.viz.com
viz media
www.viz.com

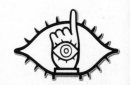